CASTING A GIANT SHADOW

NEW DIRECTIONS IN NATIONAL CINEMAS

Robert Rushing, *editor*

CASTING A GIANT SHADOW

The Transnational Shaping of Israeli Cinema

Edited by
Rachel S. Harris and Dan Chyutin

INDIANA UNIVERSITY PRESS

This book is a publication of

Indiana University Press
Office of Scholarly Publishing
Herman B Wells Library 350
1320 East 10th Street
Bloomington, Indiana 47405 USA

iupress.org

Manufactured in the United States of America

First printing 2021

Library of Congress Cataloging-in-Publication Data

Names: Harris, Rachel S. (Rachel Sylvia), 1977- editor. | Chyutin, Dan,
    editor.
Title: Casting a giant shadow : the transnational shaping of Israeli cinema /
    edited by Rachel S. Harris and Dan Chyutin.
Other titles: New directions in national cinemas.
Description: Bloomington, Indiana : Indiana University Press, 2021. |
    Series: New directions in national cinemas | Includes bibliographical
    references and index.
Identifiers: LCCN 2020043822 (print) | LCCN 2020043823 (ebook) | ISBN
    9780253056382 (hardback) | ISBN 9780253056399 (paperback) | ISBN
    9780253056405 (ebook)
Subjects: LCSH: Motion pictures—Israel. | Motion picture industry—Israel. |
    Motion pictures and transnationalism—Israel. | Nationalism in motion
    pictures.
Classification: LCC PN1993.5.I86 C38 2021 (print) | LCC PN1993.5.I86
    (ebook) | DDC 791.43095694—dc23
LC record available at https://lccn.loc.gov/2020043822
LC ebook record available at https://lccn.loc.gov/2020043823

In loving memory of
Michael Chyutin (1941–2019)

CONTENTS

FOREWORD

SITTING AT THE JERUSALEM INTERNATIONAL FILM FESTIVAL, WE noted the wide array of foreign influences that appeared in Israeli films showcased at the event and the significance the festival has always had in displaying international film to an Israeli audience. Milling around among the film scholars and general audience were also industry professionals, film stars, and international judges and distributors. What was a general observation about the transnational nature of Israeli cinema became a larger conversation about the long history of diversity in Israeli cinema and the way it has drawn on and been influenced by foreign participants within its own film industry but has also exported film stars, producers, and directors internationally—all the while being mindful of showcasing Israel through its cinema to an international audience. This book is the result of drawing others into our musings and trying to find a way to discuss Israeli cinema, which in many ways has been impacted by the inherently national mission, its changing politics and history, and its true shaping by transnational forces.

We would like to thank Indiana University Press for its long-standing support for this project and the anonymous reviewers for their helpful insights.

The book is dedicated to the memory of Dr. Michael Chyutin for his wisdom, kindness, and love of travel that inspired a local boy to think globally.

CASTING A GIANT SHADOW

ISRAELI CINEMA BEYOND THE NATIONAL

An Introduction

Rachel S. Harris

Dan Chyutin

I had first heard of the Land of Israel in 1925 and, at once, I realized the importance of letting the world know the special timbre of the country, its unique scenery and quality. . . . The solution, in my opinion, was the production of films and I at once got in touch with various companies in that field. It was my intention to establish an independent film center in the Jewish territory of Palestine.[1]

Margot Klausner's first foray into the film industry was with *Land of Promise* (1933), a propaganda documentary she co-funded that represented not only the Jewish settlement in Mandatory Palestine but also the historic and religious diversity of the country. While aiming to capture an authentic view of local realities, the film was conceived from the outset as catering to international audience's tastes. The internalization of these transnational concerns for both Jewish audiences who could be motivated to contribute to the Zionist projects and world audiences who could be made sympathetic to Jewish causes, particularly the desire for a national homeland in Palestine, shaped both the production and reception of *Land of Promise*. As Klausner discusses in her memoir, *The Dream Industry*, the realization of this film depended upon support from multiple institutional actors, investors, and artists. Her first documentary was only made possible because of the interest shown by the European Zionist Congress, who had learned of the enthusiasm of Leo Hermann, the general secretary of the Israeli fundraising organization Keren Hayesod, toward such a project. As the head of the official Zionist fundraising body, he had no film experience but understood that propaganda might serve fundraising purposes. Spurred by the enthusiasm of his sister Emily, he worked with the American company the Fox Film Corporation, which was interested in making three sixty-minute information films about the region. In the process of becoming 20th Century Fox, the studio was willing to send technicians—"a chief cameraman and a sound technician, with the recording system, as well as an assistant photographer with camera"[2]—on condition that they would be provided with a local director, suitable script, production director, and local financing in Palestine. Klausner, who put up a sizable portion of the initial funds, accompanied the documentary to the Venice Biennale in 1935, where it won the competition. But she was not there to receive the award, having already left to screen her film to Jewish philanthropists elsewhere in Europe.

Fifteen years later, as the new State of Israel was coming into being, Klausner founded its first film studio, the Israel Motion Picture Studios in Herzliya, and went on to serve as its chair and director until shortly before her death. The studio relied on the technical and artistic know-how of international filmmakers, cameramen, editors, and technicians and the purchase of equipment and film stock from abroad in order to be able to develop a local film industry. Yet its transnational nature did not stop there but rather extended to a vision that saw film as a medium for representing the Zionist vision abroad. Her aspirations are inscribed on the studio's cornerstone: "It is the aim of the founders of these Studios to draw the attention of the nations towards our way of life in Israel through the aid of movies, an art which has such a great influence in the world and reaches into all countries; to disclose to all peoples throughout the generations our spiritual and social ideas; to lead them to understand the history of Israel since the time we became a nation until this very day."[3]

This vision of an Israeli cinema placed an emphasis on its Israeliness, on the ways in which its importance lies in the ability to render visible the way of life in Israel; its realization, however, was not predicated on isolating Israel or its filmmaking from the rest of the world. In Klausner's eyes, cinema was firmly grounded in its national borders while simultaneously transcending those borders, functioning in a transnational sphere of operation and intelligibility. In this she was no different than many other players within the history of Israeli filmmaking, though at times nationalizing tendencies within the industry and culture caused one side of the dual vision to be highlighted over the other. Yet, as Klausner discovered, a tension remains between the marketing of Israel on a foreign screen and the international influences that have shaped the industry at home.

Eighty years after the international release of *Land of Promise*, the newly anointed Israeli minister of culture and sport, Miri Regev, announced a new state-sponsored, film-related initiative: the inauguration of a pavilion dedicated to Israeli cinema as part of the Village International of the 2015 Cannes Film Festival. The pavilion at Cannes, whose construction was budgeted at one million new Israeli shekels (NIS), ultimately served to showcase recent Israeli films as well as promote national film funds, film festivals, film schools, cinematheques, and filmmakers. Particular attention was given to facets of Israeli cinema that often go unnoticed—animation filmmaking, for example, as well as nationally produced technological innovations (Virtual Reality [VR] glasses, 360-degree cameras, etc.).[4] While such measures highlighted diversity, their positioning within the pavilion nevertheless submitted them to Regev's message of overarching unity—of Israeli filmmaking as "a source of national pride." Above all else, the success of the initiative seemed bound by its ability to make Israelis feel "proud of the fact that for the first time Israel's flag will fly over its national pavilion at one of the most important film events in the world."[5] To further bolster national pride, Regev also decided to time the inauguration of the pavilion with Israel's Independence Day.

Regev's comments showed clear awareness of the transnational setting in which the pavilion operates ("the Village"), as well as the festival's objectives of transnational marketing and cooperation. As opposed to Klausner, however, Regev promoted a vision and rhetoric that were nationalistic and invested in containing this pavilion and the cinema it was representing under the national heading of Israel.[6] A clear continuation of the government's ultranationalist right-wing message, this stance was critiqued by filmmakers and film reviewers from the opposite side of the political fence, who rightfully saw this as yet another state-operated attempt to circumvent the avowed pluralistic and antinationalist tendencies of Israel's leftist cultural elite.[7] Yet in spite of their opposition, what such commentators shared with Regev was a similar understanding of Israeli cinema as primarily meaningful in the context of an internal dialogue around the national shaping of Israel. Under these conditions, Israeli cinema's participation in a global dialogue and its transnational shaping as a whole were rendered insignificant.

Yet the very desire to showcase Israel at Cannes evokes Klausner's understanding of Israeli films' persistent transnationalism. Situating the case of Israel within a larger conversation about the global nature of cinema and its multidirectional shaping, this book draws its focus from Alan Williams's notion of "cinematic 'international relations.'" For "if we grant that national cinemas exist, no matter how problematic it is to define them or specify what they 'do' for a nation, then they will necessarily not be defined, or act, in isolation."[8] Our aim is thus to offer a study that considers a multitude of ways in which these transnational connections serve to shape a local industry, ultimately influencing its perception both at home and abroad.

* * *

Film came to Ottoman-ruled Palestine (referred to in Hebrew as Eretz Israel) not long after the birth of the medium. Following their celebrated screening at the Salon Indien du Grand Café in Paris, the Lumière brothers, Auguste and Louis, sent their agents to capture views in Jerusalem, Jaffa, and Bethlehem. They focused primarily on sites of importance to Christianity and on historical traces of Napoleon's Middle Eastern campaigns. While such efforts were followed by others interested in capturing a region significant for its historical and theological relationship to Europe, they themselves did not inform the emergence of a local film industry. This only came into being later, with the growth of the Jewish settlement in Palestine (the *Yishuv*) in the 1920s. Yishuv filmmaking "closely paralleled the evolution of Zionist activity, and on one level constituted an extension of that activity, thus establishing a basically harmonious extension between film pioneers and Zionist pioneers."[9] In this capacity, filmmakers

> sought to present the human drama as part of the national drama. Generally speaking, the figure of the "New Jew" is shown to be a heroic figure that triumphs all the challenges presented to him. He is deprived of almost all personal emotions and his yearnings are directed towards the deliverance of the homeland and making the barren soil bloom. In their filmmaking they created a coherent visual terminology. On the one hand, they used single images or a small series of images that glorified the heroic pioneer—shooting from unconventional angles that made the object appear stronger, offering unconventional positionings of the object, frame cuts, etc. On the other hand, they preferred the "presentation" of reality to be intelligible, distinct, easy to understand, with a simple message that provided an interpretive frame which grounds the image in concrete meaning.[10]

To the extent that these films were focused on "the construction and articulation of the evolving national identity," this identity and its articulation were influenced not only by local but also global factors. The state of flux that typified the Zionist Jewish community during this early period of development allowed it to be open to outside influences even as it attempted to close ranks around "a shared lifestyle for all its members." Accordingly, this community found itself easily influenced by the "societal and cultural systems with which it was in contact, including those of its neighbouring countries; its population's countries of origin; and countries with developed national film production that meaningfully intersected with [Palestine]— the British cinema system, which was an integral part of the dominating force in these territories during 1917–1948, and the American film system, which has unquestioningly dominated world cinema since the 1930s."[11] Such openness to the transnational manifested itself, among other things, in the fact that many of these films were shaped and mobilized by the desire "to stir Jews in the *Diaspora* to join the efforts of construction and national revival in Palestine."[12] Their creators often received training in Europe and explicitly attempted to create a local vernacular of the styles prevalent there. For example, in his direction of the Palestine-based Zionist film *Avodah* (1935), the German Helmar Lerski combined two sources of influence—the Soviet films of Sergei Eisenstein and Dziga Vertov and the Expressionist techniques of UFA, where he worked in the 1920s.[13] At times, such creators were not immigrants to Palestine but experts contracted to work on a single project, and as such, their take on the Zionist project of Israeli particularity was refracted through their "foreign" sensibilities.[14]

After the foundation of Israel in 1948, the Zionist state hegemony was faced with the challenges of expanding its nationalizing project so as to encompass a growing population of recent immigrants, most of whom were either displaced persons victimized in the Holocaust or immigrants from the Middle East. The filmmaking during this period, itself heavily reliant on the state's approbation for its existence, reflected this concern through its dominant genre—the so-called heroic-nationalist film, essentially a magnification of the cinematic articulation of the national present in the Yishuv cinema. Even as this genre worked at "'socializing' new immigrants at home" into becoming true "Israelis"[15]—like the Sabra, the indigenous Hebrew native who is enmeshed with the Israeli landscape—its framing of *Israeli* particularly remained profoundly transnational. The heroic-nationalist films "encapsulated the nationalist ethos of survival and cohesiveness."[16] Yet their form was pervasively "foreign," especially in terms of adapting the aesthetics, themes, and iconography of Soviet montage on the one hand and the popular Hollywood genres of the domestic melodrama, the war film, and the Western on the other.[17] These influences were again imported by mostly US- and European-trained filmmakers who either immigrated to

Israel or were hired for locally produced projects, including Thorold Dickinson, Larry Frisch, Meyer Levin, Joseph Leits, Joseph Krumgold, Shlomo Soriano, and Peter Frye. Their efforts fashioned the national ethos as both *Israeli*, in the sense of grounded in the local, and *Westernized*,[18] in the sense of reaching toward broader, transnational spheres.

The relationship of the state leadership to cinema during the pre-state and early statehood periods was marked by "double standards."[19] Despairing that cinema would corrupt the moral fiber of the country, Israel's first prime minister, David Ben-Gurion, was loath to offer government support, and thus the few films that appeared during the late 1940s and 1950s were made with private money. Yet Ben-Gurion was also aware of the potential benefits of building financial and cultural ties with foreign film industries and often made it possible for important transactions to occur in the transnational sphere. A look at the relationship with American producers and distributors render this ambivalence particularly evident. In 1949, for example, the fledgling government signed a lucrative theater-building contract with 20th Century Fox head Spyros Skouras following his successful visit to Israel. Yet this deal was foiled by protectionist government policies that raised import taxes on Hollywood films in the early 1950s—measures that ultimately forced American companies to keep their films in Israeli customs rather than release them to local audiences. At the same time, allowances were given to non-Israeli producers to use Israeli territories as locations for their films, including ones that dealt specifically with Israel's narrative of statehood. The most notable of this latter group was the 1960 Hollywood epic *Exodus*, which received substantial support from the government. The global success of Otto Preminger's film, as well as other like-minded Hollywood productions, such as *Cast a Giant Shadow* (1966) and *Judith* (1966), subsequently made it inevitable for the Zionist leadership to invest more funds in local filmmaking. Concurrently, many Israeli filmmakers found in these big-budget productions a source for continued artistic inspiration.[20]

In fashioning national policies regarding cinema, the Zionist hegemony was less influenced by the desires of the indigenous industry as by the demands of its indigenous audience. The proliferation of movie theaters in Palestine during the British Mandate and their equal popularity throughout Europe and the Middle East meant that both old-timers and new immigrants flocked to the silver screen. Following the establishment of the state, venues appeared throughout the country. By the 1950s and 1960s, moviegoing became the most popular form of entertainment in Israel. Along with commercial cinemas, the general trade union (the Histadrut, affiliated with the ruling party Mapai) arranged makeshift screenings with a mobile cinema in kibbutz dining halls, transit camps, and settlements, while the army provided films for soldiers and civilians in newly occupied regions such as the southern city of Eilat.[21] Audiences cultivated viewing expectations and developed a taste for escapist fantasies, which the fledgling local industry was too small to satiate. Instead, more than 80 percent of films were imported from Hollywood, while the rest came from Europe, Russia, and the Middle East. The need to import foreign films to serve audiences' demands disturbed critics, who eschewed the lowbrow content, fearing that the foreign imports were not instilling the correct values and attitudes nor serving as educational material to assimilate the populace into Hebrew culture.[22] Yet despite criticism, cinemas were filled and demand remained high; cheaper and more approachable than theater, opera, and musical concerts and without competition from television that would not arrive formally in Israel until 1968, cinema was an easily accessible luxury in a time of otherwise austerity. As such, it disrupted attempts at homogenization by reinforcing sociocultural networks that preexisted citizens' immigration. Moreover, its mass dispersal undermined efforts to shape the populations' viewing patterns. At a period when the establishment was deeply invested in the development and institutionalization of Israeli cultural forms, the filmic medium spilled over Israel's borders.

Contemporaneous Israeli audiences cared little for highbrow, mainly European content and avoided or walked out of films they did not enjoy—calling loudly for their money back. Generally speaking, they wanted to watch popular genres whose plot could be easily discernible even without familiarity with the language on screen or the language of the Hebrew subtitles projected alongside (though not necessarily in sync with the dialogue). In addition, they developed their interest further by following the lives of the stars through the news and in particular through the pages of weekly film magazines *Kolnoa* (*Cinema*) and *Olam Hakolnoa* (*World of Cinema*).[23] The increased investment of government funds led not only to a substantial growth in the industry during the 1960s but also allowed it to compete with the mass appeal of imported popular entertainment films. At the forefront of this effort were the so-called Bourekas films, formulaic comedies and melodramas that often focused on the culture and lifestyles of Israeli Jews of Middle Eastern geographical origin (Mizrahim). Positioning itself against the didactic content of Zionist propaganda films, this genre was seen as fragmenting the prominent melting-pot ideology and replacing it with a more pluralistic and multicultural vision of Israeli nationhood. As such, it drew its inspiration primarily from diasporic traditions that were otherwise repressed through Zionism's project of homogenous Israeliness.

One obvious source of influence was Middle Eastern popular cinematic traditions. From 1948 until the early 1970s, approximately nine hundred thousand Jews immigrated to Israel from Muslim majority lands. Their language, music, and culture were frequently disparaged by the Jewish European (Ashkenazi) cultural elite and marginalized on the public radio stations that made up Israel's national offerings. Moreover, the Censorship Committee had ruled that Arabic films (which were not subtitled) could only be shown at the cinemas in Arab towns.[24] Nevertheless, along with the local residents, Mizrahi Jews would frequent these cinemas in order to see the mainly Egyptian offerings. Thus, these immigrants maintained their transnational cultural connections, even as the Israeli establishment attempted to assimilate them into a Hebrewist melting pot. This particular transnationalism rarely translated itself into local filmmaking practices during Israeli cinema's period of high Zionist art.[25] Only with the arrival of Bourekas films were filmmakers able to make such influences more noticeable and put them to use in fostering a stronger bond with the local audiences of Middle Eastern descent. Of these, two filmmakers stand out as particularly transnational: George Ovadia, who worked in the Iranian film industry before immigrating, and transported the staples of that cinema into his Israeli melodramas, and Ze'ev Revach, the Moroccan-born actor and director whose work was influenced by the filmic idioms of Arabic—and in particular Egyptian—comedies.[26]

Importantly, though such texts often centered on Mizrahi Jews, with only a few exceptions, their directors were often Ashkenazi. Hence, in shaping their narratives, these filmmakers also brought to bear non–Middle Eastern influences, most notably classic Eastern European Yiddish literature. The status of Yiddish culture in Israeli-Zionist discourse was "complicated from the beginning. On the one hand, the 'negation of the diaspora' ideology . . . and the westernization project of the Ashkenazi Israeli elites . . . worked to oppress Yiddish culture. State cultural institutions defined Yiddish as exilic and anachronistic, and pushed it to the margins. On the other hand, Yiddish culture played a hidden yet vital role in structuring the Hebrew identity of the Zionist Ashkenazi elites in Israel . . . and therefore appears to have survived underneath the surface of official cultural discourse."[27] The Bourekas films came into being during a period when the ideological controls of Zionism loosened and as such were able to bring Yiddish culture to the surface. Ashkenazi directors

> used them—and offered them for the use of their peers from the Zionist-Ashkenazi elites—in three basic ways: first, the Bourekas films were means through which said elites were able to secretly partake in the Yiddish culture they once spurned; second, Bourekas films helped these elites to assuage the oedipal guilt around abandoning Yiddish culture . . . ; and third, the films were a way of reaffirming their desired identity as European Israelis. In this way Hebrew-Zionists, gained a form of legitimization that was a direct by-product of displacing the unwanted Jewish-diasporic pre-modern identity of traditional Ashkenazi Jewry from the *shtetl* (Jewish rural communities in Eastern Europe) onto a Mizrahi community.[28]

The first and paradigmatic Bourekas film, *Sallah* (1964), was an unprecedented box office success and was viewed by almost the entirety of Israel's population at the time.[29] Concurrently, it ushered in a new era of international successes to Israeli cinema, earning two Golden Globes and receiving an Academy Award nomination for Best Foreign Language Film. In subsequent years, a new enthusiasm for Israeli drama and comedy would grow outside of Israel, in no small part due to subsequent endeavors by *Sallah*'s filmmakers—director Ephraim Kishon, whose films *The Big Dig* (1969) and *The Policeman* (1971) were both nominated for a Best Foreign Film Golden Globe, with the latter winning the award in 1972, and producer Menahem Golan, who directed the Academy Award–nominated *Operation Thunderbolt* (1977) and became a key figure in the transnationalization of Israeli film production. Their efforts opened the way for other young filmmakers to achieve recognition on the global stage, though usually not in the popular genres in which they generally operated as directors—for example, Moshe Mizrahi, whose Israeli dramas *I Love You, Rosa* (1972) and *The House on Chelouche Street* (1973) were nominated for Academy Awards.[30] *Sallah*'s lead actor, Haim Topol, also managed to capitalize on his Golden Globe–winning performance and embark on an international career, which included an Academy Award–nomination and second Golden Globe for his performance as Tevye in the 1971 Hollywood classic *Fiddler on the Roof*. While being the most successful, he was not the only Israeli actor to break out on the world stage around this time. Other examples include Haya Harareet, the first international movie star from Israel,[31] who launched her career with *Hill 24 Doesn't Answer* (1954) and became known worldwide for her turn as Esther in *Ben Hur* (1959); Ziva Rodann, who played minor roles in *Forty Guns* (1957) and *Last Train from Gun Hill* (1959); Miss Universe competitor Aliza Gur, who acted in *From Russia with Love* (1962) and a host of American television shows; and Daliah Lavi, who was featured in *Two Weeks in Another Town* (1962), *Lord Jim* (1964), *The Silencers* (1966), *Casino Royal* (1967), and *Catlow* (1971), in addition to developing a very successful singing career in Germany.

Parallel to the continued-yet-weakened presence of heroic-nationalist war films and the meteoric rise of the Bourekas genre was an attempt to create highbrow Israeli cinema that would rival the contemporaneous achievements of modernist European filmmaking. Awareness of these achievements in Israel was fostered early on by critic and filmmaker David Greenberg, who in the years 1957–1963 published *Omanut Hakolnoa* (*Art of Cinema*), a limited-distribution journal featuring translated articles from *Sight and Sound, Film and Filming,* and *Cahiers du Cinéma.* Added to this was a fledgling network of cine-clubs,[32] where Greenberg and other film critics "gave lectures with information about Antonioni, Fellini, Bergman, Godard, and Truffaut . . . so as to broaden the horizons of local cinephiles."[33] This enthusiasm for European art cinema in Israel of the 1950s and 1960s, according to Judd Ne'eman, served "a historical desire" for its predominantly Ashkenazi audience; much more than with the Bourekas genre, it "reflected a yearning for the Jewish life and culture that had existed in prewar Europe and perished in the Holocaust. For many years this yearning was repressed by the Zionist ideological negation of the Diaspora [Shlilath Hagola]. Via the New Wave cinemas of Germany, Poland, and Hungary—countries imbued with anti-Semitic sentiments—the new generation of Ashkenazi Jews in Israel, who had originated in those countries, anchored themselves anew to the European Jewish life that had ceased to exist."[34]

This matrix of desire, combined with disgust at the contemporary state of Israeli filmmaking, pushed a number of young (Ashkenazi) filmmakers during the 1960s to take up European art cinema as their primary source of inspiration. All of them spent time in Paris during the rise of the French New Wave, and some also attended film schools outside of Israel (Avraham Hefner and Dan Wolman in New York, Boaz Davidson and Yigal Burstein in London).[35] Upon their return, they began drawing on these influences to create a new kind of indigenous cinema—one committed "to institute in society the freedom of artistic creation, and to disengage the arts and the artists from the political elite."[36] The resulting films, retrospectively grouped under the title *New Sensibility*, shied away from Zionist cinema's preoccupation with the national, especially in the epic context of war. Instead they focused on the existential crises of the individual, set to the background of Israel's urban centers. Additionally, rather than be bound by the staples of Zionist-nationalist iconography, these films foregrounded their transnational aesthetics, often through overt references to European (and predominantly French) films of the period. Together, such operations "created an image, often artificial, of Israel as a Western modernized state"[37]—a vision that often signaled an escape, not only to the past of pre-state Diaspora but to a potential future where Israel would become truly transnational (under a European banner). This vision, however, failed to garner audience support; certain notable achievements notwithstanding.[38] The international festival circuit did not welcome the New Sensibility films as much as it did other New Waves, perhaps judging the former to be too derivative, and domestically these works suffered box office failures, even after being hailed as artistic triumphs by the local press.

As much as these filmmakers courted European cinema culture, they shied away from participating in European Israeli coproductions, which were experiencing a surge during the 1960s and 1970s. The majority of coproductions were done with France, while others were made with the help of German, Italian, and British producers. These films often relied on Israeli studios for logistical infrastructure and incorporated Israeli film personnel at key positions. Yet their principal creators were by and large European. These filmmakers were primarily attracted to "cinematic ideas based on Israel's history and actuality."[39] Among such cinematic ideas, one can include the struggles of Zionist settlement and combat (*Give Me Ten Desperate Men*, France, 1961; *Bomb at Midnight*, France, 1965; *The Death of a Jew*, France, 1969; *Five Days in Sinai*, Italy, 1969; and *Stranger in Jericho* [also *The Death Merchants*], Germany, 1975), the impact of the Holocaust (*The Glass Cage*, France, 1965; *The Hour of Truth*, France, 1965; *The Customer of the Off Season*, France, 1970; *The Pedestrian*, Germany, 1973; and *Korczak and the Children* [also *The Martyr*], Germany, 1975), and biblical tales (*Wife of Er*, Italy, 1972; and *Rachel's Man*, UK, 1975). Though at times sporting casts of familiar international actors (for example, Richard Harris, Karlheinz Boehm, Jason Robards Jr., Maximilian Schell, Claude Riche, and Hardy Kruger), these coproductions were often financial flops both inside and outside of Israel, arguably because they were helmed by second-tier directors.[40]

By the end of the 1970s, the Israeli film industry was not only attracting international filmmakers but also exporting its own filmmaking talent internationally. A key figure in this development was Menahem Golan. From early on in his career, Golan, who studied film in the United States and interned with famed B-movie mogul Roger Corman, did not want to limit himself to the narrow boundaries of national film production and viewership. Together with his cousin Yoram Globus, he formed a distribution company (Noah Films) so as to give his products wider transnational exposure. His newfound experiences in global marketing made him aware of the possible limitations of distributing distinctly Israeli films. Though he continued to direct and produce such works and also professed the potential global profitability of such products (a position legitimized through the international successes of many of his productions), Golan gradually began to experiment with making "films according to an 'international' script."[41] The results included star-studded productions set in Israel—for example, *Operation Cairo* (also *Trunk to Cairo*, 1965) with Audie Murphy and George Sanders and *Diamonds* (1975) with Robert Shaw and Richard Roundtree. They also reflected a move to an international non-Hebrewist model—for example, *Escape to the Sun* (1973) with Laurence Harvey and Geraldine Chaplin and *Lepke* (1975) with Tony Curtis, both of which were shot in English. Israeli spectators "were reserved in their reaction to these films,"[42] possibly because it seemed as if they were not their preferred target audience. Yet these productions made enough money internationally to "open up the gates of global success" for Golan and allow him to transfer much of his operation overseas.[43]

This process culminated in Golan and Globus taking over the American production/distribution company Cannon Film in 1979 and establishing it as a force to be reckoned with. At the same time, they maintained their connections to the Israeli film industry, and even their internationally made films continued to display thematic influences that can be identified as Israeli but would go on to become important in the emergence of new styles within the United States and Europe. As Ella Shohat explains, Cannon "showed continued interest in the heroic-nationalist genre, but this time transposed into North American superpatriotic films such as *Delta Force* and *Cobra*, gratifying the desire for an American heroic image suitable to the Age of Reagan."[44] Logistically, rather than follow the trend of big-budget blockbusters that typified Hollywood operations after the success of *Star Wars* (1977), Golan and Globus focused on high-volume, low-cost production. This allowed them to sustain the business model that informed their operation in Israel: on the one hand, invest heavily in popular genre films, and on the other hand, use profits to fund a small number of artistically ambitious projects. As a result of this policy, Cannon's offerings were remarkably eclectic, combining B-movies in a variety of formats (ninja films, dance films, raunchy comedies, musicals, sci-fi fantasies) with highbrow creations by well-known filmmakers such as John Cassavetes (*Love Streams*, 1983), Lina Wertmuller (*Camorra*, 1986), Jean-Luc Godard (*King Lear*, 1987), Franco Zeffirelli (*Otello*, 1986), and Robert Altman (*Fool for Love*, 1985). Moreover, several of Cannon's more "international" productions—for example, *The Ambassador* (1984) and *The Delta Force* (1986)—were executed in Israel, and the producers also continued to invest in films made by local filmmakers not under their company's banner. Yet their greatest impact on the Israeli film industry resulted from inviting Israeli filmmakers to work with them in Los Angeles. Several of those who moved to the United States during the company's heyday in the 1980s—for example, Boaz Davidson, Avi Lerner, and Danny Dimburt—continued to maintain successful Hollywood careers years after Cannon Group fell into bankruptcy (1990) and its heads returned to Israel.

While Golan and Globus were making a name for themselves and other Israeli producers like Arnon Milchen and Avi Arad were taking their first steps in American filmmaking,[45] the Israeli film industry was going through a major transition. The Yom Kippur War (1973), which caught Israel by surprise and confronted it with the threat of annihilation as well as the rise to power of the right-wing Likud Party after thirty years of left-wing governments (1977), radicalized the political stance of many members of the local film industry's liberal ranks. Disillusioned with the path Israeli Zionism was taking, these filmmakers undertook a "vigorous revision of mainstream ideologies" through the symbolic sites that most connote them: the army, the kibbutz, the pioneer group.[46] They challenged the boundaries of the national Zionist ethos by reclaiming those figures that were excluded from it—mainly Holocaust survivors, homosexuals, and Palestinian Arabs. Particular emphasis was given to interrogating the injustices performed by the Israeli government and the Israeli Defense Forces (IDF) in the Occupied Territories—the so-called Palestinian Wave cinema—in an attempt to challenge the prevailing political climate. Rather than push toward change, however, these films usually evoked indifference, if not downright indignation, among Israeli audiences.

To the extent that these filmmakers were dealing with particular national problems and discourses, they were also professing their commitment to transnational trends within European art cinema and 1970s New Hollywood. Importantly, several of them were key figures in the Europeanized New Sensibility movement, while others were newcomers who came under the sway of new-wave European and American filmmaking as part of their studies abroad and in the newly established Film and Television Department at Tel Aviv University.[47] They wanted to create "quality cinema" in the European tradition and in this sense mimicked its turn toward political radicalism since the late 1960s (as is evident in the works of Jean-Luc Godard, Costa Gavras, Alexander Kluge, and Gillo Pontecorvo, among others).[48] Yet they also did not wish to condemn their films to the unpopularity of previous attempts at Israeli modernist cinema, so, much like filmmakers Martin Scorsese, Robert Altman, and Arthur Penn, they mixed ingredients from European art cinema "with features of the American repertoire—coherent, dynamic, and absorbing plots, as well as known generic patterns."[49] According to Nurith Gertz, "The measure of prevalence given to European ingredients in these films dictated their fate. Films whose makers were intelligent enough to combine characteristics of European and American filmmaking, or use American models that incorporated ingredients from European cinema to begin with, were the main strand in the system and some actually enjoyed wide distribution. Films which relied solely on European cinema were rejected from the system's center and failed to attract the audience's support."[50]

To the extent that it was aimed not only at domestic but also international audiences, this strategy did result in some noteworthy achievements beyond the borders of Israel. For example, Uri Barabash's *Beyond the Walls* (1984) was nominated for an Academy Award for Best Foreign Language Film; Daniel Wachsman's *Hamsin* (*Eastern Wind*, 1982) and Raffi Bukai's *Avanti Popolo* (1986) won major prizes at the Locarno Film Festival; Eli Cohen's *The Summer of Aviya* (1989) landed the Silver Bear Award at the Berlin Film Festival and the Silver Spike Award at the Valladolid Film Festival; and David Perlov's six-hour documentary *Diary* (1973–1983) was shown on Britain's Channel 4.[51] Yet more often than not, the Israeli political films failed to make a lasting mark on the global stage. The only Israeli filmmaker from this generation who did develop a successful transnational career was Amos Gitai. A director of radical political documentaries, Gitai moved to Paris in the early 1980s and gained recognition for his aesthetically complex and intellectually dense films. By the early 1990s, he had already enjoyed retrospectives in major American and European cities, and the British Film Institute (BFI) had published a volume on his work. In subsequent years, he helmed a string of high-profile feature films, several of which are multilingual and feature recognizable European and American stars (Juliette Binoche, Natalie Portman, Hanna Schygulla, Jeanne Moreau, Léa Seydoux, and Samantha Morton). These works tend to focus on Israel's past (for example, *Kippur*, 2000; *Eden*, 2001; *Kedma*, 2002; and *Rabin, the Last Day*, 2015) or critical social issues in the present (for example, *Kadosh*, 1999; *Free Zone*, 2004; *Promised Land*, 2004; and *Disengagement*, 2005), shaping them through certain formal staples of European modernist film, such as long takes and disjointed narratives. They have consistently enjoyed success at major international festivals (Cannes, Venice) to a level unmatched by the oeuvre of any other Israeli filmmaker to date.

Parallel to these developments, the Bourekas genre's presence on the cinematic landscape began to wane, and by the 1980s, it seemed that only Ze'ev Revach's films were keeping it alive. More often than not, this decline was explained as a result of the political shift, with right-wing parties taking up the cause of the disenfranchised Mizrahim and hence rendering unnecessary the Bourekas as a mode of ethnic/racial protest.[52] Yet it may also be accounted for as an outcome of the growing Americanization of Israeli culture, which raised the popularity of certain American cinematic genres.[53] The success of the American nostalgic youth film *American Graffiti* (1973) brought about a wave of similar products situated in the Israeli context, though with a greater erotic emphasis reminiscent of the American sexploitation genre. Avi Nesher's *The Troupe* (1978), a portrait of a military band during the War of Attrition (1969–1970), and *Dizengoff 99* (1979), the story of a group of youth in decadent and liberal Tel Aviv who want to strike it rich by making commercials, traded on intertextual references with American cinematic and popular culture, yet it was *Lemon Popsicle* (1978), directed by Boaz Davidson and produced by Menahem Golan, that was most representative of the trend. The film, focusing on the misadventures of three teenage friends in 1950s Tel Aviv, was seen by close to 1.5 million Israelis and led to seven sequels, most of which would gain cult status. It also became very popular across Europe (especially West Germany), Japan, and the United States (where it was nominated for a Golden Globe and remade in 1982 as *The Last American Virgin*, courtesy of Cannon Film). In addition to this franchise and its derivatives, the period also saw increased interest in contemporary youth cinema, which mostly mirrored the ascent of coming-of-age films in Hollywood of the 1980s. Like its American counterparts, these Israeli youth films often followed the trials and tribulations of teenage life, including its dark and more rebellious sides, and through them professed a "seeming revolt against all that the parents' generation held sacred and dear;"[54] yet at times they also moved beyond a generalized framework of generational struggle to address more specific social concerns (for example, in *Coco Is 19*, 1985, and *Queen of the Class*, 1986) and thus fed into the zeitgeist of politicizing cinema. The final American genre that made an impact on Israeli films of that era was that of the candid camera. Beginning with *Funny Israelis* (1978), the subsequent decade would see a proliferation of practical joke films (*sirtei metichot*), mostly directed by Bourekas actor Yehuda Barkan. These works operate around the general concept of tricking innocent bystanders while filmmakers catch it all on tape. The tricks are often of a sexual nature and as such create a more "documentary" equivalent to the Israeli youth sexploitation films of the 1980s. Irreverent in their choice of targets, such candid films were interpreted as "breaking the hierarchal, structured dimension of society and creating a social structure without distinction, sans design, a great, egalitarian, boundless community."[55] This inclusive vision of a global "society of pranks" arguably prompted producers to transcend national borders and set three of these cinematic works with a South African background, even as they were still addressing a predominantly Israeli audience base.

In the 1990s, both the raunchy comedies and the politically conscious message films were replaced by a largely somber, seemingly apolitical Israeli cinema. Rather than speak to collective identity and attempt to explicitly resurrect a clear notion of Israeliness, Israeli films during the decade often featured a society fragmented into different parts, with each part operating in a privatized state of internal exile (most evocatively represented in Assi Dayan's formative feature *Life According to Agfa*, 1993). These often include constituencies of Israeli society that the Zionist ethos marginalized and whose identities were in a state of flux. The films depicted the communities' vulnerability vis-à-vis more stable overarching forces or showed resistance serving as critique; in either case, however, thematic concerns rarely amounted to a clear and overt message for action or claim to an alternative structure of national belonging. Yael Munk has described these films as "liminal cinema," in the sense that they divulge an attempt to enact a ritual of separation from the known *communitas*. She connects these thematic directions to political events that proved traumatic for the Israeli left during the 1980s and 1990s (such as the First Intifada, 1987–1991; the assassination of Prime Minister Yitzhak Rabin, 1995; and the increasing political power of the religious establishment). Thus, the loss of faith in the power of Zionist Israeliness to guarantee not only progress and modernity but also a basic sense of stability and security engendered an atomizing effect whereby each subject had to resolve its identity away from that ethos. For those who were already displaced by the national ethos, this move marked a certain measure of relief; for those who were part of it, the break was painful.[56]

Deeply impacting this identity crisis and its cinematic expression were not only internal pressures and discourses but also external ones. The effect of globalization on Israeli society from the 1980s in particular had a decisive role in fragmenting national identity from without and promoting an agenda of global collaboration over local separatism. This force—bringing together capitalist economy and progressive politics—led to the initiation of the Oslo peace process and to innovative human rights legislation during the early 1990s. But the subsequent collapse of peace negotiations, in turn, also strengthened a profound sense of localism that clings to the traditional definitions of Israeliness as nationally bound, over and against potential global affiliations.[57] Caught between these competing pressures, Israeli liminal cinema attempted to negotiate its seemingly contradictory demands: escaping national definitions toward global membership while still holding on to a sense of local particularity overdetermined by the national but in search of other, more stable anchors.

This dynamic, which undergirds much of the filmic content of the period, is particularly evident in those films that focused on the recent immigration to Israel of approximately one million post-Soviet Jews (referred to in Hebrew as *Russim*, meaning *Russians*). Many of these texts were directed by nonmembers of this immigration wave and tended to subject filmic representation to the pattern of Bourekas cinema, reducing Russian characters to ethnic stereotypes and advocating assimilation through romantic unions between immigrant Russian women and local Israeli men. Yet as these immigrants began controlling their representation through filmmaking, the result was a more complex, "accented" Russian-Israeli cinema. This cinema unveiled the complexity of local-global/national-transnational pressures in the Israeli context, implicit in the position of "integration without acculturation." As such, these films often "walk a thin line between asserting the immigrants' place in Israel and insisting on their cultural distinctiveness."[58] The national identity is affirmed in a gesture of localism, while at the same time a transnational bond is evoked so as to assert a cultural distinctiveness—and even more importantly, a form of global citizenship that is part and parcel of the immigrant's experience.

Also evincing the effects of this glocal pressure dynamic is the cinema of second-generation Mizrahi filmmakers. Rather than submit to the reductive positioning of the Bourekas, which shaped Mizrahi identity through the codes of colonial exoticism (the Levant), these filmmakers wished to reclaim their parents' "Arab or Middle Eastern culture as inhabiting the present-day Mizrahi body."[59] Such attempts were not meant to ignore the legacy of Zionist nationalism that erased the Arabness of the Arab Jew so much as place it in critical perspective—to offer a counterbalance. This recognizes transnational affinities existing in a hybrid identity that straddles the global and the local. In making this cultural tradition visible, however, the filmmakers confronted the problematics of a language barrier and the impossibility of traveling or working within their parents' country of origin. This, in turn, according to Yaron Shemer, led to the creation of mediated constructions of the past that often turned toward nostalgia and vintage stylization. These effects are evident in the filmmaking of Hannah Azoulai-Hasfari (*Sh'chur*, 1994, and *Orange People*, 2013), Dina Tzvi-Riklis (*Three Mothers*, 2006), and Benny Toraty (*Desperado Square*, 2001, and *The Ballad of the Weeping Spring*, 2012).[60]

Even more complex in its negotiation of national and transnational cinema is the case of cinema made by Palestinians who are Israeli citizens. These filmmakers are acutely aware of their position as "enemies from within" Israeli national identity, even as they are still defined as national citizens and their projects are funded by Israeli organizations. This dislocation is further exacerbated by the erasure of Palestinian nationhood by Israel, which has made affiliation with the state and its organs an unstable relationship. Under such conditions, the transnational and national are closely (though uncomfortably) interwoven on the level of production and thematics, creating a cinema that embodies "the intricacies of fragmented lives"[61] with multiple and conflicting affiliations that also risks "a replication of a colonial and neo-colonial power dynamic."[62] For those particular reasons, the issue of whether to define Palestinian cinema made with Israeli funds, production resources, and actors as *Palestinian* or *Israeli* has become the focus of a heated debate over the past few years, both in Israel/Palestine and in the global marketplace to which these films are often marketed.[63]

The globalizing tendencies present in the 1990s came to fruition in the 2000s, when the Israeli film industry enjoyed a major boom, not only locally but in its international reputation. Israeli films now headline major film festivals such as Cannes, Venice, Berlin, Sundance, Locarno, Toronto, and Tribeca, where they have often won some of the most important awards. Since 2007, Israel has had an impressive showing at the Academy Awards, with four Israeli fiction films nominated in the Best Foreign Language Film Award Category (*Beaufort*, 2007; *Waltz with Bashir*, 2009; *Ajami*, 2009; and *Footnote*, 2011) and two Israeli nonfiction films nominated for the Best Documentary Award (*5 Broken Cameras*, 2011, and *The Gatekeepers*, 2012). Israeli cinema is now reaching bigger audiences globally, in no small part due to the development of the Jewish film festival circuit. Yet international success has also secured broad theatrical distribution for certain works without the need to rely on a "sold" Jewish/Israeli diasporic viewership—a process that has significantly accelerated with the proliferation of streaming services.

This acceptance also opens the path for many Israeli actors to play substantial roles in non-Israeli films—for example, Gal Gadot, Ayelet Zurer, Ronit Elkabetz, Alon Aboutbul, Uri Gavriel, Mark Ivanir, and Shira Haas. It also brought certain up-and-coming Israeli filmmakers, such as Ari Folman (*Waltz with Bashir*, 2008), Hagar Ben-Asher (*The Slut*, 2011) Yuval Adler (*Bethlehem*, 2013), Tom Shoval (*Youth*, 2013), Nadav Lapid (*The Kindergarten Teacher*, 2014), Aharon Keshales and Navot Papushado (*Big Bad Wolves*, 2013), Guy Nattiv (*The Flood*, 2014), Samuel Maoz (*Foxtrot*, 2017), and Joseph Cedar (*Norman*, 2016) into consideration for directing non-Israeli feature films.

These trends reflect an economic reality wherein Israeli film is becoming more and more a global *product*. This has to do, first and foremost, with a shift in the way Israeli cinema is being financed. Traditionally, filmmakers relied on financing from Israeli national and private funds and broadcast bodies. In recent years, however, the Israeli film industry has become highly dependent on funding through international coproductions, and this has created a demand to secure collaboration with non-Israeli production companies and services. Israel has official coproduction agreements with several mainly European countries, of which those with France and Germany have proved the most prolific.[64] The increased awareness of foreign interests in realizing Israeli projects has resulted in an explosion of coproduction informational conferences and pitching events in Israel, the most prominent of which is the annual Israel Market for International CoProduction, organized by the CoPro Documentary Marketing Foundation. It also led to participation of Israeli filmmakers in international film labs such as those offered by the Sundance Institute. Securing capital from overseas has not only advanced the logistics of film production but also removed certain barriers of international distribution that once handicapped Israeli cinema. Indeed, many Israeli films are selected by major festivals in the countries from which they receive financial support, thereby ensuring their widespread exposure.[65]

The importance of such international cooperation agreements is not only relegated to the artistic sphere but is increasingly serving as a diplomatic tool. In September 2020, Israel signed an historic peace agreement with the United Arab Emirates (UAE). Among the new collaborative agreements that pointed to the normalization of international relations was a partnership between the Israel Film Fund and the Abu Dhabi Film Commission. "Among bilateral workshops and training exercises, the new agreement points to a focus on co-productions and the invitation of a UAE director as a jury member at the 2021 Sam Spiegel International Film Lab."[66] In addition, selected Emirati students will be offered the opportunity to study in Jerusalem at the Sam Spiegel campus in one of three educational tracks. The announcement of this agreement was accompanied by explanations that film offers a "universal language" with the assumption that such language transcends national boundaries, while simultaneously explaining that such a collaboration is intended to promote "tolerance, education and developing a deeper cultural understanding between the Emirati and Israeli people,"[67] Thus film simultaneously works to represent the national to international audiences, and engages in a universal and transnational language that transcends those parameters.

These economic and political shifts undoubtedly affect the nature of representation in Israeli film, which is now further tasked with negotiating between the demands of the local and the global, the national and the transnational. Certain scholarly accounts noted the return of national themes—the Arab-Israeli conflict and the Holocaust, for example—to Israeli cinema in the 2000s, after their relative disappearance during the 1990s.[68] These representations have been less burdened by national specificity than their predecessors, which allowed them in turn to be more palatable for international distribution. Some achieve this palatability by divesting national themes from their particular attributes, and offering instead a universalized vision of Israeliness.[69] Others, in contrast, choose to maintain the particularity of these themes, but blatantly ignore their intricate complexities.[70] In both cases, profound literacy in Israeli social realities is not required in order to understand these works, and on occasion may even be considered a hindrance to spectatorial pleasure.

On the other hand, many Israeli films of the 2000s continue the 1990s cinematic trend of undercutting a national framework through an emphasis on transnational identity politics. What has distinguished these more recent films, however, is that they "go far beyond merely an authentic presentation of a previously unrepresented 'other'"[71] to Israel's dominant culture. For them, Israeliness ceases to be a reference point to struggle with or relate to; their particular representation of cultural identity figures it as a "detached floating" category unbound by a local determination and easily consumed by global audiences.[72] This manifests in acts of self-exoticization meant to appeal to a global perspective as can be evidenced, for example, in works dealing with the religious ultra-Orthodox Jewish community, like *Eyes Wide Open* (2009) and *Fill the Void* (2012).[73] Other films situate identity politics within genres borrowed from non-Israeli production contexts, most notably the horror film and the mind-game thriller.[74] Finally, there are also those filmic texts which overlay discussions of identity on avowedly globalized narratives that feature transnational relationships and/or overseas travel, such as *James' Journey to Jerusalem* (Africa, 2003), *Walk on Water* (Germany, 2004), *Strangers* (France, 2007), *Noodle* (China, 2007), *The Human Resources Manager* (Romania, 2010), *Tel Aviv Salsa* (Mexico, 2011), *Farewell Baghdad* (Iraq, 2014), and *Magic Men* (Greece, 2014).

In spite of these developments, transnationalism still raises controversy within contemporary discussions on Israeli cinema. Exemplary of this was the critical conversation around the release of Natalie Portman's *A Tale of Love and Darkness* (2015). The adaptation of a celebrated novel by Israeli author Amos Oz, Portman's film was shot in Israel, with all the main actors being Israeli and speaking in Hebrew (including Portman herself, who holds Israeli citizenship and was born in Jerusalem). Production funds came from various Israeli organizations, including governmental ones (it received the largest sum for a single fiction film in 2015 from the Israeli Ministry of Culture and Sports).[75] The film's distribution subsequently defined it as Israeli to Israeli audiences, as in its inclusion within the state-sponsored Israeli

Cinema Day. This definition was met with a swift and harsh rebuttal by several Israeli scholars, who declared Portman's Americanness undercut the legitimacy and authenticity of the film's supposed Israeliness.[76] According to critic and scholar Yuval Rivlin:

> The failure of *A Tale of Love and Darkness* derives from it being an artificial work that is disconnected from what goes around it. The strength and uniqueness of Amos Oz's book came not from the central plot . . . but from the social, familial, personal, and nostalgic mosaic which comprises it. The little anecdotes that Oz described were the secret to its power. Also the linguistic and behavioural nuances that he managed to capture, and which brought 1940s–1950s Jerusalem to life. I doubt it if Portman has the ability to understand the world described by Oz, its vitality, its decline, and Oz's desire to relive it through his book. Oz's ability to touch upon the Israeli undercurrent, hidden away inside everyone who grew up in little Israel, was lost in the transition to the big screen. Portman stuck to the external, universal plot, but without the local context that surrounds it the spectator remains seated in the darkness with little-to-no love toward the tormented characters presented before him.[77]

Rivlin's position exposes the challenge of transnationalism. Rather than dismiss this view as an essentialist perspective of Israeliness, we can embrace it as a means of reconsidering the limits and makeup of *Israeli* in cultural identity and its cinematic expressions. Such a reading impresses upon us the importance of moving away from a definition of *Israeli* cinema through the narrowest of national terms but instead highlights the significance of transnational questions that may enrich our understanding of how this cinema has operated artistically and structurally, as well as in terms of funding, distribution, and reception.

* * *

The following chapters operate under the assumption that "we can no longer pretend to ignore glaring gaps and blind spots in film history previously covered up or glossed over by the national cinema paradigm."[78] By this we do not mean to abolish the national and erect the transnational in its place. Such a maneuver would be problematic, first and foremost because it assumes that Israeli cinema is divorced from questions of national specificity in relation to national conditions and discourses. The reality, however, shows that this is not the case.[79] Furthermore, this position also assumes that the national and transnational are easily separated in a manner that allows us to address one while disregarding the other. As discursive formations, the *national* speaks more to an impulse of delimiting to the confines of the nation-state and its internal determinants, while the *transnational* speaks to an impulse of breaking away from such confines toward an external interstate sphere of influence and action. Yet the operation of cultural artifacts shows that these categories are almost always implicated by one another in a manner that speaks of dependency rather than disconnect. We would therefore subscribe to JungBong Choi's recommendation that "instead of looking for flat-out ruptures and frictions between the national and the transnational, one has to carefully investigate the complex structure of their mutual meditations."[80] In this sense, then, the choice to title the present introduction "Beyond the National" is meant only to signify our desire to explore more extensively the place of the transnational in this "complex structure."

The first section of this anthology focuses on filmmaking in Israel during the state's early decades—a period marked by high nationalist sentiment and substantial ideological control by the Israeli-Zionist hegemony. Rather than prove Israeli cinema narrated the nation during that time, the chapters here flesh out its transnationalism and, in the process, challenge its normative boundaries as a national cinema. In this capacity, Dan Chyutin's chapter explores Israeli film scholarship's fraught relationship with transnationalism by looking at its attempts at discussing postwar Hollywood films made about Israel's founding period. Through a close reading of Edward Dmytryk's *The Juggler* (1953), Chyutin discusses how the film subtly detaches itself from Israeli Zionism even as it celebrates its accomplishments. This disjuncture, in turn, makes it possible to imagine not only postwar Hollywood films about Israel as a bridge between national ideologies but also those contemporaneous films more commonly defined as *Israeli*. The result is a wider corpus of Israeli cinema that transcends nationally bounded concepts of Israel, even as it retains a certain commitment to and investment in them.

The transnational relationship between Israel and the United States is also explored in Julie Grimmeisen's reading of American culture and its attraction for Israeli actresses during the 1950s and the 1960s. Through a close reading of the women's magazine *La'isha*, Grimmeisen establishes the ways in which American ideals of female beauty were endorsed over and against attempts by Zionist-Socialist hegemony to vilify them as bourgeois. Of particular importance to her is the role this magazine had in promoting several Israeli actresses who fit the aforementioned model and who achieved international acting careers of various degrees of success. These valorized "beauties" were able to translate the Zionist fixation with corporeal perfection (the New Hebrew Body) into an American idiom, exchanging the former's penchant for asceticism with a celebration of luxury.

Also within an Israeli American framework, Rachel S. Harris, in her reading of several Westerns made in Israel (such as *They Were Ten*, 1960, and *Blazing Sand*, 1960), considers the tensions in importing a "foreign" genre during a time when Israel was determined to create an authentic national culture. Harris charts out a historical trajectory in which affinities between the national myths of Western and Zionist pioneering allowed for the international genre to be reimagined in a local context. But as filmmakers began to innovate outside the boundaries of acceptable pioneering narratives, the tension between importing a foreign vehicle and the expectation that film serve nationalist ends, exposed the problematics of transnational cinema. Teasing out the nationalist anxieties that plagued these productions and particularly their reception, Harris offers an examination of the threat posed by the transnational within the ideological boundaries of high nationalism.

Looking to Europe, Shmulik Duvdevani and Anat Dan's essay considers two radical documentaries—*Much'shar Bli Rosh* (1963) and *Sha'ar Ha'guy* (1965)—made by David Greenberg, a key figure in the mediation of European Art Cinema to Israeli audiences during the 1960s. These films, in their eyes, testify to their creator's expansive knowledge of modernist film aesthetics, influenced as they are by the labor of Art Cinema luminaries Alain Resnais, Georges Franju, and Luis Buñuel. Yet this influence does not define Greenberg's cinematic efforts as derivative, pale impersonations of "foreign" texts lacking in any political and social significance within the Israeli context (as has been the recurrent accusation against Israeli cinematic modernism of the 1960s). Rather, these films are unique in their mobilization of transnational aesthetics toward local political ends within the sphere of the nation, whether in delegitimizing war by comparing its carnage to the mechanics of animal butchery (*Much'shar Bli Rosh*) or in critiquing the collective rituals of memorialization and sacrifice that legitimize this carnage via a self-reflexive recovery of a particularly mythical site of combat (*Sha'ar Ha'guy*).

At the heart of this volume's second section is the fraught relationship between Palestinian and Israeli cinemas. Palestinian cinema is inherently transnational by virtue of the particular geopolitical conditions in which it operates—namely its attempt to assert a national definition under erasure by another, who also controls the territory to which both national definitions relate. This difficulty is rendered even thornier in light of the need to make films on Palestine in Israeli territories, which often also necessitates support from Israeli institutions and collaboration with Israeli filmmakers. Ariel Sheetrit's chapter addresses these complexities through its discussion of two celebrated Palestinian films: Annamarie Jacir's *Salt of This Sea* (2008) and Suha Arraf's *Villa Touma* (2014). In both cases, Sheetrit focuses on the shaping of filmic space and what it says about how a particular geography can be occupied simultaneously by multiple national identities with intertwined historical trajectories. Emphasizing the means by which these films thematize transnationalism and expose its influence on Palestinian national consciousness, Sheetrit broadens the scope of her investigation to reveal how their production and distribution were also deeply affected by transnationalism.

Mary Layoun's contribution looks at Palestinian cinema made by Palestinian citizens for ways of "imagining *otherwise* our communities." Her chapter investigates passages and sites as a potential *otherwise* that exemplifies the transnational nature of Palestinian existence, a reality of parallel worlds on a single strip of land that affords different kinds of movements while blocking others. Ibtisam Mara'ana Menuhin's documentary *Write Down, I'm an Arab* (2014) on Palestinian poet Mahmoud Darwish serves as her key example for exploring such movements and their (im)possibilities. Darwish's life was marked by (forced and voluntary) transnational positionings and negotiations, and in this he embodies the difficulties of Palestinians within the contested transnational landscape of Israel/Palestine. Yet in this film, Layoun argues, the exploration of his romantic relationship with Israeli Tamar Ben-Ari also offers viewers "signposts of living together otherwise."

Taking a more somber outlook, Yaron Shemer centers his discussion of Emad Burnat and Guy Davidi's Oscar-nominated documentary *5 Broken Cameras* (2011) on the difficulty of presenting a Palestinian narrative through the transnational cooperation of Israelis and Palestinians. Taking diegetic elements as his focus, Shemer foregrounds the "metonymic sixth camera" as that which exists outside of the raw footage of Burnat's five (broken) cameras—what essentially shows Burnat and contextualizes his political documentary work in the West Bank village of Bil'in from the perspective of his collaborator-observer, Davidi. Rather than *speak with* Burnat, the author shows how Davidi's observation *speaks for* Burnat in a manner that undermines the latter's agency. This relationship, for Shemer, is an actuation of the lopsidedness in Israeli-Palestinian transnational power relations—an attempt to narrativize the Palestinian through an Israeli perspective, the only one with the "authority to narrate" in this turbulent region.

The third section collects together chapters that deal with the ways in which Israeli filmmaking, in the broadest sense of the term, has interacted with transnational expectations and tastes, permeating through the spheres of production, distribution, and (inter)national reception. Ohad Landesman's contribution to this framework focuses on two documentaries made in and about Israel by prominent non-Israeli artists: *Description of a Struggle* (1960) by Chris Marker and *Promised Lands* (1974) by Susan Sontag. Though relating to diverse moments in Israeli history and disparate in their political agendas, these two films are nevertheless united by a decidedly Euro-American avant-garde style and an *outsider's* perspective. Yet through his careful contextualization, Landesman challenges the simplistic binary between *outside* and *inside*, revealing how both Sontag and Marker were personally invested in Israel and how their stylistic and thematic vision was largely implicated by the national narratives they encountered there.

Zachary Ingle's chapter engages Israeli cinema's expansion beyond its national borders through an examination of two key figures—Menahem Golan and Yoram Globus—and their brazen foray into transnational filmmaking with Cannon Films. Unsurprisingly, because it was deemed more American than Israeli, Golan and Globus's Cannon period has been marginalized in Israeli cinema scholarship. Providing a detailed account of Cannon's operations as a business and a forger of cinematic content, Ingle shows how Golan and Globus maintained important links between their Israeli past and their global expansion. He also reveals how their attempts to create such transnational continuation forced a backlash from local filmmakers in the United States and Europe, which was as much about critiquing the (poor) quality of Cannon films as it was about rejecting their affront to the purity of national categories.

While Cannon's story was marked by the studio's eventual downfall, Josh Beaty's discussion of Jewish film festivals in the United States brings to the fore Israeli cinema's transnational success. Beaty gives us an insider's look into these festivals' operation and specifically into their relationship with local Jewish communities, the primary audiences. Since these audiences come to the festival to experience a sense of community and articulate their ethnic identity and Israel is a key ingredient of both these activities, the measure by which an Israeli film exhibits Israeliness influences its appeal and marketability. Yet to foreground Israeliness is also to take a stand on Israel, especially in political terms, and in this, programming differs in its selections (and exclusions) depending on the particular community and organizational frameworks.

This catering to *foreign eyes* serves as the overall framework for Yaron Peleg's account of military-focused Israeli films of the 2000s. These works, according to Peleg, resonate with a traditional form of Israeli self-identification called "shooting and crying"—a position of being forced into warfare and suffering through the execution of war duties. Focusing on non-Israeli film reviews, Peleg reveals the overall attractiveness of these films' message in spite of growing transnational condemnation of Israel's militarism. This appeal elucidates the dialectic of Israel as perpetrator and victim that shapes both the understanding and interest of non-Israeli audiences. It also reveals the extent to which non-Israeli liberal elites are anxious about maintaining the balance between these polar opposites as a means of ultimately redeeming Israel amid a critique of its occupation policies.

The fourth section of the book fleshes out the effects of Israel's globalization on Israeli identity, discussing how contemporary Israeli cinema fragments traditional definitions of Israeliness so that they may function as more transnational. In this context, the films are read in light of a determination to denationalize Israeli cinema through universal tropes and an appeal to the transnational and universal, situating it within a global economy of film exchange. Nava Dushi's opening chapter argues that certain Israeli films of recent years undermine the idea of national unity, so prevalent in Israeli filmmaking of previous decades, through an emphasis on the local and on the minor. Marginalized communities stand at the focus of these works, and their alienation from the center is transposed onto the image of Tel Aviv as a fragmented, networked, globalized city. These narrative/thematic foci are refracted through a frame that at least partially challenges notions of narrational cohesiveness and causality. While such challenges force us to consider new possibilities for structure, whether it be social or narrational, what remains an open question for Dushi is the extent to which it allows us to imagine narrative or identity altogether beyond the major (by way of artistic language) and the national (by way of a collective field of reference).

The presence of a tacit dialogue between Israeli filmmakers and global(ized) markets is also what preoccupies Boaz Hagin and Raz Yosef, who analyze queer representations in Israeli films as instances of "world cinema." Drawing on Thomas Elsaesser's notion of "self-othering" or "self-exotization," the writers note a tendency for certain so-called festival films to create a distance from national identity structures and their corresponding national literacy, projecting queer representations toward broader Western definitions of how a marginal Other should look, either through a rescue fantasy shaped in light of Western neoliberal individualism, where this Other guides Israeli gays out of their homophobic society and toward an embrace of Western individualist gay identity, or through an Orientalist fantasy that sees Israel as a Middle Eastern utopia, combining a Levantine ruggedness of the land and its people with a laissez-faire attitude toward sexual orientation that extends well beyond the borders of cosmopolitan Tel Aviv. By contrast, the writers also point to several Israeli audiovisual texts that disturb these formulas of self-othering, such as in videos made for the Arisa line of monthly Tel Aviv LGBT parties. In these works, accessible on YouTube, camp sensibility and all-out irreverence abound, offering means to connect identities across borders without having to submit to notions of Western progress or Orientalist utopianism.

Concluding this section, Yael Munk's exploration of Hagar Ben-Asher's *The Slut* (2011) reveals it as yet another example of an Israeli film embracing transnational aesthetics. Munk considers the ways in which *The Slut* is rendered both visually and narratively as something not distinctly Israeli. Instead of dealing with the Holocaust or the Arab-Israeli conflict, which serve Israeli cinema as national markers even—or perhaps especially—when marketed abroad, the film engages in a contemporary international cinematic dialogue around global themes such as female sexuality and child abuse. Additionally, Munk highlights Ben-Asher's choice to draw on the aesthetics of feminist filmmaking—most clearly in female-directed French Extreme Cinema—which fosters a global awareness of patriarchal oppression and the means by which it is supported through cinema.

The fifth and final section of this anthology brings together chapters that read the effects of globalization on Israeli cinema, considering films' direct engagement with a second culture or film tradition. These chapters discuss the ways in which Israeli identity has become transnational within cinema, reflecting transcultural trends within the contemporary generation. Opening this section, Tobias Ebbrecht-Hartmann's contribution explores the creation, within the filmic diegesis, of an interzone where Israel and Germany meet—what he describes as "The German-Israeli Cinema of

Encounters." Focusing primarily within this category on the representation of Germany in films conventionally defined as Israeli, Ebbrecht-Hartmann shows how German-Israeli encounters serve primarily as a means of exploring tensions within Israel's history and cultural identity. His exploration into past representations reveals a use of the so-called German topic either in reference to the Holocaust and its affective and ethical charge on Israeli reality or in reference to the topos of journey and migration. As the treatment of these coordinates advances in time, Ebbrecht-Hartmann argues, films tend to address them more self-consciously and, in so doing, loosen Israeli identity's national boundedness—one that is reflected through a greater emphasis on the fluidity of geographical transitions and meetings that ultimately creates an evolving transnational narrative.

Tackling the notion of transnational encounter through aesthetic influence, Neta Alexander discusses a new brand of Israeli cinema—the New Violence—through its relationship with the global cinematic movement of New Extremism. She notes that the creators of New Violence all grew up during a period (1980s–1990s) marked by repeated conflicts arriving in very short order and thus were continuously exposed to violence as both citizens and soldiers. Yet when they aimed to express this experience through cinematic means, their primary source of inspiration was the confrontational aesthetics of European New Extremism rather than the more indigenous traditions of past Israeli films. Thus envisaged, New Violence seems to bridge the national and transnational in fruitful ways, both indicating the ways in which a foreign cinematic language can help address local problems and even reinterpret the idea of the local and how concurrently it can also make these local problems legible—and even interesting—to foreign audiences. Alexander's analysis of this dynamic stresses the importance of the former negotiation and uses it as means of distinguishing Israeli New Violence from European New Extremism; thus, while the latter avoids making clear political gestures and settles for a vague critique of bourgeois society, the former is committed to addressing the political conditions in Israel and to arousing Israeli audiences toward political action.

The final chapter sees Pablo Utin discussing the dialogue of three contemporary Israeli filmmakers—Navot Papushado, Aharon Keshales, and Eran Kolirin—with South Korean films. Through interviews with Papushado and Kolirin, Utin fleshes out the intricacies of this particular "transnational exchange," which could not be simplistically understood as a mere meeting of two mutually exclusive national cinemas and cultures. Rather,

Figure 0.1. Zion Cinema, Jerusalem (June 4, 1978). Courtesy of photographer Reuven Milon.

what emerges here is a complex dynamic where the Israeli filmmaker incorporates characteristics, which he defines as typically Korean, into a style that is both idiosyncratically personal and collectively Israeli, thereby creating a new hybrid version of Israeli cinema and Israeliness in general. As such, this negotiation testifies to the ways in which contemporary Israeli film maintains a transnational encounter even as it places itself, squarely and unabashedly, under the heading of the nation.

For "Israeli" is never a static and uncontested term, and this is not only due to the manifold nature of its internal ingredients, but also to the complexity of its transnational shaping. The cover image we chose for this volume speaks directly to this complicated legacy. Capturing the front of the Zion Cinema in Jerusalem, a name that reflects ideological hopes for return and redemption, we spy a familiar American film poster with credits that have been Hebraized for the local audience. Yet this is not *Gone with the Wind*'s first release in 1939, but a reissue nearly four decades after its production. Screened a decade after the Six-Day War, a war that would lead to decades of occupation of the Arab population in the land's Eastern parts and expose a legacy of racism, prejudice, and oppression for subjects who could not become citizens, this photo is a convoluted matrix of national identification and institutionalized racism that overdetermines much of "Israeliness." Israel no more imported its racism in a pure form than the United States exported it. Rather, these conceptions of nationhood, war, honor, duty, and community were translated into local contexts and framed through language and imagery that resonated with regional specificity. Thus Israeli films, like American films that had preceded them, drew cultural distinctions between those who were part of the polity and those who stood outside it, creating cinematic drama out of this tension and heroes out of those who protected and embraced the Zionist vision and rejected their own competing national interests. In the following decade, race consciousness would emerge in critical forms within Israel; this too was exported from America as a local variant of the Black Panthers. Yet whereas in the United States this movement served an African American population who had lived with centuries of slavery, discrimination, and subjugation, in Israel it was a protest movement of second-generation Jewish immigrants from North Africa and Middle Eastern countries, citizens with equal political rights who experienced economic and social discrimination. Their activism would ultimately result in a dramatic political loss for the ruling hegemony in the 1977 elections. It would take another decade before the grassroots Palestinian protest movement of the First Intifada would reshape the Israeli political landscape permanently. In the moment this photograph was taken, the national epic was no longer a rallying cry for Israeli audiences. Like *Gone with the Wind* itself, Israeli cinema would face a reckoning in the coming decades about what was represented on screen, and why.

In deconstructing the multiple sites of transnational engagement, this book ultimately sets out to offer a means to consider a small national cinema and its structural, economic, cultural, and artistic impact on a global stage. Recognizing the multiple ways in which transnationalism affects filmmaking and has become a tool for thinking about cinema, these essays explore a range of critical points of engagement. At the same time, *Casting a Giant Shadow* also makes visible the ways in which these transnational influences are drawn back into the national paradigm, thereby continually questioning and reshaping the very meaning of *national cinema.*

Notes

1. Margot Klausner, *The Dream Industry: Memories and Facts 25 Years of Israel Motion Picture Studios Herzliya Ltd. 1949–1974* (Herzliya: Israel Motion Picture Studios, 1974), 12–13.

2. Ibid., 15.

3. For an insightful account of Klausner's legacy, see Boaz Hagin, "Margot Klausner and the Pioneering of Israeli Cinema," *Screen*, no. 2 (2018): 158–175.

4. Ministry of Culture and Sport-Culture Authority, "The Ministry of Culture Unveils the Operation in the First Ever Israeli Pavilion at the Cannes Film Festival" [in Hebrew], Ministry of Culture and Sport website, April 11, 2016, accessed June 8, 2016, http://mcs.gov.il /Culture/Professional_Information/events/Pages/IsraelCann.aspx.

5. Neta Alexander, "Israel's Image-Bolstering Video to Cannes Is a Complete Mess," *Haaretz*, May 12, 2016, accessed June 8, 2016, http://www.haaretz.com/israel-news/.premium -1.719290.

6. Indeed, this point is made clear in early promotional mock-ups of the pavilion, which were plastered by banners with the title "The Israel Cinema." What may be construed as a grammatical error also offers a telling clue to the pavilion's underlying strategy of showcasing Israel to the world: placing cinema at the service of an idea of the nation (Israel), rather than using national currency (Israeli) as a descriptive of a film's territorial and societal origin.

7. For examples of this criticism, see Edna Fainaru, "Israel to Open Contentious Second Cannes Stand," *ScreenDaily*, March 21, 2016, accessed June 8, 2016, http://www.screendaily .com/news/israel-to-open-contentious-second-cannes-stand/5101635.article; Nirit Anderman, "Two Israeli Pavilions at Cannes Film Festival: A Welcomed Addition or a Waste of Public Funds?" [in Hebrew], *Haaretz*, March 23, 2016, accessed June 8, 2016, http://www.haaretz .co.il/gallery/cinema/.premium-1.2892513; Amir Bogen, "Cannes Film Festival: The Israelis Party, ISIS Threatens" [in Hebrew], YNET, May 11, 2016, accessed June 8, 2016, http://www .ynet.co.il/articles/0,7340,L-4802235,00.html; Ido Dagan, "Disappointment to Israelis at Cannes: The Israeli Pavilion Cost a Lot but Made Little Contribution" [in Hebrew], *NRG*, May 17, 2016, accessed June 8, 2016, http://www.nrg.co.il/online/47/ART2/778/897.html; and Ravit Hecht, "The Periphery at Cannes: Miri Regev's Ostentatious Quest at the Taxpayer's Expense" [in Hebrew], *Haaretz*, May 18, 2016, accessed June 8, 2016, http://www.haaretz.co.il /gallery/opinion/.premium-1.2948109.

8. Alan Williams, "Introduction," in *Film and Nationalism*, ed. Alan Williams (New Brunswick: Rutgers University Press, 2002), 10.

9. Ella Shohat, *Israeli Cinema: East/West and the Politics of Representation* (1989; rev. ed., London: I. B. Tauris, 2010), 15–16.

10. Ariel L. Feldstein, *Pioneer, Toil, Camera: Cinema in the Service of the Zionist Ideology, 1917–1939* [in Hebrew] (Tel Aviv: Am Oved, 2009), 185. In this and all subsequent quotations from Hebrew sources, unless otherwise indicated, the translation is ours.

11. Moshe Zimmerman, *Signs of Movies: History of Israeli Cinema in the Years 1896–1948* [in Hebrew] (Tel Aviv: Dionun-Tel Aviv University Press, 2001), 25.

12. Miri Talmon and Yaron Peleg, "Introduction," in *Israeli Cinema: Identities in Motion*, ed. Miri Talmon and Yaron Peleg (Austin: University of Texas Press, 2011), xi. Our emphasis.

13. Ariel Feldstein, for example, argued that the particular representation of Zionist pioneers in Aleksander Ford's 1933 film *Sabra* testifies to the filmmaker's desire to make them less an emblem of Zionist nationalism than of his Polish socialist values. Feldstein 2009, 157.

14. Ibid., 145–148.

15. Shohat 2010, 53.

16. Talmon and Peleg 2011, xiii.

17. See, for example, Nurith Gertz, *Motion Fiction: Israeli Fiction in Film* [in Hebrew] (Tel Aviv: Open University Press, 1993), 70–90.

18. Talmon and Peleg 2011, xii.

19. David Shalit, *Projecting Power: The Cinema Houses, the Movies, and the Israelis* [in Hebrew] (Tel Aviv: Resling, 2006), 46.

20. On the role of *Exodus* in shaping Israeli national mythology and its cinematic expression, see, for example, Yosefa Loshitzky, *Identity Politics on the Israeli Screen* (Austin: University of Texas Press, 2001), 1–14. Importantly, American productions shot in Israel were not only limited to films that dealt with the founding of the state; other examples include the Western *Billy Two Hats* (1974), the musical *Jesus Christ Superstar* (1973), and thrillers *Rosebud* (1975) and *The Sell Out* (1976). While these were not as impactful as the first group of Hollywood films, one can at the very least note some choreographic influences of *Jesus Christ Superstar* on the Israeli musical *Kazablan* (1974).

21. See Anat Helman, *Becoming Israeli: National Ideals & Everyday Life in the 1950s* (Lebanon, NH: UPNE/Brandeis University Press, 2014), 113–139.

22. Ibid.

23. Nathan Gross and Yaakov Gross, *The Hebrew Film: Chapters in the History of Silent and Talking Film in Israel* [in Hebrew] (Jerusalem: self-published, 1991), 395–396.

24. Helman 2014, 113–139.

25. Iraqi-born Nouri Habib's *Without a Homeland* (1956), dealing with the trials and tribulations of Yemenite Jews immigrating to Israel, is an obvious exception.

26. Sigalit Banai, "Arabic and Iranian Films in Hebrew: The Arabic Roots of Israeli Cinema," conference paper, Tel Aviv University, Tel Aviv, Israel, June 7–9, 2006.

27. Rami Kimchi, *The Israeli Shtetls: Bourekas Films and Yiddish Classical Literature* [in Hebrew] (Tel Aviv: Resling, 2012), 205.

28. Ibid., 227–228. The rise of Yiddish culture in Israel (in conjunction with the theatrical success in America of *Fiddler on the Roof*) also brought about a small cycle of Israeli films on shtetl life, including *Two Kuni Lemel* (1966), *Tevye and His Seven Daughters* (1968), and *Miracle in the Town* (1968). It may also have instigated another small cycle of comedies about contemporary Israeli-Ashkenazi Ultra-Orthodoxy that Shohat terms "'Gefilte-Fish' films (the Ashkenazi bourekas)" (110) and that include *Kuni Lemel in Tel Aviv* (1976), *The Black Banana* (1976), and *Kuni Lemel in Cairo* (1982). See Shohat 2010.

29. Yael Munk and Nurith Gertz, *Revisiting Israeli Cinema: 1948–1990* [in Hebrew] (Ra'anana: Open University of Israel Press, 2015), 41.

30. Working in France during the late 1970s, Mizrahi would eventually win the award for his French film *Madame Rosa* (1977).

31. Moshe Zimmerman, *Leave My Holocaust Alone: The Impact of the Holocaust on Israeli Cinema and Society* [in Hebrew] (Haifa: University of Haifa Press/Zmora Beitan, 2002), 156.

32. These clubs operated primarily in Israel's major metropolitan centers: for example, the Beit Lesin film club in Tel Aviv; Hebrew University's student film club in Jerusalem; and Lia and Wim Van Leer's film club in Haifa's Beit Rothschild. See Ariel Schweitzer, *The New Sensibility: Modern Israeli Cinema in the Sixties and Seventies* [in Hebrew] (Tel Aviv: Babel, 2003), 97.

33. Gross and Gross 1991, 398.

34. Judd Ne'eman, "The Death Mask of the Moderns: A Genealogy of New Sensibility Cinema in Israel," *Israel Studies* 4, no.1 (1999): 112.

35. Schweitzer 2003, 92–93.

36. Ne'eman 1999, 110.

37. Schweitzer 2003, 150.

38. Most notably, Oded Kotler receiving the Best Actor Award at the Cannes Film Festival for his starring role in *Three Days and a Child* (1967).

39. Gross and Gross 1991, 390.

40. Ibid., 386. One exception is Chris Marker, who directed his 1960 documentary *Description d'un combat* in Israel. See also Boris Trbić, "Description of a Struggle," *Senses of Cinema*, no. 52 (September 2009), accessed June 16, 2016, http://sensesofcinema.com/2009 /cteq/description-of-a-struggle/.

41. Gross and Gross 1991, 300.

42. Ibid., 303.

43. Ibid., 302.

44. Shohat 2010, 98.

45. Milchen was involved in Israeli movie production during the 1970s and became a major Hollywood player in the 1980s and 1990s with such high-end productions as *Once Upon a Time in America* (1984), *Brazil* (1985), *Pretty Woman* (1990), and *L.A. Confidential* (1997). Arad immigrated to the United States after the Six-Day War (1967), began making animation films for American TV in the mid-1970s, and founded Marvel Studios in the early 1990s.

46. Talmon and Peleg 2011, xiv.

47. Indicative and conducive of this influence is the publication of two new film journals during this period—*Closeup* (est. 1973), by Tel Aviv University's Film and Television Department, and *Kolnoa 74* (est. 1974), by the Israeli Institute for Cinema. Many of the writers and editors of these journals largely belonged to the aforementioned groups and used their position to promote cinephilic knowledge among their peers, especially surrounding European and American new waves. Helpful in their endeavors was also the establishment of the Tel Aviv (1973), Haifa (1973), and Jerusalem (1974) cinematheques. See Gross and Gross 1991, 398–402.

48. This is clearly evident in the *Kayitz* manifesto, which a group of young Israeli filmmakers published in 1977 and which called for government bodies to support quality films over popular entertainment ones.

49. Gertz 1993, 240.

50. Ibid.

51. See also ibid., 259–260.

52. See, for example, Meir Schnitzer, *Israeli Cinema: All the Facts/All the Plots/All the Directors/and Reviews* [in Hebrew] (Tel Aviv: Kineret, 1994), 16.

53. Amir Chetzroni and Shmulik Duvdevani, "On the Tel-Aviv Hedonism of the Cinema of Avi Nesher" [in Hebrew], *Resling* 7 (Summer 2000): 102.

54. Gertz 1993, 244.

55. Haim Lapid, "Flat on Its Back: A Scholarly Study of Israeli Hidden-Camera Movies" [in Hebrew], *Theory and Criticism* 2 (Summer 1992): 48.

56. Yael Munk, *Exiled in Their Borders: Israeli Cinema between the Two Intifadas* [in Hebrew] (Ra'anana: Open University of Israel Press, 2012).

57. Uri Ram, *The Globalization of Israel: McWorld in Tel Aviv, Jihad in Jerusalem* (London: Routledge, 2008); Yoav Peled and Gershon Shafir, *Being Israeli: The Dynamics of Multiple Citizenship* [in Hebrew] (Tel Aviv: Tel Aviv University Press, 2005), 40–44.

58. Olga Gershenson, "'Is Israel Part of Russia?' Immigrants on Russian and Israeli screens," *Israel Affairs* 17, no. 1 (January 2011): 167.

59. Shohat 2010, 304.

60. Yaron Shemer, *Identity, Place, and Subversion in Contemporary Mizrahi Cinema in Israel* (Ann Arbor: University of Michigan Press, 2013). See also Raz Yosef, "Restaging the Primal Scene of Loss: Melancholia and Ethnicity in Israeli Cinema," *Third Text* 20, no. 3/4 (May/July 2006): 487–498.

61. Shohat 2010, 277.

62. Yael Friedman, "Guises of Transnationalism in Israel/Palestine: A Few Notes on *5 Broken Cameras*," *Transnational Cinemas* 6, no. 1 (2015): 29.

63. In the past decade, several Palestinian filmmakers, such as Hany Abu-Assad and Elia Suleiman, have consciously worked to avoid using any Israeli financial or production resources in their works in order to bypass this conversation to the degree possible. Yet they may still use casts that include Palestinian actors with Israeli citizenship—an act that serves as its own political statement about citizenship and identity.

64. See, for example, Ofir Bar-Zohar and Hila Herzog, "Bourekas with Champagne" [in Hebrew], *Haaretz-The Marker*, July 20, 2008, accessed June 17, 2016, http://www.haaretz.co.il /hasite/spages/1004267.html.

65. For more on selling Israeli films overseas and how this relates to questions of coproduction, see Orr Sigoli, "Marking Territory: Two Israeli Producers and Two American Distributors Talk about Selling and Marketing Films" [in Hebrew], *Srita*, August 23, 2016, accessed August 23, 2016, http://srita.net/2016/08/23/israeli-movies-in-foreign-territories.

66. Joe Snell, "UAE-Israel film Collaboration Latest in Surge of Normalization Deals," *Al-Monitor*, September 21, 2020, accessed September 26, 2020, https://www.al-monitor.com /pulse/originals/2020/09/film-tv-israel-uae-emirates-collaboration-normalization-deal.html #ixzz6Z9xxGLrP.

67. Israeli 21c Staff, "Israeli-UAE Film Deal Aims to Promote Tolerance," *Israeli 21c*, September 25, 2020, accessed September 26, 2020, https://www.israel21c.org/israeli-uae-film -deal-aims-to-promote-tolerance/.

68. See, for example, Ilan Avisar, "The National and the Popular in Israeli Cinema," *Shofar* 24, no. 1 (Fall 2005): 142.

69. See, for example, Alison Patterson and Dan Chyutin, "Teaching Trauma in (and out of) Translation: Waltzing with Bashir in English," in *Media and Translation: An Interdisciplinary Approach*, ed. Dror Abend-David (London: Bloomsbury Academic, 2014), 221–241.

70. See, for example, Boaz Hagin, "Male Weeping as Performative: The Crying Mossad Assassin in *Walk on Water*," *Camera Obscura* 23, no. 2 (2008): 102–139.

71. Nitzan Ben-Shaul, "Disjointed Narratives in Contemporary Israeli Films," in *Israeli Cinema: Identities in Motion*, ed. Miri Talmon and Yaron Peleg (Austin: University of Texas Press, 2011), 117.

72. Ibid., 115.

73. See also Boaz Hagin and Raz Yosef, "Festival Exoticism: The Israeli Queer Film in a Global Context," *GLQ* 18, no. 1 (2012): 161–178.

74. See, for example, Boaz Hagin, "'Our Traumas': Terrorism, Tradition, and Mind Games in *Frozen Days*," in *Deeper than Oblivion; Trauma and Memory in Israeli Cinema*, ed. Raz Yosef and Boaz Hagin (New York: Bloomsbury Academic, 2013), 199–221; Olga Gershenson and Dale Hudson, "Nightmares of a Nation: Israeli Horror-Satires *Rabies* and *Big Bad Wolves*," *Journal of Cinema and Media Studies* 59, no. 1 (2019): 44–65.

75. Avraham Carmely and Hila Maimon, *Cinema in Israel: Yearly Review 2015* [in Hebrew] (Jerusalem: Ministry of Culture and Sports, 2016), 11, accessed January 26, 2019, https://docs .wixstatic.com/ugd/221b0b_2c6322f491354f90becd377adc2f065e.pdf.

76. Benjamin Tovias retrospectively reported that Oz "showed greater generosity toward the young artist [Portman] in her directorial debut, surely greater than that afforded to her by quite a few critics and members of the local film business who were quick to butcher it—some hours after its Cannes premiere, others in hallway conversations after seeing an incomplete cut. Several of the objectors imparted a patronizing and chauvinistic attitude: how can she, an American youth who fell in love with Oz's book and took barely a semester of studies at Hebrew University [in Jerusalem], dare to adapt our greatest author?" See Benjamin Tovias, "Give Respect to the Darkness" [in Hebrew], *Yediot Aharonot*, December 31, 2018.

77. Yuval Rivlin, "A Tale of Disappointment and Natalie Portman" [in Hebrew], *Mida*, September 25, 2015, accessed January 26, 2019, https://bit.ly/2SbU9e4.

78. Yingzin Zhang, "Chinese Cinema and Transnational Film Studies," in *World Cinemas, Transnational Perspectives*, ed. Natasa Durovicova and Kathleen Newman (London: Routledge, 2010), 123.

79. The same rule may also apply to other cinemas, for as Will Higbee and Song Hwee Lim claim, "In fact the national continues to exert the force of its presence even within transnational film-making practices" (10). Yet it may also be true that since Israel's nationhood is still in contention due to conflicts from within and without, its preoccupation with the national is potentially more heightened in comparison to that of other countries not operating under similar conditions. See Will Higbee and Song Hwee Lim, "Concepts of Transnational Cinema: Towards a Critical Transnationalism in Film Studies," *Transnational Cinemas* 1, no. 1 (2010).

80. JungBong Choi, "National Cinema: An Anachronistic Delirium?," *Journal of Korean Studies* 16, no. 2 (Fall 2011): 188.

I

MY ISRAEL: TRANSNATIONAL IMAGINING IN A TIME OF HIGH NATIONALISM

1

"I HAVE A GREAT PASSION FOR AMERICANS"

The Juggler *and the Question of National Cinema*

Dan Chyutin

WITHIN ISRAELI FILM SCHOLARSHIP, THE RELATIVE LACK OF reliance on the critical category *transnationalism* appears to bespeak of a difficulty in its integration into the existing body of work. The problem, I would argue, has its origins in the scholarship's initial investment in exploring, to quote Ella Shohat, "the agency of cinema in narrating the nation."[1] This emphasis on the nation did not exclude discussions of a transnational nature, as Shohat's formative *Israeli Cinema* (1989) clearly shows through its broader East/West perspective. Yet even if the expansion of such discussions ultimately drew scholarship further away from the narrow confines of the national cinema paradigm, the shadow of the nation still lingered in the attempt to submit these to localized explanations of Israeli film. In this sense, a frequent implicit assumption is that Israeli cinema is made most meaningful in relation to its national territory and society, particular history, particular language, and cultural codes; that it is, after all, "Israeli" and thus requires a specific kind of Israeli literacy to be best understood. And while such an assumption may be correct, it has arguably prevented studies from exploring the full scope of Israeli cinema's transnational operation and meaningfulness.

A particularly telling example of this difficulty, in my mind, can be found within scholarship's treatment of cinema in Israel's founding period

(1947–1967). As this was a period when the Israeli film industry concentrated on making heroic-nationalist films that foreground the tenets of Israeli-Zionist nationalism, it also makes itself particularly amenable to analysis through the national cinema perspective. Yet rather than submit to this perspective and its exclusionary tendencies,[2] scholars often challenged it by including Hollywood films made in and about Israel during that period as part of their consideration of postwar Israeli cinema. So brazen and exceptional was this inclusion—blurring rather than maintaining the commonly defined demarcation lines between *Israeli* and *non-Israeli*—that it often necessitated the concomitant inclusion of special explanatory caveats. Yosefa Loshitzky, for one, devotes a whole chapter to *Exodus* (Preminger 1960) in her book on Israeli cinema (2001), justifying this choice with the explanation that "although *Exodus* is *not an Israeli film*, it has become an inspiring model text for the heroic-nationalist genre in Israeli cinema."[3] For her recurrent references to *Exodus*, Nurit Gertz used similar terms: "Though *Exodus* is an *American film*, made by an *American director*, it succinctly captures the ideology of the national cinema and *plays a role in the history of Israeli cinema*: the creators of films that were produced in its aftermath saw it as part of the repertoire of Israeli cinema and incorporated some of its ingredients."[4] For his part, Moshe Zimmerman went so far as to argue that the title of "Hebrew or Israeli film" should be given to all films "that have some meaningful bearing on the country (they are set in it, their plots are relevant to its inhabitants, or the bulk of their creators are its residents)."[5] Accordingly, he includes in his analysis of Israeli cinema such movies on Israel as *Exodus, Sword in the Desert* (Sherman 1949), *Judith* (Mann 1966), and *Cast a Giant Shadow* (Shavelson 1966), which are often associated with Hollywood studios—and by implication with America. Yet even as Zimmerman is reluctant to follow other scholars in seeing these texts as strictly American, he still sections them off from other postwar films that fall more comfortably under the heading of "Israeli cinema."[6] As such, his and other similar maneuverings testify to a certain uncomfortableness with speaking about "foreign" film texts, which a resolutely transnational theoretical framework could alleviate.

This chapter centers on postwar Hollywood cinema about Israel, using it to explore not only this phenomenon's transnational workings, but also the limits of scholarship's attempt to incorporate transnationalism into its consideration of Israeli film. For these purposes, I offer a close reading of *The Juggler* (Dmytryk 1953), an early Hollywood film about Israel. The

Figure 1.1. Kirk Douglas on the set of *The Juggler*
(Dmytryk 1953). Collection Christophel / RnB © Stanley
Kramer Productions (licensed by Alamy).

first part of my argument follows the general model of past scholarship,
which often has related to such films as capturing the constitutive myths of
Zionist "Israeliness" while inflecting them toward particular "American"
sensibilities. Yet it also moves beyond past scholarly efforts in its attempt to
provide a more rigorous contextualization of these sensibilities in relation
to the realities of postwar America. This allows me to counter readings of
The Juggler as an unequivocal celebration of Zionist myths, foregrounding instead those dimensions of mythology that the film problematizes or
ignores in order to avoid collision with contemporaneous American ideology. Armed with these insights, the second part of the argument draws on
the film's reception history to uncover its complex matrix of transnational
identification. Such complexity, I stipulate, has been largely marginalized
in Israeli cinema scholarship's analysis of postwar Israeli-themed Hollywood productions, circumscribed as it is by national coordinates.

Israeli-Zionist Values and Postwar American Sensibilities

In the aftermath of the Holocaust, American popular opinion on the Jewish people exchanged past traditions of antisemitism with an unabashed embrace. First and foremost, this shift affected the public perception of American Jews, who began to be recognized as "consummate insiders in American culture."[7] For Jews themselves, recognition came hand in hand with the desire to "be like everyone else"[8]—most explicitly in the move to the suburbs, whose call "for a homogenization of differences . . . led them to diminish community and tribal ties while emphasizing continuing mobility and the individual pursuit of happiness above all else."[9] Concomitantly, American acceptance of Jews extended its reach to include an acceptance of Israel. The foundation of the Israeli state offered Americans a way out of seeing Jews only as emblems of victimhood, dependent on America's good graces for their survival. Israel's successful struggle for independence made the fledgling state appear, if not an equal, then at least a powerful ally to America. In the framework of Cold War pragmatic internationalism, it consequently became important to stress in the public sphere how American and Israeli "cultures were kin,"[10] articulating a shared basis for geopolitical collaboration. Vocal in promoting this message were American Jews, who searched in cultural kinship for means of associating themselves with a positive image of Jewry while "affirming their 'Americanness.'"[11]

Hollywood played a major part in this process. Though many Jews inhabited its ranks, the American film industry before World War II—and especially during the 1930s[12]—tended to downplay Jewish particularity due to fear of alienating its mainstream audience base. Things changed in the immediate postwar period, when an atmosphere of racial tolerance allowed studios to produce two films dealing with American antisemitism—*Crossfire* (1947) and *Gentlemen's Agreement* (1947). Yet even as these movies addressed a specific cause of concern, the Jewish community "felt that [they] would do more harm than good" by undercutting Jews' status as all-Americans.[13] Later, as American Jews became more accepted, their presence on the American screen grew while concurrently becoming "de-Semitize[d] and de-Judaize[d]" in order "to avoid challenges to a homogeneous view of American life."[14] This strategy made it difficult for the main studios to deal with Israel, a context that could potentially emphasize Jewish particularity over a universalized American ethos. As a result, the burden of representing Israel fell on the shoulders of "those at the beginning of successful careers, and especially left-liberal writers, directors and producers," who were less encumbered by the reservations of Old Hollywood. "Eager to reassert themselves in the wake of the Holocaust and its painful passive imagery," these cineastes gravitated toward Zionism's image of the New Jew and committed themselves to helping Israel "by dramatizing its story and heroes for Americans."[15]

A direct result of this newfound commitment was *The Juggler*—the second Hollywood fiction feature about Israel and the first to be shot in Israel.[16] For the film's principal creators—Michael Blankfort, who adapted his eponymous novel to the screen, and Stanley Kramer, who served as producer—Israel's struggle for statehood had been a powerful social drama as well as a way of reconnecting with their Jewishness. They therefore fervently believed in the value of giving it cinematic expression and making it an object of widespread veneration. Sharing in this belief were other members of the production. The film's (gentile) director Edward Dmytryk, for one, explained that he "did the film in order to see Israel, a country that was pulling itself up and doing *wonderful* things for the world."[17] Similar sentiments were retrospectively expressed by the film's (Jewish) star, Kirk Douglas, who was excited "to be in the land of my ancestors, my heritage," and recognized that in spite of the various hardships besetting the country, "it was *wonderful*, finally, to be in the majority."[18] It is this sense of "wonderful" that the filmmakers wanted to bring out—though perhaps only in very broad strokes, since, as Kramer asserted, it would have been wrong for the picture to "get caught up in 'Zionism'" and marginalize the "universal dimensions" that apparently made Israel "the closest place to the United States."[19]

The Juggler follows Hans Muller, a Holocaust survivor who lost his wife and children and seeks refuge in Israel. The Israeli immigration relocation camp causes Hans to feel claustrophobic, and he escapes its close quarters. While roaming the streets of Haifa, he flees an Israeli policeman, after mistaking the latter for a Schutzstaffel (SS) guard. Hans wounds the officer and, thinking him dead, decides to head for the border. On the way, he encounters Yehoshua, an orphaned boy who offers to be his guide. The two travel the countryside until they reach a kibbutz, where Yehoshua is injured by a land mine. While the child is recuperating, Hans remains in the kibbutz under the false identity of an American tourist and falls for one of its members, Yael. Growing more comfortable, he even agrees to resume his past profession—a juggler—and perform for the local children. At the height of the performance, however, police detective Karni, who has led the manhunt after Hans, arrives on the scene. The juggler barricades himself with a rifle; Yael attempts to convince him to come out peacefully, saying that the policeman was in fact only wounded. Hans undergoes a psychic breakdown; he lays down his arms, ultimately collapsing to the ground and into Yael's embrace.

These basic narrative coordinates offer the infrastructure to which the filmmakers apply much of Zionist ideology on the nature and function of Israeliness, modulated through their particular American emphases. In this engagement, like contemporaneous films defined more conventionally as Israeli, *The Juggler* foregrounds Zionism's three main symbolic foundations: immigration (Aliyah), the Sabra ideal, and ingathering (Kibbutz Galuyot). In terms of the first foundation, the emphasis on Aliyah as the means and emblem of national redemption is most notably present in the opening sequence, titled "The Refugees Arrive," which features refugee boats entering the Haifa port. The interaction between the refugees and the Israelis portside, made either through crosscutting or shared frames, establishes this immigration as a return—not to a foreign land but to a home where family and friends are already present to greet them. The jovial music, smiling faces, and waving hands provide affirmation of the supreme positive value of this meeting. Such affirmation, in turn, helps contextualize the appearance of refugee maladjustment in subsequent scenes as something that must be endured for a worthy cause.

This framing of Aliyah interacts with postwar American discourses in a variety of important ways. Most significantly, the film's reliance on the Zionist valorization of immigration seems intent on resonating with the contemporaneous conception of "the United States [as] a nation of immigrants, some persecuted, all coming to better their lives, experience freedom, and achieve economic success."[20] While this strategy ensured legibility for a broad American audience, it held particular relevance for American Jews, who at that period highlighted their immigrant heritage as part of "a similar drama of acceptance and assimilation."[21] By linking the narratives of immigration, the film then implicitly positioned American Jewish experience as a privileged site where the commonalities between Israel and America become apparent.

At the same time, so as to afford this kinship, certain dimensions of Zionist immigration had to be modified and/or elided. Firstly, *The Juggler* only speaks of Aliyah in the context of the Holocaust. In this, the film recapitulates the postwar American position on Israel as being less a national project with particular geopolitical ambitions and more a solution for the global humanitarian problem of Jewish genocide. This framing is also meant to address the tension surrounding American Jewry's reluctance to immigrate to Israel. As Jacob Neusner reminds us, "American Jews take very seriously indeed the existence of themselves as a distinctive community and the continued existence of the State of Israel as well." These two commitments nevertheless find themselves in conflict when this constituency fails to take to heart "the challenge of Aliyah" and voluntarily renounce their exilic affiliation.[22] By speaking of immigration only through the terms of the Holocaust, the film thus offers American Jews a Zionist Israel where that challenge is nonexistent. The call for Aliyah is made pertinent solely to the victims of recent European persecutions—and not to an American Jewry undergoing an unprecedented golden age. At the same time, since the American Jewish story has its origins in European antisemitic persecution, a certain level of helpful parallelism is still maintained between American Jews and the recent arrivals at Haifa port, imagined more as refugees than as voluntary immigrants (Olim).

The Israel that the film's immigrants meet, and that supposedly provides remedy for their ailments, is shaped in light of the second symbolic foundation of Zionism—the Sabra ideal. *The Juggler* foregrounds several aspects of this golden standard in a manner that is indicative of its American concerns. In relation to Sabra asceticism, the film shows how Israelis often deprive themselves of luxury due to the challenges of founding a state, as when Yael introduces a small shack without an indoor bathroom as her house. Importantly, on this latter occasion, as in several others, a contrast is established between such bare conditions and the affluence of America. These allusions seem to evoke the contemporaneous fear that the shift toward suburban middle-class existence has made Americans unable to cope with hardships such as those endured by their forefathers in their struggle to build a nation. At the same time, however, *The Juggler* also bolsters American self-image by presenting Israeli characters as evocations of America's Puritan/Protestant work ethic. Paradoxical in a sense, this representation exposed American audiences to both the challenge and the inherent possibility of recovering their traditional national ethos.

The asceticism of Sabras is linked to their investment in a socialist vision of egalitarianism, most clearly represented in the ethos and practice of the kibbutz. *The Juggler* highlights this vision through various kibbutz scenes featuring group activities: for example, when all the members form a human chain to lead Hans and the child away from the minefield after Yehoshua is injured, or when members dance the hora around the campfire in synchronized motions. Significantly, however, even as such events are foregrounded and contextualized, their socialist underpinnings are ignored. Considering that McCarthyism was at its height during the film's release, this disavowal could best be understood as an attempt by the filmmakers to rid Israel of the stigma of communist affiliations, turning it into an idealized nonpolitical democratic society.

This whitewashing of socialism, in turn, not only makes the kibbutz seem more democratic but also more pioneering. By placing Israeli pioneers front and center, *The Juggler* attempted, in the spirit of the contemporaneous public discourse, to surface an analogy with "the mythic heritage of the American West" and "remind Americans of their own rugged past." Yet in so doing, the film also brushed against the postwar fear around how "American society was becoming 'soft.'"[23] This is evident, for example, in a scene in which the kibbutz "head of cows" Mordechai tells Hans of his impression of New Yorkers: "Such crazy people," he says; "No room for trees, for cows, just people. Push, push, push." This invocation comes to portray Americans as fundamentally dissimilar to Israelis. They are defined not in relation to the Western frontier's rugged pioneer tradition but to a supposedly unnatural and unproductive East Coast metropolitan lifestyle. One may also find in this a more specific comment on the debilitated state of American Jewry based on the traditional perception of New York as a Jewish stronghold.

The Juggler also engages another archetypical role that the Sabra played in the context of nation building—that of the hero warrior. In addressing the Arab-Israeli conflict as the context of warfare, the film makes its presence known throughout via images of encirclement, as when Lucy, a little refugee girl, denotes the names of Arab countries surrounding Israel or when Yael tells Hans that "the only way to get out of Israel these days is by plane or by boat." In this, the film adopts "the David and Goliath metaphor"[24] prominently featured in American public discourse on Israel's geopolitical situation and uses it to paint a picture of a country "continually threatened by its more numerous and brutal neighbors"[25] and of its inhabitants as "tough fighters who use violence only as a last resort."[26] As with references to pioneering, the vision of an Israeli "warrior nation" complemented the American frontier myth where "a modern people set out to tame a wilderness of 'savages.'"[27] Moreover, it also connotatively referenced

"America's own story of independence more than one hundred fifty years earlier,"[28] in which a small nation in the making had to fight against greater states for its survival.

Yet it is also important to note that unlike subsequent Hollywood films about Israel, such as *Exodus*, *The Juggler* does not foreground Israeli combativeness. Indeed, the actual presence of the conflict exists in only one scene, when Hans and Yael encounter an enemy patrol near a destroyed Arab village; as he tries to fire upon the unsuspecting soldiers, she stops him by stating, "We don't kill people in cold blood." The depiction of this event departs mainline Zionist mythology, representing a desire to underplay Israeli military heroism through avoidance of spectacular battle scenes and through subsuming it *exclusively* under the heading of defensiveness, if not passivity. This strategy shows the limits of analogizing Israel and America as sister warrior nations, for it all too closely relates the former to the persistent image of Jews as universal symbols of vulnerability and the latter to the position of robust protectorate of the free world. In this, one finds echoes not only of the criticism leveled by the early Eisenhower administration against Israeli militarism for being an obstacle to Middle Eastern stability but also of a broader American hesitancy to ascribe the role of aggressor to the generation of Holocaust survivors that had suffered so much from aggression.[29]

Zionism's third foundation—ingathering as the desired outcome of a meeting between Aliyah and Sabra culture—is expressed in the film primarily through Hans's journey. Hans is a man whose chosen profession acts as a metaphor for his existential state. Like the juggler's bouncing balls, he is everywhere and nowhere; he can never have a home, since, in his mind, "a home is a place you lose."[30] The narrative's objective is to prove him wrong—to show that a person must always have a home and that for the recently displaced Jew, this home must be Israel. Because *The Juggler* positions Israel as a resolution for Holocaust traumas, its treatment of home appropriately takes on therapeutic terms. Accordingly, Hans follows the commonplace cinematic trope "of the survivor as a psychologically wounded soul."[31] The locus of his agony is the memory of being tortured by and losing his family to the Nazis. His journey toward acquiring a home is therefore a journey toward reclaiming sanity by letting go of such recollections. The achievement of this goal, as the film notes occasionally, is contingent on Hans being able to acknowledge his problem (personal transformation) and seek help from others (social transformation).

This process of psychic amelioration, which is synonymous with accepting Israel as a therapeutic home, is mapped onto a physical traversing of Israel, thereby reflecting the Zionist emphasis on journeying through the landscape as means of Sabra indoctrination. Yet the film's treatment of the journey trope diverges from the Zionist ethos in important ways. Thus, for example, if the Zionist ethos figured wandering as a cure for the ailments of Holocaust survivors, *The Juggler*, invested as it is in the American image of Jewish vulnerability, uses this activity to explore Hans's psychological resistance to assimilation. Also significant in terms of divergence is the choice to structure the journey as a police procedural—a popular Hollywood genre that made little impact on early Israeli film. *The Juggler*'s use of this narrative form asserted its *distinct* American flavor. Moreover, it also served to move away from issues of Zionist indoctrination and tackle the unique postwar American problem of anticommunist blacklisting. Thus, in one telling sequence, Lucy's father asks that she hand over her autographed picture of Hans to Detective Karni for identification purposes, explaining that "sometimes, for the sake of the law, we have to give up our friends." Read in light of Dmytryk's role as a friendly witness to the House Un-American Activities Committee (HUAC), this moral lesson therefore becomes an implicit apologia about "naming names,"[32] rather than a statement about Israeliness.

Being that the journey is insufficient in curing Hans of his malaise, the film supplies two characters who amplify its salubrious effects. The first of these is Yehoshua, who becomes Hans's travel guide. The choice of having a child fulfill this role relates to Zionism's cult of youth, which set the perennially young Sabra apart from old diasporic Jewry. Yet beyond this general connection, Yehoshua's age makes him a suitable surrogate son to Hans, a replacement for the children he had lost. Yael, the other major figure in Hans's assimilation story, plays a similar function. She supplants Yehoshua's guidance with further initiation into the Israeli-Zionist value system in the context of the kibbutz. Even more importantly, however, her romance with Hans, according to the film's logic of replacement, renders her a proper substitute for the wife who perished and helps him assimilate by "reconstitut[ing] his family in the New Land."[33]

The process of reconstitution is made possible not so much because of Hans's psychic agility but because he seems innately equipped to be part of the national body. Though an immigrant, Hans is not representative of the physical frailty and excessive erudition that Israeli Zionism associated with diasporic Jewry. Rather, as portrayed by a virile Douglas, he captures the essence of the Israeli-Zionist "tough Jew." Accordingly, his assimilation does not require any substantive change, for the raw material of Israeliness is already there, buried under a layer of psychic maladjustment. This understanding is expressed forthright during the hora dance scene, when Hans and Yael become part of a greater ensemble of kibbutz members engaged in the Zionist ritual of circle folk dancing. Through careful synchronization of music and physical movement, the scene puts forward the rite's symbolic function of engendering harmonious collectivity. Hans is overwhelmed by such intense inseparability, declaring that "we danced together, as if we were practicing for years." Rather than feel removed from the collective rhythm, he identifies with it as something that has been a part of him all along. Israeliness need not be learned—only recovered.

The definition of this new family as Israeli Zionist, in turn, coincides with its (paradoxical) definition as American. Thus, upon their first encounter, Hans Muller assumes the identity of Hans Schumann, an American who is a friend to the stars. And all through the remainder of the film, he is treated as an American, offering several occasions for Israeli characters to explain to him their national differences. Additionally, as Hans's interlocutor, Yehoshua is turned into Josh, a Sabra who is literate in American popular culture, including *Hopalong Cassidy* and Rita Hayworth. Yael is perhaps the least noticeably American of the family's members. Nevertheless, her blond locks and formfitting outfits still make her appear closer to the stereotypical representation of the White Anglo-Saxon Protestant (WASP) shiksa, later exemplified by Eve Marie Saint's character in *Exodus*. In this characterization, for Patricia Erens, "the freedom and equality of the Israeli woman is coopted and transformed into a symbol of sexual freedom (*cum* promiscuity)."[34] Yet even while trading upon the conventional voyeuristic pleasures of Hollywood cinema, Yael connotes a traditional domestic ideal, as when she says to Hans, "I want a husband. And children. To build a good home in a good country." Such aspirations seem to speak more to the American fantasy of the white-picket-fenced suburban bourgeois home than to kibbutz communalism, where traditional family structures were eschewed.

Though such overlaying of Americanism onto the Israeli-Zionist ideational structure seems cosmetic in nature, it points to deeper changes the film performs in the Zionist concept of ingathering. If for Zionism this concept was founded on a "negation of the diaspora" whose traditions must be forgotten, here amnesia is supported only partially. As the symbol of ingathering, Hans is pushed toward forgetting only a segment of his exilic past—the Holocaust. Once this element is erased, however, other elements of the past may be fully accepted—most notably his juggling, which he had forsaken because it reminded him of his fatal miscalculation, staying in Nazi Germany so as to hold on to his precious career. When he juggles in front of the kibbutz kids, Hans effectively demonstrates that Israeli-Zionist society has room for vestiges of his diasporic history. As such, the film seems to imagine Israel away from the prevailing melting-pot ideology and fashion it as a pluralistic nation of immigrants.

This rendering of Israeli-Zionist assimilation chimed with the contemporary American national image, which had substituted traditional melting-pot commitments with a pluralistic acknowledgment of (certain) difference. Furthermore, it carried special resonance for American Jews, who like Hans were also becoming insiders in their society and were similarly challenged in maintaining their cultural heritage. By permitting Hans to abandon only part of his diasporic past, *The Juggler* thus offered American Jewry a way out of this predicament—"an ethos of controlled acculturation" that preserves markers of distinction.[35] Finally, and even more narrowly, this representation held particular relevance for Hollywood Jews. Both Hans and Jewish Hollywood used entertainment as a means of assimilating into a foreign society. By allowing Hans to reclaim his juggling in a national context that values productive work, *The Juggler* legitimized entertainment as an occupation of substance and by extension positioned Hollywood Jews as key players in America's national drama of pluralism and assimilation.

Yet as much as this version of Israeli-Zionist ideology is brought forth to garner American popular support, its distance from the actual ideological reference point renders it fundamentally unstable. For this reason, perhaps, *The Juggler* cannot offer the cathartic ending traditionally provided by the Israeli-Zionist cultural metanarrative, wherein the outsider becomes a full member of its host society. Rather, more than catharsis, the film ends with a crisis: the mental breakdown of its main character, which prompts him to ask for assistance but hardly guarantees recovery. This crisis proves that like Hans, *The Juggler* also struggles with the task of bringing two national value systems into dialogue, and of negotiating the complex matrix of identification and removal that is engendered as a result. The film's open-ended denouement, in turn, attests to a basic sense of unrest in the transnational relationship between Israel and America and between American and Israeli cinemas during a formative period of their historical development.

The Juggler between Israel and America

In accounting for postwar Hollywood films that narrate Israel, Israeli cinema scholarship largely coalesced around two complementary claims: on the one hand, that these films were *Americanizing Israel* by foregrounding for an American audience those Israeli-Zionist myths that resonate with American mythology; and on the other hand, that their impact on Israeli culture, and specifically cinema, was in *Israelizing America* by allowing Israelis to imagine that America can also be theirs. The fact that such filmic texts surfaced points of divergence between Israeli and American national images has occasionally been acknowledged. Yet the scholarly emphasis was placed on how postwar Hollywood cinema exposed similarities between these images and thus enabled a transnational mode of identification that ultimately serves to *solidify a viewer's own national definition*. This, by extension, helped scholars maintain their commitment to the national within the Israeli cinematic context, essentially by arguing that postwar Hollywood films about Israel and contemporaneous Israeli heroic-nationalist films similarly buttress the nationalist model of Zionist Israeliness, even as they appeal to American models and traditions.[36]

While not dismissing scholarship's investment in trans/national sameness, I would nevertheless like to offer a counter-reading that highlights "difference and disjuncture" in global cultural operations.[37] As already shown, *The Juggler* not only sustains conventional Zionist-Israeli myths through their similarity with American perspectives—it also discloses a misalignment between these national mythologies. This misalignment, in turn, creates a complex and fractured web of transnational identification, one that arguably typifies both *The Juggler* and other contemporaneous Hollywood "Israeli" movies. A testament to that effect, I would argue, can be found in the film's reception, which exposes dimensions of filmic experience that have so far been neglected by Israeli cinema scholarship's limited engagement with the transnational. Studying this pattern of reception, then, may give credence to Andrew Higson's point about the need for scholars to shift "emphasis away from the analysis of film texts as vehicles for the articulation of nationalist sentiment . . . to an analysis of how local audiences construct their cultural identity" vis-à-vis the screen.[38]

The Juggler received a lukewarm response in the American press. Critics did point to some redeeming dramatic qualities but also observed faults. Of the film's rendering of Israel, recurring compliments were given to the filmmakers for faithfully depicting the Israeli landscape in a manner that revealed the young nation's challenges and triumphs. Indeed, it is in such scenes that an authentic vision of Israel seemingly came to the fore—a portrait "of the youthful, ancient land and of the young idealists who have come to wrest a living from the time-eroded soil."[39] Yet for these reviewers, Israeli authenticity was nevertheless compromised by employing the conventions of Hollywood genres. Thus, for example, *Monthly Film Bulletin* noted with distress that "the original idea . . . of pursuing the fate of so socially a useless figure as a juggler through the new Israel, needing only manual workers, is a promising one. But the film's conflicts arise not so much from this as from a completely conventional man-on-the-run story."[40] *The Christian Science Monitor* expressed comparable sentiments when describing the filmmakers' decision to not capitalize on "the pioneering atmosphere of the new state, plus the fact that its cherished sites are known only by name to most of us."[41] This avoidance, according to the reviewer, turned *The Juggler* into "a chase film which, for all its psychological pretensions, follows a standard pattern."[42] Otis L. Gurnesy Jr. from the *New York Herald Tribune* was more generous yet still faulted the film along similar lines: "As a story, 'The Juggler' is a psychological melodrama, and it is doubtful whether the adventures of a psychopath, however pitiable, are quite the right glass through which to view modern Israel. The device causes the film to stress the qualities of hope, compassion and brotherly love, but it filters out the subtler realities and strengths of this environment."[43]

Such evaluation shows critics to be conscious of potential dissonance between Israel's national image and their own foreign framing devices. This becomes an explicit theme in Nathan Glick's extended article on *The Juggler* for the Jewish American journal *Commentary*. At the outset, Glick argues for an affinity between American and Israeli cultural images: "The themes of the 'Western,'" he writes, "are the themes of Israel: refuge from tyranny and from city life, the crude settlement carved out of a wilderness, the drawn-out guerrilla warfare with a primitive native enemy, the conflict between individualist and communal ethics, the hope of a new beginning."[44] The writer does not dismiss such thematic affinities but rather sees the "virtues of *The Juggler*" as originating from them. Yet at the same time, he also recognizes that occasionally the desire to find cultural commonalities also pushes the Hollywood film to blatantly misrepresent Israeli realities. Such is the case in the choice to figure the traumatized Holocaust victim, who does not sit comfortably in the American-Israeli cult of pioneering, as a Hollywood insider—a strategy that "neutralizes the American spectator's presumed resistance to the foreignness of the subject by assuring him that the hero is, after all, only Kirk Douglas acting a part." Other examples, in his mind, include how "the whole meaning of the concentration camp is squeezed into the claustrophobia of close quarters, and the hero's reaction becomes a variation of the 'Western' theme, 'Don't fence me in,'" or how "the Israeli kibbutz comes to resemble a comfortably appointed American adult vacation camp."[45] Manipulations of this nature, according to Glick, profess the "inability of the American film-makers to absorb what is alien to American experience."[46] Accordingly, so as to avoid aggressive appropriation, the writer seems to argue that a proper "Hollywood approach" to Israel must account not only for sameness but also for difference.[47]

American audiences did not flock to see *The Juggler*.[48] Like the critics, they may have felt disappointed that the film presented an inorganic attempt to Americanize or Hollywoodize Israel's national image, rather than an organic attempt at surfacing an authentic common ground of identification. Such feelings would have emerged as a result of the film's release during a transition period in general American attitudes toward Israel, when Jews were gradually seen less as perennial victims and more as tough fighters or pioneers, mirror images of America's idealized self. *The Juggler*'s focus on a tormented Holocaust victim was therefore out of step with the times; consequently attempts to bring this protagonist closer to the American ideal—"a tough hombre in the kibbutz"[49]—appeared forced and foreign. Yet even if we accept this claim, it would be wrong of us to argue that audiences were entirely unconvinced by the film's message. American Jews, for one, may have found ample ground for connecting with its narrative. As Deborah Dash Moore explains in the context of two representative postwar Jewish communities:

> *The Juggler* affirmed convictions of Miami and L.A. Jews that survivors belonged in Israel, the one Jewish home and homeland. Its vision of rebirth amid pioneering struggles offered solace to Jews who had uprooted themselves from their homes. As permanent tourists, Jews in Miami and L.A. *peered into the distance for a redeeming image of a homeland with which they could identify.* Israel promised to heal the wounds of the Holocaust not only for survivors, who had suffered as grievously as Hans, but also for American Jews, who had

observed the disaster from afar. If Yael could win Hans, who pretends at several points in the movie to be an American from Hollywood, then the fair and beautiful Israel surely could capture the hearts of American Jews.[50]

What this account reveals is that the film's depiction of vulnerable Jewish immigrants to Israel held sway over an equally vulnerable Jewish American constituency struggling to become an American insider. This identification, in turn, did not necessarily bolster identification with America as a national home. If anything, American Jews "peered into the distance" toward a nation that seemed more accepting of vulnerability and hence more appropriate to their needs than a postwar America invested in national robustness. As a result, for them, *The Juggler* activated the particular transnational conundrum of "dual loyalty."[51]

This conundrum was seemingly resolved in later years as American and Israeli national images became more closely aligned around the trope of robust pioneering. For American Jews who were now feeling more like insiders, this meant that identifying with Israel served as an avenue to strengthen their identification with America. Common wisdom stipulates that 1960s films on Israel such as *Exodus* helped facilitate this process by encouraging the American Jew "to overcome the split in his [sic] identification" through their celebratory presentation of hardened Israelis.[52] Yet one could argue that these subsequent works did not overcome the tension of dual loyalty visible in *The Juggler* but rather repressed it. For as much as American Jews wanted to identify with the vigorous American pioneering spirit, this was not part of their particular heritage; the only way to participate in this ethos was through a proxy with a similar yet distinct national narrative. The similarity, articulated through the trope of pioneering, made possible this vicarious identification; yet it is an acute recognition of national difference that sustains vicariousness, for otherwise the inability of direct identification would assert itself too forcefully. In short, even if the aforementioned alignment helped American Jews feel like regular Americans, the process seems to have necessitated that they detach themselves from their national boundaries and feel like regular Israelis. Even more paradoxically, this alignment may not have potentially prevented non-Jewish Americans from entrapment in their own dual loyalty. Perhaps to a lesser—yet in no way insignificant—degree, Americans used "images of Israelis [to] construct their self-image at mid-century."[53] This need for foreign images to solidify one's own self-image was arguably motivated by anxiety surrounding the ability to realize America's pioneering spirit. Indeed, at certain junctures, *The Juggler* surfaces this fear when explicitly contrasting American laxity with Israeli productiveness. Such contrasts arguably moved to the background as Hollywood films became increasingly invested in professing similarity between Israel and America. Yet tropical alignment did not elide a basic imbalance—that Israelis were not just similar to Americans in terms of pioneering spirit but were *distinctively better*, a superior Other with which to identify beyond American borders.

The Israeli reception of *The Juggler* (*Ose Halehatim*) presents equally complex patterns of identification. Like their American counterparts, Israeli critics saw the film as projecting a foreigner's perspective that distorted Israel's national image. Such distortions made the work unserviceable for Israelis in the solidification of Israeliness; whether implicitly or explicitly, the Israeli reviews saw *The Juggler* as catering primarily to non-Israeli audiences. *Herut's* critic Yizhar Aharon, for one, abhorred this "foreign" vision, with its "typical plot of hunters and hunted, characteristic of the Hollywood film."[54] The film's inaccuracies testified "to the filmmaker's ignorance of Israeli existence," leading the writer to exclaim that *The Juggler* "did not justify all the publicity that was given to it and all the hopes we had placed upon it as a film about Israeli life."[55] Uzzi Ornan, critic for *Haaretz*, was a bit more forgiving in his evaluation. He reports of having been able to "breath the dry dust of the Galilee mountains" during the screening, even while pointing out that the film's limited perspective "undermines its claim to represent Israel." He particularly notes that "there is no great feeling of the Israeli motif in the movie, and it seems as if Stanley Kramer was focused mostly on the work itself than on the background."[56] This strategy, Ornan explains, could alienate Israeli viewers, who may find the film's representation of Israel "too polished." But if such polish was for Aharon a distortion that hurt the film, for Ornan it was what made *The Juggler* "a work of art."[57] Even more supportive was *Davar* contributor B. David. Though noting various inconsistencies that deprive the film of Israeli authenticity, David failed to see them as a major impediment. Rather, in his opinion, "What simultaneously evokes our amazement and admiration is that—in spite of minor faults, and without hurting the interesting story and the high level of filmmaking, the screenwriter and director succeeded . . . in casting a sympathetic light onto life in Israel and address—superficially at face value, but succinctly—some of the major problems that occupy our mind in the days of ingathering."[58] Importantly, he doesn't ask that the film produce verisimilitude but rather encourages the very polish which characterizes a foreigner's perspective, recognizing that this can help rally international support to the Israeli cause.

Though not as popular as the later *Exodus*, *The Juggler* did run for five consecutive weeks in Tel Aviv during October and November in 1953, with additional screenings being held there and in other cities (Haifa, Jerusalem, etc.) as late as October 1956. Such relative acceptance by the general Israeli audience raises questions about the particular nature of identification that stood at its basis. One could follow the argument of Israeli film scholarship and claim that *The Juggler* gave Israeli viewers the opportunity for self-identification, solidifying their own national identity as Israelis vis-à-vis a mirror image. To agree with this perspective is to presume that reviewers overemphasized the film's divergence from Israeli national definitions and that for regular viewers this departure was not apparent or at least was minor enough so as not to upset their self-image. Yet even if such a claim holds water, audiences could not have been so blind as to not recognize that they were identifying with themselves through *foreign* images. And perhaps the foreignness of such images, even if submerged in familiarity, made them more appealing for identification than homespun representations. Evidence to this dynamic may be found, for example, in famed Israeli novelist Amos Oz's retrospective account of his relationship to Hollywood. Here, Oz describes how during his childhood, "Tarzan and Flash Gordon films" represented a "world [he] would like to live in, the 'paradise lost,' where order reigned supreme." Such "larger than life" images "fit marvelously with [his] Zionist education. . . . That is to say: there are few idealists surrounded by a host of savages. They're solitary, but they're just. They seem weak, but in fact we are assured that they're not really weak."[59] Yet this nice fit did not necessarily eliminate a hierarchy. For even if both Hollywood and Zionist indoctrination professed an idealized existence, only the latter was in continuous friction with Oz's familiar reality. The American dream of Hollywood could remain untested and untainted, while all else appeared "a partial and flawed realization of a perfect template."[60] It is for this reason that Oz stresses his identification with the heroes of Hollywood over those of Zionism. And it is for this reason, as well, that to identify with the Hollywood version of Israeli life in *The Juggler* does not so much signal a desire to access Israeliness as it imagines a more perfect Israeliness, one that cannot exist but *elsewhere*. Thus, as was insinuated by the critic B.

David, what attracts Israelis to the film is not the prospect of the *same* but of the *better.*

It may also be possible, however, that this *better* was conceived as a radical departure from, and challenge to, the underlining sameness of Israeli and American national ideologies. Here one can trace a different route of fascination through the various items about *The Juggler's* production in the Israeli film fan magazines *Kolnoa* and *Olam HaKolnoa.* These publications catered to an Israeli population whose average yearly attendance in cinemas during the 1950s was only surpassed by that of the British and who resided in a country where "about 80 percent of the movies shown . . . were American."[61] The government feared that Hollywood's power over Israeli audiences could be detrimental to the causes of cultural and moral indoctrination; national press critics, often holding themselves up as educators, also "slighted American movies and their popularity even as they recognized that the cinema provided an escapist break."[62] *Kolnoa* and *Olam HaKolnoa,* on the other hand, celebrated Hollywood, providing Israelis with accounts of glamour that countered not only postwar Israeli austerity but also the socialist ideology used for its justification. Such was the nature of articles on *The Juggler's* production, which chronicled the arrival and departure of key personnel,[63] activities on set,[64] and public events with the film's actors and how they were received by the local crowds.[65] Expressions of audience enthusiasm on such occasions were registered throughout, indicating a mode of identification that aligned itself with the cult of the stars rather than that of pioneering. Such is the gist behind one "slightly cynical but typical detail" noted about the film's Israeli crew members: they "walk just like Americans, while the Americans opened an offensive upon the short khaki pants, and walk in them to their heart's delight."[66] Thus, if enjoying a signifier of Israeli national culture allowed Americans to experience themselves as more pioneering than their lifestyle afforded, identification with Americans permitted Israelis to imagine an Israeliness liberated from the stern parameters of Israeli-Zionism. *The Juggler,* in this view, may not therefore be read as an affirmation of conventional national definitions; its foreign perspective, if anything, opened up the possibility for Israelis to rework these definitions in light of a different set of values—one that glorified beauty and materialism. And in so doing, these audience members were able to acknowledge more fully what Yehoshua declares at one point during the film—that they "have a great passion for Americans."

With an acknowledgment of such divergence, we may finally ask: Should *The Juggler* be included in scholarly considerations of postwar *Israeli* heroic-nationalist cinema? And, for that matter, what about the inclusion of other contemporaneous Hollywood films about Israel, which all share similar divergences in representation and reception (though perhaps not to the same degree)? If one imagines the heroic-nationalist cinema as a genre whose purpose is teaching Israelis the Zionist definition of *Israeliness*, then such Hollywood pictures may not be neatly incorporated into its corpus; quite simply, they are *too American* to perform this educational role properly. Yet one could also talk differently about heroic-nationalist Israeli cinema—to draw on how it was defined by the postwar Israeli film industry as a product meant mainly for export.[67] In this view, heroic-nationalist cinema was not expected to stand on national particularity like an internal socializing agent; rather, it needed to bridge one national culture with others, creating a transnational space of intelligibility, even at the cost of courting tension and disjuncture among its ingredients. To look at this cinema in such a way allows us to better ascertain its affinity to postwar Hollywood films about Israel, which were equally invested in the precarious project of creating transnational bridges. Even more than the national currencies they traded upon, it was the nature of this transaction that made these cinemas kin and allowed postwar film critics to mention *The Juggler* in the same breath as Israeli cinema, even to the extent of claiming the Hollywood movie to be "a remarkable *Israeli* achievement in the international arena, whose influence is greater than that of many emissaries."[68] And if such categorical confusion compromises the national purity of heroic-nationalist Israeli cinema, seemingly the most national of all Israeli film genres, then what may be said about Israeli cinema at large? In overly localizing Israeli film, do we not risk containing it to the nationally bounded concepts of Israeliness, in spite of the fact that it has persistently eluded them throughout its short history?

Notes

1. Ella Shohat, *Israeli Cinema: East/West and the Politics of Representation* (1989; rev. ed., London: I. B. Tauris, 2010), 250.

2. Over and against such scholars who wish to define a national cinema by differentiating it from Hollywood, Andrew Higson rightfully reminds us that "Hollywood is not only the most internationally powerful cinema—it has also, of course, for many years been an integral

and naturalized part of the national culture, or the popular imagination, of most countries in which cinema is an established entertainment form." See Andrew Higson (1989), "The Concept of National Cinema," in *Film and Nationalism*, ed. Alan Williams (New Brunswick: Rutgers University Press, 2002), 56.

3. Yosefa Loshitzky, *Identity Politics on the Israeli Screen* (Austin: University of Texas Press, 2001), 2. My emphasis.

4. Nurit Gertz, *Motion Fiction: Israeli Fiction in Film* [in Hebrew] (Tel Aviv: Open University Press, 1993), 51. My emphasis. In this and all subsequent quotes from Hebrew sources, the translation is mine.

5. Moshe Zimmerman, *Signs of Movies: History of Israeli Cinema in the Years 1896–1948* [in Hebrew] (Tel Aviv: Dionun-Tel Aviv University Press, 2001), 112.

6. Ibid., 343–362.

7. Michelle Mart, *Eye on Israel: How America Came to View Israel as an Ally* (Albany: SUNY Press, 2006), 138.

8. Samuel C. Heilman, *Portrait of American Jews: The Last Half of the 20th Century* (Seattle: University of Washington Press, 1995), 16.

9. Ibid., 19.

10. Mart 2006, 59.

11. Ibid., 121.

12. Eric A. Goldman, *The American Jewish Story through Cinema* (Austin: University of Texas Press, 2013), 2.

13. Ibid., 80.

14. Mart 2006, 119.

15. Deborah Dash Moore, *To the Golden Cities: Pursuing the American Jewish Dream in Miami and L.A.* (Cambridge, MA: Harvard University Press, 1994), 229.

16. The first Hollywood film about Israel, *Sword in the Desert* (1949), was entirely shot on the studio lot. Of *The Juggler*, only the exteriors (about 40 percent of the film) were shot in Israel, while the interiors were done in Hollywood. For more on the production process, see Nathaniel Gutman, "American Films in Israel" (MA thesis, University of Southern California, 1971), 12–18.

17. Quoted in Donald Spoto, *Stanley Kramer, Film Maker* (New York: G. P. Putnam's Sons, 1978), 141. My emphasis.

18. Kirk Douglas, *The Ragman's Son: An Autobiography* (New York: Simon and Schuster, 1988), 203–204. My emphasis.

19. Idan Tadmor, "With Stanly Kramer" [in Hebrew], *Olam Hakolnoa*, August 7, 1952, 13.

20. Mart 2006, 132.

21. Ibid., 134.

22. Jacob Neusner, *Stranger at Home: "The Holocaust," Zionism, and American Judaism* (Chicago: University of Chicago Press, 1981), 125.

23. Mart 2006, 58.

24. Ibid., 26.

25. Ibid., 67.

26. Ibid., 65.

27. Ibid., 58.

28. Ibid., 69.

29. Ibid., 78–79.

30. Lawrence Baron, "The First Wave of American 'Holocaust' Films, 1945–1959," *American Historical Review* 115, no. 1 (February 2010): 103.

31. Ibid.

32. Blankfort, who had initially been assigned to direct *The Juggler*, was refused a passport to travel to Israel in early 1952 after being named a communist in Congress proceedings. Kramer then reassigned the film to Dmytryk, a member of the Hollywood Ten who by then had been exonerated as a friendly witness. Margot Klausner, the head of Israel's Herzliya Studios, asserted that Dmytryk got the job as a reward for "becoming a 'king's witness' and giving up the names of his friends." See Margot Klausner, *The Dream Industry: 25 Years to Herzliya Studios LTD, 1949–1974* [in Hebrew] (Herzliya: Herzliya Studios, 1974), 42; "State Dept. Nixes Passport to Mike Blankfort for Israel, Snagging Kramer," *Variety*, May 7, 1952, 3.

33. Patricia Erens, *The Jew in American Cinema* (Bloomington: Indiana University Press, 1984), 216.

34. Ibid., 217.

35. Heilman 1995, 23.

36. See, for example, when Shohat retrospectively (2010) defends the choice to include the postwar Hollywood "Israel" films in her *Israeli Cinema* by asserting the need "to broaden the discussion of 'national cinema' generally, and 'Israeli cinema' in particular," while at the same time, as further legitimization, arguing that these texts' "narrative movement *replicated* the official [Israeli-Zionist] metanarrative" (Shohat 2010, 271; my emphasis). For a rare and remarkable counterexample that foregrounds discrepancy, see Boaz Hagin, "'The Catskill Mountains with Arabs': Pluralizing the Meanings of Melville Shavelson's *Cast a Giant Shadow* (1966)," *Jewish Film & New Media* 6, no. 1 (Spring 2018): 1–27.

37. Arjun Appadurai, "Disjuncture and Difference in the Global Cultural Economy," *Theory, Culture & Society* 7, no. 2 (June 1990): 295–310.

38. Higson 2001, 65.

39. Richard L. Coe, "Israel Is Setting for 'The Juggler,'" *Washington Post*, July 3, 1953, 8. For positive references to the representation of landscape in contemporaneous reviews, see, for example, Hollis Alpert, "Kirk Douglas's Journey Back; an Italian Repeat," *Saturday Review*, May 9, 1953, 29; "Review: The Juggler," *Variety*, December 31, 1952, accessed August 21, 2016, http://variety.com/1952/film/reviews/the-juggler-1200417369/.

40. "Juggler, The, U.S.A. 1953," *Monthly Film Bulletin*, January 1, 1953, 101.

41. "Kirk Douglas Star of Film from Israel," *The Christian Science Monitor*, May 25, 1953, 4.

42. Ibid.

43. Otis L. Gurnsey Jr, "The Juggler," *New York Herald Tribune*, May 6, 1953, 22.

44. Nathan Glick, "The Juggler: Hollywood in Israel; *Tough Hombre in the Kibbutz*," *Commentary* (January–June 1953): 615.

45. Ibid., 617.

46. Ibid., 617.

47. Ibid., 615.

48. Edward Dmytryk retrospectively defined *The Juggler* as "a modest success with the public" (171). Contrastingly, film historian Tony Thomas included it in a group of films made by Kramer for Columbia in 1952–1953, all of which "were disappointments in the box office" (103). See Edward Dmytryk, *It's a Hell of a Life but Not a Bad Living* (New York: Times Books, 1978); Tony Thomas, *The Films of Kirk Douglas* (Secaucus, NY: Citadel, 1972).

49. Glick 1953, 615.

50. Moore 1994, 247. My emphasis.

51. On dual loyalty in the context of American Jewry, see for example: David Nathan Myers, "Dual Loyalty in a Post-Zionist Era," *Judaism* 38, no. 3 (Summer 1989): 333–343.

52. Loshitzky 2001, 6.

53. Mart 2006, 176.

54. Yizhar Arnon, "The Juggler" [in Hebrew], *Herut*, October 13, 1953, 3.

55. Ibid.

56. Uzzi Ornan, "The Juggler" [in Hebrew], *Haaretz*, October 9, 1953.

57. Ibid.

58. B. David, "The Juggler" [in Hebrew], *Davar*, October 16, 1953, 14.

59. Amos Oz (1968), "The Lost Garden" [in Hebrew], *Keshet Kolnoa* [reissue] (Jerusalem: Sam Spiegel School, 2013), 198.

60. Ibid., 199.

61. Anat Helman, *Becoming Israeli: National Ideals & Everyday Life in the 1950s* (Lebanon, NH: UPNE/Brandeis University Press, 2014), 113.

62. Ibid., 134.

63. See, for example, "'The Jugglers' Have Arrived" [in Hebrew], *Kolnoa*, October 2, 1952, 1–2; Yaacov Baal Teshuva, "The Makers of 'The Juggler' Leave the Country" [in Hebrew], *Olam Hakolnoa*, October 30, 1952, 3, 16.

64. See, for example, Bela Dor, "'The Juggler' Is Coming to Us" [in Hebrew], *Kolnoa*, September 18, 1952, 2; R. Natan, "'The Juggler' Shoot Coming to an End" [in Hebrew], *Olam Hakolnoa*, October 16, 1952, 12–13.

65. See, for example, Idan Tadmor, "Kirk Douglas Conquers Tel Aviv" [in Hebrew], *Olam Hakolnoa*, October 9, 1952, 3; Sylvia Keshet, "Amidst the Stars" [in Hebrew], *Kolnoa*, October 26, 1952, 1.

66. R. Natan, "On the Set of 'The Juggler'" [in Hebrew], *Olam Hakolnoa*, October 9, 1952, 18.

67. Nathan Gross and Yaakov Gross, *The Hebrew Film: Chapters in the History of Silent and Talking Film in Israel* [in Hebrew] (Jerusalem: self-published, 1991), 265.

68. David 1953, 14.

2

LONGING FOR HOLLYWOOD

Israeli Beauties on International Film Stages in the 1950s and 1960s

Julie Grimmeisen

IN A TELLING SCENE FROM VINCENTE MINNELLI'S *Two Weeks in Another Town* (1962), Veronica, a young Italian girl, asks Jack Andrus, a fallen movie star and recovering alcoholic, for the reasons someone like him would want to become an actor. Jack's response points neither to fame nor to accomplishment but rather to a different, more pedestrian cause: the desire to hide from the world.

"Everybody likes to hide once in a while," Veronica affirms. To which Jack replies: "Sure, they do. Look in any movie theater, what's the audience doing there. Hiding in the dark, trading their problems for mine and the screen. Actors, what a job."

In going to the movies, viewers are invited to forget their problems and identify with the often exciting and adventurous lives of characters and, by extension, of actors. Accordingly, the actor's challenging task is to realize the audience's dreams every time he or she stands in front of a camera. Minelli's film serves to articulate the actor's relationship between audience expectations and his own aspirations, drawing attention to the unsavory aspects of the industry, but only three minutes after Jack's fearful confession, he leans over a young Veronica, declaring "I like girls with black eyes, soft mouth," and kisses her passionately. Veronica submits willingly, as did many other attractive and exotic female characters during Hollywood's heyday. This shift in which the rewards of an actor's life are demarcated (often predicated on the availability of a willing female) constructs a cinematic fantasy that indulges the spectator's dreams of a more exciting and more fulfilling existence.

The actress pressing her full red lips against the mouth of the dashing Kirk Douglas was nineteen-year-old Daliah Lavi, a native of Northern Israel's Shavei Zion cooperative settlement (moshav). Capitalizing on Hollywood's long-standing interest in "foreign beauties," Lavi was not the only—and not even the most prominent—Israeli actress who answered the call. Indeed, during the first decades after the founding of the Israeli state, several other Israeli women—most notably Ziva Shapir-Rodann, Haya Harareet, Elana Eden, Aliza Gur, and Gila Golan—made the transnational leap into mainstream American and European cinema. They were all celebrated as talented "beautiful girls," both abroad and at home. Israel's female population especially followed their careers closely, cheered for their successes, and longed to become global movie stars themselves. These impulses were encouraged by commercial Israeli women's magazines, most prominently *La'isha* (*For the Woman*), which encouraged readers to follow these women's footsteps and imitate Hollywood's way of expressing femininity. They instructed young Israeli women how to dress, wear makeup, work out, and use their bodies alluringly. In reading the instructions and looking at the accompanying photographs, the dream of becoming an overnight Hollywood success and leaving the harsh reality of one's own country behind did not seem so far-fetched.

This chapter considers the ways in which young Israeli actresses became role models for the new Israeli woman by tracing their position on national and international stages. In particular, the following discussion will surface a certain ambivalence *embodied* in these glamorous female figures—how on the one hand, they came to signify the young Israeli nation through their "beautiful body," portraying the new country for an international audience who regarded them as foreign and exotic, and on the other hand, they served to give Israelis a sense they had been accepted within Western spaces and were normalized within them. In the process, by courting careers overseas, these actresses opened Israel up to the effects of transnational mass media, which reimagined Israeli femininity and shaped it in line with foreign values and aesthetics.

Watching the American Body

In Israeli culture's formative years, the socialist Zionist hegemony constructed a nationalist ideology around the mutually supportive idealized visions of pioneer spirit, agricultural and manual labor, kibbutz life, collectivism, modesty, and strong civil commitment to the state. These visions, as scholarship has long attested, tend to converge in the cult of the "new Jewish body." The proposed alternative for the supposed frailty of diasporic Jewry, the body of the "new (Israeli) Jew" was imagined as strong and upright, the product of gradual hardening via physical labor. When military conflict became a dominant theme in the life of the Jewish settlement and state, combativeness and bravery were added to this body's list of necessary traits, establishing it as the promise for the continued survival of the state.[1] While the male body was foregrounded in this context, the female body was nevertheless imagined as equal, enjoying the same rights and obligations (most prominently through universal conscription to the army). But at the same time, female bodies were still singled out as responsible for procreation and caregiving for the new Jewish generation.[2] As a dominant social construct, this vision of a nationalized body held considerable influence on the deportment of Israeli women during the state's early days. It created expectations for behavior and dress that included limitations with regards to adornment, ideals about women's hairstyles, and expectations about the ways in which women were expected to sacrifice their bodies to the national project. While this image dominated the discourse within the Labor-socialist hegemony that was instrumental in creating the new state, in real life this image was often in conflict with external influences. The prevalence of foreign films and magazines and the prominence of American popular culture's depiction of femininity offered an alternative model that allowed women to dream of an ideal lifestyle apart from that framed by Zionism. In this vision, women's bodies were made up, dressed in the latest fashion, and desired by the most attractive men, which included not only heroic pioneers, as in the Israeli tradition, but also tortured artistes, cowboys, and biblical heroes all played by Hollywood's leading men.

During the twentieth century, the growth of global mass media outlets allowed for the rise of an American body-centric popular culture that had immense transnational reach and "that celebrated the beauty, athleticism, and mobility of individuals and promoted a widely attractive consumerist ethos of self-improvement."[3] The American body at the center of this culture was associated with modernity, strength, health, and the constant desire for self-improvement, most importantly through reliance on the latest fitness-related commodities and trends.[4] Shanon Fitzpatrick demonstrates that at the beginning of the century, health and fitness periodicals such as

Physical Culture reached readership all over the world. They encouraged subscribers to imitate the many visual representations of the modern white body and, thereby, fostered the image of the United States as a robust superpower. At the same time, through bodybuilding manuals and ads for various beautification products, they disseminated the promise of an impressive physique that could be attained by almost anybody, regardless of ethnicity or nationality. In practical ways, they invited the consumer to participate through the institution of, for example, sponsored photo competitions in which they would tell their own personal story about physical transformation through adherence to a fitness ideal.[5] This activity was, however, tantamount to a steamrolling of local cultures. America's globalized popular culture, in Fitzpatrick's understanding, engaged in a "transnational participatory pastiche," displaying openness to "messages about bodies and nations that seemed to be every bit as flexible as the physical culture movement's ideal bodies themselves."[6] The meaning of the modern fit body was thus constantly reshaped within this transnational, interactive, and multivocal circulation.

With the growing popularity of movies, more and more American and international Hollywood celebrities communicated the message of body-centric self-improvement and self-fashioning across the global marketplace. In this framework, American and European filmmakers were constantly on the lookout for women with nonwhite bodies and faces that could interact with and become somewhat enmeshed in the white body-centric ideal. Successful actresses, such as the Chinese American star of the 1920s and 1930s Anna May Wong, parlayed their "exotic beauty" into glamorous, modern careers and became "transnational symbol[s] of cosmopolitan femininity."[7] They offered seductive invitations of participation in this cosmopolitan femininity for women across the globe, including in the fledgling State of Israel.

The challenges of building a new state did not stop Israelis from attending the cinema in droves. Without television, which only came into use in Israel in 1968, this attendance was seen as a necessity, particularly as every screening also included newsreels. Yet beyond providing updates on actuality, as historian Anat Helman explains, "for adult Israelis as well as youths, movies provided a diversion from daily hardships and concerns."[8] The low costs meant that it was one of the few forms of affordable entertainment in Israel at that time. City audiences often had to wait in line for hours to purchase a ticket and occasionally were forced to compromise on overpriced tickets from scalpers. In development towns and agricultural settlements outside of Israel's metropolitan centers, watching movies was as popular as in the cities, despite the attendant hardships. There were usually only open-air cinemas with projectors that often broke down during the screening. Regardless of where the screening was held, people did not only come to watch the film; they smoked, ate, argued, and interrupted the show by whistling, shouting, and even assaulting cinema workers.

Although movie critics and the intellectual elite asked for artistic and quality films, the majority of Israeli moviegoers wanted commercial fare, mainly from Hollywood, to satisfy their desire for an "escapist break."[9] Viewers "went to the cinema to fulfill their aesthetic and emotional needs, notwithstanding the numerous inconveniences;"[10] they wanted to see strong men battling it out in crime and adventure stories, attractive actresses in tantalizing love scenes, and happy endings that would divert their attention from harsh realities. Hollywood carried the promise of excitement, joy, sexual stimulation, and satisfaction; more specifically, it gave Israelis a taste of another life—of over-the-top heroes marked by physical beauty, exceptional careers, and modern lifestyles.[11]

Early Israeli society was confronted not only with many external challenges concerning the security of the young state but also with internal ideological frictions along collectivist and individualist modes of living. After the founding of the state, even certain key adherents of the pioneering ideal opted for personal freedoms, such as higher wages and living standards and the end of compulsory sacrifices by the individual, especially in the context of the postwar austerity regime (*tzena*). Israel's budding bourgeoisie began looking to Western, particularly American, culture and dreamt of living in a society where individual ambition was financially and socially rewarded over commitment to the collective.[12] A sign of such defiance was noticeable in the outcry among Israel's female population against the rationing of clothing and shoes in July 1950. Middle-class Israeli women did not want to dress according to the pioneering model, in a simple, ascetic, and androgynous style, but craved fashionable and cosmopolitan looks that would reflect their new social standing. These were offered by the stars of foreign cinema, role models to be emulated.[13]

La'isha, Israel's first successful commercial women's magazine, featured articles on and photographs of famous Hollywood actors, such as Rock Hudson, Peggy Dow, Julie Adams, Tony Curtis, and Piper Laurie. These celebrities, according to *La'isha*, had started with almost nothing, but after years of hard work and playing small parts, they had ascended to the coveted position of world-renowned stars.[14] Such sensational stories about Western high society attracted younger and older women (as well as men).[15]

In these narratives, *La'isha* often foregrounded the role beauty pageants held in facilitating a Hollywood career. For example, in its discussion of Donna Reed, daughter of a Midwest farmer and Academy Award winner for Best Supporting Actress in 1953, the magazine was quick to mention that the actress began her career by winning a beauty contest. After her coronation, newspapers published Reed's picture, and several of the biggest film studios contacted her immediately. She decided to sign a contract with Metro-Goldwyn-Mayer and landed her first on-screen appearance in *The Get-Away* (1941). More than an insignificant stage, then, "Donna's election as 'College Queen' was the chance of a lifetime. The doors of the studios opened before her and she found herself on the path to becoming a star."[16] This particular chance of a lifetime was not hers alone but was figured as the catalyst for the successes of such retired beauty queens as Ann Sheridan, Mary Murphy, and Bess Myerson.[17]

The images of those smiling, healthy, and, groomed women with long legs, slim waists, white teeth, and lustrous hair represented the so-called "American Look" and projected a national image of the United States as "wholesome, fun-loving, friendly, resourceful, and self-confident." They were the symbol of a "desirable modernity,"[18] an ideal of a future that promised freedom, abundance, health, youth, and openness. Moreover, the American Look promised a better life for anyone who invested in bodily beautification.[19] *La'isha* encouraged Israeli women to imitate the American model of femininity and its "body beautiful," sealed in the recognition that came with a beauty pageant win.

Instructing the New Israeli Woman

La'isha started as a supplement to the daily newspaper *Yediot Ahronot* in January 1947. Its initial popularity was low, but it soon appeared as an independent magazine and gained a loyal readership, reaching a circulation of 72,000 copies in the 1960s.[20] Across this period, the magazine defined itself as an advisor on the "special world" of women,[21] intending to instruct the Israeli woman on "how she can maintain her charm (*chen*) and increase it."[22] In this capacity, *La'isha* promoted Western fashion, seen as modern and up-to-date, and declared a pleasant femininity to be the golden standard for dressing in Israel; particular attention was given to the latest trends from abroad, including illustrations from American magazines and tips on how to revive old dresses, over and against the official austerity policy.[23] Indeed, the same day the government's restrictions on clothing and shoes were enacted, the magazine published a story about a glamorous French fashion parade in Tel Aviv, accompanied by photographs of strapless, slim-waisted, long evening gowns that pronounced a woman's "gentleness."[24] "There is no doubt that, despite everything, women in Israel will not stay behind other countries in the field of fashion," wrote the correspondent with confidence. "Now, we will utilize every piece of cloth, every old dress to alter and adjust to the new fashion trends."[25]

Extravagant clothing and the application of cosmetics were condemned as "bourgeois vanity" in Zionist-socialist ideology.[26] *La'isha*, on the other hand, propagated the right use of creams, lipsticks, makeup, hairsprays, and perfumes. In a published letter from January 1950, a young woman asked whether the use of cosmetics should be allowed even in agricultural settlements like the kibbutz, seen as emblematic of Zionist ideals. In its answer, the magazine only recommended a "basic treatment" that took the conditions of farm life into account.[27] It suggested "not to apply all colors of make-up" but face and hand creams that would fight against the dangers of working long hours in the sun. If that would not be enough "to guard her beauty" and preserve her youth,[28] *La'isha* told the letter writer to visit a beauty salon. Seeking professional help in a beauty parlor was for many Israeli women and housewives, especially in the cities, a weekly ritual. Getting one's hair done was an important sign of taking good care of her home and herself. The haircuts of the 1950s and 1960s resembled those of Hollywood actresses and were made with the help of gifted stylists, hair curlers, and a lot of hairspray.[29] Although *La'isha* was careful in advising against the overuse of cosmetics in an intolerant kibbutz environment, its pages were nevertheless filled with advertisements for all kinds of beauty products. Consuming them, according to the magazine, was a necessary step toward the declared goal of increasing an Israeli woman's charm, which in turn would help in finding a husband and starting a family.

In an article titled "Every Young Woman Is a Beauty Queen," Ela Atzmonit explained that when a man chooses a wife, "the inner soul of the woman" is a decisive factor in his decision.[30] But "first, the man is attracted to the exterior of the woman, which serves as the entrance to the garden of her soul. . . . Therefore . . . every woman, from early age on, needs to . . . take care of her beauty and her charm."[31] Atzmonit advised her readers to attend to their hair, face, hands, fingers, body, and legs. "Yes, there is a lot of work, but it is worthwhile,"[32] she concluded. The article couched beauty care in the need to find love and simultaneously communicated the message that every woman could be beautiful by taking extensive care of her body and using appropriate products.

The notion of every-Israeli-Woman-as-beauty-queen reached its most literal and influential expression in *La'isha*'s annual Miss Israel Competition (*Malkat Ha'yofi shel Israel*), which began in 1950 with support from local cosmetic producers, fashion designers, and cosmeticians.[33] Establishing a nationwide beauty contest was no easy feat with austerity being the order of the day. With this in mind, the organizers defended their undertaking by stating that they not only wanted to protect "the beauty, vitality, and charm of the Israeli woman" but also to help Israel "live like all the other [nations],"[34] which had been organizing beauty pageants since the beginning of the twentieth century.[35] *La'isha* wanted their girls to be able to compete with the standards of "international beauty,"[36] understood in terms of a perfect proportional and delicate female body, a pleasant facial expression, good skin, health, youth, intellect, polite manners, and graceful, captivating charisma.[37] These standards were searched for primarily in European and American contexts. In its first year, French advisors and European beauty queens took part in the preparations and helped crown the first Miss Israel.[38] During the following years, however, the focus shifted to the United States: thus, in 1951, an American expert taught the twenty finalists how they could enhance the "enchantment" (*kesem*) of their walking;[39] in 1952, an Israeli representative was sent to the international Miss Universe pageant in Long Beach, California, for the first time; and in 1954, *La'aisha* informed its Israeli readers that Miriam Stevenson, Miss America 1954 and future Miss Universe, had "the perfect figure of 36-24-26 inches,"[40] setting this as a model to which Israeli contestants had to aspire. The absolute archetypes of beauty queens were Hollywood actresses. *La'isha* emphasized this in no uncertain terms: "Those [women] who do not adapt to [Hollywood's] 'style' will not win the longed-for title,"[41] as a contract with one of Hollywood's film studios was seen as a guaranteed result of winning a major beauty contest.[42] During the California-based Miss Universe competition in particular, international beauty queens were able to meet their screen idols and experience firsthand Tinseltown's "splendor and glory."[43] This opportunity was but a stepping-stone toward becoming the Hollywood stars of tomorrow, the magazine would have its readers believe.

La'isha's beauty politics during this period testify that the Americanization of Israeli society was not an exclusively late-1960s phenomenon, as other scholars have argued, but had its beginnings much earlier.[44] The successful magazine circulated American body-centric popular culture from its inception and promised Israeli women a life full of excitement, love, personal success, and the richness of modern society. Its main concern centered on questions of how to maintain and cultivate a "modern"—that is, beautiful—female body. Obtaining the desired figure and lifestyle was in principle open to anyone, as long as she was willing to imitate the American example and consume the right fashion and beauty products.

Becoming the American Body?

La'isha attracted even more readers when some Israeli beauty queens realized their dreams and began acting abroad. One such article discussed the newfound international success of Israel's first Hollywood starlet, Ziva Shapir (later Rodann):

> It is wrong to think that beauty is only naturally given. It can also be an artificial product. Every woman that is basically beautiful, has charm, and personal charisma can improve her look until she reaches perfection. Ziva Shapir serves as the irrefutable proof for that assumption. The young Israeli woman came to Hollywood not only because of her acting talents but particularly thanks to her extraordinary beauty.... By chance, she encountered the cosmetic salon of the sisters NinaBella. They recognized immediately the "wonderful material" before them. A girl that, with the right treatment, could turn into an international beauty. And they tackled the work.[45]

The article highlighted the role of two cosmeticians who, according to the magazine, decisively influenced the direction of Shapir's career. They perfected her external appearance—they even advised her to have plastic surgery done on her nose—and thereby paved her way to Hollywood.[46] Shapir sang, danced, and acted. But her international career took off once she was crowned Israeli Wine Queen in 1954.[47] While promoting Israeli wine in the United States, she was able to attract American film producers and sign a contract with Universal-International. Shapir then became a staple of television bit parts during the late 1950s and '60s, also acting in several films, such as *Pharaoh's Curse* (Lee Sholem, 1957), *Forty Guns* (Sam

Fuller, 1957), *Last Train from Gun Hill* (John Sturges 1959), and *The Giants of Thessaly* (Riccardo Freda, 1960). In Israel, she was mentioned alongside the greatest film beauties of her time, like Marilyn Monroe, Sophia Loren, Anita Ekberg, and Kim Novak, and was repeatedly dubbed "the Israeli Ava Gardner."[48] Shapir's fame was short-lived, however; her reputation suffered from rumors about romantic affairs with several costars, including Cary Grant,[49] and she was photographed in the nude and appeared on the pages of American men's magazines (*Scamp* and *Esquire*). When the photographs were presented to the Israeli public in the controversial weekly news magazine *Ha'olam Ha'zeh*, they caused an uproar and elicited letters of complaint. The publisher Uri Avnery later recalled that 1950s Israeli society was very puritanical and not yet prepared for such female liberalities.[50] Israelis wanted to be entertained by beautiful and successful actresses but in keeping with bourgeois, conservative morality, which vehemently disapproved of sexual escapades by women in real life.

Aliza Gur (née Gross), Gila Golan (née Goldberg), and Daliah Lavi (née Lewinbuk) followed in Ziva Shapir's footsteps and went to Hollywood. Gur had first come to prominence as Miss Israel (1960) and was a semifinalist in the Miss Universe pageant. Golan, first runner-up of the Israeli beauty pageant that same year, placed second in the 1960 Miss World competition held in London.[51] Both Israeli women parlayed their public exposure as beauty queens to gain access to the international film business. In Hollywood, Gur would make several television appearances and play parts in *From Russia with Love* (Terence Young, 1963), *Night Train to Paris* (Robert Douglas, 1964), *Agent for H.A.R.M.* (Gerd Oswald, 1966), *Kill a Dragon* (Michael D. Moore, 1967), *The Hand of Night* (Frederic Goode, 1968), and *Tarzan and the Jungle Boy* (Robert Gordon, 1968). After Golan's modeling contract took her to New York, she signed a deal with Columbia Pictures.[52] She appeared in *Ship of Fools* (Stanley Kramer, 1965), *Our Man Flint* (Daniel Mann, 1966), *Three on a Couch* (Jerry Lewis, 1966), and *The Valley of Gwangi* (Jim O'Connolly, 1969). But probably the most well-known of this generation was Lavi. Working as a model and fluent in several languages, she was hired as lead actress for the German-Israeli film *Blazing Sand* (Raphael Nussbaum, 1960). In the following years, her career took off, and she appeared in a large number of European and American productions, such as *The Whip and the Body* (Mario Bava, 1963), *Il Demonio* (Brunello Rondi, 1963), *Lord Jim* (Richard Brooks, 1965), *The Silencers* (Phil Karlson, 1966), *Casino Royale* (John Huston et al., 1967) and *Catlow* (Sam Wanamaker, 1971). The role of Veronica in *Two Weeks in Another Town* earned her a Golden Globe nomination for Most Promising Female Newcomer. In the 1970s, she would go on to have a successful singing career in Germany.[53]

La'isha celebrated these women as heroes who, in appearing in international films as ideal forms of beautiful women, became part of the American body. It mentioned their perfect measurements, according to international/American standards, and their ability to captivate the audience with their beauty and charisma.[54] Journalist Dvora Namir met Gila Golan in New York after she'd shot her first film and described her as "shining, charming, beautiful as ever, pleasant, and admired."[55] The description of Golan's life story resembled an adventure movie with a happy ending. As a small child, she survived the Holocaust in Poland but lost both her parents. After the war, she immigrated to Israel, lived in a small apartment in Tel Aviv, and barely scraped a living. Then she took part in *La'isha*'s beauty pageant. "Gila had enough of the cloudy past. She decided to face the future. Now, she is a beautiful young woman who advances confidently towards the status of a movie star. She is a much talked about young actress in Hollywood. Her pictures are displayed in every important American journal."[56]

Thanks to her looks and ambition, she attracted international attention, was invited to auditions, and "became the Princess of Hollywood." She was even compared with the British American actress Elizabeth Taylor.[57] The Israeli magazine also took it as confirmation of their accomplishment that the girls received compliments everywhere they appeared, as well as expensive presents and hundreds of marriage proposals from American men.[58]

At the same time, however, *La'isha* pronounced the *Israeliness* of their beauty. It highlighted Aliza Gur's "long, black hair"[59] and "her dark brown face with its exotic look,"[60] which were seen as authentic traits of women coming from a Middle Eastern country.[61] Furthermore, the magazine described Israel's progressive politics of gender equality contributing to the women's physical perfection through the state's mandatory military training.[62] These stars were thought of as personifying a hybrid aesthetic, bringing the best of Western and Eastern cultures together.[63] *La'isha* was proud of their "mysteriousness" and was convinced that the girls not only imitated American standards but also glorified Israeli female beauty—and by extension, the beauty of the state. It therefore declared them to be "special ambassador[s] of good will."[64]

The actresses' foreign success was regarded as a triumph at home, placing the women in the international spotlight as representatives of a small and still relatively unknown country. Their advancement within the highly competitive cinema industry also reflected the country's desire to move to the center of the Western world. The actresses' bodies on the screen reflected this desire by seemingly molding together Israeli and American beauty standards. Yet in spite of *La'isha's* best intentions, it was not the interweaving of seemingly comparable standards that brought these actresses success but rather the definition of these standards as resolutely dissimilar. Although they were working within a Western idiom of beauty, what made such women attractive to Hollywood was the measure by which they were not fully assimilated into this idiom—that is, the extent to which their exotic and erotic beauty could evoke, in the minds of international filmmakers and audiences, associations of the seductive and dangerous Eastern *other*.

In the horror film *Pharaoh's Curse*, for example, Ziva Shapir plays Simira, an Egyptian woman who tries to stop a group of archeologists from desecrating a holy tomb. The men do not listen to the black-haired, partly veiled woman with dark eyes and exotic jewelry, and subsequently strange things begin to happen, leading to the death of several of them. During the film, one man expresses his attraction and fear toward the foreign woman coming from the desert: "That beautiful mirage is a walking nightmare." Shapir is clearly presented as a desirable woman but one representing the primitive, barbaric, and superstitious East, distinct and not wholly approachable to the "enlightened" West. In her most famous role, as a Native American woman in the Western *Last Train from Gun Hill*, the actress did not fare much better. She is married to a US marshal (Kirk Douglas) and is a good mother and well groomed, symbolizing the bridge between Indian and Western culture and the possibility of assimilation to modern life.[65] The plot of the film is driven by her rape and killing, after which the marshal sets off to avenge her death. Her Native heritage is visualized through her dark skin, long black hair, and moccasins. Her new civilized lifestyle is shown by her European dress and two long braids, which tame her hair. When she tries to escape the two aggressors, they corner her and rip off her clothes. Before the sexual abuse takes place, the camera turns away. The violence enacted on her stereotypical "savage" body underscores her position outside the realm of the accepted. Elise Marubbio discusses how 1950s films reflect America's repressed anxiety of miscegenation and racial integration in the civil rights and Cold War era.[66] She states: "In the context of the United States' formation as a nation, Whiteness represents the color of civilization."[67] This ideal needed the "polarity to the primitive,"[68] the national *other*, who was used to set the boundaries of national inclusion and exclusion—progress and decay—and who reasserted America's self-image of a strong, white nation-state. Israeli actresses like Shapir stood as exotic figures on this line of demarcation and dramatized the ambivalence between openness to and, more often, subjugation of the *other*.

Aliza Gur's performance as a gypsy girl in *From Russia with Love* became iconic, in no small part because of its trading on exotic tropes. She stages a "catfight" with another girl (played by Martine Beswick) over a man they both love. She is dressed in only a belly top and very short pants, and the spectator can easily see her athletic body, well-formed breasts and legs, delicate arms, and slim but muscular waist as she lunges forward and jumps on her rival. For a British gentleman, Sean Connery as James Bond is exceedingly rapturous about the abnormal spectacle and only leaves the scene's sexual fantasy to stop another megalomaniac villain. In the British thriller *Night Train to Paris*, Gur receives a comment on her extraordinary looks from the film's protagonist, former Office of Strategic Services officer Alan Holiday (Leslie Nielson), before she joins a group of models for her cover on a secret mission. He says that she "might make other women obsolete," meaning that she will endanger the mission by being too beautiful. Throughout the film, Gur is shown with stylish haircuts, expensive jewelry, and extravagant dresses that draw attention to her body. Within a similar vein, in the two James Bond parodies, *Our Man Flint* and *Casino Royale*, Gila Golan and Daliah Lavi respectively play exotic international spies, and their beauty is emphasized. Both have scenes in which they lay practically naked in bed so the viewer can gaze at their perfectly proportioned bodies and soft skin.

Despite the proliferation of these representations of Israeli actresses as sexual vehicles that proved to be contingent props or facilitated the plots while having relatively marginal roles, an interesting exception is Brunello Rondi's *Il Demonio* (1963), in which Lavi played Purif, a country girl in Southern Italy. After being rejected by the man she loves, she is taken hold of by a demon. Purif is cursed as a witch by the village, abused, and raped by different men. At the end, she undergoes a violent death. The sexual interactions of the film are presented as horrifying and deterring. In one scene, she is screaming while having a nightmare, tosses her head and hair around, and starts touching herself. The camera closely follows the movements of her trembling body. Although Purif's body is shown as appealing and lascivious, the tragic film about a young woman's horrible fate courts not sexual stimulation but fear.

Resisting the films' narratives, *La'isha* did not perceive the actresses' representation as degrading and discriminatory but instead as inspiring and nationally satisfying. As Ann Kaplan, Jackie Stacey, and others have argued, spectators' positions, desires, pleasures, and resistances are diverse as well as multiple, varying across time and place and producing different cultural meanings in specific contexts.[69] The Israeli women's magazine hailed the pleasure of seeing "one of their girls" on the same screen with Hollywood stars, notwithstanding her inferior and passive role. It valorized her as a symbol of Hollywood, a beautiful, admired, and successful actress leading the same glamorous life as her famous colleagues. At the same time, Israeli women and men could identify with the "male gaze"— that is, with the male protagonist and *his* looks and activities to civilize the world.[70] The American narrative of quelling the Wild West mirrored Zionism's dream of rebuilding the East. Israelis liked to compare themselves with adventurous, crafty but noble Western heroes who did not always adhere to the rules but were driven by morality.[71] The positioning of Israeli actresses helped make this comparison possible, as if inviting them toward such identification. This becomes clear in the German cinema booklet (*Neues Filmprogramm*) for *Blazing Sand*, an adventure film about a group's trip to the archeological city of Petra in Jordan, which describes the role of Dina (Daliah Lavi) as follows: "She lures [all the men of the expedition] with her calculated female shrewdness. She offers promises and seductions. The men's blood begins to boil."[72]

Normally, Israeli actresses embodied the ideal exotic adornment for every James Bond–type hero who surrounded himself with international beauties, which made his adventurous life seem even more exciting and enviable. This female admiration and submission emphasized the strength, power, and virility of white men and justified Western dominance and control over the world. But despite their subsidiary roles to white men, Israeli actresses found their physiques being celebrated by American and European film directors as fit and attractive, equal to and at times even surpassing Western beauty. These women were introduced as representatives of a cosmopolitan femininity that served as a basis for Hollywood's global outreach. Their regular appearances on international film stages invited women of the world to cross borders and follow their own paths to beauty, celebrity, and a glamorous lifestyle. Like "exotic" actresses before them, they became a symbol of self-fashioning and self-improvement. They had successfully trained and adapted their bodies and learned how to dress elegantly, use makeup, attract an audience, mingle in high society, and converse in different languages. They were able to control and transform their otherness into a desirable transnational personality—an image in which Western and Eastern attributes harmoniously coexisted.[73] In this ambition of changing and modernizing a woman's body, American/European and Israeli representations of Israeli actresses' beauty overlapped.

Conclusion

Both at home and abroad, Israeli actresses' "beautiful bodies" on the screen satisfied unfulfilled desires by embodying a contradiction: the self and the *other*, West and East, the future and the past. The construction and interpretation of their beauty served different needs for different spectators and were not limited to national criteria. Israeli society after 1948 not only wanted to become recognized as a sovereign state in the Middle East but also dreamt of Western comforts and luxuries. Israeli actresses who appeared in Western films seemed to make such dreams feasible. Popular culture's promise that a woman could transform her body to fit American beauty standards and lead a better, modern life appealed to the Israeli public and was a welcome diversion from the harsh conditions of postwar reality. It also influenced the image of the new Israeli woman—a combination of fierce soldier and alluring beauty queen. For American and European audiences alike, Israeli actresses were exotic and sexy women who flattered their white male heroes and reinforced the supremacy of the West over the rest. Their ambivalent representations between otherness and modernity, expressed through their modern fit bodies, stimulated sexual tension and delivered satisfaction. Simultaneously, the celebration of their bodily beauty within the American and European film industry revealed the openness of transnational popular culture toward new forms of self-fashioning.

Notes

1. See, for example, Oz Almog, *The Sabra: The Creation of the New Jew* (Berkeley: University of California Press, 2000); David Biale, *Eros and the Jews: From Biblical Israel to Contemporary America* (Berkeley: University of California Press, 1997); Daniel Boyarin, *Unheroic Conduct: The Rise of Heterosexuality and the Invention of the Jewish Man* (Berkeley: University of California Press, 1997); Tamar Mayer, "From Zero to Hero: Masculinity in Jewish Nationalism," in *Gender Ironies of Nationalism: Sexing the Nation*, ed. Tamar Mayer

(London and New York: Routledge, 2000), 283–307; George Mosse, *The Image of Man: The Creation of Modern Masculinity* (New York: Oxford University Press, 1996); Boaz Neumann, *Land and Desire in Early Zionism* (Waltham, MA: UPNE, 2011); and Anita Shapira, "The Origins of the Myth of the 'New Jew': The Zionist Variety," *Studies of Contemporary Jewry* 13 (1997): 253–268.

2. Rachel Elboim-Dror, "The Ideal Zionist Woman" [in Hebrew], in *Will You Listen to My Voice? Representations of Women in Israeli Culture*, ed. Yael Azmon (Tel-Aviv: Hakkibutz Hameuchad, 2001), 95–115; and Margalit Shilo, "The Double or Multiple Image of the New Hebrew Woman," *Nashim*, no. 1 (1998): 73–94.

3. Emily Rosenberg and Shanon Fitzpatrick, "Introduction," in *Body and Nation: The Global Realm of U.S. Body Politics in the Twentieth Century*, ed. Emily Rosenberg and Shanon Fitzpatrick (Durham: Duke University Press, 2014), 10.

4. Ibid., 11–12.

5. Shanon Fitzpatrick, "Physical Culture's World of Bodies: Transnational Participatory Pastiche and the Body Politics of America's Globalized Mass Culture," in *Body and Nation: The Global Realm of U.S. Body Politics in the Twentieth Century*, ed. Emily Rosenberg and Shanon Fitzpatrick (Durham: Duke University Press, 2014), 83–108.

6. Ibid., 85.

7. Shirley Jennifer Lim, "'The Most Beautiful Chinese Girl in the World': Anna May Wong's Transnational Racial Modernity," in *Body and Nation: The Global Realm of U.S. Body Politics in the Twentieth Century*, ed. Emily Rosenberg and Shanon Fitzpatrick (Durham: Duke University Press, 2014), 112.

8. Anat Helman, *Becoming Israeli: National Ideals & Everyday Life in the 1950s* (Waltham, MA: UPNE/Brandeis University Press, 2014), 133.

9. Ibid., 135.

10. Ibid., 137.

11. Almog 2000, 79, 136–137; Oded Heilbronner, "'Resistance Through Rituals'—Urban Subcultures of Israeli Youth from the Late 1950s to the 1980s," *Israel Studies* 16, no. 3 (2011): 35–36.

12. Orit Rozin, *The Rise of the Individual in 1950s Israel: A Challenge to Collectivism* (Waltham, MA: UPNE, 2011), 99, 130–132.

13. Ibid., 19–26; Anat Helman, *A Coat of Many Colors: Dress Culture in the Young State of Israel* (Boston: Academic Studies Press, 2011), 51–88.

14. *La'isha*, "These Hollywood Stars Will Host the Beauty Queens" [in Hebrew], March 26, 1952. Hereafter, all *La'isha* references are in Hebrew.

15. Hanna Herzog, "Women's Press: A Place for Reproduction or for Critical Reading?" [in Hebrew], *Kesher* 28 (2000): 51.

16. *La'isha*, "At the Beginning—Beauty Queen!," March 24, 1954.

17. *La'isha*, "Mary Murphy: From Beauty Queen to Hollywood Starlet" and "They Are All Beauty Queens," June 15, 1955.

18. Emily Rosenberg, "The American Look: The Nation in the Shape of a Woman," in *Body and Nation: The Global Realm of U.S. Body Politics in the Twentieth Century*, ed. Emily Rosenberg and Shanon Fitzpatrick (Durham: Duke University Press, 2014), 189.

19. Ibid., 196–198.

20. Ziviah Cohen, "Women's Magazines in Israel" [in Hebrew], in *Yearbook of the Journalists* (Tel-Aviv, 1971), 233, 237.

21. *La'isha*, "From the Editorial Staff," January 22, 1947.

22. Ibid.

23. Sonja Leiden, "'*La'isha*'—Israeli Weekly for Women: Domesticity, Self-Representation, and Reality" [in Hebrew], *Kesher* 28 (2000): 41.

24. Ibid.

25. Miriam, "Miss Lyon Presents the Latest Parisian Fashion," *La'isha*, August 9, 1950.

26. Helman 2011, 156.

27. *La'isha*, "Beauty Care in the Kibbutz," January 4, 1950.

28. Ibid.

29. Oz Almog, "From Blorit to Ponytail: Israeli Culture Reflected in Popular Hairstyle," *Israel Studies* 8, no. 2 (2003): 91–93.

30. Ela Atzmonit, "Every Girl Is a Beauty Queen!," *La'isha*, August 16, 1950.

31. Ibid.

32. Ibid.

33. These professionals also provided a great number of gifts for the beauty queen and other contestants. See, for example, *La'isha*, "Every Beauty Queen Wanted to Travel to Israel," July 26, 1950; "These Are the Presents, Which the Beauty Queen Received," July 29, 1953; and "These Are the Presents for the Beauty Queen," June 16, 1954. All the candidates visited a beauty parlor before the contest, where they were professionally prepared for the show. See *La'isha*, "They Are All 'Queens' on a Small Scale!," June 16, 1954.

34. *La'isha*, "*La'isha* Announces the Competition for the Election of Miss Israel 1950," December 28, 1949.

35. Colleen Ballerino Cohen, Richard Wilk, and Beverly Stoeltje, "Introduction: Beauty Queens on the Global Stage," in *Beauty Queens on the Global Stage: Gender, Contests, and Power*, ed. Colleen Ballerino Cohen, Richard Wilk, and Beverly Stoeltje (New York and London: Routledge, 1996), 4; Sarah Banet-Weiser, *The Most Beautiful Girl in the World: Beauty Pageants and National Identity* (Berkeley: University of California Press, 1999), 35.

36. *La'isha*, "Rules, Conditions, and Admission for the Candidates of the Election of the Israeli Beauty Queen," January 30, 1952.

37. *La'isha*, "The Battle over the Beauty Queens" and "What Is International Beauty?," June 29, 1955.

38. *La'isha*, "That Way Miss Israel of 1950 Was Elected," August 2, 1950.

39. *La'isha*, "The Battle over the Beauty Queens," September 12, 1951.

40. *La'isha*, "'La'isha's' Emissary in Long Beach Tells You How the Most Beautiful Girl of the Universe Was Elected," July 28, 1954.

41. *La'isha*, "Beautiful Women and Their Painters," September 17, 1952.

42. *La'isha*, "Rules, Conditions, and Admission for the Candidates of the Election of the Israeli Beauty Queen," January 30, 1952.

43. *La'isha*, "Beauties of the World in Hollywood's Film Studios," December 9, 1953.

44. Uzi Rebhun and Chaim Waxman, "The 'Americanization' of Israel: A Demographic, Cultural and Political Evaluation," *Israel Studies* 5, no.1 (2000): 81.

45. *La'isha*, "The Good Luck Card of Ziva Shapir: From the Candidate for a Beauty Queen until . . . Hollywood!," November 9, 1955.

46. Ibid.

47. *La'isha*, "Ziva Shapir Carries the Title Israeli Wine Queen," August 18, 1954.

48. *La'isha*, "The Good Luck Card of Ziva Shapir," November 9, 1955; *Davar*, "About People and Films: A Soldier with Lipstick" [in Hebrew], December 7, 1956.

49. Charles Higham and Roy Moseley, *Cary Grant: The Lonely Heart* (San Diego: Harcourt Brace Jovanovich, 1989), 260.

50. Hagai Matar, "Bar Refaeli, Before You: The First Glamour Girl of Israel" [in Hebrew], *Maariv NRG*, April 15, 2012, accessed April 5, 2016, http://www.nrg.co.il/online/54/ART2/356 /960.html.

51. *La'isha*, "The Crown Was Placed Twice," June 5, 1960; "The Girl Who Won Twice," July 17, 1960; "Victory at the Weekend," November 13, 1960. The Miss World competition was founded in London in 1951 and is, as of this writing, the biggest rival to the American Miss Universe competition.

52. *La'isha*, "The Cinema Discovered Gila," April 13, 1965.

53. Elmar Kraushaar, "Daliah Lavi: I Was Not Particularly Happy" [in German], *Frankfurter Rundschau*, October 11, 2012.

54. *La'isha*, "Victory at the Weekend," November 13, 1960.

55. *La'isha*, "The Cinema Discovered Gila," April 13, 1965.

56. *La'isha*, "The Israeli Beauty Queen Became the Princess of Hollywood," May 3, 1966.

57. Ibid.

58. *La'isha*, "300 Marriage Proposals," January 22, 1961.

59. *La'isha*, "The Girl Who Won Twice," July 17, 1960.

60. *La'isha*, "300 Marriage Proposals," January 22, 1961.

61. Julie Grimmeisen, "Halutzah or Beauty Queen? National Images of Women in Early Israeli Society," *Israel Studies* 20, no.2 (2015): 41.

62. *La'isha*, "The Good Luck Card of Ziva Shapir," November 9, 1955.

63. Irit Rogoff, *Terra Infirma: Geography's Visual Culture* (London: Routledge, 2000), 165.

64. *La'isha*, "The Cup Is Ours," March 12, 1961.

65. M. Elise Marubbio, *Killing the Indian Maiden: Images of Native American Women in Film* (Lexington: University Press of Kentucky, 2006), 61–62.

66. Ibid., 61–85.

67. Ibid., 81.

68. Ibid., 84.

69. E. Ann Kaplan, *Women and Film: Both Sides of the Camera* (New York: Routledge, 1983), 26–27; Judith Mayne, *Cinema and Spectatorship* (London and New York: Routledge, 1993), 63; and Jackie Stacey, *Star Gazing: Hollywood Cinema and Female Spectatorship* (London and New York: Routledge, 1994), 33–34, 36.

70. Laura Mulvey, "Visual Pleasure and Narrative Cinema," *Screen* 16, no. 3 (1975): 12.

71. Almog 2000, 111.

72. *Neues Filmprogramm*, "Brennender Sand" [in German], August 1960.

73. Lim 2014, 115–118.

3

NEW FRONTIERS

Creating a Nation through the Israeli Western

Rachel S. Harris

D URING ISRAEL'S EARLY STATE YEARS, CINEMATIC EXPERIMENTATION with genre films in Hebrew, particularly during the 1960s, sought to bring large audiences to the cinema in order to inculcate them into national values. These musicals, film noirs, and Westerns were vehicles that helped guide neophyte filmmakers in plot, styling, and mise-en-scène, while the need to provide ideologically rich narratives and characterizations impacted film subtexts and distanced Israeli-led productions from their international counterparts. Translating Hollywood genre staples through the lens of the local national experience speaks to Will Higbee and Song Hwee Lim's contention that "a critical transnationalism does not ghettoize transnational film-making in interstitial and marginal spaces but rather interrogates how these film-making activities negotiate with the national on all levels—from cultural policy to financial sources, from the multiculturalism of difference to how it reconfigures the nation's image of itself."[1] Using the few Western films made in Israel, mainly in the early 1960s, we can see the tension between the genre film with its international conventions and the specificity of Israel's national ideology, exploring both the efforts to combine the aesthetics and ideology and the limits of such a possibility. In the process, I want to consider upending Hamid Naficy's notions of "accented cinema" as taking place outside a geographic homeland and responding to a cinematic classic and argue for considering genre as a place for accenting film, bringing the local into a phenomenon that is already global, even in the homeland. In this way, genre filmmaking offers a way of articulating the particular through a vehicle of the international. "Consequently," as Naficy argues, "they are simultaneously local and global," but rather than "resonating against the prevailing cinematic productions"[2] that are produced locally, these films resonate against the prevailing cinematic productions that are produced globally.

The Israeli Western is neither diasporic nor deterritorialized but rather is concerned particularly with framing both territory and territoriality. Moreover, the Western is particularly well suited for elegiac celebrations of the physical and geographic landscape. As Naficy ultimately reminds us, "The study of a transnational cultural phenomenon such as the accented cinema is always haunted by the particularity of its autochthonous cultures. Within every transnational culture beats the hearts of multiple displaced but situated cultures interacting with one another."[3] Even in importing this global genre, in each context in which it plays out it is shaped by other encounters with the same vehicle of delivery while simultaneously being contoured by the specific context of the place in which it is remade. Moreover, in the Israeli context there is no doubt that audiences and filmmakers alike would have been well acquainted with manifestations of the genre from different national and linguistic origins.

In the 1950s and 1960s, Israel had the second highest per capita film viewing in the world behind Britain. Television would only emerge in the country in the late 1960s, and even then there would only be one official channel until the 1990s, when channel two arrived and there was an opening of the airwaves to two domestic cable companies, Hot and Yes. Thus, in the state's early years, cinema served as cheap, easily accessible entertainment. Cinemas boomed in cities and towns, and makeshift screenings were also common in kibbutzim, through labor unions, and on army bases. Israel's two major film studios were established soon after independence—United Studios commonly known as Herzeliya Studios began in 1949 and Geva a year later, though they would take some time to become operational. In the early years, it was Hollywood, Europe, and the Middle East that provided the vast majority of cinematic offerings, with the first full-length feature film, *Hill 24 Doesn't Answer*, not appearing until 1955. In general, the local studios managed to make around five or six films per year—certainly inadequate for the rapacious appetites of local filmgoers. At the same time, the local films held a higher cultural status and played a significant role in inculcating the two million new immigrants into the values, humor, culture, language, and expectations of the country.

Ilan Avisar explains that filmmaking was integral to shaping Israeli nationalism by constructing it in simplistic and easily digestible formats for an audience that was only semiliterate in the Hebrew language and "as a popular medium enunciates national identity."[4] The fledgling industry began in the wake of the battle for the country's independence, but without studios, sound stages, meaningful budgets, or trained film actors at a time when the country was still under postwar rationing and austerity, the output was small and generally of poor quality. Given the technical limitations of the age, using the natural landscape, making films in outdoor spaces, and requiring more action than dialogue circumvented some of the most problematic issues of filmmaking. By creating films about the contemporary reality there was little need for costly sets and costumes; the sun provided lighting, and by limiting dialogue there were fewer technical issues, such as shooting around the shadow image of the boom microphone. More importantly, less dialogue also solved the problem of casting. Filmmakers could choose between trained actors who had worked in theater but often bore heavy diasporic accents or untrained actors who were native Hebrew speakers. While the former clashed with the national ideology the films wished to represent, the latter undermined the films' effective exportation to an international market who were more discerning about plot, character, and acting and less invested in the heavy nationalistic messaging. Films were marketed not only in Israel but also to European and American audiences, with films entered into Cannes and the Academy Awards and frequently receiving at least limited global cinematic release.

Along with solving the technical issues of filmmaking, the Western as a genre provided a recognizable vehicle for the film's subject matter for international viewers and, like the epic and war film, proved popular. Moreover, as a medium, the Western interrogated many of the issues that were central to Israeli national ideology during its heyday of the 1950s and 1960s. These films offered an opportunity to construct a Jewish masculinity based on loyalty, courage, and sacrifice that was fundamental to the idea of the Sabra, the native hero. Simultaneously, it offered an opportunity to consider racial conflict (Arabs against Jews) and even ideological conflicts (Zionists against Diaspora Jews), and it employed the language of new frontiers, border-crossing, and the settlement of immigrants.

The creation of an Israeli form of the Western can be seen in light of other international Westerns that employed imagery of lone heroes, myths of origin, and racial conflict within a regional and national paradigm that also engages with local film culture, such as the Australian bushranger films or those about the Canadian Pacific Northwest. The Western, "although widely known as a distinctly American phenomenon, has a universal function, marking the genre of films that trace the origins of the nation by celebrating the pioneering phases of settlement and communal formation."[5] In this spirit, the Israeli form of Western films represented the "experience of developing a civilized, value-ridden society" through battles "against hostile forces of wilderness and human enemies" translating the nation's pioneering history into the genre film.[6] Yet even with the transnational and at times global identity of the Western, it was the American form that Israeli filmmakers looked to in creating their own local variant. Thus, the traditional image of the cowboy was reimagined and "accented" by images of the halutz (pioneer) or the Sabra (native-born), the Western town with saloon and store was represented through a Zionist agricultural project (moshava or kibbutz), the rifle was now a machine gun, the Stetson and boots were replaced with the *kova tembel* and sandals, and suede chaps became khaki work clothes. These recognizable allusions marketed Israeli identity abroad while creating a homegrown popular entertainment in Israel.

Western films that showcased pioneering narratives, such as *House in the Desert* (1949), which depicted efforts to make the desert bloom, and *They Were Ten* (1960), the story of a late-nineteenth-century agricultural outpost, show the ways in which the Western could be denatured of American elements while retaining the visual and atmospheric impact of the Western landscape and lone hero. The new plot focus now resonated for an Israeli public invested in nation building as the international turned inward into the national.

The American cowboy was never entirely antithetical to national ideology as long as he could be brought into the collective. The lead in *I Like Mike* (1960), a popular Israeli comedy nominated for the feature film competition at Cannes (1961), is a rich Jewish Texan complete with Stetson who visits Israel. Using the language of the contemporary Western, the film sets up a romantic plot (common to the subgenre) that pits bourgeois modernity against traditional Zionism through the threat of the diasporic Jewish community as an alternative to the national homeland. The film's plot revolves around a matriarch's efforts to matchmake her daughter to the wealthy foreigner, but Mike has fallen for Nilli, an Israeli woman on a magazine cover who is a soldier and works on a kibbutz, preferring cattle to people. Meanwhile, her daughter is in love with a Sabra, who appears frequently in uniform and also lives on the kibbutz. As Mike falls for Nilli, he is brought into the Zionist collective, and the plot also draws on the already existent pattern in Israeli cinema of paralleling women, the land, and fecundity. Through its main character's love for the native Sabra woman and his decision to stay rather than return to America, the film diffuses the threat that Americanization and the American Western pose to national ideology. In this way, the film maintains the figurative attraction of the cowboy without threatening nationalistic messaging. Moreover, it draws a direct connection between the lone cowboy and the land in which the land is now Israel and not the American West.

The First Israeli Western

One of the very first Israeli films made, *A House in the Desert* (1949), which won a medal for Best Documentary at Cannes in 1948, interwove the prototypical pioneering narrative with conventional elements from the American Western. The film's opening panning shot captures the desolate, hostile, and barren landscape, finally focusing on a single man looking out upon it. After a voice-over explains that there is no water and none can be expected to come from the heavens, the solitary figure mounts his horse in front of a tent that resembles a teepee. He slings his rifle over his shoulder, mounts his horse, and rides off. Thus established, the film never really returns to the imagistic motif of the Western genre, but it has already encapsulated the genre's value: any man in this landscape is a lone hero fighting nature—and if necessary, man. Revisiting the agricultural-propaganda films made for the Jewish National Fund and Keren Hayesod both before and after the establishment of the state, the film then embarks on the story of creating an agricultural settlement in the Negev Desert near the Dead Sea and desalinating the soil so that it can hold crops. Only once the project is advanced do women join, and the community becomes a collective. This parallel between the arrival of water and the appearance of women and children had already been drawn in Helmar Lerski's social-realist film *Labor* (*Avodah*, 1935) and directly links the new filmmaking with propaganda films.

The narration in *House in the Desert*, we learn later, is provided by the character playing the scientist who helps the settlement think through the problems of the soil and find appropriate seedlings that will thrive, connecting the intellectual urban Jews with the agricultural pioneers. The need to paint all of Israel as working toward communal goals, highlighting a

shared collective, disrupts the traditional tensions of the American Western between the city dweller and the pioneer settler. The embedding of ideology, even where it disrupted the Western as a genre, was indicative of
the local filmmaking industry's interests. This also applied to extradiegetic
concerns. The film was made in at least two different language versions
(with voice-overs in English and Hebrew) with the goal of inculcating the
local audience into the nation's value system while simultaneously serving
a propaganda purpose for international audiences that included recruiting
new pioneers and fundraising. This early experimentation with fiction film
built on the conventions of prewar nationalistic documentaries, newsreels,
propaganda films, and the few early feature films made in the Yishuv that
depicted the pioneering efforts of the new settlers and their military responsibilities for protecting the Jewish people from attack.

During the 1940s and 1950s, depictions of the Western were widespread
in Israel, appearing in a variety of mediums, including films, fiction, and
serialized comics.[7] The Western fit the "myths and ethos" of the period, but
while Israeli film "leaned on the Western because it was a model of cinema
that was easily copied and its components translated into its particular situation," it only adopted "those components of the Western that it needed,"
changing many of the original features to "fit their new function"—and
these too changed in time.[8] While Nurith Gertz has considered the ways in
which the Western's imagery morphed into other Israeli film styles particularly informing the war films of the late 1960s and fundamentally served
a national Zionist vision, the Western was also a framework embraced by
the Canaanite movement. Founded in 1939 by Yonatan Ratosh, the movement rejected Judaism as a diasporic religion and sought to identify with
the Land of Israel through a Hebrew identity that drew on a Canaanite past.
This philosophy distanced the group from traditional Zionism, and though
it remained small, it was composed of mainly writers and artists who would
proceed to have an outsized influence on culture. Included among its members was the author Amos Kenan, who would write the script for Uri Zohar's *Hole in the Moon* (1964).

Ratosh evoked the connection between Israel and America in his call
for an authentic local culture that would be as authentic to Hebrew youth as
the Western was to American culture.[9] If, in his formulation, the Americans
could derive an identity that was rooted in the place, connected to the land,
and had a quality of originality about it that embodied the very spirit of
the pioneering adventure, then the young Hebrew should aspire to nothing

less. In both the Zionist vision and the Canaanite one, there were material similarities between the American Wild West and the pre-state and under-developed Land of Israel. These were represented in iconographic depictions, such as the empty land that needed civilizing, the lone hero, and the struggle against the hostile elements (nature as well as man). Moreover, the shared ideological similarities between the American concept of Manifest Destiny and the Zionist national revival movement lay in ideas of nationalism, group exceptionalism, and a sense of divine mission. A. D. Gordon's writings, which would inform both popular Zionism and the Labor Zionist movement, developed from Victorian ideas about the merits of agrarian labor redeeming the individual worker, an activity that in turn redeemed the land. Thus, the Zionists' expression of dedication to the soil was seen in an embodied relationship to the land that was physically determined through a religion of agricultural work. The image of blood and sweat watering the earth was, in Boaz Neuman's formulation, part of the erotic relationship by which the earth was inseminated and fertilized as part of its acquisition.[10] The connection between land, myth, and divinely granted authority connected the Zionist project to the ideological underpinnings of the Western. In the conclusion to his analysis of the American Western genre, Will Wright explains:

> It seems this land has become our tradition—a tradition based not on the West itself but on the myth of the West. The meanings of this tradition are to be found in the Western, particularly in the Western film, where the land's natural beauty is photographed with magnificent significance by such masters as John Ford, Anthony Mann, and John Sturges. In these films, the wilderness/civilization opposition establishes associations with the land that we can then experience in our contact with it. As we have seen, the land is the hero's source of strength, both physical and moral; he is an independent and autonomous individual *because* he is part of the land. The strength that makes him unique and necessary to society and the beauty that makes him desirable to the girl are human counterparts to the strength and beauty of the wilderness. Moreover, the weakness of society and the villainy of the villains stem from their ignorance of the wilderness and their identification with the trappings of civilization. Thus, the man who accepts the wilderness, believes in it, and communes with it is stronger than civilization and capable of make it into something worthwhile. . . . Respect, friendship, and love are available to people who associate with the land, who may work in or for society . . . but whose understanding and comfort derive from the wilderness.[11]

The adoption of the Western genre within Israeli cinema during the formative period of both cinema and the country's development worked

because beliefs about the land and man's relationship to it and their representation in the Western genre coalesced. As Boaz Neumann claims, working the Land of Israel creates an "esthetic and spiritual relationship" that
transcends that which can be achieved by mere purchase.[12] Gordon's radical position held that labor leads to a "state of diffusion" between man and
landscape through which "an ineffable moment always arrives when the
laborer senses his entire being interwoven with the work of nature," providing "a kind of eternal elation, divine purity."[13] Physical contact actualizes
the relationship to the land as both desire and destiny, creating the identity
of the people upon it.

In the American context, the Western had already depicted this connection between man and agricultural labor or husbandry through images
of men driving cattle or farming the range. But it could also be created
through physical sacrifice. The image of the cowboy being shot is embedded in our cultural memory, but it is accompanied as often by images of the
body being buried in the land, the picture of the boot hill cemetery on the
edge of town, and later the passage of time shown in the cemetery's incorporation into the town ultimately built around it. In the Zionist context,
sacrifice is part of a narrative by which the land is made fruitful, worked by
the living body and fertilized by the dead.

Agricultural labor was not only about the desire for homesteading or
even physical sacrifice but also contained an additional element that was
specific to the Israeli context: it tied labor to scientific advancement. This
can be seen in descriptions of sanitation, advanced irrigation or desalina-
tion techniques, and scenes set in laboratories with wise scientists. The
youth and vigor of the pioneers is juxtaposed with the elderly man who
facilitates the pioneering experience, though he does not physically participate in it, or when the audience discovers the American hero in *I Like Mike*
is not just a cowboy but also a qualified economist with a degree.

Raphael Nussbaum's *Blazing Sand* (*Holot Lohatim*), a German Israeli
coproduction, was released in 1960, followed a year later by Baruch Dienar's
They Were Ten (*Hem Hayu Asarah*) and Peter Frye's *I Like Mike*. The new
films nodded at Zionist pioneering, and *I Like Mike* and *Blazing Sand* were
particularly focused on bringing the cowboy narrative into the present and
tackled issues that were relevant to the period—the conflict between diasporic Jewry and Israel and the trend of young thrill-seeking adventurers
risking their lives to cross the Jordanian border and visit the ancient city
of Petra ("The Red Rock"). These films consciously imported American

imagery into the local Western. For the critics, this created an incongruous and imported style that jarred with the locally based story. But audiences enjoyed the popular cultural form and the illusion of a locally made "authentic" Western.

In contrast to the mid-century contemporary Westerns, Baruch Dienar's *They Were Ten* offered a traditional pioneering Western. Working in the editing room while a film student at Columbia University when *A House in the Desert* was being processed, he witnessed the earliest efforts at filmmaking and, returning with his foreign training, would make one of the first Israeli epics. In *They Were Ten*, nine men and one woman set out to establish a new settlement in the Galilee in the late nineteenth century. The film's poster directly alluded to the Western through its visual evocation of a wagon train carrying tools and a small band of settlers walking in its wake as they follow an armed guard on horseback. Translating the conflict between Native Americans and the new settlers, the need for water, and the hostile landscape, the film depicts the Zionist pioneers beset by difficulties that include hostility from the neighboring Arab village that controls the local water source, a troublesome Turkish official, internal feuds, and drought. Its focus on the community's internal feuds in addition to the more conventional Zionist propaganda films' attention to agricultural labor and armed resistance to attack raises the film from propaganda to compelling drama.

Manya, the only woman in the group, is married to Yosef. Many of the plot's tensions specifically arise around this union. At first they share their sleeping quarters with the other men at the site. In this way, their marriage and its celebration of individuality are marginalized in the collectivism of the pioneering enterprise. Taking on a traditional domestic role, Manya cares for all the men at the site, providing meals, washing clothes, and nursing them through malaria. Ella Shohat has argued that the pioneer woman in Israeli films is an exalted Madonna becoming the "great mother" and is "an exemplar of self-abnegation."[14] Without privacy in the shared house, she must go to great lengths to be alone with her husband in nature, and it is here, looking out at the land the men have tilled and turned from a barren landscape into a fruitful harvest, that she seduces her husband and predictably falls pregnant. Having fulfilled her role as mother, she dies shortly after "suffering the fate of the frontier woman in many Western films."[15] In this spirit, the film draws on the legacy of Hollywood Westerns in which male camaraderie and the pursuit of danger "tests the heroes as men." But it is also characteristic of the genre that "women are always a threat, a potential danger,"[16] since the woman's presence disrupts male bonding. This becomes evident in *They Were Ten* when one of the other pioneers falls in love with her or when the men risk the wrath of the Turkish official and endanger the entire settlement by building the woman a private room. Despite her physical sacrifices to care for the men, her need for a separate space marks out her bourgeois sensibilities and undermines her actual role within the pioneering project, since she threatens its destruction. While the men engage in backbreaking labor, fight their enemies, and perform heroic acts, women remain in domestic roles (even at the frontier), supporting men in their endeavors. These films institutionalized the expectation that true heroism was men's work while the Israeli woman was expected to serve, procreate, and sacrifice.

The nationalist mythology that underpinned most of Israeli cinematic culture had positioned women as factotums of a male hegemonic structure in which they provided succor. Women channeled their needs, wants, and desires into caring for men, and thus their bodies were offered up in service to the patriarchal culture. This tendency to represent the kind of women who accorded with Zionist archetypes as sexually available was in many ways restricted to contexts in which a woman's body served as a reward for the heroic male and thus spelled her martyrdom. Depictions of sex were not usually graphic, and often cutaway shots implied that which had taken place without displaying it on the screen. The sublimation of sexual desire into labor or the use of sexual metaphor in images of a man's sweating brow and torso and a woman's shining face might also be substituted for explicit erotica. The life-giving sources (food, water, and woman) were paralleled, and sexual seduction (always heterosexual) frequently took place outdoors within nature, creating a triangular sexual economy between the female body, the heroic male pioneer/soldier, and the land.

Long after the pioneering days had drawn to a close, the image of the halutza (female pioneer) continued to resonate as an archetypal role model with her simple garb and sacrificial character. As part of this ideal, women were "portrayed either as equal partners in agricultural settlements or as equal partners in military organizations," serving as "proof of the realization of the new, revolutionized society based on equality."[17] The rift between this ideology and the asymmetrical reality was deftly disguised. The few women who would attain this *masculine* ideal were celebrated, but increasingly women's magazines focused on women's *femininity*, and a culture grew up around beauty parlors and women's fashion.

I Like Mike reiterates the conventional mythologization of the kibbutz pioneer hero in the young beau who steals the daughter's heart, a pattern that was to appear in several films of the period. But it is in the American rancher's lover, Nilli, that we see the overdetermined presentation of the land-as-woman. Presented as ethnically "Oriental," a coded but unspecified Middle Eastern origin, she represents the earth and the connection to it. She is the very extension of the soil—the physical manifestation of it—and as such connects him to his authentic Jewish roots. As a Mizrahi (an Oriental), she is a metonym for the Jewish relationship to the land of Israel, since her family's presence (theoretically) predates nineteenth-century Ashkenazi-led Zionism.[18] Rather than being viewed as a newly transplanted pioneer, she is identified with a long history of Jewish settlement. The film then ties together the image of the "don't-fence-me-in" nomadic cowboy—who is actually seen singing "Home on the Range"—while roaming the landscape with the diasporic wandering Jew figure. Once Mike has arrived in Israel, he no longer needs to exist as a foreign cowboy, since he can now sublimate this identity into his newfound role as a Zionist connected to the homeland.

Unlike the other two films, which were generally well received by audiences and critics alike, *Blazing Sand* pushed at the boundaries of what was acceptable and sparked a national debate. The film details an expedition organized by Dina (Dahlia Lavi) to rescue Yoav, her boyfriend, from the caves in Jordan. His dangerous search for the lost scrolls, which are compared to those found at Qumran and which began to trade at high values during the 1950s and 1960s, suggest a regional interpretation of the search for gold that had become a convention of the Western. Recruited to this mission are the Mizrahi nightclub owner from Jaffa, Zadik, who supplies the funds and is induced to participate with the promise not only of profit but the potential to consummate his lustful desire for Dina, which she seductively throws into the negotiation; Yoav's best friend from the kibbutz, David (Uri Zohar); Rubin (Gert Günther Hoffmann), an archeologist and scholar of ancient textual fragments; and Mike (Oded Kottler), a young friend from Tel Aviv who works in a record shop. Dina, the film's main protagonist, is not only female but is a woman depicted to be of loose morals. We first meet her as a dancer in Zadik's nightclub, suggesting connections to an illicit underground and particularly to Middle Eastern culture. Though several early scenes (in a hospital, at a kibbutz) attempt to return her to a conventional Zionist space, her behavior in these spaces positions her as an outsider. At the hospital, she becomes hysterical in front of the Israeli soldier and then appears calculating as she plots her next move. At the kibbutz, she uses her sexuality to seduce David, even though he is clearly involved in a relationship with Hannah, the kibbutz dairy hand played by Gila Almagor. Almagor, who is represented as Lavi's antithesis, evokes the traditional representation of a good Zionist woman: she is dressed modestly, relatively unkempt and unadorned with makeup or jewelry, working in the mud.

As Dina systematically builds a team of men to find the treasures at Sitra (a thinly veiled allusion to Petra),[19] she must use her wiles to lure each man into the project by appealing to his greatest desires; for David, it is leadership and honor, for Mike, it is adventure, for the scholar, it is historical Jewish texts, and for Zadik, it is herself. Each of these desires appeals to personal vanity rather than an ideological collective project. The journey to Sitra through the hostile landscape is ultimately a quest for personal enrichment (for Dina it is to find her boyfriend), and the landscape is across the border in Jordan, thereby disconnecting the narrative from a pioneering effort or a project of settlement and instead evoking a dangerous adventure—one that the band has no ideological or nationalistic right to engage in.

Choosing a more conscious engagement with the Western that attempted to formulate the film as a Western made in Israel—perhaps even an Israeli Western—rather than a film that incorporated but transmogrified Western film imagery within a Zionist nationalist frame, Nussbaum's film received a great deal of negative press. The prime minister, David Ben-Gurion, believed that the film would negatively influence the country's youth.[20] Of particular concern, expressed mainly by parents whose sons had died trying to reach Petra, was the idea that the representation of youths in nightclubs or engaged in sneaking across the border romanticized the danger. A popular song of the late 1950s, "Sela HaAdom" ("The Red Rock"), written by Haim Hefer, a short-story writer and veteran of the Palmach, evoked the mystery and danger of the quest to find the red rock, a synonym for Petra, and exemplified the very real fate that had befallen youths attempting to cross into Jordan. The song, with its Western rhythm that evokes a horse's gait, simple melody, and dominant guitar part, called up images of the traditional cowboy and signaled the ubiquity of the Western in Israeli popular culture. But it was ultimately banned from the radio for fear of inciting further misadventure.

More generally, Ben-Gurion was concerned that the characters' failure to express any sense of national duty or sacrifice reflected badly on the country. The parents and the prime minister were united in wanting the film banned and appealed to the censorship board, where they had an ally in acclaimed poet Nathan Alterman, who described the film as "sensationalist" at the censorship committee's meeting and expressed concern that it would offend the feelings of the families whose sons had died.[21] Ben-Gurion wrote a stern letter to Minister of Internal Affairs Haim-Moshe Shapira, appealing to him to influence the censorship committee he was responsible for overseeing and complaining that the film "insults travelers, is full of pornography and desecrates the memory of the dead."[22] Shapira responded by schooling Ben-Gurion in democracy, contending that he had no right to influence the committee, and declaring "the film is worse than mediocre, but it is not the committee's purpose to ban films on the grounds of their lack of artistic merit even if they are terrible—that task falls on critics and the public."[23] The committee pushed back against Alterman, and its chair, L. Grey, declared that there was no basis in the rules governing the committee or the law that established it to ban the film and that if families were offended, it was their right to sue the filmmakers. Their verdict to allow the film's screening silenced the public debate. Nachman Ben-Ami wrote in a review of the film after it appeared at Cannes that "the script is mediocre, but there's something in it that engages interest. The direction and acting are mediocre, but not grating. The musical score is above average, and the camera work—which displays the vistas of the Negev to us—is first class. And as such, there's no doubt that it's an Israeli film that can and should be screened globally."[24] *Blazing Sand* would ultimately launch Lavi's international career, as well as encourage a move away from depicting Israeli women as prudish and wholesome. But rather than resulting in cinema that focused on women's subjectivity, creating women who were empowered leading characters, as Lavi had been, Israeli film would produce more sexually provocative films and displays of nudity while continuing to situate women at the margins as objects of male lust, incidental to the story of the nation.

Blazing Sand deconstructed the elements of the Western, identifying particular qualities such as the quest, the band of heroes, the femme fatale, the barren landscape, and the thrill of danger, and then reconstructed them from an Israeli perspective, thereby accenting the Western genre. The film trailer claims that Israel's own mythology serves as outstanding material for cinematic exploration (and that audiences have no need to hunger for American exploits), and it served the local Israeli audience's desire for the Western. By taking up the genre in numerous plot points, atmospheric music, and cinematic landscape shots, it evoked the Western association with heroism, frontier life, and danger. But the tension in the film's reception can be understood in terms of the film's attempts to Hebraize the Western while simultaneously rejecting the tropes of national ideology. The film's physical landscape is beyond the boundaries of the State of Israel, there was no pioneering element, and the film Judaized Western imagery, linking the narrative as much to a diasporic past as to a Canaanite one. *Blazing Sand* questions the disconnection that had been portrayed between Judaism and Hebrewism. The search for the lost scrolls of Qumran inside a fictionalized Petra becomes an effort to recover Israel's Jewish identity. In these ways, it operated outside of the traditional land/labor/hero triangle. Furthermore, whereas sacrifice had always been connected to protecting the land and the settlement, the deaths in *Blazing Sand* happen outside of a national paradigm. In fact, in many cases they are the result of greed, willful stupidity, and abandoning the group rather than working in its interest. The ignobility of the characters, their motivations, and ultimately their deaths works against the nationalist-heroic genre of the period.

The public outcry against these elements and the abandonment of a national identity were central to the criticism. And yet in many ways, the film works to invent Israeliness, providing representation of the different sectors of Israeli society and moving beyond the valorization of the agricultural laboring minority to a representation of the diversity of the country by 1960. The participants represent the major cleavages in Israeli society—Oriental (Mizrahi), kibbutznik, secular city dweller, diasporic Jew—and their names evoke these identity markers. The characterizations are archetypes conventional in the period; the association with Jaffa and an exotic Orientalism, encapsulated in the dance Dina performs in the nightclub, connects Zadik to an underworld culture common to the representation of urban Mizrahim in films of this period, such as the film noir *El Dorado*. The young blonde Almagor is the ideal female kibbutz member, a role she would repeat in several comedies, such as *Not a Word to Morgenstein* (1963) and *A Gang Like This* (1963). David's Sabra characteristics are shown in his defense of the kibbutz (he's first shown on guard duty at the water tower), his knowledge of the land, his wisdom about surviving in dangerous situations, and his military tactics, and he serves as the de facto leader of the expedition. The archeologist scholar is associated with Jerusalem—the country's scholarly, religious, and intellectual heart. He is first shown among his books at the Hebrew University campus on Givat Ram and serves as a metonym for a pan-Jewish national identity whose roots lie not only in the pioneering present that the kibbutz member represents but also in a historical connection to the region and the diasporic intellectualism of the Jew. The final member of the ragtag band is the uninitiated Tel Aviv urbanite, the youngest member of the group and the source of much of the comedy and light relief of the film. This character visually allies the adventures of the film to the Western genre and situates the urbanite as a consumer of popular culture who is disconnected both from the land (and the present and ancient past) and from religion (the Diaspora and the recent past).

He first appears for the journey with a Stetson and six shooters, the rolled-up cuffs on his jeans marking him as a contemporary cowboy. In the film's trailer, he's shown with a bottle of whiskey, which David immediately empties out and refills with water to highlight the seriousness of the expedition but which also directs attention to the imagery of the Western while simultaneously undermining it as improbable and irresponsible. Mike's desire to view this dangerous mission through the lens of American popular culture highlights the break between Israel's own heroic past and the inculcation of its youth with this national sense of belonging and the invasion of Western culture exemplified in the imagery of the cowboy film, which becomes the projection site for identification. Thus, the Tel Aviv youth is shown disconnected from the land, Jewish history, Judaism, and national ideology. His lack of fortitude during the film's climax and his regular expressions of fear mark him out negatively as unheroic by comparison to the kibbutz members. Thus, the homage to the imagery of the Western creates a problematic tension between the desire to make a local genre film with popular appeal and the erasure of a distinctly Jewish Israeli national cultural history.

Yael Zerubavel identifies a tendency in the films of the 1950s and 1960s to frame the dissonance between the more moderate present, in which borders of a state are defined, and the wilderness of an earlier mythological period in the Israeli cultural lexicon:

> At the official level, the national-military and the individual-adventurous border-crossings of the 1950s offer significant differences in their meanings: whereas the former was glorified as a sacrifice for the national cause, the latter was criticized as senseless brushing with death and considered a violation of the law. At the popular level, however, the two forms of border crossing share a defiant, dare-devil spirit that was cultivated in the prestate youth culture and

continued in the special combat units. This spirit blurred the distinction between the national and the adventurous border-crossing, especially for young
people who fit the mold of those who serve as combat soldiers.[25]

But by picking this Petra trope and accentuating its for-profit goal, the
film highlights the individualistic over the nationalistic and creates a break
between the two forms of daredevil antics. Using the historical context, the
film creates a Jewish ownership of the past that occurs through the references to biblical events and the construction of Jewish worship practices
and is ultimately tied to the search for the scrolls. On the map, David refers
to the valley of Abraham. Rosen explains as they follow a path through the
desert, riding in single file, that "this is the path the children of Israel took
when the Adumin barred their way." Zadik responds dismissively that he
didn't expect to find the Tanakh (the collected works of the Jewish biblical
tradition) to be the map. Mike will later comment during the period of danger in Sitra that "this is part of our history and now we are even forbidden
from coming here." As they navigate the archeological site looking for the
wounded Yoav, Rosen guides them to him by using Jewish religious history
in order to explain the caves: "He will be found in one of the small rooms
which is where the holy texts were always located." He calls one area, where
the Cohen Hagadol was based, the Mikdash (Sanctuary). He says that Yoav
should be found there and that the cave will be under the altar, and it is he
who will eventually find the way in. The fact that all these references are
fictional and bear no relationship either to the religious text or to the particular areas referenced in the landscape is immaterial to the ways in which
this Israeli Western was calling on conventions in which archeology was
read through the Bible as part of the Israeli narrative of belonging.

That the actual biblical text bears no relationship to any reality the film
constructs misses the importance the film ascribes to the landscape. As with
the American Western, it is the land that becomes the defining relationship,
not the textual history that once evoked it. Moreover, this is exemplified in
the final scene; as the expedition falls apart due to greed, attacks by Bedouins, and the desert heat, only Rosen is left. He carries the dead Dina's body
back to Israel, but the scrolls, which were his incentive (and the ploy used
by Dina to seduce him with the promise of professional acclaim), blow away
in the dust. Hence the film concludes that Jewish heritage lies not in the
dusty books and textual fragments of a bygone era but in the land and the
men who stand upon it, ultimately proffering the audience a nationalistic

salve to what is otherwise a radically antinationalist film. Rosen, as the only survivor, will return the story of this band of brothers to the chronicles of Israel, continuing his role of chronicler of the Jewish people; thus, a new chapter is being written, and it is one more immediate than the texts of the past. In this conclusion, the film ties together the Jewish identity of the place with the national identity of the country overlaid into the tragedy of the Western, thereby achieving the very mission of creating an authentic, local, and particular Jewish expression of the Western genre. Thus, the film uses the transnational genre of Western to ultimately recover Zionism by creating an authentic local expression, even as it challenges the accepted notions of what such a local expression ought to have been.

Irreverent Satire in *Hole in the Moon*

By the time the comedy *Hole in the Moon* appeared in 1964, the conventions of pioneering mythology were well established in the Israeli collective memory, and their translation into the Western that Zohar was satirizing was comfortably familiar to Israeli audiences. Made in a style that nodded at both Italian neorealism and French Nouvelle Vague through its focus on hyper-stylization, the film has an abstract quality and fragmented cameos that referenced the films of the early 1950s using classical Zionist imagery. The film opens with a newly arrived immigrant who travels to the Negev desert. Quickly he sets up a kiosk evoking the first images of Rothschild Boulevard. Soon, a second man arrives and sets up a competing kiosk opposite him. After an encounter with Haim Topol, who had recently played the titular character of Sallah Shabbati to international acclaim, they decide to make films. Moments later, an entire two-dimensional Western-style town has developed. The flat fronts of the set are exposed as the camera follows the action behind the scenes to show the wooden stakes holding the fronts upright. The ludicrous cast of characters, including Charlie Chaplinesque figures, dancing saloon whores, and Western cowboys outfitted with Stetsons and gun holsters, evokes a parody of the old-style American Western.

In light of Naficy's claim that accented film challenges the classical tradition, we see in Zohar's film not only a satire of many of the conventions of the American Western in general but also the way the genre was appropriated within a local Israeli context. Its self-consciousness as a critical medium is part of the film's engagement with the historical nature of Israeli cinema as propagandistic entertainment. Employing the language of the spaghetti Western, which was still in its infancy as a genre, Zohar offers a meta reading both of the Western-as-genre and the Western-as-vehicle for depicting Zionist nationalism. As Ella Shohat explains, "*Hole in the Moon* allegorizes both filmmaking itself and the Zionist master-narrative. Its anti-illusionistic strategies raise questions not simply with regard to the coherence of the fictive world it creates, but also . . . with regard to the coherence of Zionist-realist fiction."[26] Zohar's use of the grotesque under-cuts the established repertoire for conveying heroic sentiment as he pil-lories the pioneering mythology of the young country, simultaneously spotlighting the bastardization of its values following its encounter with mid-twentieth-century modernity.[27] At the same time, his film also pays homage to this cinematic heritage in an ostentatious effort by which the film "calls attention to its own status as a fictive construct, and more gen-erally, to the status of all films as artifacts."[28] The film frequently employs the alienating technique of interspersing extreme long shots with extreme close-ups without providing narrative logic for this editing work, evoking the alienating style of the European Western that Sergio Leone would go on to define. But it had none of the hallmarks that made the genre famous on an international scale. The resonant Ennio Morricone soundtracks, the spectacular cinematographic panning landscape shots, and the richly satu-rated color film stock were possible because of Hollywood studios' support for Westerns, even those filmed in Italy and Spain. Such enterprises were far beyond the budget and practical filmmaking equipment and resources available in Israel.

Zohar's modus operandi involved a large degree of improvisation on set; he frequently cast off Amos Kenan's scripts and instead worked from notes he had made for the day's shooting. The filmmaker's generally er-ratic behavior and his habit of treating the entire enterprise as a game further affected the fractured experimental quality of the film. Yet *Hole in the Moon*'s strength lies in this dialogue with Zionist elements and its disruption of the traditional mythology. Whereas once sexuality was only represented in chaste heterosexual encounters or more often in the homo-erotic camaraderie between brothers-in-arms and in the erotic association between women's bodies, fecundity, soil, and water, women were increas-ingly being displayed sexually on screen. Daliah Lavi's erotic dance in *Blazing Sand*—and particularly her move from local celebrity to interna-tional Hollywood star—had embedded this new female sexuality into the national consciousness. But the images that redirected past sexual desire into militarism and agricultural pioneering had become so ubiquitous that Zohar could parody this motif while using the newly represented permissiveness to upend the sanctity of pioneering Zionism.

In an iconic scene, the camera pans over a woman in a bikini carrying a gun and driving a hand plow harnessed to a horse, which is led by a man wearing long robes (who in a second shot is shown holding an umbrella and the leash of a pet dog). The woman is singing the Zionist pioneering song "God Will Build the Galilee." Her curious procession is spliced with a shot of several men dressed in traditional Bedouin garb who are racing on horses waving guns and appear to be giving chase as they ride into the camera. The woman is startled and appears to slip while reaching for her rifle. In a jump cut, the Bedouin men are suddenly angrily marching into a tent standing in a barren landscape with a sign above reading "film director." Before Zohar, who is posing with a cigar in the style of a big shot producer, and the film director of the mise en abyme, who is wearing a colonial safari hat, the Arab men beg for a different kind of role. Chattering wildly, they proclaim: "We are always the bad guys. We want to be the good guys for once." A conversation between Zohar (as Tzelnik) and the reluctant director Mizrahi ensues. Zohar ascents and gives the Bedouin one scene. Next we see the Arab men dancing on the landscape that previously held the tilling, bikini-clad woman holding rifles and singing "God Will Build the Galilee." Men dressed as Cossacks with ammunition belts slung around their bodies suddenly appear and point guns at the Bedouin, but this is supposedly a comic pretense, and they then throw down their weapons. Subsequently, in a montage of stills, the men embrace with large gesticulations that can be taken as much as a fight as the implied embrace. Are these "Cossacks" allusions to the marauding bandits who murdered Jews in pogroms and therefore dangerous aggressors who ally with the Bedouin with the ultimate goal of Jewish destruction? Or do they refer to the early Jewish guard organization Hashomer, whose men dressed in the clothes of the local Bedouin, Druze, and Circassians, and therefore appear in the guise of Jewish protectors who hope to build relations with the local Arab population for a shared future? Zohar never tells us.

In this rapid juxtaposition of scenes, the film breaks down the traditional elements of Zionist imagery, which also became the staple of the Israeli Western: working the land, bearing arms to defend it, the existential threat of the Arab, the need for a national homeland that is tied to a diasporic history of persecution—in this case exemplified by the Ukrainian

peasants who want to enact a pogrom—and equality between the sexes signified by the woman driving the plow. At the same time, Zohar is able to
satirize the violence and women's sexual availability because *Blazing Sand*
had opened the door to questioning their role within the national iconography. But the scene also offers an opportunity to examine ethnic relations
in Israel. In naming the reluctant director Mizrahi (the term for Jews from
Middle Eastern and North African countries) and having the character remain at the mercy of the producer Tzelnik (a characteristically Ashkenazi
name referencing Jews from Europe who were the social and political elite),
the filmmaker is offering a nod to the ethnic power dynamics in the early
years of the state, dynamics that will take decades to be fully articulated
and realized critically in Israeli cinema.

Mizrahi's protest against the Arabs' request for positive representation,
when he denies them on the basis that they are Arab, presupposes a convention, understood by the audience, that Arabs are the country's existential
enemy and as such can never enjoy any other role but a negative one. *Blazing Sand* had already challenged this stereotype by making the Bedouins
the characters who ultimately allow the final survivor of the expedition
to return to Israel. Building on this challenge to what had become a racist stereotype, Zohar uses the scene to highlight the nation's acceptance of
prejudice toward Arabs. In character, he responds to the Arabs' request by
arguing that this is a movie that they are making and is therefore the representation of fantasy in which anything is possible. But Mizrahi's repetition of *it is the movies* reminds the audience that films in Israel established
social expectations and were not inherently an object of the imaginary but
an articulation of values that established a set of norms within the normative discourse.

Returning to Higbee and Hwee Lim's assertion that the study of transnational cinema offers an opportunity to consider the relationship between
the national and the transnational, we can see that the use of the Western
in Israeli cinema serves as an ideal case study. The films were made with
foreign audiences in mind, such that *House in the Desert* was produced in
both an English and Hebrew soundtrack version and *Blazing Sand* was a
German-Israeli coproduction made in both a Hebrew version and a German version titled *Brennender Sand* (with a German composer creating the
score and a German actor in one of the lead roles). Ultimately, the film was
only well received back in Israel after it had been screened at Cannes and
would later have a cult following because it introduced the singers Esther

and Abi Ofarim, who became international musical sensations and cult figures in Germany. Both *Blazing Sand* and *I Like Mike* were made by foreign
directors—a German and a Canadian, respectively. Though this chapter focuses on the thematic elements within the diegesis of genre films, considering the interplay between national and transnational, many extra-diegetic
issues surrounding the films' appearance, production, and reception reflect
a transnational shaping that helped mold national sentiments.

By the time Zohar made *A Hole in the Moon*, audiences had become
tired of the valorizing narratives of the long-lost pioneers. It wasn't that this
national imagery was no longer important but that it had been relegated
to memory to be sanctified and preserved. For entertainment, audiences
wanted to see something real that reflected their own lives and contemporary reality, and in many ways the filmmaking turned inward, creating
local comedies and dramas. Zohar's film, with its evocation of pioneering legends, was of no more interest than the mythologizing films it was
mocking. And Zohar's backward-looking imagery coupled with the film's
idiosyncratic style made it unwatchable. It was rejected by the public and
tanked at the box office. The Western no longer provided a meaningful engagement for Israeli audiences, who had no interest in a local variant when
they could watch the many international versions that were being imported
into screens around the country. As such, the industry would turn toward
satirical comedies that represented the problems of immigration during the
middle of the decade and then, following the war in 1967, return to the less
controversial heroic-nationalist genre in several war epics. It would take
until Dan Wolman's *Valley of Strength* (*Gei Oni*, 2010), fifty years after *They
Were Ten* was made, for another Israeli pioneering Western to appear.

Notes

1. Ilan Avisar, "The National and the Popular in Israeli Cinema," *Shofar: An
Interdisciplinary Journal of Jewish Studies* 24, no. 1 (Fall 2005): 131.

2. Hamid Naficy, *An Accented Cinema: Exilic and Diasporic Filmmaking* (Princeton, NJ:
Princeton University Press, 2001), 4.

3. Ibid., 6.

4. Avisar 2005, 131.

5. Ibid.

6. Ibid.

7. Nurith Gertz, *Motion Fiction: Israeli Fiction in Film* [in Hebrew] (Tel Aviv: Open
University Press, 1993), 70.

8. Ibid., 71.

9. Dan Laor, "American Literature and Israeli Culture: The Case of the Canaanites," *Israel Studies* 5, no. 1 (Spring 2000): 287–300.

10. Boaz Neumann, *Land and Desire in Early Zionism* (Waltham, MA: UPNE Press, 2011), 50.

11. Will Wright, *Sixguns & Society: A Structural Study of the Western* (Berkeley: University of California Press, 1975), 189.

12. Neumann 2011, 50.

13. Ibid., 51.

14. Ella Shohat, "Making the Silences Speak in Israeli Cinema," in *Israeli Women's Studies: A Reader*, ed. Esther Fuchs (New Brunswick, NJ: Rutgers University Press, 2005), 292.

15. Ibid., 292.

16. Elizabeth Cowie, *Representing the Woman: Cinema and Psychoanalysis* (Minneapolis: University of Minnesota Press, 1997), 28.

17. Julie Grimmeisen, "Halutzah or Beauty Queen? National Images of Women in Early Israeli Society," *Israel Studies* 20, no. 2 (2015): 29.

18. While "Mizrahi" has become an umbrella term for referring to Jews of Middle Eastern and North African descent (MENA), the original meaning of the word "Eastern" echoes the European term "Oriental" as distinct from "Occidental." That many of the Jews came from areas to the geographical west of Israel highlights the degree to which this term is laden with orientalist prejudice.

19. The name can also be read as a thinly veiled allusion to the "dark side" (devil): the *Sitra Achra*.

20. Rafi Mann, "Holot Lohatim (film)" [in Hebrew], *The 7th Eye*, June 17, 2015, accessed July 30, 2017, http://www.the7eye.org.il/163022. All translations from Hebrew are my own unless otherwise indicated.

21. Committee for Overseeing Plays and Films, "Minutes from the committee meeting 20/9/60 at the Ministry of the Interior," Israel National Archives file, ISA-MOIN-InteriorFilmCensor-000cbap.

22. David Ben-Gurion, Letter to Haim-Moshe Shapira, September 19, 1960, Israel National Archives file, ISA-MOIN-InteriorFilmCensor-000cbap.

23. Haim-Moshe Shapira, Letter to David Ben-Gurion, September 27, 1960, Israel National Archives file, ISA-MOIN-InteriorFilmCensor-000cbap.

24. Mann 2015.

25. Yael Zerubavel, "Passages, Wars, and Encounters with Death: The Desert as a Site of Memory in Israeli Film," in *Deeper Than Oblivion: Trauma and Memory in Israeli Cinema*, ed. Raz Yosef and Boaz Hagin (New York: Bloomsbury, 2013), 312.

26. Ella Shohat, *Israeli Cinema: East/West and the Politics of Representation* (1989; rev. ed., London: I. B. Tauris, 2010), 169.

27. See for example, the discussion of the binding of Isaac in Anat Zanger, "'Hole in the Moon' or Zionism and the Binding (Ha-Ak'eda) Myth in Israeli Cinema," *Shofar* 22, no. 1 (2003): 95–109.

28. Shohat 2010, 170.

4

THE RUST OF TIME

*The Apparition of Memory in
David Greenberg's* Sha'ar Ha'guy *(1965)
and* Much'shar Bli Rosh *(1963)*

Shmulik Duvdevani

Anat Dan

E VER SINCE ITS INCEPTION, ISRAELI CINEMA WAS A site of heterogeneity—a national cinema that was highly influenced by other cinematic vernaculars with no cultural heritage of its own. In short, it was a national cinema conceived solely by translations. Pioneer Zionist filmmakers immigrating from Russia and other Eastern European countries shaped their films in the spirit of the Soviet social realism of the 1930s, which resulted in their being termed *Zionist realism*. A key film among these early propaganda films is Helmar Lerski's *Avodah* (1935), which follows the story of a typical pioneer who arrives to the Land of Israel. While this film determined most of the images associated with early Zionist cinema (especially that of the New Jew, who is tall, healthy, suntanned, and masculine), it is also a landmark film for the integration of Zionist ethos and modernist aesthetics drawing from the Soviet montage and German expressionism. This interplay between modernist aesthetic and national ideology is the subject of this chapter. Our understanding of modernist aesthetics leans on Miriam Hansen's notion of "modernist vernacular" that was assigned to account for the ways in which "an aesthetic idiom developed in one country could achieve transnational and global currency."[1] We argue that European modernist aesthetics were used not only to shape the images of Zionist ethos but also—thirty years later—to question the role of collective memory and to create critical texts regarding the heroic-nationalist ideology and its related images. In other words, in adopting the post–World War II modernist aesthetic that originally informed particular sociopolitical concerns in Western European states like France, Italy, Britain, and later in Germany, Israeli documentarists began to question their own nationalist ethos as a part of the broader decline of the national imaginary's domination. There should be no surprise, therefore, that collective memory, which is an essential component of nationhood, is one of the first themes to be deconstructed. Coping with the national—whether in an attempt to shape its imagery or in an attempt to criticize it—cannot be considered, therefore, without taking into account cross-cultural tendencies, as Andrew Higson notices: "The degree of cultural cross-breeding and interpenetration, not only across borders but also within them, suggests that modern cultural formations are invariably hybrid and impure."[2]

Since our discussion should be located in the context of the ongoing debate about the connections between the fictional Israeli cinema and the European Modernist cinema, we shall briefly present it before elaborating on our own intervention. A particularly important polemic focused on the question of the existence or lack thereof of sociopolitical criticism in films of the Israeli New Wave—films that were inspired by the French New Wave and Italian modernism between the years 1965 and 1974 and are known today as part of the New Sensibility.[3] These films' creators—young directors who spent periods residing in Europe and got to know European cinema up close—adopted the characteristic contents, themes, and styles of modernist works. They stressed their inspiration through specific references to the films of Jean-Luc Godard and the poet of modernist alienation, Michelangelo Antonioni.

The appearance of an artistic cinema that places at its center the individual and his (or later her) subjective experience—in contrast to the heroic-nationalist cinema, which portrayed the laboring, warring Israeli collective, and the popular ethnic films that presented the family and the Jewish tradition—was perceived rather as a strong political reaction to a dominant Zionist cinema. The mere attempt to create a dialogue with a different culture with different values was considered in and of itself an act that challenged the Zionist enterprise.

The debate regarding the cultural significance of the New Sensibility commenced two decades later, with the publication of two comprehensive studies on Israeli cinema around the early 1990s: Ella Shohat's *Israeli Cinema: East/West and the Politics of Representation* (1989) and Nurith Gertz's *Motion Fiction: Israeli Fiction in Film* (1993). Both these scholars criticized the New Sensibility films (which they titled in their books "Personal Cinema") for not having harnessed the foreign models that they rooted themselves in for the creation of a local critique expressed within the work itself. Failing to address the true essence of this transnational wave, Shohat argued that "the apparent modernism of the style of the personal films is somewhat misleading."[4] Furthermore, Shohat explained that the Brechtian strategies that the European directors adopted turned into a meaningless tribute in the Israeli films, since the use of these strategies was made "in a kind of social and historical vacuum."[5] She claimed that the distancing strategies of French, Italian, and German modernist cinema were used to study sociopolitical structures and to reveal the "relationship between realism and bourgeois ideology or between illusionism and capitalist culture." By contrast, Israeli cinema failed to use these strategies to critique the Israeli reality or its cultural tradition.[6] According to Shohat, the efforts of the Israeli filmmakers to repress local characteristics expressed their intentions to assimilate completely within the "universal"—that is, within the West—while expressing no awareness of the established compilation modes and discursive arrays regarding regional provincial cinema—that is, the East.[7] This cultural blindness, Shohat concluded, resulted in extraterritorial provincialist filmmaking without the kind of critical bent that is evident in its European counterparts.[8]

The image that arises from the above criticism—one of a local artistic cinema that for the most part fails to recruit the European cinematic language in order to express a critical stance toward the sociopolitical situation in Israel or toward the cultural system within which it operates—was challenged by Judd Ne'eman, whose film *The Dress* was specifically noted in Shohat's critical account. Ne'eman focused on Shohat and Gertz's critiques regarding the frosty and distant implementation of the modernist aesthetic in the New Sensibility films and claimed that essentially, this was a "collective emotional defense mechanism involving a reaction formation: an indifference expressed for the sake of self-preservation in the face of a youth death wish."[9] Ne'eman showed that the existentialist alienation that characterizes European modernist works received unique local expression: "Members of the State Generation set out on their life course with an unconscious objective of materializing their death wish through war. . . . They were enabled to give up on this fantasy, namely, on the implementation of the death wish, through literature, art, and cinema. From the moment the filmmaker gave up on his unconscious death wish, he endowed his fantasy with a spirit of life, [countering] the Mask of Death of the fallen Palmach fighters."[10]

In his article, Ne'eman draws on Frederic Jameson's relations between modernism and mass culture to connect the modernist aesthetic, with the social, cultural, and political distress of its creators.[11] Ne'eman's study does not refute the claim that the New Sensibility films (at least in the second half of the 1960s) lack any political content; rather, it suggests that the choice of modernist aesthetics be interpreted as that which provides the sociopolitical context for the films. As such, the modernist language in Israeli cinema serves as a mechanism for coping with the (unconscious) trauma of the ethos of martyrdom. On the basis of this claim, Ne'eman argues that the radical critique offered by New Sensibility films "is a stressful coping, potentially also not self-aware, whose meaning is—to say 'no' to the yearning to integrate into the [tradition of] 'here our corpse lies,' [. . .] so as to live, to negate the negation, to oppose the death wish with the help of a Mask of Death."[12] In line with Ne'eman, Ariel Schweitzer argued that "the ideological and cultural nuances prove that this cinematic school was not merely comprised of a pure imitation of Western models, but rather succeeded in developing an original and dynamic dialogue with the Israeli reality."[13] Significantly, while a few documentary films were mentioned in this controversy, the discussion primarily focused on self-financed fictional cinema.[14]

Moving away from the focus on fictional filmmaking, here we turn toward documentary cinema. Despite the Israeli Film Service's virtual monopoly on documentary filmmaking and its attendant upholding of the classical modes of narrative and cinematic expression that were reflective of the earlier Zionist propaganda and promotional films, we claim that a few filmmakers insisted on a modernist aesthetic even in commissioned films, despite the rigid production framework in which they created their works. We argue that the modernist aesthetic enabled documentary filmmakers to criticize the nationalist ethos of Zionist Realism not only from outside the establishment but also from within. In this sense, we concur with Ne'eman's claim that the modernist documentary filmmakers—some of whom are among the artists of the New Sensibility—"created political cinema that predated the works of the New Historians and Sociologists."[15] In essence, Israeli documentary cinema of the early 1960s began sketching out the chapter headings of Zionism's new historiography. Thus, by turning to modernist aesthetics and highlighting the transnational relations with modernist cinema, such criticism became effective.

Historical Background on Israeli Documentary Film

The Israeli Film Service, founded in 1956, is a governmental institution that deals with the production and distribution of documentary films made for government offices, Israel Defense Forces, and other state and public institutions. These documentaries from the 1950s and 1960s deal with issues such as national development, immigration, housing and agriculture, natural resources, education, water supply, tourism, and other public interest issues. Most of them run for approximately twelve to thirteen minutes and were intended for public screening, mainly in film theaters (before the feature-length film).

Another state institution that played a major role in the production of documentaries in Israel during that period was the Histadrut Labor Federation, which initiated films on the foundation of new settlements, road building, youth rehabilitation, sports, and the lives of working people. These works highlighted the Histadrut's role in the development of the young state and its actions in caring for the workers.

The Zionist films were modeled on the documentaries produced under the supervision of John Grierson in 1930s Britain. These state-sponsored films "were both idealistic and practical in their treatment of social issues and problems."[16] Narrated by men with authoritative voices, they serve propaganda purposes of education and mobilization while making drama out of ordinary lives. What the Israeli Film Service and the Histadrut documentaries shared was the optimistic spirit and male-voiced commentary that reflected Zionist institutional discourse. However, their focus celebrated collective effort and achievements and, unlike Grierson's films, placed greater emphasis on the community than on the struggles of the individual, with the purpose of projecting a positive vision of a rapidly developing young country in accordance with the dominant socialist-Zionist ideology.

The films' focus on Zionist enterprises and their institutional perspective marginalized nonhegemonic voices. Mizrahi Jews (Jews of Middle Eastern and North African descent), women, Arabs, and immigrants were absent except as symbols of the challenges they pose to Zionist institutions—challenges that had to be managed or overcome. Moreover, even in films that appeared to present other voices, the commentary adhered to the dominant ideology. One such example is *Dimona* (Nathan Gross, 1962), which depicts the rapid development of a city in southern Israel that was populated mainly by Mizrahi immigrants. The first-person commentary is provided by a Mizrahi construction worker named David Levi. However, this apparent nod at representing ethnic diversity is belied by the actor chosen for the part—the popular Israeli actor and singer Arik Lavie, an Ashkenazi (Jew of European descent). Moreover, the film's content is full of optimism and pride and emphasizes the role of the Histadrut (which commissioned the film) in the city's growth while ignoring the unhappiness many of the new immigrants felt at being exiled to the country's periphery.

The shift toward modernist documentary filmmaking was heralded by David Perlov and David Greenberg. Perlov's *Old Age Home* and especially *In Jerusalem* and Greenberg's *Much'shar Bli Rosh* (1963) and *Sha'ar Ha'guy* (1965) present a self-reflexive, lyrical point of view and an aesthetic highly influenced by the cinematic inventiveness of the French New Wave, among others. These new ideologies and aesthetics contradicted those of earlier documentaries.

Thus, for example, *In Jerusalem* strives to attain an unprecedented formalism. Instead of adhering to an objective (i.e., providing an institutional perspective on the city with its holy places and importance to Jewish history and tradition), Perlov documents hidden corners, bystanders, children playing, stonemasons, old peddlers, and even beggars. The film offers experimental correlations between sound and music and a rare interview with the long-forgotten pioneer Zionist filmmaker Murray Rosenberg, who made *The First Film of Palestine* (1911). Perlov, who is much influenced by modernist documentary filmmakers such as Joris Ivens and Alberto Cavalcanti, creates an abstract and impressionistic documentary that undermines the informative and didactic approach of earlier propaganda Israeli documentaries.

David Greenberg

Although David Greenberg's cinematic work has never been sufficiently discussed and academically acknowledged in Israel, he was, as Igal Bursztyn noted in *Face as Battlefield* (1990) and *Intimate Gazes* (2007), a trailblazer of independent production in the Israeli film industry.[17] Greenberg (1931–1990) managed cine-clubs in Tel Aviv as of 1954, long before the Israeli

Cinematheque was founded in Tel-Aviv in 1973.[18] In 1965, he established the first film school in Israel, where he was the sole lecturer and taught only two courses: film editing and film acting. In 1981, he also started teaching film history and screenwriting. During the years 1957 to 1963, he founded and edited the journal *Omanut HaKolnoa* (*The Art of Cinema*) and published the books *Kolnoa* and *Omanut HaKolnoa*. *Omanut HaKolnoa* was the first Israeli journal on cinema in the vein of *Cahiers du Cinema* and *Film Culture*.[19] It referred to film as art and included essays on film from theoretical and aesthetic perspectives, seeking to bridge the gap in film criticism between Israel and Europe. Greenberg was also an obsessive film archivist. Cognizant that Israeli distributers in the 1960s were required by law to burn prints once the rights for public screenings expired, he chose to preserve them instead, amassing a significant private film archive of about five hundred titles.

Greenberg was also the first truly independent filmmaker in Israeli cinema. According to Chen Sheinberg, his film *Total Sale* (1959) was the first independently financed film made in Israel, as well as the first attempt to make an experimental documentary in Israel.[20] He directed many documentary films after that, among them *Museon Yisrael* (1965), *Yosef Trumpeldor—A Diary* (1971), *Blood Libel through the Ages* (1975), and *Mauritzio Gutleib* (1979). In addition, he directed the fictional film *Iris* (1968).

Yet, as influential as he was at the time and though he may be considered the "Israeli Henri Langlois,"[21] Greenberg is nearly unmentioned in scholarly literature. This absence is particularly glaring in light of what we consider to be Greenberg's crucial role in introducing European art cinema to the ever-growing number of Israeli cinephiles during the 1960s. Such mediation did not only take place in his lectures, public screenings, and writings but also in his filmmaking, which shares similar aesthetic and thematic factors and engages in dialogue with some of the flagship creations of the European modernist documentary cinema.

Greenberg's unconventional filmic choices—to avoid voice-over, to make use of minimalist music, to apply a fragmentary structure that distorts the linear progression of time, and above all to create a sense of reality through the exclusive reliance on *"surface images* that do not refer to an underlying continuous process of development, which is commonly manifested in classical narrative"[22]—all hint at a clear influence of European modernist cinema. These choices deconstruct the collective memory that is integral to the creation of nationhood and instead offer transnational identification reaching across borders, thereby universalizing experience. What collective themes are discussed may signal a certain national particularity that also cannot be dismissed and distinguishes between Greenberg's films and those of European filmmakers.

The present discussion explores this relationship through two of Greenberg's films. *Sha'ar Ha'guy* serves as an example for the way these modernist strategies operated in the framework of a state-commissioned film in order to create a cinematic essay that deals with the question of collective memory—an issue that was addressed by many European writers, playwrights, and filmmakers after World War II, such as Marguerite Duras and Alain Resnais in France; Heinrich Böll, Günter Grass, and Alexander Kluge in Germany; and Alberto Moravia in Italy. This film demonstrates a process of decomposing collective memory and iconographic components of an historical event (the liberation of besieged Jerusalem) and recomposing them through a melancholic outlook that preserves the fragmentation of the cinematic structure. *Much'shar Bli Rosh*, which was independently produced in a manner uncharacteristic of many Israeli documentaries at the time, is a modernist allegory just like the Mask of Death that Ne'eman referred to. Through a presentation of the chicken-slaughter industry, this film criticizes the ethos of sanctifying death through surrealistic means that stress the banal, industrial aspects of death in war and the fragmentation of the body.

A Site of Distorted Memory: *Sha'ar Ha'guy*

Sha'ar Ha'guy (the Ha'guy Gate) is a narrow entranceway leading from the flatlands toward the Jerusalem Mountains. During the period of the War of Independence, various bloody battles were fought along this route, which served as one of the only ways for supply convoys to reach the besieged city and prevent its Jewish inhabitants from starvation. Remnants of the armored vehicles that were destroyed in the battles have been preserved and displayed along the road as a living testament to the bravery of the combatants. Seventeen kilometers from Jerusalem, over the remains of the demolished Arab town of Hirbat A'Zankula, stands a memorial that was established at the initiative of the Israeli Ministry of Defense's Unit for Commemorating Soldiers. The film returns to the battlefields to tell the story of the combatants' great courage; yet, in contrast to other fictional and documentary films dealing with the War of Independence, *Sha'ar Ha'guy* does not comply (at least not fully) with the ideological commandment of its era to mythologize the death of young soldiers in battle and immortalize them in a national pantheon of heroism.[23] The following lines comprise a short part of the voice-over narration that Greenberg originally wrote for this film:

> Can you hear me? Do you hear me, over? . . .
>
> Let me feel your growth in my flesh, the pulse of life that flows anew,
>
> the wonder of creation, the force of rejuvenation.
>
> Let me look again at the growth of the bush, the song of birds, the leaves shivering in the wind.
>
> Bring me back my youth that was washed in iron, the rusty iron, the burning iron, the iron that became
>
> part of the scenery, part of its being, of its flesh, a bush growing in its soil.
>
> Let me feel the twilight wind, the song of birds.
>
> I hear you, I hear you, I hear you, over.

As opposed to his peers—the heroes of the Israeli films of the 1950s—Greenberg's fallen soldier functions as neither mythic figure nor martyr. Instead, the voice-over demands the return of his lost youth: "Let me feel your growth in my flesh, the pulse of life that flows anew, the wonder of creation, the force of rejuvenation." Yet, these narrated lines did not make their way into the final film. In fact, Greenberg chose to forgo narration altogether, thereby making *Sha'ar Ha'guy* the first state-funded Israeli documentary film to reject the rhetorical means most commonly associated with the voice of institutional Zionist authority. The reading of the film as an open text—integrating extratextual documents, such as the film's screenplay—provides above all a hermeneutic richness but also assists in identifying more precisely the moment at which the modernist mode was born in Israeli documentary cinema.

Greenberg's strategy of filming scenes at a site of historical significance so as to address questions of memory (or forgetfulness) is found in two other documentaries: Alain Resnais's *Night and Fog* (1955) and Alexander Kluge and Peter Schamoni's *Brutality in Stone* (1961). Resnais's film pits archival materials filmed at the Auschwitz and Majdanek concentration and extermination camps during World War II against images of the deserted camps of the present. Both nature and time threaten to extinguish the remnants of the place, and as such in this context, they materialize the Nazi mission that aimed at eliminating any memory or trace of the atrocities on one hand and of the industry of death on the other hand. The juxtaposition of these two types of images raises questions regarding memory, the connection between memory of the past and the conceptualization of the present, and the role of cinematic imagery in relation to these issues.

Brutality in Stone also returns to a place commonly associated with barbarity: the Nazi congress site in Nuremberg. This site, which served as the backdrop for Leni Riefenstahl's film *Triumph of the Will* (1935), is decomposed into brief shots that portray fragments of the neoclassicist structures that were initially intended to symbolize life in heroic proportions and to mirror the strength of the dictator and of his modern state. Whereas the film is composed exclusively of images shot in the present at the time it was made, its soundtrack mixes in numerous archival materials: the noise made by a cheering crowd from Riefenstahl's film; the voice of Hitler, recorded at various occasions; the voices of radio hosts from the Nazi era; a recording of the singing of the Hitler Youth Choir; and a reading from the memoir of Rudolf Höss, the commander of Auschwitz, that describes the murderous industry of demolishing Jews at the camp. Thus, in a similar manner to *Night and Fog, Brutality in Stone* confronts images from the past (Nazi architecture and recordings featured in its soundtrack) with images of the present (the remnants of the buildings and the deserted camp square). Eric Rentschler describes Kluge and Schamoni's film as a "deconstructed museum of memories" intended to assist us in understanding the role of the tangible historical materialist reality that continues, unobstructed, into the present.[24] As such, it takes issue with the assumption that Nazism is fully sealed off and confined to Germany's past.

We argue that much like these European films, *Sha'ar Ha'guy* also returns to the site of historical happenings so as to reassess the relationship between past and present—and, more specifically, the components of collective memory. The final product is a composition of images, music, and sound effects divided into four chapters. The first chapter was filmed in the (contemporaneous) present era of the Sha'ar Ha'guy valley. The second chapter is composed entirely of stills and describes daily life in besieged Jerusalem. The film's third chapter portrays the movement of the combatants toward the besieged city, while the fourth and final chapter returns to the present and discovers the cacti that grow amid the steel remnants from the war.

The film opens with images of a grove at the outskirts of the road to Jerusalem. Greenberg focuses on minor occurrences: ants crawling on the remains of old clothing, a spider weaving a web between branches, rays of sun shimmering behind the treetops. The forest is alive—it grows and expands all around the remains of recent history, threatening to erase it. The editing creates a dialectic between the artificial (metal) and the organic (nature), which alludes to what Walter Benjamin defined as "the return of history to nature" in his discussion of the notion of ruins. In *The Origin of German Tragic Drama*, Benjamin portrays the image of the architectural ruin—a motif identified with the Baroque arts—as an image that represents radical change in the conceptualization of history.[25] Whereas the classical tradition imagined redemption as establishing a new utopian order, the Baroque expressed the messianic element as the return of history to nature by decomposition and destruction. Notably, even if this approach contains a melancholic element, it is not necessarily a pessimistic worldview, as it inevitably implies beauty—the beauty of that which is passing.[26]

The dialectic comprises an allegory for the conflict between the present and the past. The living, ever-transforming nature threatens to cover the remains of the past and to erase them in the void of forgetfulness—or, as Pierre Nora phrases it, threatens to remove them to the realm of the synthetic, the dead, which is the realm of history. All the while, the desire to remember remains: "Lieux de Mémoire [sites of memory] are created by a play of memory and history, an interaction of two factors that result in their reciprocal over-determination. To begin with, there must be a will to remember."[27] Hence, Sha'ar Ha'guy itself comprises what Nora labels a *lieu de mémoire* in which an ongoing conflict exists between the historical moment and the movement of history: "no longer quite life, not yet death, like shells on the shore when the sea of living memory has receded."[28] Thus, the first episode of the film rejects the association of the site with a place of commemoration that elevates its status to that of national myth and makes it a rallying cry of national collective memory. Instead, Greenberg prefers to read it as a site of ruins in which death wipes away all commentary in an act that returns everything to nature.

The second part of the film is comprised of still shots—archival photos of Jerusalem under siege. The expressive use of cinematic tools such as the image of a sharpshooter's eyepiece wandering over the photos revitalizes the representations and releases the past from its frozen state. In this context, we note Georges Franju's *Hotel of Invalids* (*Hôtel des Invalides*, 1952), which was requisitioned by Henri Claudel, cultural relations spokesman and manager of the funding of cultural projects at the Ministère des Affaires Étrangères. The selection of the army museum as the topic of the film (which was intended to deal with French culture) enabled Franju to create a pacifist work that contests any and every war. The film describes the museum through two perspectives, which are related to the viewers through two types of narration; the first is the film's official narration, which focuses on the historical and architectonic elements of the place, whereas the second focuses exclusively on the museum's collection and is told from the fictional perspective of a museum guide who is himself a veteran (Franju authored the voice-over narration, which is read by the actor Michel Simon). Franju breathes life into inanimate objects—helmets, armor, flags, arms, and even the paintings on the walls—through the use of dramatic film angles, the movement of the camera through the museum room, the dynamic editing, and the music of Maurice Jarre. Yet in addition to the effect of objects coming to life, which unleashes the past from its frozen state as discussed above, Kate Ince notes the film's featuring of "the prominence in memory's operations of looking, the gaze and visual technologies."[29] In *Sha'ar Ha'guy*, the pictures that provide historical witness—deserted streets, barricades, and barbed wire—are presented through the sharpshooter's eyepiece. This is the enemy's perspective, which is not seen in the pictures themselves. Like the museum guide in *Hotel of Invalids*, the sharpshooter here too creates the presence of a ghost—even more so in Greenberg's film, since he has no voice. The documentarist, just like the anonymous sharpshooter, seeks out a sign of life in the urban realm through the pictures. The double meaning of the verb *to shoot* serves as a reflexive characteristic connected to modernist cinema.

Another series of stills appears, starting with pitchers and bowls of water and oil and moving to a group of women standing facing a closed store, waiting to fill up their baskets and buckets with supplies. The sharpshooter's target disappears, and in its place, the camera wanders around through the photos, telling a new story—that of people living under siege. The impression of the siege that the pictures create is based on the contradiction between the still shots and the movement of the camera, which seeks to realize the past in the present of the filmmaking. Light and sound effects provide additional artistic means that support the attempt to extract the historical event from the moment in which it was frozen. In the series of photos that describes life in the besieged city, Greenberg weaves in images of water pipes filmed from a low perspective. These pipes bear a double

Figure 4.1. The anonymous sharpshooter seeks out a sign of life in *Sha'ar Ha'guy* (Greenberg 1965).

connotation: the first involves the specific context of the montage—the absence of water; the second involves the fact that these pipes are reminiscent of other pipes—those of the gas chambers—and resultantly, the entire sequence arouses associations of the ghetto. The sequence hints at an analogy between the life of Jews in the ghetto and the siege on Jerusalem. Thus, we argue that Greenberg expands the boundaries of collective memory with the aim of including imagery that does not correspond with the Zionist myth. The passive, victimized image commonly identified with Jews of the Diaspora, which the Zionist collective memory sought to repress, is presented for the first time in Israeli cinema alongside images from the battlefield.

The third part of the film returns to Sha'ar Ha'guy—this time to the armored vehicles. The segment is composed of three separate sequences that are thematically connected. The first sequence presents the armored vehicles that have been deserted along the side of the road. Here, the camera is static, but the editing moves at a fast pace, to the point that the motion

Figure 4.2. Water pipes filmed from a low perspective in *Sha'ar Ha'guy* (Greenberg 1965).

begins to take place within the shots themselves—the doors and the cracks of the armored vehicles are closing. In the second sequence, the camera enters into the armored vehicle and mimics its trip up through Sha'ar Ha'guy. Between the staged shots of soldiers jumping out of the armored vehicles in the midst of battle, Greenberg integrates archival shots of soldiers that we assume traveled in these vehicles. This sense of movement is reminiscent of the "phantom ride" from cinema's early days. This notion, coined by Tom Gunning, relates to the placement of the camera on the nose of a train's engine so that the viewer experiences the attraction of the travel experience.[30] The phantom ride integrates motion (i.e., life) with the absence of that which creates the motion (i.e., the phantom, the existence of a ghost). On one hand, this is the perspective of the anonymous fallen soldier, discussed above, whose voice was silenced in the decision to forgo narration. On the other hand, the trip in the armored vehicles transforms into an experience taking place in the present moment, and we bear witness to the failure that is inherent in any attempt to breathe life through myth. That is to say, the

Figure 4.3. The cactus that grows between the vestiges of that war in *Sha'ar Ha'guy* (Greenberg 1965).

phantom ride reveals the unbridgeable gap between historical memory and the attempt to bring it to life. This interpretation may explain Greenberg's choice of melancholic music that accompanies the sequence.

The fourth and final chapter of the film returns to the valley—to the cactus that grows between the vestiges of that war. The cactus, like the steel remnants, is an object bearing very strong symbolic connotation in the Israeli consciousness. Both the cactus and steel symbolize the toughness of the native-born Israeli. Simultaneously, however, in particular because the first part of the film stressed the referential aspect of nature, the cactus demands a reinvestigation of its denotative, initial meaning as a plant that grows in its natural environment. With this pendulum swing between the symbolic and referential spheres of the cactus, Greenberg concludes *Sha'ar Ha'guy*. The project of decomposing the collective memory has been completed. Like the skeletal armored vehicles and institutional monuments, *Sha'ar Ha'guy* becomes a *lieu de mémoire* of a *lieu de mémoire*.

The Production Line of Death: *Much'shar Bli Rosh*

While death in *Sha'ar Ha'guy* involves the heroic memory of combatants who were killed on the way to liberating besieged Jerusalem, functioning as a shadowy presence, in *Much'shar Bli Rosh* (1963), death is constant and concrete. It is represented in almost every shot, whether directly or indirectly, as it captures the work process of a chicken slaughtering facility in southern Israel.

This earlier documentary, whose title is a play on words regarding the kosher slaughtering process, was an independent film produced without institutional support. Though it was not Greenberg's first self-financed film (the earlier documentary *Total Sale* was), this second self-financed film proved successful globally, winning prizes at several international film festivals (San Francisco, Los Altos Hills, and Barcelona). For his part, Bursztyn claimed *Much'shar Bli Rosh* was naïve in its portrayal of the beauty of violence. He disliked the editing (by Jacquot Ehrlich), which demonstrated "a not insubstantial self-delight," but viewed the film in the "context of the era" as containing "cinematic awareness—an innovation in the Israeli landscape of the time." Moreover, Bursztyn notes that "never before has a film in Israel (certainly not a documentary) dared to present as brutal, evil, and stupid faces as those of the slaughterers that appeared in *Much'shar Bli Rosh*."[31]

Greenberg's stylistic choices made *Much'shar Bli Rosh* an abstract film. It was shot without any synchronized sound recording, and Greenberg's initial intention was to edit the film to the tunes of Sergei Prokofiev's Fifth Symphony. However, after completing the filming, the filmmaker decided to give up on this idea and approached the composer Yehezkel Braun with the request that he compose an original score for the film. Greenberg's choice to film in color was an important artistic choice. The bold red color that will evoke blood screams out from the first shot that portrays a field of blood-red anemones surrounding the slaughterhouse. This focus on the red color is a deliberate aesthetic choice that accompanies the entire film—red is the color of the truck that brings the chickens to the slaughterhouse, of the subtitles, of the bloodied aprons of the slaughterers, of the crests of the chickens being led to slaughter, of the container of machine oil, and, of course, of the chickens' spilled blood.

Franju's *Blood of the Beasts* (1949) comprises a clear and dominant influence on Greenberg's film. Both films are based on what Jeanette

Figure 4.4. A field of blood-red anemones surrounding the slaughterhouse in *Much'shar Bli Rosh* (Greenberg 1963).

Sloniowski has termed "the aesthetics of cruelty." Franju's film describes the slaughterhouses and butcher shops of the Paris suburbs, particularly in the Quartier de la Villette (the 19th Quarter). For Franju, just like for Antonin Artaud—creator of the Theater of Cruelty—the role of art is to be intensive and painful so as to lead the viewer to drown in it, yielding a masochistic loss of subjectivity. Sloniowski claims that *Blood of the Beasts* rejects any attempt to define a moral statement about cruelty toward animals or about the survival of humans at the expense of the death of other creatures—or even as an allegory on the Holocaust (and a similar claim can be posited regarding *Much'shar Bli Rosh*). Had the viewing of these films been accompanied by a clear moral statement, she notes, "it would be far more comfortable for spectators to suffer the pain."[32]

The immediate connotation that arises from viewing Franju's film is that of World War II (which ended four years before the film was produced). One cannot help but recall the Nazi death camps while watching the film's portrayal of the death industry. Indeed, Raymond Durgnat suggests that the cold and methodological cruelty taking place at the featured slaughterhouses can be compared to that of the German SS officers.[33] In contrast, Sloniowski posits that although the film could have served as a metaphor for the mass murders that spread wildly throughout Europe, nothing in the film creates any direct connection to the war or to the death camps.

However, other film critics, such as Siegfried Kracauer, note the associative connection between the queues of calves awaiting their slaughter in *Blood of the Beasts* and the piles of tortured corpses that were photographed at the concentration and death camps. Kracauer claims that these images "beckon the spectator to take them in and thus incorporate into his memory the real face of things too dreadful to be beheld in reality."[34] In this regard, Franju's film, just like Greenberg's that followed it, describes horrors that are present, even if hidden, within daily life.[35]

Much'shar Bli Rosh shows crates tightly packed with live chickens being unloaded off of a truck. Laborers carry them and hang the chickens from their legs on moving hooks. Slaughterers take them off the hooks, assess them, cut their throats with a sheath, and throw the quivering chickens into a huge tub in which they bleed. From there, the chicken corpses get taken, placed again onto a system of moving hooks, and transferred into a machine that plucks them of their feathers. The next stage in the production line is the placement of the plucked chickens in a machine that washes them, followed by the amputation of their feet and heads. Through the depiction of these stations, Greenberg's film criticizes the brutality of kosher slaughtering, the suffering that the chickens undergo, and the lack of empathy that the slaughterers express toward the chickens. For this purpose, the director makes sure to film them mainly from low perspectives in a manner that stresses the slaughterers' smiles (which in this context seem cruel) or their callous, aloof expression regarding efficient, mechanical labor. The use of close-up shots of the slaughterers' faces stresses this message of cruelty and separates the events taking place from a concrete context, yet the name and location of the slaughterhouse is never mentioned. In contrast to other documentary films of the era (certainly in Israel), the film lacks any informative narration. Just like *Blood of the Beasts*, the cold efficiency of the slaughterers contrasts with the shock the viewer experiences. The film presents the routine of labor as a routine of death. The existential involvement with the meaning of life and death is reduced to the cruel, banal, and unromantic image of the production line. *Much'shar Bli Rosh* demands its viewers perceive it through the same kind of distancing as the one with

Figure 4.5. The routine of labor as a routine of death in *Much'shar Bli Rosh* (Greenberg 1963).

which Greenberg's camera follows the miserable chickens—allegedly absent of any attempt to preach, advocate, or make any statement whatsoever.

Just like Franju's film, *Much'shar Bli Rosh* demands that its viewers cope with representations of real death on the screen. In her analysis of representations of death in documentary cinema, Vivian Sobchack argues that "death presents a special problem in representation."[36] The removal of natural death from the public space and discourse "leaves only violent death in public sites and conversation."[37] In Franju and Greenberg's films, death is first and foremost "the thing itself"—not a fictional image that enables the comforting distancing of an allegorical or symbolic reading. "The documentary representation of death seems experienced as a visualization of the real,"[38] claims Sobchack, while fictional death is nothing but a "simulacrum of a visual taboo."[39]

Sobchack stipulates that "the most effective cinematic signifier of death in our present culture is violent action inscribed on the visible lived-body."[40] This is the third dictum in a typology of ten propositions that she offers for the representation of death in documentary cinema, and this is the one that requires of the viewer an ethical response, since it involves a break with the above-noted visual taboo. The viewer passes ethical judgment over the gaze onto death that is represented by documentarians as "an inscription of their humanity and moral responsiveness to a social world shared by filmmaker and audience."[41]

Absent this ethical response, *Much'shar Bli Rosh* prompts a reading as a surrealistic work deeply influenced by the early efforts of the Spanish surrealist director Luis Buñuel and particularly by his documentary *Las Hurdes* (*Land without Bread*, 1932). The absence of (institutional or other) voice-over narration prevents the viewer from creating a context for the abstract images—or the aim of the film—and from attaching any meaning to the human cruelty presented in it. The images of the "production line of death" seem to be random and pragmatic, whereas the viewer is requested (unsuccessfully) to attempt to interpret the film and its meaning on his or her own. The absence of voice-over narration places the viewer in an uncomfortable position, as the viewer expects some reaction to the cruel aesthetics presented. The lack of a human voice represents the absence of humanity in the act of slaughtering itself. Moreover, similar to the dialectical usage Buñuel made of Brahms's Fourth Symphony as a background for the human wretchedness and illness that he describes in his film about the peripheral Hurdes tribe, Greenberg uses modernist music that pleasantly and shockingly shifts to a cheerful jazz tune that accompanies the scene in which the dead chickens' feathers are plucked (i.e., a contrapuntal use of sound).

This surrealism is rare in the documentary cinematic tradition of its era. It avoids the deductive, informative basis identified with propaganda and informational films of the Griersonian model while appearing to be more aligned with an ethical and aesthetic attack on the viewer. The film even attacks the passivity of the viewer, who finds him or herself wondering about the meaning of the images presented. In this sense, Sloniowski's statement regarding *Blood of the Beasts* can be said to apply to this film as well: it "might be read as an assault on safe, aesthetic spectatorship and the Griersonian school of moral improvement."[42]

Nevertheless, we posit a reading of the film that perceives it as a provocative challenge regarding the ethos of sacrifice and sanctity of death that is present in Israeli fictional and documentary cinema of the era. The involvement of *Much'shar Bli Rosh* with the "production line of death" in fact turns into a criticism of the sanctification of death on the altar of the nation. The death industry that Greenberg describes contradicts the heroic spirit of sacrifice that the national cinema of the time glorified. In contrast to the hegemonic Zionist discourse that addresses stories of brave opposition to going "like sheep to the slaughter" and glorifies the ideal of "beautiful death" and sacrifice, Greenberg presents a distant image of wholesale death lacking real meaning. The film never once leaves the premises of the slaughterhouse. It ends with an extraordinary montage (forty-five shots in forty seconds) of the chopping of chickens' heads, which are tossed one after another into a pile, with a seemingly scared look of a live chicken integrated into the frame, raising the association of the livings' fear of death.[43]

This is the point where the film's meaning is achieved. It deals with the "conveyor belt" of death as an allegory for a society in which the living commemorate and immortalize the dead. "Symbolic suspension of death or the elimination of the experience of death are essential to the existence of a society that comes into being," argues Israeli historian Idith Zertal. Commemoration of the dead (the fallen heroes in the battlefields) "suspends the sacrifice from his historic death turning him into the symbolic dead, the eternal living."[44] The film thus posits a secular perspective of death that detaches it from the sacrificial and heroic significance it has in Zionist collective memory and national rituals.

As mentioned in the introduction, the New Sensibility films are characterized by themes that engage in discourse with the ethos of martyrdom into which its creators were born and raised. Terrifyingly, this ethos identifies youth with death (notably, the youth that died in the 1948 Arab-Israeli War) and develops this notion through national and private commemoration initiatives. Ne'eman argues that Israeli modernist films presented an antithesis to the "death wish" of those who were raised on the myths of the 1948 Generation. In fact, the sequence of aesthetic images and the rhythmic montage with which *Much'shar Bli Rosh* is sealed—the dead eyes of the chickens whose heads are dumped in a pile, the bodies skinned of their feathers being led off in a cart, the smile of a slaughterer, the field of anemones accompanied by music based on percussion and wind instruments—seemingly ridicule the image of "beautiful death" (heroic death in the service of the nation). Simultaneously, the contrast between the visual beauty of the film and the horrors it describes, between the peaceful "outside" and the terrifying "inside," evoke the contradiction in *Night and Fog* between the bold color images of Auschwitz in the present and the black-and-white archival images of the corpses piled at that site in the not-so-distant past.

Conclusion

This article is indebted to the important polemics on modernist Israeli cinema, which coped with a number of critical questions regarding the adoption of transnational strategies within the national context. We sought to uncover the influence of documentary modernist European cinema on Israeli documentary cinema of the 1960s. The two films under discussion in this article provide a vantage point to Greenberg's work mode: one is a commemoration film that opposes the conventionality of commemoration films; the other is an independent, experimental film, which, by the nature of its effect on the viewer, calls for an allegorical reading of its contents that releases it from its sensational, shockumentary, daily realm. Both films deal with the role of collective memory and the construction of Israeli national tradition. In this sense, it is clear that the films do not ignore the social, political, and cultural contexts in which they are made. In fact, one might even argue that Israeli documentary cinema was ahead of its time in relation to Israeli fictional cinema in that it adopted foreign influences so as to create aesthetic critical texts regarding the heroic-nationalist ideology and its related images.

Moreover, this chapter sought to reposition and recognize David Greenberg as a trailblazer of writing, conceptualization, teaching, and filmmaking—a genuine leader at the cutting edge of the cinematic discourse in Israel—after many years of exclusion and neglect. He should be placed alongside such important filmmakers as David Perlov and Emil (Milek) Knebel as an innovator of Israeli documentary cinema. His work is a pure expression of modernism in this mode during the 1960s, which cannot be defined as mere imitation of or simple inspiration from the works of others. On the contrary, he uses characteristics of modernist European cinema so as to reassess the collective memory of the 1948 War and the ritual of sacrifice and death in the fledgling Israeli state.

This research was supported by the Israel Science Foundation (grant no. 794/12).

Notes

1. Miriam Hansen, "The Mass Production of the Senses: Classical Cinema as Vernacular Modernism," *Modernism/Modernity* 6, no. 2 (1999): 59–77.

2. Andrew Higson, "The Limiting Imagination of National Cinema," in *Transnational Cinema—The Film Reader*, ed. Elizabeth Ezra and Terry Rowden (London and New York: Routledge, 2006), 19.

3. Yehuda Judd Ne'eman, a director associated with the New Sensibility and a scholar of Israeli cinema, coined this term in his article "The Moderns: The Genealogy of the New Sensibility," first published in French (1992) and later in Hebrew (1998). His choice of the term was meant to stress the change in internal Israeli values that brought about this particular cinematic movement. See Yehuda Judd Ne'eman, "The Death Mask of the Moderns: A Genealogy of 'New Sensibility' Cinema in Israel" [in Hebrew], in *Fictive Looks—On Israeli Cinema*, ed. Nurith Gertz, Orly Lubin, and Judd Ne'eman (Tel Aviv: Open University of Israel Press, 1998), 9–32.

4. Ella Shohat, *Israeli Cinema: East/West and the Politics of Representation* (Austin: University of Texas Press, 1989), 202.

5. Ibid., 201.

6. Ibid., 202.

7. Ibid., 201.

8. Ibid., 204.

9. Ne'eman 1998, 25.

10. Ibid., 27.

11. Ibid., 26.

12. Ibid., 29.

13. Ariel Schweitzer, *The New Sensibility: Israeli Modern Cinema of the Sixties and Seventies* [in Hebrew] (Tel Aviv: Babel, 2003), 218.

14. In particular, David Perlov's films *Old-Age Home* (1962), *In Jerusalem* (1963), and *Tel Katzir* (1964); yet overall, the documentary films produced in that period were rarely discussed. Despite the common acceptance of *In Jerusalem*'s contribution to the maturing of the personal mode within New Sensibility films, the literature on Israeli cinema tended to view such films as a direct continuation of the newsreels and short propaganda films of Zionist Realism—cinema in the service of the Zionist ideology, namely the same cinematic movement toward which sentiments of loathing spurred the New Sensibility.

15. Ne'eman 1998, 29.

16. Richard M. Barsam, *Nonfiction Film: A Critical History* (Bloomington: Indiana University Press, 1992), 89.

17. Igal Bursztyn, *Face as Battlefield* [in Hebrew] (Tel Aviv: Hakibbutz Hameuchad, 1990), 101–102; Igal Bursztyn, *Intimate Gazes* [in Hebrew] (Haifa: Magnes, 2007), 10.

18. Though Lia Van Leer, the mythological founder of the Jerusalem Cinematheque, managed a cinema club in Haifa since 1955, Greenberg founded similar cine-clubs in many cities and kibbutzim across Israel.

19. It was not, however, the first cinema journal in Israel. It was preceded by *Kol-Noa* (1931–1935), the weekly *Kolnoa* (*Cinema*) that started being published in 1939, and *Olam Ha'Kolnoa* (*The World of Cinema*), which was first published in 1950. These publications mainly addressed young film buffs and mostly provided gossip and behind-the-scenes information on American movies.

20. Avant-garde filmmaker and researcher Chen Sheinberg reissued a volume of *Omanut HaKolnoa* that accompanied a cinematheque retrospective of Greenberg's films in July 2016. Some of the details brought here are taken from his insightful introduction to that special issue.

21. As Israeli film historian David Shalit refers to him, relating to the mythological founder of the Cinematheque Français.

22. Andràs Bàlint Kovacs, *Screening Modernism: European Art Cinema 1950–1980* (Chicago: University of Chicago Press, 2007), 121.

23. For further elaboration, see also Na'ama Sheffi's study of the Israeli Educational Channel and its ideological role in shaping the nation's new identity by those who were chosen as its model figures. Na'ama Sheffi, "Israeli Education System in Search of a Pantheon of Heroes, 1948–1967," *Israel Studies* 7, no. 2 (2002): 62–83.

24. Eric Rentschler, "Remembering Not to Forget: A Retrospective Reading of Kluge's *Brutality in Stone*," *New German Critique*, no. 49 (Winter 1990): 35.

25. Walter Benjamin (1928), *The Origin of German Tragic Drama*, trans. John Osborne (London: Verso, 1998), 81.

26. Judith Butler, "Critique, Coercion, and Sacred Life in Benjamin's 'Critique of Violence,'" in *Political Theologies: Public Religions in a Post-Secular World*, ed. Hent De Vries and Lawrence E. Sullivan (New York: Fordham University Press, 2009), 218.

27. Pierre Nora, "Between Memory and History: Les Lieux de Mémoire," *Representations*, no. 26 (Spring 1989): 19.

28. Ibid., 12.

29. Kate Ince, *George Franju* (Manchester: Manchester University Press, 2005), 29.

30. Tom Gunning, "Landscape and the Fantasy of Moving Pictures: Early Cinema's Phantom Rides," in *Cinema and Landscape*, ed. Graeme Harper and Jonathan Rayner (Chicago: Intellect Books, 2010), 31–70.

31. Bursztyn 1990, 101. The film's photographer, Asher Mullet, recalls a virtuoso shot in which the camera turned around nearly a full 360 degrees to document the slaughterers during their meal. The lighting was softer, offering less contrast, and for the first time in the film, a background noise was audible. In this manner, the atmosphere was instantaneously altered, creating the impression of regular people taking a break from their daily chores. This shot does not appear in the known version of the film.

32. Jeanette Sloniowski, "'It Was an Atrocious Film': Georges Franju's *Blood of the Beasts*," in *Documenting the Documentary*, ed. Barry Keith Grant and Jeannette Sloniowski (Detroit: Wayne State University Press, 1998), 172.

33. Raymond Durgnat, *Franju* (Berkeley: University of California Press, 1967).

34. Siegfried Kracauer, *Theory of Film: The Redemption of Physical Reality* (New York: Oxford University Press, 1960), 306.

35. Adam Lowenstein identifies *Blood of the Beasts*, as well as Franju's fictional film *Eyes without a Face* (1959), with what he labels "shock horror": "The employment of graphic, visceral shock to access the historical substrate of traumatic experience." See Adam Lowenstein, "Films without a Face: Shock Horror in the Cinema of Georges Franju," *Cinema Journal* 37, no. 4 (Summer 1998).

36. Vivian Sobchack, "Inscribing Ethical Space: Ten Propositions on Death, Representation and Documentary," *Quarterly Review of Film Studies* 9, no. 4 (Fall 1984): 283.

37. Ibid., 285.

38. Ibid., 290.

39. Ibid., 291.

40. Ibid., 288.

41. Ibid., 291.

42. Sloniowski 1998, 177.

43. Chen Sheinberg notes that this scene analogizes between the cutting of the chicken and the process of cutting and editing the film.

44. Idith Zertal, *Death and the Nation: History, Memory, Politics* [in Hebrew] (Or Yehuda: Dvir, 2002), 37.

II

PALESTINIAN CINEMA
"MADE IN ISRAEL"

5

TRANSNATIONAL IMAGININGS IN *SALT OF THIS SEA* (2008) AND *VILLA TOUMA* (2014)

Ariel M. Sheetrit

THIS STUDY EXAMINES TRANSNATIONAL POSITIONINGS AND CONCEPTU-
ALIZATIONS of space in the Palestinian films *Salt of This Sea* (Annemarie
Jacir, 2008) and *Villa Touma* (Suha Arraf, 2014). Both films are preoccupied
with representations and conceptualizations of the spaces of Palestine and
Israel; whereas *Salt of This Sea* is a road movie that cuts across vast spaces,
Villa Touma is set in a claustrophobic landscape confined almost entirely
to a villa in Ramallah. In *Salt of This Sea*, a third-generation Palestinian
woman born in America visits Israel and Palestine for the first time. Her
expectations from the places she visits clash not only with those of local
Jews but also with those of the local Palestinians she meets, as her Diaspora
consciousness informs her conception of space. *Villa Touma* depicts three
sisters who confine themselves to their villa for over thirty years in an effort
to forestall the personal and national implications of Ramallah's annexa-
tion by Israel in 1967. That *Villa Touma* emanates from sensitive interstices
is reflected not only by its content but also by the brouhaha it caused when
its director labeled it *Palestinian*—not *Israeli*, despite having received Israeli funding. This positioning and its reception brings out the real-world
implications of the national and cultural ambivalences within the film.

Given that Palestinians still do not have their own independent
nation-state, classifying a film as Palestinian raises fascinating and important questions. In what sense can a national cinema emanate from a people

whose national sovereignty is unsettled, precarious, still wavering? In what sense is a national cinema a product of cultural identity? As has been asked, "In what sense do Palestinians have a claim on a 'national cinema,' given their global dispersion, dispossession, exile, and life in refugee camps?"[1] As Livia Alexander observes, "The Palestinian national struggle, on the one hand, and experiences of exile and displacement, on the other, place any discussion of Palestinian cinema between two existing bodies of literature: that of national cinemas, which focuses on films produced within the defined geographic boundaries of the nation-state, and that of exilic, or transnational, cinema, that operates beyond national boundaries."[2]

Hania Nashef articulates a different perspective, arguing that Palestinian film cannot be viewed as a national cinema, "simply because historic Palestine no longer exists, and the issues tackled are human narrative that transcend Palestinian-specific matters. . . . Internal and external exile has resulted in the emergence of a transnational cinema that narrates the Palestinian story."[3] After observing that there is "no entity or institution that can unambiguously be identified as Palestinian cinema," Carol Bardenstein notes that, "There are Palestinian filmmakers." Yet, many films by Palestinian filmmakers fall into the category of exilic and diasporic filmmaking.[4] These controversial perspectives reveal the indeterminate and ambivalent positioning of Palestinian cinema vis-à-vis national or transnational classification and characterization.

Palestinian cinema produced in Israel complicates this picture even more. When a director labels his or her film *Palestinian*, does this imply a strictly geographic association, and if so, does it apply equally to all parts of the land considered part of historical Palestine or only territories governed by the Palestinian Authority? In what way are the nationality and cultural identity of the director implicated? Does designating a film Palestinian necessitate an association (funding?) with Palestinian institutions? Might such a categorization bespeak an irony that is pointedly and purposely subversive—namely that in order to take a stand in the Palestinian struggle for national self-determination, one must overlook or even undermine notions of essentialist national affiliation in the sense of an independent nation-state? How, then, does this designation evoke a sense of identity that is ethnic, linguistic, cultural, political, and somehow tied to the geopolitical space of Palestine?[5]

Many studies have addressed the problematics of "national cinema" more broadly, not only in the context of peoples without national sovereignty but also in light of national affiliations that are multiple or not straightforward. Studies have examined how national cinema boosts a particular national collective identity or, conversely, how it reflects diversity or subverts a particular collective identity. It has been argued that "another challenge to the 'essentialist' concept of national cinema is growing academic enthusiasm for the 'transnational'—a concept that seems to serve as a kind of benevolent counterpart to the perceived evil of globalization."[6] This view persists in seeing national versus transnational largely in opposing, dichotomous terms. However, some thinkers conceptualize the categories of national cinema and transnational cinema as interconnected and imbricated within each other. Andrew Higson formulates this conceptual continuity by calling into question Benedict Anderson's conceptualization of the nation as "limited, with finite and meaningful boundaries." Moreover, Higson argues that "when describing a national cinema, there is a tendency to focus only on those films that narrate the nation as just this finite, limited space, inhabited by a tightly coherent and unified community, closed off to other identities besides national identity."[7] In migrations across borders and within identities, transnational cinema emerges not only to describe cinemas detached from a stable national coherence but also—perhaps surprisingly—indigenous communities. In Higson's words: "It is difficult to see the indigenous as either pure or stable."[8] This view conceives of modern "indigeneities" in terms of works in progress that are hybrid, dynamic products of interpenetrations of diverse traditions, languages, and cultures. Even cinemas established in specific, circumscribed nation-states are rarely autonomous cultural industries. Higson points out transnational tendencies that emerge in two predominant ways, particularly in coproductions and distribution/reception of films. These two tendencies often occur in films that are categorized from a predominantly national perspective. While this problematizes an assumption of a purely monolithic national cinema, it nevertheless does not succeed in completely uprooting the usefulness of the concept of national cinema.

Crucial to our discussion of Palestinian film is the idea that transnational and national tendencies need not be mutually exclusive. More to the point, cinema marked by transnational tendencies can (paradoxically) shape a *national* consciousness or map out a homeland, especially for a nation without circumscribed geographic borders. Beyond coproductions and distribution/reception, the transnational is also expressed thematically in narratives of exile, migration, and displacement, as well as in the border crossings, diversity, and multiplicity of cultural formations experienced by the films' protagonists. National identity, as Higson stresses, "is not of course dependent on actually living within the geo-political space of the nation." Especially in the Palestinian context in which the Diaspora is scattered throughout the world (not a single Diaspora), national film can serve as a cultural conduit for transforming broad experiences of dispersal and variegation into "a meaningful national collectivity."[9] In this vein, Elizabeth Ezra and Terry Rowden point out, "Indeed, in many films that can be fruitfully considered from a transnational perspective, identification with a 'homeland' is experienced and represented as a crisis . . . national identity often becomes a placeholder for idealized sites of cultural memory and imagined social security."[10] In his book *An Accented Cinema* (2001), Hamid Naficy has brilliantly conceptualized and worked through characteristics of diasporic and transnational cinema that occur in the interstitial and marginal spaces of national cinemas.[11] Will Higbee and Song Hwee Lim build on Naficy's conceptualization but argue that although such cinemas transgress and transcend national boundaries, they also have the potential to occupy or influence mainstream national cinema.[12] They suggest that a critical transnationalism "does not ghettoize transnational film-making in interstitial and marginal spaces but rather interrogates how these film-making activities negotiate with the national on all levels—from cultural policy to financial sources, from multiculturalism of difference to how it reconfigures the nation's image of itself. . . . It scrutinizes the tensions and dialogic relationship between the national and transnational, rather than simply negating one in favor of the other."[13]

This fraught interaction between the national and the transnational and their interpenetration underwrites the twofold goals of my study of *Salt of This Sea* and *Villa Touma*. First, I will explore the expression of transnational tendencies in the dual rubric delineated by Higson that relates to issues of production and distribution in each film. Second, I will delve into the filmic content to analyze how the tension between national and transnational perspectives mobilizes conceptions of place and space in each film. How do the films reify national borders as either bounded or unstable? How do migration, border crossings, multiple national longings, and belongings affect the notions of individual and collective Palestinian identity and Palestinian space expressed in the films? I will examine how space is molded and imagined in both films and how space is constructed to enfold within it multiple, even contradictory, significances.

In conjunction with theories of transnational cinema, I will draw from Doreen Massey's theoretical engagement with conceptualizations of space in her book *For Space* (2005). Her conceptualization of spatialities as unstable, dynamic, subjective, and political provides a rich theoretical framework for working through the relation between power and space, which is particularly relevant for the politics of space that suffuse both films. Crucial ideas include the "temporality of space" that exposes the significance of time on connection between the changes in conceptualizing a particular space over time.[14] "Coeval existence" deconstructs the idea of a single linear world history and allows for spatial heterogeneity.[15] According to this idea, "the spatial, crucially, is the realm of the configuration of potentially dissonant (or concordant) narratives. Places, rather than being locations of coherence become the foci of the meeting and the nonmeeting of the previously unrelated and thus integral to the generation of novelty."[16] "Radical contemporaneity" asserts the multiple trajectories including fractures, ruptures, and divides in constructing space.[17] She builds on José Rabasa's concept of "imperfect erasures,"[18] arguing that the heterogeneous multiplicity that a particular space may encompass need not be imagined *only through layers, surfaces, and superimposition* but in the "discontinuities of the multiplicity in contemporaneous space."[19] She suggests a shift in perspective that entails moving from a "concern with horizontalities to a focus on coeval trajectories."[20] In other words, the multiple significances of a particular space are not constructed only or necessarily by layerings (i.e., how the space was conceived differently in different periods) but by how the same space is multiply conceived at the same moment—how it is imagined, produced, viewed, experienced, delineated, codified, and named. Massey's emphasis on the different positionings that shape conceptions of space is crucial for grasping differentialized perspectives toward landscapes of the Palestinian homeland.

Salt of This Sea

Both the opening scene and the final scene of *Salt of This Sea* occur at Israel's Ben Gurion Airport, thereby framing the film within transoceanic border spaces. In both scenes, the main character, Soraya, a third-generation American whose grandfather was a Palestinian refugee, uses the word *here* to refer to the place she is visiting, rather than naming it Israel or Palestine. This articulates the film's preoccupation with the indeterminacy and instability of space and its drive to problematize and expose the multiple narratives through which individuals conceive of their affiliation to place. Soraya visits Israel for the first time, crossing into the West Bank ostensibly to claim the money her grandfather left in a British bank in pre-1948 Palestine. Upon discovering that the bank has confiscated the money, she decides to hold up the bank for the precise amount, aided by her new West Bank friends, Marwan and Emad. After the heist, they dress up as American Jews and escape across the border into the Green Line (Marwan and Emad do not have permits), beginning a journey that includes the beach, Tel Aviv, Jerusalem, and two visits to lost homes within the homeland—one to Soraya's ancestral home in Jaffa and the other to Emad's ancestral home in the destroyed village of Duwayima. In the first of the two significant homecoming scenes, Soraya, Emad, and Marwan visit Soraya's grandfather's house in Jaffa. The present owner is a liberal Jewish woman who invites them in. Marwan stays on with her, while Emad and Soraya (now romantically involved) proceed to the second homecoming scene in which they spend the night in the ruins of Duwayima, from which Emad's family fled in 1948. The next day, the police apprehend them both. Soraya is deported because her visa has expired, and Emad is imprisoned for entering Israel illegally.

The film's transnational premise is manifested not only in Soraya's hybrid identity and the characters' multiple border crossings but also in the technical aspects of production, filming, and language. *Salt of This Sea* was the first feature film of Annemarie Jacir (and the first Palestinian fictional feature film by a woman), a filmmaker whose peripatetic biography encompasses the themes of travel and exile apparent in the film. Born in 1974 into a Christian family in Bethlehem, she then moved as a child with her family to Saudi Arabia, where they "lived as alien outsiders in Riyadh's closed society."[21] At sixteen, she was sent to school in Dallas, Texas. She studied in California and New York and returned to Palestine to teach in 1992 and once again to film *Salt of This Sea* over a decade later. She has been living in Jordan since being denied entry into Palestine in November 2007.[22] She has made two subsequent films: *When I Saw You* (2012) and *Wajib* (2017).

Jacir's biographical trajectory, when taken with the film's preoccupation with "dislocatory feeling structures," would suggest that Naficy's framework of "accented cinema" could inform an analysis of this film's relation to place.[23] In fact, the all-too-real effects of actual political constraints impacted and expanded the transnational scope of the film, since when Jacir was denied entry into the West Bank to finish the filming, she was forced to shoot one of the film's main scenes outside of Palestine and chose to re-locate to Marseilles, France.[24] Such political imbalances are often at work in transnational filmmaking, which, instead of implying a broadening of horizons and navigable, permeable borders in fact sometimes implies the opposite. It exemplifies that transnationalism is often not a choice—artistic, personal, or otherwise—but conscripted. Although transnationalism can be cast as a celebratory and euphoric confirmation of open borders and multicultural understanding and tolerance, it is in fact often the corollary of creative (or necessary) solutions to closed borders, discrimination, and inequality. Philip Crang, Claire Dwyer, and Peter Jackson aver that "there is nothing inherently 'given' about the politics of transnationality, and those who make appeals to concepts of non-fixity, in-between-ness, and third spaces as inherently progressive construct transnationality in . . . one dimensional terms."[25] The particular scene filmed in France evokes trans-nationalism as displacement since it is out of place, an imagined replica of the on-site shooting of the rest of the film. Beyond this particular scene, real-life politics and asymmetrical power situations affected the shooting overall. Jacir notes that the Israeli army blocked the shooting and denied permissions for the locations requested. To resist these aggressive policies, they resorted to filmmaking "guerilla style,"[26] shooting on location with crewmembers who themselves were often refugees from the specific places in which they were filming. Thus, the film, in its insistence on filming in Israel, embodies both an act of resistance and of return.

Aside from the scene filmed in France, the film was shot mainly in Ramallah, Jerusalem, Jaffa, and Haifa. While this implies a specific national territorial focus on the expanse of historic Palestine, the political reality subverts such a national unity and necessitates crossing international bor-ders. Ramallah has a distinct national affiliation from the other three cities, and the road between Ramallah and the cities located within the Green Line (pre-1967 borderline) entails crossing borders controlled by Israelis in order to enter into territory under jurisdiction of the Palestinian Author-ity. This further complicates the transnational quality of the film's produc-tion. In addition, Jacir explains, "Due to the lack of film schools and re-strictions on Palestinian movement, assembling a crew was challenging, most having never been on a film set before. . . . Other on-the-ground pro-duction difficulties stemmed from the fact that most of the crew carried Palestinian identity cards and were denied permission to leave the West Bank, therefore a new crew had to be formed for the sequences shot inside

Israel. Additionally, we were denied permission to shoot in several places and therefore had to compromise on locations and even actors."[27]

The transnational underpinnings of *Salt of This Sea* are exposed in the opening production credits, which list seven countries: Palestine, Switzerland, Belgium, the United States, the United Kingdom, the Netherlands, and Spain. The film is a coproduction between Paris-based JBA Productions, Spain's Mediopro, Switzerland's Thelma Film, Belgium's Tarantula Films, Ramallah-based Philistine Films, Danny Glover, and Joslyn Barnes.[28] Contrasting with this expansive amalgamation of financial support is the fact that this film represented Palestine (*not* the Palestinian Authority) as the 2008 submission for the Academy Award for Best Foreign Language Film, submitted by the Palestinian Ministry of Culture. This blurs a dichotomy of local and global, since the local here in itself is a political entity-in-formation, and as such, it raises the question of art—and film, specifically—not in *representing* Palestine but in defining it and bringing it about, both as an onscreen construct and as a political, internationally recognized reality.

Moving from production to filmic content, I would like to draw attention to issues surrounding the languages spoken in the film. The main language in the film is Arabic; English is also spoken, as well as a smattering of Hebrew. Jewish Israelis speak to Soraya, Emad, and Marwan in accented English within the Green Line. At checkpoints and borders, Israeli soldiers speak in accented Arabic and among themselves in Hebrew. The security checkers at the airport do not resist the chance to take advantage of the language divide to crack a joke at her father's expense in an aside unintelligible to Soraya but translated in the subtitles. When Soraya tells the Jewish Israeli security staff at the airport that her grandfather was from "Yaffa," using the city's Arabic name, they hesitate and then reply "Ah, Yaffo" using the Hebrew appellation.

Naficy points out that multilingualism, a characteristic of the accented mode of film, "makes intelligibility more complex. . . . Importantly, in these films, language is almost never taken for granted. In fact, it is often a theme and the self-reflexive agent of narration and identity."[29] This is true not only regarding the main character, Soraya, who speaks Arabic with an American accent and who is most visibly transnational, but also regarding other characters, such as Marwan. On the way to the beach near the end of the film, Soraya, Emad, and Marwan get lost, driving in the wrong direction on the Israeli Road One. "I thought you learned Hebrew," Soraya berates him. "We didn't learn 'sea' in jail," Marwan retorts. This exposes a great irony—that within prisons in which Palestinians from the West Bank are jailed, inmates learn Hebrew, thereby actually taking part in Israeli culture. This language acquisition gives them leverage and power in dealing with their captors, which Marwan now uses in order to navigate inside the Green Line. However, his disorientation points to the limits of his Hebrew and his answer to the fact that prison Hebrew is not congruous with the vocabulary needed for excursions. This disorientation is intensified by the skewed reflections of the buildings visible in the car windows. At first, as they drive, the camera captures cars driving along the road, shot from the perspective of the cars themselves, suggesting an equality among them in their anonymity. The scene cuts to a close-up of Soraya shot through the window of the car, the buildings reflected such that they seem superimposed on her. This expresses her disorientation and displacement in a homeland that is both hers and also not hers: she heads in the wrong direction, the buildings springing out of the side of the frame and mapped onto her face embodying her nightmarish predicament.

Throughout the film, Soraya moves easily between English and Arabic, depending on her interlocutor. Her language use and her accent demonstrate a subjectivity that stretches beyond a binational dual affiliation with two nation-states. Her Arabic is a spoken argot that she has acquired from her father (we know nothing of her mother!); she speaks it with the ease of a native speaker and yet with the accent of a foreigner generations removed from them, a Diaspora Palestinian. It simultaneously expresses belonging and unbelonging. Her standing as an outsider in Palestine is articulated when she receives compliments on her Arabic while in Ramallah—a compliment that bespeaks her foreignness by identifying her as someone whose Arabic is not a given. Only rarely are there words she does not know in Arabic or blurts out in English—like *speed bumps*. This reveals more than a linguistic gap. Emad does not even seem to know there is a word for the bumps they ride over (in Arabic or any language). This exposes Emad's parochial perspective—he thinks Israelis put speed bumps on the road to vex the Palestinians. "Do they have them in Canada?" he asks incredulously. This humorous revelation manifests the divergence between Emad's indigenous Palestinian perspective and Soraya's worldlier Diaspora-Palestinian perspective.

Soraya's American accent in Arabic articulates the connection between the two distinct places through which Soraya identifies—Brooklyn, New

York, and Palestine. Her identity is not neatly divided into two parts represented by the two places with which she identifies but rather intertwined, her Palestinian identity filtered through her American identity, thus accented. This accent is also used in a richly ironic way, as this marker of foreign affiliation allows her freedom of movement within Israel and the West Bank. It bolsters her costume of a religious American Jew that allows her to cross the border into Israel proper with Emad and Marwan. As Emad says toward the end of the film as he whips his *kippah* (Jewish head covering) out of his pocket: "With your accent and my look, we have it made." They are able to pass for American Jews and therefore seamlessly pass across the border from the West Bank into the Green Line. This passing is subversive and allows for infiltration of hegemonic social and national boundaries.[30]

The film draws out a differentiated relation to place between Soraya—the Diaspora Palestinian—and the local Palestinians. Soraya's enthusiasm for being in Palestine—for "claiming for herself the right of return," as she puts it—clashes repeatedly with that of the local Palestinians whose hearts are set on "abroad." This is reinforced by the conversation with upper-class Palestinians minutes after her arrival in Ramallah; by the woman showing her an apartment who proudly notes that the neighbors' son lives in Michigan; by the aspirations of her lover Emad to go study in Canada ("Life is better in other places," he says); and by the Palestinian Authority representative who cannot grant her citizenship ("You have an American passport? What could be better than that?").

Soraya is entitled to freedom of movement that West Bank Palestinians are not—until her visa runs out. Emad and Marwan need permits to leave Ramallah. When Soraya and Emad reach the border overlooking Israel, he says that this is as far as he can go, since he has not been issued a permit to leave Ramallah in seventeen years. When they eventually cross into Israel together, they do so illegally, dressed as American Jews. Emad also faces restrictions on travel abroad and is repeatedly refused a visa to leave for Canada in order to make good on his university scholarship there. A significant difference between Soraya and local Palestinians is that while their connection to the land is based on their own lived experiences on it, her connection is based on "postmemory." Hirsch conceptualizes postmemory, or the remembering of other people's traumatic memories, as follows: "Postmemory characterizes the experience of those who grow up dominated by narratives that preceded their birth, whose own belated stories are evacuated by the stories of the previous generation, shaped by traumatic events that can neither be understood nor re-created."[31] Soraya recites her grandfather's daily schedule, complete with the names of places and streets that were his stomping grounds. This dramatizes that Soraya has inherited and internalized her grandfather's memories of life in Jaffa and expulsion from there. The places are frozen in time, in her postmemory of his memory, including Arabic names of streets and places now replaced by Hebrew names—or demolished entirely. This enacts Soraya's connection to Palestine; through her memories of his memories, through the spaces he has mapped in the stories he has shared, she looks out onto the spaces she sees for the first time in actuality.

Kamel Dorai has noted, with regard to Palestinians living in the Diaspora, that oral history acts as an account of the Nakba "and also transmits the land, the Palestinian landscape."[32] This is crucial to understanding the rupture experienced by Soraya as she travels within the present-day landscape of her grandfather's memories. She sees the landscape superimposed by the recollections and narrations of the place that have been passed down to her. In contrast, Emad's connection to Palestine is visceral, drawn from immediate lived experience. Although Emad is an internal refugee (his family was originally from the destroyed village Duwayima), his Palestinian identity is not shaped by a primarily diasporic consciousness. *Salt of This Sea* reveals a radical contemporaneity in constructing spatiality. Soraya presupposes an undivided land, whereas Emad does not question the limitations of present-day boundaries and associated restrictions on movement; he is resigned to the two-state solution, which is presented (by him and by the Palestinian elite sitting in the restaurant) as a matter of reality.

Power Geometry and Space-Time in *Salt of This Sea*

The image of the sea is employed to connect the first sequence in the film, archival footage of the destruction of homes in Jaffa and the fleeing of the Palestinian residents, to the present-day images of the same area. The camera pans from images of the destruction of houses portrayed in black and white, to the sea, also in dark grainy gray. Then cut to the sea in color, a sparkling azure, as if to convey that the place is the same, but the time (and the technologies) have changed. The image of the sea is used as a transition, first in black and white and then in color, to symbolize a connection between past and present on the same physical space and also to embody the transformation of that same space over time. The sea demarcates national boundaries and also can be read as an expression of the difference in outlook between Soraya and Emad; she crosses the ocean from North America to reach her homeland, whereas he dreams of crossing the same ocean in the opposite direction, hoping for a visa to Canada. The ocean symbolizes something different for each of them; for him, it symbolizes the world of possibilities beyond his homeland, and for her, it brings her to her homeland.

The film's transnational inclinations are exposed not only through its border crossings and transoceanic premise but through casting the entire space of "here" in terms of the superimposition of the State of Israel onto Palestine. This is brought out in the opening archival shot of the destruction of homes in Jaffa. This encapsulates the rupture of the Palestinian Nakba and the moment when Soraya's family was uprooted. Such acts of destruction are not relegated to the past, the film shows us, but are ongoing, exemplified in footage of Israeli tractors destroying Palestinian homes and by the news broadcaster who states that Israelis demolished eighteen homes in the Balata refugee camp that day. Thus, the lines between past and present are sometimes obscured. Such spatial heterogeneity is revealed briefly when Emad and Soraya whiz past a grove of olive trees in the midst of which a Muslim family is picnicking. The postcard-like moment is timeless and could be happening now or generations earlier.

The film oscillates between portrayals of the fractured, modernized landscape that emphasizes the technologies of power and domination, brought out, for example, in traveling shots against the background of the Separation Wall, and sweeping olive-tree-filled panoramic shots that recall an idyllic Paradise Lost before the 1948 Nakba. These shifts disrupt the internal coherence of the modern spatial configurations but also portray the postmemory (her grandfather's inherited memories) through which Soraya views the landscape. Soraya's doubly outsider perspective—as a Palestinian in Brooklyn and an American in Palestine—is given concrete expression in the yellow shirt that she wears that reads *Brooklyn* on it in Arabic letters. Pressing the point home, she later wears a different shirt that says *Brooklyn* in English letters.

In its representation of the landscape, the film destabilizes a claim to a single order and a uniform view of the land (i.e., only Israel). The land is revealed as enfolding within it fragments and shards of a past that is there for whoever takes the trouble to look for it. As Massey puts it: "We know then that the 'presentness' of the horizontality of space is a product of a multitude of histories whose resonances are still there, if we would but see them, and which sometimes catch us with full force unawares."[33] Soraya's keen eye uncovers remnants of the Palestinian present in Israeli everyday reality.

In West Jerusalem, Emad, Marwan, and Soraya notice a plaque revealing the political identity of the place on which they are now standing as it once was back in 1924, when the British Mandate referred to it as Palestine. The sign is trilingual, with English central and largest, representing the British control of the region, and on either side of the English, a translation into Arabic and Hebrew respectively. Soraya focuses only on the three Arabic words—Yaffa (Jaffa), al-Quds (Jerusalem), and Filastin (Palestine)— but does not stop to think of the implications of either the content (the British high commissioner and British governor) or the additional two languages, both of which would be enough to shatter her idealized view of the pre-Nakba Paradise Lost. The camera supports her view by its attention to this plaque that has melted into the background and by its unaccustomed, disorienting angle that accentuates the Arabic.

Especially inside the Green Line, the camera repeatedly defamiliarizes the Israeli landscape by exposing such "imperfect erasures" of an obliterated Palestinian past.[34] When Soraya enters what used to be her grandfather's house in Jaffa, the camera imbibes the Ottoman tiles as though from Soraya's perspective, drawing the audience in through an extreme close-up panning up to the arched Ottoman windows. Soraya and Emad then find similar tiles on the Jaffa beach, hidden in piles of stones. The destruction of the remnants of Palestinian culture and life is foregrounded when Soraya asks the current owner of her grandfather's home in Jaffa what they did with the furniture. The owner's answer is that her parents apparently got rid of it, but the film answers by cutting to the montage at the Jaffa flea market. The long takes of this lyrical scene are accompanied by the soundtrack of a song sung by Asmahan, unfolding the place through sounds of another era. The montage excludes people almost entirely, focusing only on items that bear signs of an Arab past, including an oud, furniture, a tarbush, and Arabic writing on brass instruments. The montage ends at the pile of debris on the beach, the same extra-diegetic music still playing, as though to show that this pile is where the items at the flea market will end up. These discarded fragments, cast away as old junk, juxtapose the Palestinian past with the Israeli present.

When Soraya visits her grandfather's house in Jaffa, her shirt matches the aquamarine color of the house's shutters, implicating her in the place itself. Sitting in front of the shutters, she asks Marwan, "Is this my house or not?" The camera gives the answer, blending her into the shutters. As powerful as this imagery is, the attire of the Jewish owner Irit is similarly symbolic, showing that space can be multiply conceived: her orange shirt matches the color of the oranges she is squeezing in the kitchen. Oranges symbolize Palestine, as Soraya specifically says, and so the Jewish owner is—like Soraya—also visually integrated into the landscape. The grandfather's house is a microcosm of the land itself, incorporating natural browns and greens, brimming with plants, decorated with large landscape pictures.

The scene in Soraya's grandfather's house, along with the scene of the night spent in the destroyed village of Duwayima, represent two key moments in the film. By staging an actual return of third-generation refugees to their ancestors' dwellings, both scenes bring the themes of home and return into sharp relief. The scene in the Jaffa home is particularly crucial because it stages the issues surrounding the Israeli-Palestinian conflict from subjective perspectives of two individual women, one from each side of the conflict. It then breaks the duality by showing that Soraya does not represent a monolithic Palestinian perspective, as her view is not shared by Marwan, who makes himself at home in Irit's house even after Soraya leaves in anger.

Irit, the Israeli, acknowledges the Palestinian past—to a certain extent— but sees it as over and finished. She is portrayed as a leftist Israeli, bemoaning the violence of the current situation, sporting mugs with the inscription "Peace Now—End the Occupation." From the inscription on the mug, it is clear that she supports Palestinian national sovereignty in the West Bank. However, she rejects the Palestinian-ness of the space in which she lives. For her, the Israeli present is built on top of the Palestinian past, and they do not—and cannot—coexist within the Green Line; they are not contemporaneous.

Soraya overlooks the present, the Israeliness of the landscape, her probing examination of the landscape constantly uncovering shards of Palestinian-ness. It would be naive to compare the views of both women on equal terms, as one is from the dominating side, which expelled the other side. While Irit understands this power dynamic regarding the West Bank, she cannot see it in terms of her own house. Soraya's perspective cannot incorporate Irit's ownership of the house, at least without an acknowledgement of the injustice presupposing this ownership. "You want to speak about history, the past—let's forget it," Irit tells her. Soraya's response sums up her perspective: "Your past is my every day, my right now. . . . This is not your home." Soraya grants Irit the right to stay in the house—on the condition that she admits that it is stolen. In *Salt of This Sea*, space is multiply conceived and used to show contradictory symbols of subjectivity. Taken separately, the perspectives of Irit and Soraya seem to represent a layered approach to spatiality wherein each history and each perspective is temporally overlaid upon the other, Israel upon Palestine.

Irit and Soraya do not come to an understanding, their views as intractable as the conflict itself. Soraya says she wants recognition of the grievances, but her outburst shows that the feelings exploding inside her are not just contingent on Irit's recognition of the Jews' role in uprooting Palestinians. She expresses an older anger, the product of her generations-old trauma.

Soraya vents her pent-up fury by hurling the potted plant (a symbol of the land) onto the floor. The act is an expression of the blowup engendered by the contact between the two unconditionally opposing perspectives—the one that can only see the present and the other that must frenetically unearth the past (if not her, then who?). Ultimately, *Salt of This Sea* is a declaration of rage—rage in the face of injustice, rage upon discovering that there is no going back to the place that once was.

Massey emphasizes that time and space are necessarily connected—that space is not "a collage of the static."[35] Rendering space static, one-dimensional, and frozen leads to "the stabilisation of others, their deprivation of a history."[36] In Massey's conceptualization of space-time, different trajectories meet up. It is in such terms that we can conceptualize the encounter between Soraya and Irit. Jacir's words are illuminating here: "Palestinian cinema has been relegated to the West Bank and Gaza or to stories which take place within historic Palestine . . . but certainly not about the fact that Israel is still Palestine to us."[37] This is the main thrust of the film's preoccupation with space: it is about representing space beyond a surface or a pile of surfaces but as it enfolds within it multiple histories.

Soraya refers to Israel (several times throughout the film, when talking to Jewish Israelis) with a resonant, meaningful, almost sung-out *here*. Where are you from? *Here*. This undermines the present-day name *Israel*, but she does not replace it with the word *Palestine* until the final scene, when she answers, "Here—Palestine." She challenges the conception of space as singular by declaring the space that is the State of Israel to be Palestine. Does that mean that Israel does not exist—or that for her, this same land is *also* Palestine? Does this undermine the sense of layered spatiality that

Soraya seems to otherwise express in the film, instead relating to space in terms of "coeval trajectories"?[38] Rather than casting the multiplicities that may exist in a single space in terms of horizontality, superimposition, and layering, such that one reality replaces another, this approach assumes that space can entail a contemporaneous plurality in which distinct trajectories coexist, therefore comprising a sphere of coexisting heterogeneity.

In the sequence in which Emad and Soraya spend the night spent in Duwayima, they take cover in one of the few structures still partially intact. Officially, the place does not exist: "They call it Amatzya now!" Emad and Soraya are woken up and forced out by an Israeli Jewish guide (Juliano Mer-Khamis) showing his students vestiges of the ancient history of the land in what is a national park in the present of the film.

This echoes the forced evacuation of the families of Soraya and Emad three generations earlier. It also prefigures Soraya's imminent deportation from Israel. It enacts the power dynamics of who is and who is not allowed to be in this particular space and who controls it. The casting of actor Juliano Mer-Khamis is purposeful here. The son of a Palestinian father and a Jewish mother, he embodies the juxtapositions of difference played out in this scene. This can be considered in light of the phenomenon of "cross-casting," which Bardenstein discusses in her study of Israeli and Palestinian film of the 1980s and '90s. She argues that cross-casting can interrogate or transgress category boundaries, but the degree to which they do so can be established only on a case-by-case basis.[39] This case is particularly interesting because it is not a case of boundary crossing from one identity to another, but it is a case of a person with a hybrid identity, both Palestinian and Jewish Israeli. Therefore, his role here is not so much transgressive as it is symbolic; his body can be seen as emblematic of the land itself—one land (and one body) with multiple simultaneous identities. This casting choice reflects the film's tendency toward destabilization of binary, fixed identity categories and of a clear-cut demarcation between *Palestine* and *Israel*.

This scene powerfully brings out how individual perspectives shape how space is conceived differently. For Emad and Soraya, they are in Duwayima, whereas for the guide and his students, they are in a national park composed of ruins of an ancient biblical landscape. The film uses this space to show the opposing significance of this space to Israelis and Palestinians—as a national park or as a destroyed, usurped home. By waking them and telling them to leave, the guide is echoes the historical usurping, thereby revealing the power dynamics underlying each perspective on the land's identity.

Villa Touma

Villa Touma unfolds a story of three sisters—Juliette, Antoinette, and Violette—who have lived cloistered in Villa Touma since 1967. They construct an anachronistic space that is ostensibly unaffected by the changes wrought by the war. They cling to their prewar lives, blocking out all transformations that occurred in the wake of the war. The way that they have frozen time inside of Villa Touma clashes with present-day reality in Ramallah in 2001, which is when the film takes place. The sisters are from a landed Palestinian Christian family who lost both their land and high status in the aftermath of the 1967 Six-Day War, when Israel conquered and occupied the West Bank, previously under Jordanian sovereignty. The sisters embody the trauma of national loss; its repercussions have taken a toll on their personal lives. Each has a background story of unfulfilled love. Juliette's engagement is broken off when her mother dies so she can raise her two sisters and brother; Violette is widowed, having married a much older man who becomes paralyzed only two days after their wedding and dies; and Antoinette is not allowed to marry her lover because he is not from an aristocratic family.

The sisters' monotonous routine is thrown off kilter by the arrival of their teenage niece, Badia, their late brother's daughter. Badia, who was raised in an orphanage, is sent to live with them. Her appearance at their doorstep shakes them out of their stultified existence. At first they try to incorporate her into their idiosyncratic, sterile, near-silent, humorless, and austere repetition of unvarying quotidian tasks. Their attempts at vivifying the aristocratic lives they once led are reflected by their wardrobe, daily timetable, furnishings, and customs (such as incorporating French into their speech, playing the piano, and observing "proper" etiquette). They try to teach Badia the basics of an aristocratic life long-ago defunct. When she arrives, Juliette burns Badia's meager clothes and possessions, including the only photo of her mother, who, as a Muslim, symbolizes for them their brother's disloyalty to their status and religion. They condescend to those they consider lower than them, notably to Abu Hasan, their gardener and handyman, who is Muslim and from a peasant background.

The sisters decide that they must marry off Badia, and to this end, they take her to church to meet the local Christian society families. As they are seen as out of touch and snobbish, their efforts, which include throwing a tea party and attending weddings and funerals, come to naught. At one of the weddings, Badia meets and falls in love with Khalid, a wedding singer who is Muslim and a refugee living in the Qaalndia refugee camp. They meet secretly until Badia learns he has been shot and killed by the Israeli army. Badia is pregnant with their child and dies in childbirth, leaving her aunts with the baby.

The film was written, produced, and directed by Suha Arraf, an Israeli citizen born in the village of Maaliya on Israel's northern border. Arraf has directed three documentaries to date, and this is her first feature film. She wrote screenplays for two acclaimed Israeli films, *Lemon Tree* (2008) and *The Syrian Bride* (2004), both directed by Eran Riklis. Although in the storyline of *Villa Touma*, no international borders are crossed, the filming involved multiple border crossings, not least because it was filmed both in Haifa and Ramallah. The villa itself is an estate located in Haifa, not Ramallah, and only the shots of the Ramallah streets were actually filmed there.

The film's transnational positioning is embodied in the controversy that Arraf incited when she labeled the film *Palestinian* at its Venice Film Festival premiere. Given this controversy, it is important to bear in mind Arraf's years of work in both Arabic and Hebrew as a Palestinian artist working in concert with Israeli Jews, a fact also reflected in the film crew, which, unlike *Salt of This Sea*, consisted of both Israeli Jews and Palestinians. Arraf's decision to classify the film's nationality as Palestinian was considered problematic, since most of her funding came from the Israel Film Fund—an Israeli public organization—which threatened to sue her to force her to return the funding. In the end, Arraf changed the classification of her film from *Palestinian* to *stateless*, presenting it only under her name.

The brouhaha that erupted when Arraf first labeled her film reveals how sensitive the politics of identity can be. It demonstrates the explosive connotations of declaring a particular identity in certain contexts and the disparity and overlap between national versus artistic identity. The uproar exposes transnational aspects of Arraf's personal identity, the identity of the film, the national affiliation of Ramallah residents, and the interrelation between them. Whereas *Salt of This Sea* implicates identification with countries separated by borders and seas, *Villa Touma* is concerned with multiple identities that emanate from the same strip of land, revealing how multiple nationalities may inhabit the same geographic area. Her characterization problematizes the hybrid identities of Palestinian Israelis and undermines the injunction that official country of citizenship must comprise the sole articulation of one's national identity. This film can be—or could have been—classified as Israeli, since the director carries Israeli citizenship and since a large part of the funding came from the Israel Film Fund, with the participation of other Israeli sources (including the Israel Lottery Council for Culture and Arts and the Jerusalem Cinematheque). On the other hand, justifications for labeling it Palestinian include Suha Arraf's personal identification as Palestinian (and Israeli), the language (Arabic), and the setting (Ramallah). The most compelling reason for labeling it Palestinian is that the director classified it as such. This raises the question of the role of directors in classifying the national identity of their films. Arraf justified classifying her film as Palestinian: "Films belong to those who create them—the producer, director, screenwriter. They never belong to the foundations that helped to fund them, and they certainly never belong to countries. I define my film as a Palestinian film because I am first of all a Palestinian, and its story is told from my point of view, which is a Palestinian point of view. It's a story about four Christian women living in Ramallah. Only Arabic is spoken in the film, which has no Israeli-Jewish characters."[40]

These criteria are not axiomatic when deciding the national orientation of a film, and therefore they bear not only on this specific film but also on classification of films in general, particularly those that preempt a singular national identity. At the Sundance Film Festival, for example, the rules state that if more than 50 percent of film financing comes from a specific country, the film is categorized accordingly.[41] In contrast, the Foreign Language Film Award Committee of the Oscars does not consider the source of the film's funding, focusing instead on the nationality of its creators. What is interesting in the case of Arraf is that if her own passport-based nationality decides on the nationality of the film, then technically, the film should be labeled Israeli. In light of this, the controversy here transcends the question of what criterion is more crucial—the nationality of the director or the main source of funding. Arraf phrases it in terms of the film's "artistic identity."[42] By classifying this film as Palestinian, not Israeli, Arraf asserts a Palestinian identity that is supranational, evincing a sense of linguistic, ethnic belonging connected to territory but not necessarily in its nation-state sense. Arraf's classification is a statement about the significance of Palestinian identity for Arab citizens of Israel, and this is her main achievement in calling her film Palestinian.

Despite Arraf's insistence that the film is Palestinian, the film was not screened at the Alexandria International Film Festival in Egypt "because of the film's 'Israeli' origin."[43] This adds yet another set of questions regarding classification. In this case, the consequences led to a ban on the screening of the film.

"Static" Transnationalism in *Villa Touma*

The sisters' clinging to the prewar era inside their villa effectively creates an isolated enclave bounded by walls to maintain the conventions of a different epoch and of a bygone national emplacement. This is what imbues the storyline with a transnational dynamic, given that "border-crossing is the raison d'être of . . . transnational cinema."[44] As such, this film recalls other Palestinian works that present place as static but space as dynamic—that is, where the geographic territory is constant, but the spatial identity undergoes change. This occurs in the Palestinian novel *She, I, and the Autumn* (Salman Natur, 2011), in which a woman who has not left her house in sixty years walks out the door to discover that her homeland of Palestine has become a foreign country—Israel. The film similarly is imbued with a transnational consciousness in which exilic and transnational identities are generated by a change in the identity of the same piece of land over time (the space outside of the villa), rather than by the movement of people across boundaries and borders. In this sense, the villa embodies what Crang, Dwyer, and Jackson call "transnational space," reconfiguring attachments and distancings more broadly and considering "symbolic and imaginary geographies."[45]

In *Villa Touma*, the quotidian efforts of the sisters within the villa reflect an attempt to maintain the same lifestyle as they had before the war, although they no longer have the means to do so—and despite the changes in the demographics of the city. This is reflected visually by the dated furnishings, by their old-fashioned clothes, and most pointedly by the shifting shadows that reveal the pictures of dead people on the wall as ghosts, making them seem eerily alive in the house, almost moving in the shadows. Similarly, the soundtrack blocks out outside noises until the end of the film, when the outside world encroaches on their own, and the illusion of dissociation from the outside world is shattered.

The way the sisters imagine the space and craft it clashes with present-day reality in Ramallah in 2001. This is exemplified in the scenes when the sisters venture out of the villa. The people on the streets gape at their anachronistic attire; the members of the church community shun them. "More often than not," Ezra and Rowden argue, "transnational cinema's narrative dynamic is generated by a sense of loss . . . by a sense of being 'out of place.'"[46] That the sisters are out of place is articulated when Violette agrees to teach Badia French but for naught—"How many families are there like ours in Ramallah since the war?" The upper-class Christians, the film reminds us repeatedly, have moved to America. Ironically, this makes the sisters feel like *they* are living a Diaspora existence because the fabric of their social community has disintegrated. The men return only to be buried, thereby equating return with death. In this film, life is possible only where there is the possibility for change, for overturning stereotypes and static mores. Of the return home, Massey contends that you can never really go back because although you may be able to return to the space, time will always have changed it.[47] This is crucial for conceptualizing the sisters' ultimate failure to cling to pre-1967 Ramallah.

The attempt to stop time is symbolized by the mirror in Violette's room that remains covered, signifying endless mourning. Time stands still for her because she cannot view the changes wrought on her face and body. When Badia uncovers her mirror, Violette has a psychotic breakdown. The "radical contemporaneity" of how the sisters conceive of space versus Ramallah's transformation post-1967 generates a disjunction that traumatically isolates them. The noises from outside of the villa are not heard inside the villa. The near-silence of the background is gradually penetrated by the sound of helicopters, the presence of which reflects Israeli domination. The first time outsiders enter their house since 1967 occurs when the sisters hold a tea party that ends in disaster. The boundaries of the house are penetrated, and life inside the house loses its pristine pre-1967 temporality. However, in clashing with the sisters' expectations, the guests, like visitors from another country, reveal the gap between the sisters and their surroundings. As such, in this film, place is evoked as a contradictory symbol of displacement and rootedness.

Conclusion

Taken together, these two films challenge and broaden the boundaries of Palestinian film and bring out space as the sphere of the possibility of the existence of multiplicity in the sense of contemporaneous plurality. My analysis interrogated space as the sphere in which distinct trajectories coexist, revealing the multiple layering and significances imbued within the same physical space. Home in both films provides neither security nor comfort. Both films end in tragedy. In *Salt of This Sea*, Soraya's dual love affair with the land and with Emad is cut short, and, in turn, his dreams are shattered when he is imprisoned. *Villa Touma* also ends in an ill-fated love affair and in Badia's death—the baby's presence symbolizing new life but within the same stagnated space. Both films bring out how transnational concerns shape Palestinian *national* consciousness, uncovering, recovering, imagining, and dramatizing different aspects of the Palestinian homeland. They show how space is shaped by diverse points of view and how these same points of view also shape, circumscribe, and constrict individual lives on this land.

Notes

1. Annemarie Jacir, "I Wanted That Story to Be Told," *Alif: Journal of Comparative Poetics*, no. 31 (2011): 245.

2. Livia Alexander, "Is There a Palestinian Cinema? The National and Transnational in Palestinian Film Production," in *Palestine, Israel, and the Politics of Popular Culture*, ed. Ted Swedenburg and Rebecca L. Stein (Durham: Duke University Press, 2005), 153.

3. Hania A. M. Nashef, "Demythologizing the Palestinian in Hany Abu Assad's Omar and Paradise Now," *Transnational Cinemas* 7, no. 1 (2016): 83.

4. Carol Bardenstein, "Cross/Cast: Passing in Israeli and Palestinian Cinema," in *Palestine, Israel, and the Politics of Popular Culture*, ed. Ted Swedenburg and Rebecca L. Stein (Durham: Duke University Press, 2005), 106.

5. The films of filmmaker Cherien Dabis refocus the spotlight from Palestine to the Diaspora. Her first film, *Amreeka* (2008), is filmed and takes place mostly in America, and her second film, *May in the Summer* (2013), takes place in Jordan. Both films evoke Palestinian identity in different ways, particularly Palestinian Diaspora identity, and as such, they enrich and, I would argue, extend the signification of the label *Palestinian*.

6. Ian Christie, "Where Is National Cinema Today (and Do We Still Need It)?," *Film History* 25, no. 1–2 (2013): 24.

7. Andrew Higson, "The Limiting Imagination of National Cinema," in *Transnational Cinema: The Film Reader*, ed. Elizabeth Ezra and Terry Rowden (New York: Routledge, 2006), 18.

8. Ibid., 19.

9. Ibid., 16.

10. Elizabeth Ezra and Terry Rowden, "General Introduction: What Is Transnational Cinema?," in *Transnational Cinema: The Film Reader*, ed. Elizabeth Ezra and Terry Rowden (New York: Routledge, 2006), 8.

11. Hamid Naficy, *An Accented Cinema: Exilic and Diasporic Filmmaking* (Princeton, NJ: Princeton University Press, 2001).

12. Will Higbee and Song Hwee Lim, "Concepts of Transnational Cinema: Towards a Critical Transnationalism in Film Studies," *Transnational Cinemas* 1, no. 1 (2010): 10.

13. Ibid., 18.

14. Doreen Massey, *For Space* (London: SAGE, 2005), 118.

15. Ibid., 68.

16. Ibid., 71.

17. Ibid., 99.

18. Ibid., 109.

19. Ibid., 110.

20. Ibid., 114.

21. Nicholas Blincoe, "Annemarie Jacir: An Auteur in Exile," *The Guardian*, June 5, 2014, accessed May 31, 2017, https://www.theguardian.com/film/2014/jun/05/annemarie-jacir -auteur-in-exile-palestinian-director-when-i-saw-you.

22. Jacir 2011, 241.

23. Naficy 2001, 27.

24. Annemarie Jacir, "Another Denial of Entry for a Filmmaker," *Denied Entry*, May 1, 2008, accessed May 31, 2017, https://deniedentry.wordpress.com/2008/05/01/another-denial-of -entry-for-a-film-maker.

25. Philip Crang, Claire Dwyer, and Peter Jackson, "Transnationalism and the Spaces of Commodity Culture," *Progress in Human Geography* 27, no. 4 (2003): 443.

26. Jacir 2011, 248.

27. Ibid.

28. Annemarie Jacir, "Salt of This Sea: Notes on a Shooting," *Vertigo* 3, no. 7 (Autumn 2007), accessed May 31, 2017, https://www.closeupfilmcentre.com/vertigo_magazine /volume-3-issue-7-autumn-2007/salt-of-this-sea-notes-on-a-shooting/.

29. Naficy 2001, 50.

30. Some of my remarks in this paragraph are inspired by Carol Bardenstein's illuminating study on cross-casting and role switching in Palestinian and Israeli cinema (2005).

31. Marianne Hirsch, "Past Lives, Postmemories in Exile," *Poetics Today* 17, no. 4 (1996): 659.

32. Kamel Dorai, "The Meaning of Homeland for the Palestinian Diaspora Revival and Transformation," in *New Approaches to Migration: Transnational Communities and the Transformation of Home*, ed. Nadje Al-Ali and Khalid Koser (New York: Routledge, 2002), 92.

33. Massey 2005, 117.

34. Rabasa's term, cited in ibid., 110.

35. Ibid., 119.

36. Ibid., 122.

37. Jacir 2011, 249.

38. Massey 2005, 114.

39. Bardenstein 2005, 101.

40. Suha Arraf, "I Am an Arab, Palestinian and Citizen of Israel—I Have the Right to Define My Own Identity," *Haaretz*, August 24, 2014, accessed May 31, 2017, http://www .haaretz.com/opinion/.premium-1.612195.

41. John Anderson, "The Hand That Feeds Bites Back: Israel and Suha Arraf Differ on Nationality of 'Villa Touma,'" *New York Times*, October 16, 2014.

42. Ibid.

43. Creede Newton, "Villa Touma: The World's First 'Stateless' Film," *Middle East Eye*, October 16, 2014, accessed April 20, 2016, http://www.middleeasteye.net/in-depth/reviews /villa-touma-world-s-first-stateless-film-489386955.

44. Higbee and Lim 2010, 17.

45. Crang et al. 2003, 9.

46. Ezra and Rowden 2006, 7.

47. Massey 2005, 123–124.

6

HERE AND THERE, NOW AND THEN

Nations and Their Relations in Recent Palestinian Cinema

Mary N. Layoun

People make their own history but they do not make it of their own free will or as they choose but under already existing, given, and transmitted circumstances. The tradition of all dead generations weighs like an Alp on the brains of the living.

—**Karl Marx**, *The Eighteenth Brumaire of Louis Napoleon*

"WE COULDN'T DO WHAT WE DIDN'T SEE TO do. We couldn't enter where we had no vision to go," reflects Aldrick, the central character of Earl Lovelace's 1979 novel, *The Dragon Can't Dance.*[1] In prison after an indecisive and circumscribed protest against the poverty, discrimination, and underdevelopment in postindependence Trinidad, Aldrick provides an insight that is not only a sober assessment of a truncated rebellion but also suggests the importance of vision, of imagining *otherwise* our communities, our lives in them, our relations with one another, and those structures that frame and emerge from those relations and communities. Without those visions, we can't see what to do or where to enter. And, as Lovelace's novel illustrates, we certainly can't dance. In its own powerful literary accomplishment,[2] *The Dragon Can't Dance* points at and itself illustrates a critical source for that imagining or visioning otherwise—in culture, in literature, in film, in visual art, and, as in the novel itself, in music and dance.

Yet, as the narrative arc of Lovelace's novel suggests, such vision otherwise is no simple proposal or straightforward directive. It is not a mundane allegory of equivalences. And it might not appear where or as what we expect. For such unexpectedness resides not just in the visions of an otherwise that emerge from cultural forms[3]—for my present purposes, from Palestinian cinema by Palestinian citizens of Israel.[4] Rather, it is that the character and shape of those visions emerge in a form—Palestinian cinema—that simultaneously registers, explicitly and implicitly, the ongoing violence and coercion of occupation, the despair and anger of oppression. And in the crux of the contradiction between excruciating material circumstances and possibility, Palestinian cinema—in its stateless diversity, in its range of visual and narrative registers, in its widely situated stories—offers rich and diverse suggestions of an otherwise.

Given the grim and unrelenting if different "facts on the ground" for Palestinians in the Occupied Territories, in Israel, in Lebanon, in Jordan, in Syria and their refugee camps, or in the broader Diaspora, such visions of an otherwise seem themselves unlikely, if not impossible. But they are visible in precisely this context of apparently grim impossibility and that especially, though not only, in the last ten or fifteen years. So, though it might seem unrealistic or perhaps even frivolous to point to traces of an otherwise in more recent Palestinian cinema, that is what I will do in selective citation of documentary and imaginative films.[5]

Traces of an otherwise are there in torturous relation to the brutal now and here of everyday humiliation, to a past and present of Israeli state violence, and to violent and nonviolent responses to that state violence. They are there in celebrated and world-famous poetry, and fiction, and film, and music. They are there in small and large acts of humanity between neighbors and cohabitants, Palestinian, Israeli, and others. *Here and there, now and then*—the point in that titular reference, though, is not only the localized and nonsystemic.[6] It is also temporal and spatial multiplicity. Here, in Palestine/Israel. There in the Occupied Territories. There in the Diaspora. Now in the present. Then in the near and in the not-so-near past. The nonsystemic and multiple—an awkward mouthful or eyeful of words. An impossible landscape. An excruciating network of relations. A folding-over of nations and peoples and spaces and times.[7] Another understanding of the workings of the transnational, "across nations" (or between them), another understanding of the very landscape of nations themselves, of parallel worlds on the national landscape, and of ways to move across that landscape and between those parallel worlds.[8]

It is perhaps precisely our task at present to recognize the effort to conjure passages across the landscape through the apparently impassable—or to recognize the effort to map the landscape of the impassable and the impossible and the effort to persist—"Like twenty impossibles," as Tawfik Zayyad's poem of over fifty years ago avows.[9] For Palestinian citizens of Israel, the harsh conditions on the ground, their up close but complicated and manifestly unequal relations with the Israeli state, their no less complicated relations with Jewish citizens of the Israeli state, their relations with Palestinians in the occupied territories of the West Bank and Gaza, and the profusely complex relations between Palestinian citizens of Israel and diaspora Palestinians are unequivocally dense with impossibility. And maps of or conjured passages through the apparently impassable seem high on the list of those impossibilities.

Still, on that impossible impassable landscape, how is it that Palestinian cinema visually renders its narratives and stories? How is it that it frames what it presents for the viewer's eye to *see*? While these are questions that could be—and are—asked of any visual form, it is intensified in the case of film, complexifying questions asked of the earlier technology of the photographic camera or of earlier forms of visual art. Film—"moving pictures"— deepens such questions of mechanical/technological frame and content at the same time as it seduces the eye and ear with the apparently immediate content of what it frames, with the visual, aural, verbal stories situated in its human and mechanical capture. And Palestinian film, given where and how it casts its filmic eye, deepens such questions yet further.

For central to the by now familiar complexity of the human-machine interaction is the equally familiar question of perspective—what can be seen from where one stands. It's a truism that perspective shifts depending on that *where*, on one's angle of vision, on one's distance from—or proximity to—that which is seen, on what one is "trained" to see or to ignore.[10] The perhaps overly vaunted openings (which are for some a relentless mandate) of mobility notwithstanding, we still stand *somewhere*, look from *somewhere*, are seen from *somewhere*— literally and metaphorically. If the convention of perspective is that everything centers on the eye of the beholder—the ruse of the all-seeing eye[11]—that eye doesn't exist in the world of mortals nor yet in the world of mechanical or technological sight.[12]

It is, though, this very trope and material technology of the film camera and the perspectives from which the human and mechanical eyes see—behind the camera, in front of the camera as well as in front of the film itself—that are at the heart of some of the most compelling Palestinian films of the last ten or fifteen years. In the exploration of that trope and its material rendition of images, our more familiar understanding of proximity and distance is challenged. Our understanding of our roles as viewers and audiences for visual images is challenged. Our attention to perspective and standpoint is challenged and sharpened.

Though these are familiar stories of mechanical and human seeing, of distance and proximity, of perspective, I cite them again as a way to trace a small path to the "trans/inter/national" and Israeli cinema, which is our collective focus here. For this focus, too, is predicated on proximity and distance across and within and between nations. On the one hand, it's clear enough to what *transnational cinema* refers. The transnational is a now widely exercised force in funding, producing, distributing, and marketing film. And the transnational is equally at work in the very stuff of what is funded, produced, distributed, and marketed.[13] And that "stuff" is not simply reducible to the intentions of the filmmakers or of film funders and distributors. Nor is it simply the reception by transnational audiences of a film. The transnational *is* those things. But I would focus here on the equally present, if more figurative and nonsystemic, traces in the films themselves—*here and there, now and then.* That is on the otherwise of visually imagining trans/inter/national relations within, between, and among peoples or communities or nations.

In the dialectic of transnational and localized contexts, the accomplishments—aesthetic, narrative, political, cultural—of a diverse range of Palestinian filmmakers and video artists are stunning. To discover again or for the first time the work of Rashid Masharawi, Tawfik Abu Wael, Suha Arraf, Eyad Burnat, Annemarie Jacir, Larissa Sansour, Amer Shomali, Najwa Najjar, Scandar Cobti, Anan Barakat, Ibtisam Mara'ana Menuhin, Hany Abu-Asad, Elia Suleiman, or Michel Khleife is to appreciate anew the rich diversity in form and content, in aesthetic style, in distributive channels, in expanding and diversifying audiences of recent Palestinian film and videos.[14] Their renderings of narratives and stories of Palestine and Palestinians challenge, whether implicitly or explicitly, not just the boundaries of filmic convention, of perspective, of distance and proximity, of linear narratives, of the work of memory and desire. They also challenge, implicitly or explicitly, an impossible material present: the seizure of homes and land, the social and judicial and political processes of "the only democracy in the Middle East," the impossible situation of refugeehood seemingly without end. From where the camera and the cameraperson stand, from where the eyes of the camera and of the cameraperson see, from where the audiences see the mechanically reproduced moving pictures—these multiple standpoints frame and narrate Palestinian (and, simultaneously, Israeli and international) stories. And they do so with acute and often ironic insight into diverse lives, with a complex and rich narrative aesthetic and with moments of tenderness and beauty amid pain and frustration that is not only compelling in its own right but also in the context in which it is evinced. The camera eye is often proximate to the details of everyday life under occupation, whether or not it is the occupation itself that is the story that the film tells. And the same camera eye distances those details of everyday life by its very framing of them for viewing and reflection. In parallel worlds, infinitesimally close to that of the camera eye, the eye of the filmmaker brings close and makes distant the stories she tells. This contradiction is at the heart of filmmaking and film viewing. It is a different, though not unrelated, proximity and distance from that of transnational circuits of funding, production, distribution, and reception.

A striking example of the intertwining of the near and the distant, of the mechanical and the human eye is Eyad Burnat and Guy Davidi's acclaimed 2011 documentary, *5 Broken Cameras*/خمس كاميرات محطمة.[15] The five-year span of its narrative frame traces numerous proximate parallel worlds: the "life and death" of the five cameras of the title, the first of which Emad acquires on the birth of his and Soraya Burnat's fourth son Gibreel; the first years of young Gibreel Burnat's life; the continuing Israeli seizure, in that same period, of Bil'in village land and the bulldozing of their olive trees for the Israeli settlement of Modi'in Illit[16] and for the infamous Separation Wall; and the establishment and development of nonviolent resistance to the illegal settlement and wall in the Bil'in Popular Committee against the Wall.[17] Also within the narrative arc in *5 Broken Cameras*, though at a distance from the film's central stories, are further parallel worlds indicated by persistent presence of Israeli allies in the Bil'in nonviolent demonstrations each Friday as well as the intermittent presence of international allies.

At the heart of this film—of all film—is distance, no matter how close the content of the stories. That distance lives simultaneously with the filmic projection of immediacy and proximity for audiences located in other times and places, with experiences of similar situations, or with experiences radically different from the stories presented. The village of Bil'in is brought visually near and audible; distance is apparently overcome by the camera eye. But in that very apparent overcoming, distance is accentuated, even when the stories the film narrates are familiar to or shared by some audiences. Emad Burnat notes on showing 5 *Broken Cameras* in Palestine: "The people [in Palestine] know more about this; they related to the place and they related to the situation. This is how the life is in many parts. They were more touched by the story, to see the village to remind them what happened."[18] Here proximity and relationship are predicated on familiarity; distance is generated by time and memory.[19]

If distance and proximity, literal and metaphoric, are a fundamental part of the technology with which any visual narrative is constructed, they are filmic conventions and tools that Palestinian filmmakers put to work in particular ways to tell their stories of nations and inter- and trans-nations. For if Burnat's five broken cameras themselves constitute the narrative frame for the parallel worlds noted above and for selected stories within and across those worlds, those broken mechanical eyes are belied by the film and by the very stories it tells. Broken mechanical eyes (and injured human eyes) are not blinded altogether but rather see and tell of the transformation of intensely localized stories, of Burnat and his family and friends in their injured but unbroken stance against the efforts to enclose and strangle their village. The broken cameras are belied by Burnat and Davidi's working relationship itself, proximate but respectfully and insistently distant. They both maintain, though differently, that their work together is distinct from the category of "Israeli-Palestinian collaboration."[20] They bridge the distance between them as an Israeli activist and filmmaker and a Palestinian activist and filmmaker by characterizing the film as Burnat's on which they work together. In a joint interview with Tom White for the International Documentary Association, Burnat explains their relationship and refusal of the rubric of Palestinian Israeli collaboration: "The reason I decided to work with Guy—his sense of origin is as an Israeli activist and not to represent [the conflict of] Arabs against Israel. When I approached him to join the project, we agreed that we were not making it political, it was not Israeli-Palestinian collaboration. I told them you'd come and support and help, and this is my film; it's a Palestinian film. It's my story, my family's story, my village's story."[21] In another interview by Elizabeth Wood with Burnat and Davidi, the latter explains, "Israelis and Palestinians work together and it's mediatised, it's used as propaganda to show that Israelis and Palestinians are able to work together. So we didn't want to put much emphasis on that. Personally, I want to normalise that in the film, that the Israelis are helping Palestinians in their struggle because it's also their struggle. But we didn't want to idealise it or put it at the centre. Even if I'm Israeli and Emrad [*sic*] is Palestinian, for us it was a natural decision to work together, because there's a movement around us."[22]

There are, then, other eyes, national and beyond, and other nonlocal categories at work in the funding, production, distribution, and reception of films, leaving their traces in the film itself, as Burnat and Davidi both indicate.[23] And the transnational in this small instance is but not only funding and distribution streams and diversely located and trained audiences. It is also the reluctance to cross specific borders on someone else's terms. The transnational of "Palestinian-Israeli collaboration" is what Burnat and Davidi refuse in the name of a shared struggle, of a recognition of radically differential access to resources, to authority, and to the very stories the film seeks to tell in the name of "a movement around us."

In this context of already existing visual and verbal categories that not only cross boundaries but stop or are brutally stopped short of them, Scandar Cobti and Yaron Shani's explicitly Palestinian-Israeli collaboration in their film *Ajami* (2009) is an interesting counterpoint in reflecting on distance and proximity, on perspective, and on the literal and metaphoric force of the trans-, inter-, and intra-national in recent Palestinian cinema. The debates around Israeli "branding" of the film duly noted,[24] *Ajami*'s achievement in visual narrative and in stories sequenced within that narrative is remarkable. So too is Cobti and Shani's filming process: employing intensely talented, nonprofessional actors from the Ajami neighborhood, working without a script, and accomplishing it all in an amazing twenty-three days.[25] The nested stories in the nonlinear narrative arc foreground, as the arc itself, the gritty everyday detail of Israeli-Palestinian interactions in an Arab Palestinian ghetto neighborhood in Yafa. With depictions of violence, poverty, crime, drugs, and exploitation, *Ajami* could be set almost anywhere—except for the Arabic and Hebrew dialogue and explicit if uncontextualized location references. The film's Cannes Festival Pressbook in its gloss on the film's content is astonishing in its ignoring of any context at all, except the very familiar one of religious affiliation: "Jaffa's Ajami neighborhood is a melting pot of cultures and conflicting views among Jews, Muslims and Christians. The tragic fragility of human existence is experienced in the enclosed community of Ajami, where enemies must live as neighbors."[26]

In its universalizing public relations rhetoric and the decontextualization of both its narrative frame and the stories embedded therein, as well as in its distinct difference from the production and filming of *5 Broken Cameras* and its very different reception, *Ajami* proves Burnat's and Davidi's point about the category of Palestinian-Israeli collaboration.[27] And it proves their point not only in its production and distribution but also in the content of the film itself. In his *Occupation Diaries*,[28] Jaffa-born Palestinian attorney, author, and human rights activist Raja Shehadeh writes of the film: "The film portrays Arab men as noble savages given to hugging each other, evidencing how tender these cut-throat murderers can be with one another . . . men who are sitting around smoking nergila in the street . . . have the effrontery to stab him to death. Simple. It's their way, it's who they are and how they normally behave as Arabs."[29]

One of the most striking illustrations of the limitations of a narrow close-up filmic focus within a radically diminished context is the nested story of Binh, a Palestinian restaurant chef (played by Cobti himself). As a Palestinian citizen of Israel, Binh moves more freely, both literally and metaphorically, than most of the Palestinian men in the film. He is at his job, joking and good-natured, trying to help the young West Bank boy, Malek, smuggled into Israel and working illegally at the restaurant with Binh, or imagining a future with the Jewish girlfriend he loves, or dancing and drinking in bars, or snorting cocaine—foolishly, naively, or stupidly thinking he will single-handedly outwit not just individuals, Palestinian or Israeli, but systems of domination and occupation that have been in place far longer than him. Against those systems, his individual desires, dreams, and illusions of escape are insignificant and largely inexplicable—if poignant. *Ajami*'s considerable filmic accomplishments noted with admiration, it is remarkable how such poignant stories of the gritty everyday—as compelling a story as they tell—offer very little in the way of interrupting or contextualizing already existing stories of what Shehadeh calls "Arab men as noble savages [and] cut-throat murderers." It offers very little in the way of locating the poverty and violence of the Ajami neighborhood in the continued destruction by the Israeli state of what was once the cultural, economic, and industrial center of British Mandate Palestine, a prosperous, sophisticated city of over one hundred thousand people, Yafa, the "Bride of the Sea."[30]

Perhaps, though, one of the central things we can learn from Palestinian cinema of the last decade or two is that the attempt to visually account for the impassable and impossible landscape *is* itself to begin to imagine otherwise. It *is* to trace a series of signposts on the landscape and, in doing so, to suggest, explicitly or implicitly, ways of shifting those signposts, of cohabiting on and moving across the landscape differently, or at least to suggest a *need* to do so. But those accountings and their signposts in the narrative frame and in the stories situated therein are not some fixed surety. They are subject to being seen and recognized. They can be unseen and un- or mis-recognized. And they can erode. Juliano Mer-Khamis's 2004 documentary, *Arna's Children*, on the work of his mother, Arna Mer-Khamis, is a poignant reminder that transnational relationships painfully, patiently woven and retraced can be rent by unrelenting violence and despair.[31] The conclusion to that film and to the stories of the young men who participated in the Jenin Theater project and the assassination of Juliano Mer-Khamis himself are clear markers for the incredible visions that can be built at a specific historical moment and their brutal extermination in another moment.[32]

If *5 Broken Cameras* narrates a series of parallel stories of a community's resistance to Israeli state violence, *Ajami* narrates the discontinuous stories of the violence and anguish of individual lives in a single devastated neighborhood, and *Arna's Children* conveys the lifework of a Jewish Israeli woman in the Palestinian refugee camp of Jenin, Ibtisam Mara'ana Menuhin's سجل أنا عربي/*Write Down I Am an Arab* (2014)[33] turns around the life of a single man, albeit a very famous man—the internationally celebrated poet Mahmoud Darwish.[34] *Write Down I Am an Arab* narrates—most often through Darwish's own comments and poetry—his life and the lives of those close to him. Framed by Darwish's poem and life, it is also a visual narrative of selected moments in Palestinian history, threaded through Darwish's person and work as well as through Mara'ana Menuhin's narrative construct. And its beautifully configured filmic narrative of the life and work of Darwish and of Palestinian history is simultaneously a delicate suggestion of the relationship of the narrator herself—most especially in those moments when it is her voice-over that questions or comments—with the person and work of Darwish and, by extension, with Palestinian and Israeli history.

The documentary begins not with Darwish himself but with his identity papers, an Israeli passport with the photograph and signature of a young Darwish. The highlighted details of Darwish's passport—first name, birth year and place, nationality ("Arab"), full name, and signature—are underscored by the sounds of rustling papers, footsteps, scraping chairs, and equipment. There is a hesitant exchange that opens this segment of the film, an initial awkwardness that positions what is to follow:

> INTERVIEWER: Yes. Alright, I—
>
> DARWISH: Fine.
>
> INTERVIEWER: Look, you—[35]

The woman's voice (Mara'ana Menuhin) addresses Darwish with a statement about his position as "the Palestinian national poet." As she speaks to him, the visual image shifts from Darwish's passport to a sky of clouds over which is superimposed a young Darwish sitting on the ground lighting a cigarette. Their exchange continues:

> INTERVIEWER: —For several years you have been considered the Palestinian national poet. You are greatly revered in the Arab world.
>
> DARWISH: I think that every poet dreams of being the voice of others.
>
> INTERVIEWER: Of course. Doesn't it bother you?
>
> DARWISH: It depends on the meaning. I'm telling the story of a sad winter's night in Paris. Sadly, or gladly, every Palestinian thinks that I represent him. I don't like to represent. I barely represent myself.[36]

It is only after this exchange that the film's title and the name of the director emerge on the screen. And as the documentary concludes, we see Darwish, the distinguished senior poet, in Ramallah at the last poetry reading before his death. He reads his "If You Walk on a Street."[37] From behind the audience, at the back of the hall, the camera moves forward to Darwish himself. And as the reading concludes, the scene shifts to Darwish's funeral; the camera lingers on the figures and faces of young boys lining the street, flashing peace signs and holding flags, banners, and photographs of Darwish. This narrative arc for the film, then, opens and closes with Darwish in the documents and images that represent him, as it opens and closes with his poetry.

Aurally situated in between this frame of images and words for the life and work of Mahmoud Darwish is the soundtrack for another of his poems, "Rita and the Rifle."[38] The song points to and underscores a parallel universe in *Write Down I Am an Arab*, as it serves as a signpost for the story of Darwish's love for Tamara Ben-Ami, a young Jewish Israeli woman.[39]

Figure 6.1. A young Mahmud Darwish in the opening of *Write Down I Am an Arab* (Mara'ana Menuhin 2014).

As the film credits conclude after the sequence above, the scene shifts to Ramallah, and "Rita and the Rifle" plays as the backdrop for street scenes of the city. And from the street scenes in Ramallah and a man smoking as he walks alongside the graffiti-covered wall that blocks in Ramallah on the southwest side of the city, the camera moves in close to a woman carrying an armful of red flowers and walking along another wall—that of the Darwish memorial and museum in Ramallah. As the as-yet unidentified woman lays flowers on Darwish's grave and subsequently moves through the museum, Darwish's voice-over narration explains his use of the name *Rita*. The camera, meanwhile, follows the woman through the museum exhibits and then fades out to the home of Darwish's older brother, Ahmed. There is no voice-over narration, and the song "Rita and the Rifle" fades away to complete silence. The camera lingers briefly here on another kind of testimony to Mahmoud Darwish and the Darwish family—photos, beautiful objects, book-filled shelves. In the previous segment, Tamara Ben-Ami is not explicitly identified. Mahmoud Darwish's older brother is, with "Ahmed Darwish, Jedideh (Galilee region)" appearing on the screen. The film concludes in the same city, Ramallah, with the same song, "Rita and the Rifle," as soundtrack accompanying the images of Darwish's funeral. Privilege of aural place then is given to the song that is a signpost for the relationship between the poet from Palestine and the young Jewish Israeli woman he loved as a young man.[40]

Write Down I Am an Arab presents a beautifully configured, poetic series of introductions to Mahmoud Darwish's life, work, and reception. And the narrative sequence in which it does so is as suggestive as the stories themselves. On the one hand, following the chronology of a life, the film begins not with Darwish's birth but with the Israeli document that records his presence and status in what has become Israel. Concluding with Darwish's death, it returns aurally to his love for Tamar Ben-Ami—even though their late reconnection in Paris a few years before Darwish's death is fleeting and conflicted. Moments of possibility can be lost. Still, a young Palestinian man's love affair with an even younger Jewish Israeli woman is tenderly recorded visually and verbally.

The sequence in which Tamar Ben-Ami is introduced by name—though we've already been visually introduced to her at Darwish's memorial in Ramallah and aurally introduced by the metaphoric reference to her in the song created from Darwish's poem "Rita and the Rifle"—is preceded by Darwish himself accounting for his relationship with Hebrew, "the language of the foreigner who came to my land."[41] He accounts for his use of the language "with the policeman, the military governor, the Hebrew teacher, and the beloved."[42] For nearly the final ten seconds of this clip, the visual as Darwish speaks is the photo of a young Darwish standing with his arm around Tamar Ben-Ami—a photo that appears multiple times in the film, a signpost for the love between the two and for a possibility passed, if not completely lost. And then, for what is initially some ten minutes of a seventy-three-minute film,[43] we are introduced directly and by name to Tamar Ben-Ami in her Berlin apartment as she sifts through her letters from Darwish. But the material presence of Darwish's love letters to Ben-Ami as an archival artifact is not quite the focus here. Rather, occasionally accompanied by photographs of the young couple, selections from the letters are read by a man's voice as the images of his letters being written in Hebrew on a pad fill the visual screen. A particularly tender passage from one of Darwish's letters has Tamar herself reading the passage over the voice of the male reader.[44]

And then it is Tamar Ben-Ami who narrates the story of Darwish's reading of the poem "Identity Card," with its opening lines that constitute the title of Mana'ara Menuhin's film, and his subsequent arrest.[45] With archival film footage and stills sequenced with Darwish's reading of that poem, the segment concludes with Ben-Ami's pointed if patient explanation to the off-screen interviewer of Darwish's arrest and the significance of his "Identity Card" poem.[46] The relationship between Ben-Ami and

Darwish continues to be foregrounded in his letters to her before he leaves for prison and while he is there. His last letter to her in this segment of the film marks a second ten-minute sequence focused on Ben-Ami's relationship with Darwish,[47] recording the forceful ending of their relationship. After the 1967 War, Ben-Ami joins the Israeli Navy and works as a member of the navy band. By 1970, Darwish leaves Israel for the Soviet Union.[48] By 1973, he is in Beirut, where he lives through the Lebanese Civil War, leaving with the PLO leadership almost a decade later, after the Israeli invasion and the 1982 siege of Beirut.

There is one further extended segment with Tamar Ben-Ami toward the end of the film; she recounts her public defense of Mahmoud Darwish in the face of the hysteria with which his poem "O those who pass between fleeting words," written at the beginning of the First Intifada in 1987, was greeted in Israel. He calls to thank her for standing up for him and invites her to visit him in Paris. As she describes that last meeting, the interviewer questions Ben-Ami's ecstatic account of realizing that she would see him the next day.

BEN-AMI: I was happy and excited and—
INTERVIEWER: Why?
BEN-AMI: I was going to see him! Ibtisam, I loved that man very much.[49]

This is the only time the off-screen interviewer, the film director, is addressed directly by name. But it is not the only or the first time that her questions provoke for her interviewees' emphatic clarification to her of what they saw, heard, experienced, or understood. And as they provoke such clarifications for the interviewer, they also emphasize those clarifications for the film's audiences.

This third not-quite-five-minute segment with Ben-Ami ends, though the images remain of rainy Paris streets. But the audio transition and sound-over for the next brief segment of Darwish at a book signing is "Rita and the Rifle." This delicate filmic concatenation of repetition, image, words, and sound is a powerful poetic testament not only to the compelling and evocative life, work, and relationships of Mahmoud Darwish, though it is certainly that. It also exemplifies the remarkable accomplishment of the film itself—a delicate, difficult, and beautiful balance of violence, love, desire, and anger—and subsequent generations, such as the filmmaker herself, who learn of and respond to others' stories and histories.

In a consideration of cinematic distance and proximity of the position from where one stands, sees, and narrates, there are two further moments to which I would draw attention in Mara'ana Menuhin's documentary. In the lingering focus on Tamar Ben-Ami's international or transnational relationship with Darwish, there is also a subtle and astute commentary on the international and transnational Palestinian national struggle. Darwish's older brother, Ahmed, recounts Darwish's departure for Moscow, noting without affect, "He told no one he wasn't planning on returning."[50] The elder Darwish's statement is followed by an interview with the Palestinian Druze poet Samih Al-Qasim in the village of Rama in the Galilee, where he lived virtually all of his life. Al-Qasim notes his "complex anger" on learning of Darwish's departure and decision not to return to Palestine. Their relationship of intense closeness was "severed," al-Qasim notes. "Some people said, let him go . . . I reacted harshly; poetry will never evolve if it means renouncing your homeland."[51] Punctuated by a clip of Darwish reciting two lines of poetry—"Sarhan was fodder for war. / Sarhan was fodder for peace."[52]—the interview with Al-Qasim is followed by another with Ahmed Dahbour. Dahbour, a Palestinian writer, journalist, and poet who lived most of his life in exile, sits with Palestinian writer Ziad Khadash, watching a Darwish poetry recital on a laptop. Khadash applauds. The off-screen interviewer asks Dahbour when he first learned of Mahmoud Darwish and his poetry "and made the connection between Palestine and Mahmoud."[53] Dahbour responds by referring to other poets and writers of the Occupied Territories in the late 1960s. He narrates the story of Darwish's trip to Egypt on the eve of Nasser's death (1970) and the rumors that Arafat was angry with him. Dahbour faces his on-screen interlocutor, Khadash, who nods his head as he listens. Khadash asks Dahbour if Arafat was angry with Darwish "because he left?" "No," Dahbour responds. "You must be with your people . . . Nasser was the flag of 'Arabness.' But now that Nasser is dead you should return to your home." "Which is where?" the off-screen interviewer asks. "Beirut," Dahbour answers without hesitation. And he expands, "The revolution was managed from Beirut."[54] The scene then shifts without comment to archival film footage of Beirut.

But in these three sequenced responses to Darwish's departure for the Soviet Union and his decision not to return to Palestine/Israel, are three very different standpoints on *home* and *homeland, exile* and *abandonment.* Those three juxtaposed responses expand ever farther outward. They make implicitly explicit the diversely located positions of home and homeland. And by implication they make implicitly explicit the *trans-* of the nation.[55] As with Emad Burat's *5 Broken Cameras* and its narrative arc, Mara'ana Menuhin's film captures and is captured by the stories that it tells. Her biographical documentary of Mahmoud Darwish—closely and intimately focused on the here of an individual life—is also a story of distant places and times, of international currents, of transnational relationships. And that is as much the story that *Write Down I Am an Arab* tells as it is the story of Mahmoud Darwish's life. In between Darwish's Israeli passport that opens the film and his death and burial that end it, woven into the framework of biographical chronology and locations are parallel universes of perception, of memory, and of desire. Those parallel universes serve as signposts on the very same landscape (though understood radically differently). They are bound together, though subtly and almost but not quite imperceptibly, in the film itself and with that at which the film directs its eye—the life and work of Mahmoud Darwish.

And there is a second—and here final—instance of cinematic distance and proximity of the position from where one stands, sees, and narrates in this rich and suggestive filmic narrative in words and images and sounds. A further exchange between the off-screen interviewer and Darwish occurs toward the end of the film, after the onset of the First Intifada is introduced.[56] The scene shifts from street scenes of stone-throwing Palestinians and houses being blown up by Israeli tanks to a cluster of Israeli soldiers in a field, one of whom is using a stone to break the arm of one of a group of captured and bound young men lying on the ground.[57] The voice-over of the first visual presentation of that incident is Darwish reading his poem "To Those Who Pass between Fleeting Words."[58] The Arabic poetry reading, dated March 11, 1988, continues as the images shift now to Darwish reading the poem. Footage of the same excruciating incident is played for a second time ninety seconds later,[59] this time with the voice-over of Darwish explaining to the off-screen interviewer his response to seeing a video of the incident. As the replay of the incident ends, the scene shifts to Darwish sitting in a café with coffee and a cigarette, reading a newspaper and turned away from the camera and the interviewer. The voice-over exchange with the interviewer continues.

DARWISH: —I felt very bitter.
INTERVIEWER: Yes.

Figure 6.2. Mahmud Darwish in *Write Down I Am an Arab* (Mara'ana Menuhin 2014).

DARWISH: Because all my Israeli friends took part in the attack on me . . . the Israeli foreign ministry translated it [the poem] to every language and distorted the poem. I never said . . . I challenge whoever finds it. "Take your dead and get out." I didn't.

INTERVIEWER: "The graves," is there no such line?

DARWISH: There is no such line! There is no such line.

INTERVIEWER: That's the line that killed me.

DARWISH: There is no such line! What can an occupied people say to an occupier?[60]

The proximity and the distance between a life lived, remembered, and narrated to another (Palestinian Israeli) and represented in film are both brought close and capaciously expanded by the carefully complex interweaving in images, dialogue, and sound of interlocutors from near and far, of lovers, of family, of friends, and of adversaries. Darwish's story is captured by Mara'ana Menuhin's eye—mechanical and human—and it captures the interviewer herself. Her film lingers on and repeatedly returns to a story of love across nations, of friendships and intimacies possible and impossible, of a vision of cohabitation that sets out from the titular imperative of the film. The interviewer is "killed" by a fictional attribution to a poem. The rapid shift between proximity and distance running throughout the film is accentuated here.

Write down! I am an Arab. From that imperative in Darwish's poem and in Mana'ara Menuhin's film, perhaps we can then engage in a dialogue otherwise, in a shared effort otherwise, in a common struggle of imagining *otherwise* our communities, our lives in them, our relations with one another, and those structures that frame and simultaneously emerge from those relations and communities. Perhaps as the truncated relationship, repeatedly cited in Mara'ana Menuhin's film, between Mahmoud Darwish and Tamar Ben-Ami suggests, perhaps precisely even *in* its truncation, we can see visions of where to enter. We can see what to do. We can see, as Guy Davidi notes, "Israelis are helping Palestinians in their struggle because it's also their struggle."[61] But that co-laboring for "real peace," as Darwish characterizes it to the interviewer in his reflections on the profound limitations of the Oslo Peace Accords, "must be founded on a dialogue between two versions of the same history. It's our fate to be settling in the same metaphor."[62] With ferocious inequality in the same land, in the same historical moment, in the same metaphor, and in spite of the onerous weight of the past, the imaginative materiality of Palestinian films—whether or not they are documentaries—flash traces across the screen, fleeting but discernible signposts, of "living together otherwise."

For *Write Down I Am an Arab*, as, in fact, for Earl Lovelace's *The Dragon Can't Dance* cited in the opening, one of those flashes of possibility is in the heterosexual relationships that gird both film and novel.[63] In that regard, localized proximity takes precedence over distance. And moving to meet across a contested landscape from different vantage points proves impossible to sustain—in spite of moments of intense connection. But perhaps that is where—here and there, now and then—we can begin to see where and how to enter, how and what to do, as cohabitants of the same history, the same land, the same metaphor. Those signposts of connection across (ferocious) differences are surely one of the rich possibilities discernible in the compelling creative accomplishments of recent Palestinian cinema. In that body of work, the very technology of film offers a vision of—offers a chance to *see*—those imaginative flashes, if only we are able to discern them from where we stand, while there is still a chance to do so.

Notes

1. Earl Lovelace, *The Dragon Can't Dance* (1979; repr., New York: Faber and Faber, 1998), 179.

2. For an insightful discussion of Lovelace's novel and its implications, see Joelle Tybon, "Moving across the Landscape: Bodies, Space, Mobility, and the Reconfiguration of Community," PhD diss., University of Wisconsin–Madison, 2018.

3. For a compelling and suggestive analysis of and reflection on hope diversely located, see Ernst Bloch, *The Principle of Hope*, trans. Neville Plaice, Stephen Plaice, and Paul Knight (Cambridge, MA: MIT Press, 1995).

4. What defines Palestinian cinema is a powerful, suggestive, and intensely debated question—both in its own right and for what it suggests about national cinema in general. See, for example, Livia Alexander, Ella Shohat, Anan Barakat, Sabah Haider, or the furor around Suha Arraf and her film فيلا توما / *Villa Touma* (2015; Israel and Palestine: Belssan), as she insisted that it was a Palestinian and not an Israeli film. (See Ariel Sheetrit's chapter in the present collection.) Some part of that debate is, as Arraf's situation illustrates, also about the moves of the Israeli state to claim as Israeli films made by Palestinian citizens of Israel and/or films that received Israeli funding in one way or another. (I would note that this nationalist claim because of funding lines—especially with the tremendous rise of transnational funding of various kinds—is hardly a norm.) The question that logically follows is, of course, what defines Israeli cinema? See Raphaël Nadjari's excellent two-part documentary, *A History of Israeli Cinema* (2009; Israel and France: Amir Feingold Productions), for a suggestive address to this question. As Shohat has astutely and persistently noted, Israeli cinema is crucially defined in its relation to what it postulates as its *other* but what is, in fact, at the heart of the concept of the Israeli itself. But for the moment, here, in keeping with the context in which this essay is offered, my focus will largely be on Palestinian cinema by Palestinian citizens of Israel. See Livia Alexander, "Is There a Palestinian Cinema? The National and Transnational in Palestinian Film Production," in *Palestine, Israel, and the Politics of Popular Culture*, ed. Ted Swedenburg and Rebecca L. Stein (Durham, NC: Duke University Press, 2005), 150–171; Anan Barakat, *The New Wave: Palestinian Cinema* [in Arabic] (Jerusalem: El-Jundy, 2013); Hamid Dabashi, *Dreams of a Nation: On Palestinian Cinema* (New York: Verso, 2006); Nurith Gertz and George Khleifi, *Palestinian Cinema: Landscape, Trauma and Memory* (Edinburgh: Edinburgh University Press, 2008); Sabah Haider, "Palestine Already Exists on Film" [in French], *Le Monde Diplomatique*, March 2010; Sabah Haider, "'Palestinian Cinema Is a Cause': An Interview with Hany Abu-Assad," *The Electronic Intifada*, March 7, 2010, accessed March 25, 2020, https://electronicintifada .net/content/palestinian-cinema-cause-interview-hany-abu-assad/8708; Sarah Irving, "Israel's Movie-Funders Ban Recipients from Calling Themselves Palestinian," *The Electronic Intifada*, January 30, 2015, accessed March 25, 2020, https://electronicintifada.net/blogs /sarah-irving/israels-movie-funders-ban-recipients-calling-themselves-palestinian; and Ella Shohat, *Israeli Cinema: East/West and the Politics of Representation* (1989; rev. ed., London: I. B. Tauris, 2010).

5. For in their imaginative materiality, literature, film, and art—words, images, frames to which we can point—offer markers for those traces of hope.

6. I would argue that the *systemic* presence of those traces would indicate a different historical moment of possibility than the one in which we now find ourselves.

7. See Michel Khleife and Eyal Sivan, dirs., *Route 181: Fragments of a Journey in Palestine-Israel* (2003; Paris France: momento! films Ltd.; coproduced by Sourate Films SPRL [Belgium], Sindibad Films Ltd. [UK], WDR [Germany]), written by Michel Khleife and Eyal Sivan.

8. Scandar Copti and Yaron Shani's film, *Ajami* (عجمي [2009; Germany and Israel, and UK: Inosan Productions], also written by Scandar Copti and Yaron Shani), its narrative arc and the stories therein, poignantly (and brutally) visualize a rendition of parallel worlds.

9. From Tawfik Zayyad's 1965 poem, "هنا باقون/Here We Will Remain." For an English translation, see *Modern Arabic Poetry, An Anthology*, ed. Salma Khadra Jayyusi (New York: Columbia University Press, 1987), 486. See also Annemarie Jacir's short film *Like Twenty Impossibles*, a powerful reflection on (blocked) movement across the landscape (كأننعشرون مستحيل / *Like Twenty Impossibles* [2003; Palestine: Philistine Films], written by Annemarie Jacir and Kamran Rastegar).

10. China Miéville's *The City & the City* (London: Macmillan, 2009) is an astute imaginative fiction of the training of sight and the dangers of seeing beyond what is proscribed.

11. John Berger's *Ways of Seeing* (New York: Penguin Classics, 2008), first published in 1973, is still one of the most compelling introductions to this configuration.

12. The more recent surveillance and military technology of "smart drones" notwithstanding.

13. Randall Halle, *German Film after Germany: Toward a Transnational Aesthetic* (Urbana: University of Illinois Press, 2008). In his *The Europeanization of Cinema: Interzones and Imaginative Communities* (Urbana: University of Illinois Press, 2014), Halle has also compellingly demonstrated the potential for visions of an expansive cohabitant community in the transnational language of film.

14. Amid those compelling filmic efforts, there is also a powerful commitment to the training of younger generations of filmmakers and to expanding audiences for film and video: Rashid Musharawi's Cinema Production and Distribution Center, Anan Barakat's Arab Film School, the Ramallah-based NGO Shashat's training and support program for Palestinian women filmmakers, or Omar Al-Qattan's Palestinian Audio-Visual Project.

15. Emad Burnat and Guy Davidi, dirs., خمس كاميرات محطمة / *5 Broken Cameras* (2011; France and Palestine: Alegria Productions, Burnat Films, Guy DVD Films), written by Emad Burnat and Guy Davidi, filmed and narrated by Emad Burnat.

16. One of the largest Israeli settlements in the area, Modi'in Illit's population is 58,000 as stated on the *Nefesh B'Nefesh* website, accessed March 25, 2020, http://www.nbn.org.il /aliyahpedia/community-housing-aliyahpedia/community-profiles/modiin-elite-kiryat-sefer/.

17. Meeting every Friday for over ten years, the Bil'in Popular Committee against the Wall is led by Emad Burnat's brother, Iyad. See his account of that ongoing effort in Iyad Burnat, *Bil'in and the Nonviolent Resistance* (self-published, 2016).

18. Qtd. in Tom White, "Seven Years, '5 Broken Cameras': Documenting the Occupation," *IDA/International Documentary Association*, February 2013, accessed March 25, 2020, http:// www.documentary.org/magazine/seven-years-5-broken-cameras-documenting-occupation.

19. And, in Palestine in particular, spatial distance is exacerbated for Palestinians even within a few kilometers of one another in the maze of checkpoints and impassable barriers, let alone the infamous Wall. See Khaled Jarrar's متسللون / *Infiltrators* (2012; Ramallah: Idioms Film), filmed by Khaled Jarrar.

20. Unlike, for example, Cobti and Shani's characterization of their shared work in *Ajami*.

21. White 2013.

22. Elizabeth Wood, "Five Broken Cameras," *Vertigo Magazine*, no. 31 (Winter 2012), accessed March 25, 2020, https://www.closeupfilmcentre.com/vertigo_magazine /issue-31-winter-2012-in-conversation/five-broken-cameras/.

23. A photo of the two men from White's IDA interview with Burnat and with Davidi illustrates the complexity of their self-presentation in their work together. Davidi, facing the camera, looks at it from an angle, out of the corner of his eye; Burnat, seated to the side of Davidi and turned sideways to the camera, looks at himself in the mirror. His reflection is caught by the camera eye as looking directly at that camera. See White 2013 and Kino Lorber press photos for the film, which includes this image: https://www.kinolorber.com/sites /5brokencameras/photos.php, accessed September 13, 2020.

24. Not least of all by Cobti himself, as indicated in his 2009 *al Jazeera* interview, where he accounts for the filming process and, interestingly, astutely tells the story of the Israeli state renditions of and claims on Palestinian Israeli collaborations. See Sousan Hammad, "Interview: Palestinian Cinema," *Al Jazeera*, September 28, 2009, accessed March 25, 2020, http://www.aljazeera.com/focus/2009/09/200992891013627492.html.

25. Ibid.

26. *Ajami: A Film by Scandar Copti and Yaron Shani*, pressbook (Cologne: The Match Factory, 2009), 2, accessed March 25, 2020, http://www.the-match-factory.com/films/items /ajami.html.

27. A quick survey of European and American film reviews for *Ajami* reveal an astoundingly uninformed understanding of even simply the literal events in the film, never mind the context of those events. Roughly half of the reviews, for example, parrot the "conflicting views among Jews, Muslims, and Christians" of the film's pressbook.

28. Raja Shehadeh, *Occupation Diaries* (London: Profile Books, 2012). For an astute review of Shehadeh's book see, Sarah Irving, "Review: Tortured Optimism in Raja Shehadeh's *Occupation Diaries*," *The Electronic Intifada*, August 31, 2012, accessed March 25, 2020, https://electronicintifada.net/content/review-tortured-optimism-raja-shehadehs -occupation-diaries/11631.

29. Shehadeh 2012, 72.

30. For historical accounts of the neighborhood of Al-Ajami in Yafa, see *Remembering Yafa's al-Ajami Neighborhood* (Tel Aviv: Zochrot, 2007), accessed March 25, 2020, http:// zochrot.org/uploads/uploads/cd7c6d613af3226ebb1b0c6a285ace01.pdf; Sami Abu Shehadeh and Fadi Shbaytah, "Jaffa: From Eminence to Ethnic Cleansing," *The Electronic Intifada*, February 26, 2009, accessed March 25, 2020, https://electronicintifada.net/content /jaffa-eminence-ethnic-cleansing/8088.

31. Juliano Mer-Khamis and Danniel Danniel, dirs., *Arna's Children* (2004; Netherlands and Israel: Pieter van Huystee Film & Television, Trabelsi Productions), written by Juliano Mer-Khamis and Danniel Danniel, with Arna Mer-Khamis and Juliano Mer-Khamis. Juliano Mer-Khamis was assassinated by masked gunmen in Jenin on April 4, 2011.

32. I have noted elsewhere the suggestive implications of two brides for/of Palestine, for example—a fiercely circumscribed possibility rendered visually in the narrative of Michel Khleife's film عرس الجليل / *Wedding in Galilee* (1987; France, Belgium, and Palestine: Marisa Films, Les Productions Audiovisuelles, Zweites Deutsches Fernsehen), written by Michel Khleife. But there are also fierce limitations on such filmic visions. The material context in which that poetic possibility was imaginable has receded ever more strikingly

in the years since the production and circulation of that film. See Mary Layoun, *Wedded to the Land? Gender-Boundaries-Nationalism in Crisis* (Durham, NC: Duke University Press, 2001).

33. Ibtisam Mara'ana Menuhin, dir., سجل انا عربي / *Write Down I Am an Arab* (2014; Jaffa, Tel Aviv: Ibtisam Films), written by Ibtisam Mara'ana Menuhin. "Write down! / I am an Arab" are the opening lines of Darwish's 1964 poem "Identity Card"/"بطاقة هوية".

34. See also Simone Bitton, dir., *Mahmoud Darwich, Et la terre, comme la langue/Mahmoud Darwish: As the Land Is the Language* (1997; France: France 3, Point du Jour), with Elias Sanbar, music by Marcel Khalife.

35. Mara'ana Menuhin, 0:0:56–0:0:58.

36. Ibid., 0:0:59–0:01:38.

37. "إن مشيت على شارع"; for an English translation, see Mahmoud Darwish, *Almond Blossoms and Beyond*, trans. Mohammad Shaheen (Northampton, MA: Interlink Books, 2009), 11.

38. "ريتا و البندقية," famously set to music by the Lebanese composer Marcel Khalife, is here sung by Mira Awad.

39. Parallel universes, the side-by-side existence of universes alternate to the one we occupy, are a persistent and striking feature of comics and graphic narratives, as they are a question of theoretical physics—visually for the former, hypothetically for the latter.

40. That song was not infrequently misunderstood as referring to love for the homeland, for Palestine is often metaphorized as a woman. In the film itself, Darwish is emphatic. Rita is the fictional name for a Jewish woman. But, after all, perhaps it can be both. Tamara Ben Ami, too, is a (Jewish Israeli) woman of Palestine, an im/possible citizen of a not-yet state. See note 2 above.

41. Mara'ana Menuhin, 0:09:09–0:09:10.

42. Ibid., 0:09:10–0:09:28.

43. Ibid., 0:09:34–0:19:20.

44. Ibid., 0:19:01–0:19:15.

45. Ibid., 0:20:04–0:22:56.

46. "Why?" asks the off-screen female interviewer (the director, Mara'ana Menuhin), about Darwish's arrest. "What did he do?" (0:20:25). Ben Ami responds with patient emphasis, "'What did he do?' He was an Arab and a poet and the 'I Am an Arab' poem,' the 'Identity Card' poem, was very powerful."

47. 0:20:02–0:30:07. Interviews in London and in Paris with Darwish's first wife, the Syrian writer and scholar Rana Kabbani, occupy some ten minutes of the film (0:36:49–0:47:25). Darwish's brief second marriage in the mid-1980s to the Egyptian translator Hayat Heeni is not mentioned in Mana'ara Menuhin's film.

48. Samih Al-Qasim's rueful account of his intense closeness to Darwish and surprised anger and dismay at Darwish's sudden departure from Haifa for the Soviet Union is a differently gendered story of love, complexity, and separation.

49. Mara'ana Menuhin, 0:57:26–0:57:38.

50. Ibid., 0:33:03–0:33:06.

51. Ibid., 0:33:10–0:34:37.

52. Ibid., 0:34:38–0:34:47.

53. Ibid., 0:34:55–0:35:05.

54. Ibid., 0:35:45–0:36:04.

55. This is decidedly not an argument for the irrelevance of a homeland and a state structure that governs that space. It is, though, to note the diversity of location in and on that homeland and to insist, in the Palestinian instance, on the necessarily nonexclusive cohabitation that must occur there—in the Palestinian instance but *not only* in that instance.

56. Poignantly, that introduction follows a rather awkward exchange between the Finnish Israeli writer, Daniel Katz, who lives in Darwish's village, and Darwish himself. Though the exchange begins with a question in Arabic put to Katz by Darwish, most of the exchange is in English. Katz is manifestly uneasy. And Darwish repeatedly turns to look at the camera rather than at his interlocutor (0:51:15, 0:52:15, 0:52:18, 0:52:38–39). Darwish concludes with an offer to and claim on Katz of friendship and his hope that peace is possible. This occurs seconds before the film shifts to the First Intifada. The unspoken implication of the narrative sequence here is deafening.

57. Mara'ana Menuhin, *Write Down I Am an Arab*, 0:52:58–0:53:13.

58. "أيها المارون بين الكلمات العابرة," a direct address to those referred to in its title, was first translated into Hebrew in February of 1988. Subsequently, as Darwish points out in the film, the poem was translated into many languages, not least of all into Hebrew by the Israeli government itself. For an astute commentary on the responses to the poem's translations and mistranslations, see Ammiel Alcalay, "Who's Afraid of Mahmoud Darwish?," *Middle East Reports* 154, no. 18 (September/October 1988): 27–28. In the same issue of *MER* as Alcalay's article, the editors published an English translation of the poem from the *Jerusalem Post*, April 2, 1988.

59. Mara'ana Menuhin, 0:54:35–0:54:43.

60. Ibid., 0:54:43–0:55:17. Ellipses here are in the film's English subtitles.

61. Qtd. in Wood 2012.

62. Mara'ana Menuhin, 1:02:11–1:02:26.

63. In Mara'ana Menuhin's film, the differently gendered and differently configured relationships between Darwish and Al-Qasim or Darwish and Katz, for example, don't quite signal the same possibility—in spite of Darwish's rather awkward claims of friendship and peace in that segment of the film. Nor in Lovelace's novel, as Joelle Tybon shows, do the relationships between the defiant young men of Calvary Hill or other cohabitants reach such a suggestive force.

7

FIVE BROKEN CAMERAS AND THE METONYMIC SIXTH CAMERA

Time, Narrative, and Subjectivities in Emad Burnat and Guy Davidi's 5 Broken Cameras

Yaron Shemer

THE BULK OF 5 BROKEN CAMERAS IS EYEWITNESS documentation by a Palestinian farmer and self-taught cameraman Emad Burnat. There are five cameras—each with its own story and chronology. When his fourth son, Gibreel, is born in 2005, Burnat gets his first camera. Burnat uses his cameras to document the protests of his village, Bil'in, against the erection of the Separation Wall, the encroachment of Israeli settlements in the West Bank into his people's lands, and the brutality of Israeli police, military, and settlers against the villagers' nonviolent resistance.

During the course of filming, some of Burnat's closest friends and coactivists from the village are shot by Israeli military and police. Ashraf (Dabah) is arrested and shot in the foot while lying down blindfolded and with his hands tied; his brother, Bassem (Al-Fil, "the elephant"), who becomes a second father figure for Gibreel, is shot dead. Burnat himself is arrested and later, after his release, is injured seriously when a tractor he is riding crushes into the barrier wall. Israeli soldiers then rush him to the Tel Hashomer hospital in Tel Aviv. In one scene, Israeli soldiers raid the village in the middle of the night to arrest children.[1] Each time Burnat's camera is shot by Israeli soldiers (or damaged by other means), he obtains a new one in an act that resonates with Palestinian *sumud* (steadfastness).

The idea of developing a film out of the hundreds of hours of footage shot by Burnat was broached by the Greenhouse Development Project, a Mediterranean development enterprise initiated by an Israeli foundation and sponsored by the European Union.[2] In 2009, Burnat approached Guy Davidi, an Israeli filmmaker who had already made the documentary *Interrupted Streams* (2010) in Bil'in, to codirect the film with him.[3] After some hesitation, Davidi joined the project as codirector and editor. Importantly, Davidi wrote the entire first-person narration voiced in the film by Burnat. The narration was written in English and then translated into Arabic by a Palestinian friend living in Berlin. The informative part of the voice-over is guided by the raw footage shot by Burnat (and other Palestinians from the village) and is also based on the encounters Burnat and the villagers conveyed to Davidi. Additionally, since Davidi had lived in Bil'in for the purpose of researching and making *Interrupted Streams*, he was already familiar with the struggle of that village against Israeli authorities. The reflective and more poetic segments of the voice-over narration (for example, articulations about the victim's duty to heal quoted below) were strictly of Davidi's making. Burnat did not accept certain sections of the voice-over narration Davidi had drafted, and the film's text was finalized after Burnat and Davidi agreed to make certain changes to the initial version.[4] The film came out in 2011 and won several prestigious awards and recognitions.

Around the time the film was nominated for the Academy Award Best Documentary Feature in 2013, Israeli media engaged in and eventually became part of the debate and controversy about the national marking of the film—Israeli or Palestinian. More specifically, there were voices critiquing the appropriation of the film as an Israeli film for the purposes of public relations, a concern not very different than that aimed at pinkwashing, namely the strategies Israeli opinion leaders have employed to project an image of a multicultural, multiethnic, liberal, progressive, tolerant, and accommodating Israeli Jewish society.[5] This is all the more significant given that it seems to be the only film codirected by an Israeli Jew and a Palestinian from the Occupied Territories rather than with a Palestinian Israeli citizen.

In various interviews, Israeli codirector Davidi conveyed his view about this issue by circumventing the question and posing it in terms other than the either-or form.[6] He emphasized that although the Israeli press referred to the film as an Israeli film (a fact that was highly disturbing for Burnat), documentaries, unlike feature films, do not enter the Oscars as the official submissions of the country. For Davidi, the issue of national marking or

representation was a moot one. Conversely, Burnat shunned this equivoca-
tion about the national marking of the film. In an interview for the Israeli
daily newspaper *Yediot Ahronot*, journalist Alon Hadar addressed the question of national marking by suggesting to Burnat that, in light of funding
sources and other factors, *5 Broken Cameras* should be considered an Israeli
film. Burnat responded pithily: "[This] is a 100% Palestinian film."[7]

The references in the press to the collaboration between the two codirectors render an intriguing case study for the well-rehearsed dilemma of
speaking for the subaltern broached by Gayatri Chakravorty Spivak and
further pursued by Linda Alcoff and others. To an extent, the first-person
voice-over narration Davidi wrote for Burnat literalizes the act of *speaking for*. In "The Problem of Speaking for Others," Alcoff attempts to avoid
sweeping generalizations about this dilemma that pertain to the power
to represent. Alcoff attempts to demystify and even critique the notion of
"speaking only for myself."[8] Her attack on proponents of that "solipsist"
position is threefold: (1) "It assumes that one can retreat into one's discrete
location and make claims entirely and singularly based on that location
that do not range over others, that one *can* disentangle oneself from the implicating networks between one's discursive practices and others' locations,
situations, and practices;" (2) "The declaration that I 'speak only for myself'
has the sole effect of allowing me to avoid responsibility and accountability
for my effects on others;"[9] and (3) All speech acts involve the subject-object
relations, and therefore, in this sense, speaking for the *other* and speaking
for one's self are merely two aspects of the same discursive mechanism (a
critique informed by Bakhtin's utterance).[10]

In accordance with Spivak's affirmation of the *speaking for* act,[11] Alcoff
challenges its detractors for their assumption that "the oppressed can trans-
parently represent their own true interests."[12] Even though Alcoff concurs
with Spivak that it is preferable to supplant *speaking for* with *speaking with*
or *speaking to*, she maintains that "it is not *always* the case that when others
unlike me speak for me I have ended up worse off, or that when we speak for
others they end up worse off."[13] What are we to make, then, of the *speaking
for* (mainly through the voice-over Davidi wrote for Burnat) and the *speaking with* (the two are codirectors) in the case of *5 Broken Cameras*?

Those dilemmas and the debate about whose film it is—Israel's or Palestine's, Burnat's or Davidi's—bring to the fore the issues of lopsided power
relations in cases of collaborative transnational cinema when the parties
involved are members of two national entities in strife. In her analysis of

Figure 7.1. Filmmaker Emad Burnat displaying his five broken cameras in front of the invisible sixth camera run by codirector Guy Davidi. From *5 Broken Cameras* (Burnat and Davidi 2012), courtesy of Guy Davidi.

5 Broken Cameras, Yael Friedman discusses the shortcoming of a celebratory transnational cinema. Guided by Andrew Higson, Will Higbee, and Song Hwee Lim, she demonstrates how the national "does not cease to exist, but continues to exert the force of its presence" in these films.[14] For her, despite the promising liberating potential of the Greenhouse Project, it ultimately reinforced and reproduced post-colonial power structures with Israel as a European patronage carrying out the "civilizing mission."[15]

Notwithstanding the importance of attending to the structural non-diegetic aspects (namely, elements from outside the filmic space) of Israeli/Palestinian power relations, appropriation, and national marking in *5 Broken Cameras,* in this essay my interest lies instead mostly in diegetic elements that pertain to the dilemmas of the speech act, agency, and subjectivities as they transpire in the film's constructed narrative and time. To explore this, I will examine what I would dub the metonymic sixth camera in relation to Burnat's five cameras. My use of *the metonymic sixth camera* is meant to signify all the elements that are not captured by Burnat's five cameras, which include the voice-over narration and the intertitles as well as the actual camera Davidi and non-Palestinian videographers employ to film Burnat documenting with his cameras.[16] My choice of *metonymy* is in line with its use in Roman Jakobson's language theory and Jacques Lacan's psychoanalytical conceptualization to suggest two words (in our case, *objects* and *subjectivities*) that are associated by occupying the same lingual (cinematic) function and the *displacement* of one with the other.[17]

The Construction of Subjectivities and Time

In the film's opening, the camera moves erratically; the image is discontinuous and seems to suggest that the camera is about to stop functioning. There is a commotion; an ambulance siren and possibly gunfire and shelling are heard in the distance. In Arabic, someone refers to the camera, but just like the image, the sound is mostly indistinct and unintelligible. Then the camera cuts to a medium close-up of Burnat, and his voice-over in Arabic states, "I film to hold on to my memories." Burnat is standing behind his broken cameras, and against the voice-over "these are my five cameras; every camera is an episode in my life," he is displaying them strategically for full view of the sixth camera—the camera documenting Burnat and his cameras.

This opening sets out the film's various subjectivities, namely that of filmmaker Burnat and his cameras and the omniscient sixth camera operated or directed by Davidi. Whereas Burnat's five cameras are not only a means of delivery but, collectively, an object within the film diegesis—each of the cameras is referred to individually, and one of the cameras probably even saved Burnat's life when he was shot at and the bullet lodged in the camera he was holding—the sixth camera remains unspoken of, transparent, impersonal, and not anchored in time. Put differently, whereas each of the five broken cameras "is an episode in my life," the sixth camera connotes distance and detachment. Arguably, while the active filming by Burnat's five cameras is threatening to Israeli authorities (and that is precisely why they are shot at by soldiers and smashed by settlers), Davidi's sixth camera turns the threat—the cameras—into an object of observation and thereby mitigates their force and agency.

The five broken cameras in the film render time in terms opposite to Walter Benjamin's "empty time"—the homogenous and detached chronological temporality. By centering his experiences around the stories of each camera, Burnat discards "empty time" in favor of what I would call "camera time," where temporality is marked by interruption and rupture. The epitome of this temporality is when, in the midst of the homogeneous time (itself dense and explosive), each of the five cameras records its own finality in turn. The *Jetztzeit* (*here and now* or *now-time*)[18] and *Stillstellung* (*zero-hour, stop-time*, or *cessation of happening*), to use Benjamin's terms, and the punctuating and puncturing of time are ipso facto disruptive and subversive and interject new subjectivities and connections.[19] This is exemplified in the connection between the personal and the political (e.g., the first camera was bought to document the life of Burnat's newborn baby, Gibreel, and the fifth camera marks the child's fifth birthday) and in the organic cycle of life of the village, with its connections to seasons and olive harvesting that the cameras document. This organic time is the binary opposite of the rather rigid, nonnatural calendar time of the intertitles/the metonymic sixth camera, as in "the first camera witnessed winter 2005 to autumn 2005. When it was shot, Emad also injured his hand." It is worth noticing here that in the raw materials of the five broken cameras, Burnat, even if not seen, is at the center of the action by the very fact of filming what is around him. However, the following discussion questions the apparent narrational power Burnat possesses in *5 Broken Cameras* and relates the film's narrative strategies to the Israeli-Palestinian divergent subjectivities it ends up reifying.

The placement of Burnat at the center stage of action in the diegetic space only seemingly offers unequivocal empowerment. Immediately after the *Stillstellung* moment when a camera is crashed (literally, each destroyed camera creates "stop-time"), in the intertitle, Burnat turns into a third-person object and, in the abovementioned case, agency is actually given to his camera—the camera, not Burnat, is the one that witnesses "winter 2005 to autumn 2005." As mentioned earlier, the voice-over narration Davidi wrote for Burnat is in first person. This switching back and forth between Burnat's first-person narration and third-person references in the intertitles (again, the elements of the metonymic sixth camera) amounts to an obfuscated and unstable subjectivity that the film renders for Burnat.

Narrative and Agency

Ever since the publication of "The Permission to Narrate," in which Edward Said lamented over the failure of the Palestinians to make their narrative known and visible,[20] the impossibility or reluctance of the Palestinian filmmakers to narrate or to create a cogent and cohesive narrative has become a prominent trope in the scholarship on Palestinian cinema.[21] Is this film then another instance of the Palestinian master anti-narrative and of the intrinsic impossibility for the Palestinians to tell their story? In her article on *5 Broken Cameras*,[22] Yael Ben-Zvi Morad suggests that the Hebrew title *Ḥamesh Matzlemot Shvurot*, which is a literal translation of the English title, is misleading—the verb form *nishbarot* (*being broken*) would have been more appropriate for the title than the stative form (*pa'ul*) *shvurot* to connote action, agency, victimizer, and victim. Also the film's Arabic title *Khamis Kamerat Muḥtama* (*Five Destroyed Cameras*) uses the adjective/stative form, not a verb. But perhaps the choice of the stative form *shvurot* is precise and deliberate to connote a condition rather than action. As Ben-Zvi Morad points out, the opening is repeated with slight differences toward the film's end (Emad standing behind the cameras and Gibreel sitting next to the open front door of the house) to render a story of trauma with a circular structure that favors repetitions. In psychoanalytical terms, the traumatic raw material is necessarily non-agential and anti-narrational—it is repressed and does not lend itself into storytelling (unless heavily guised and displaced), and more importantly, the ferociously repetitious nature of the traumatic event makes time stand still, and a denouement or a linear movement forward are all but untenable.[23]

Given that narratives are couched in teleological terms, the issue of narrative strategies in *5 Broken Cameras* is clearly bounded by the dilemmas of the film's purposefulness of action and agency. Importantly, Burnat renders his insistence on filming purposeful both personally and politically as it weaves into the here and now the wounds of the past and his people's future aspirations. For example, at the beginning, Burnat states, "So I decided to film in order to hold onto my memories," and then, in the penultimate scene, he reflects, "Barriers can be removed, but the land will always bear the scars. . . . Healing is a challenge in life. It's a victim's sole obligation. By healing you resist oppression. . . . Forgotten wounds can't be healed, so I film to heal." Seemingly, then, at least to an extent, the film attests to purposefulness and a specific accomplishment that resulted from nonviolent resistance—the tearing down of the existing separation barrier and the rebuilding of a wall farther west of the village of Bil'in to allow the farmers access to their fields. Yet again, we need to remember that in the film diegesis, this purposefulness, as we have seen, is provided primarily by the context and abstraction the voice-over and the sixth camera provide, not by the raw footage of the five broken cameras.

This brings to the fore various dilemmas pertaining to the issue of power disparities and lopsided access.[24] Most relevant to our discussion are the choices made for particular narrative strategies that give the film its form and structure. In an extended interview for the Israeli film magazine *Cinematheque*, Israeli filmmaker Davidi explains, "I wrote the script. . . . Emad doesn't write, it's hard for him to talk about himself. It was a big relief for him that I wrote his voice. It was a huge responsibility, because what one sees [in the film] is actually my interpretation of Emad's condition. It's not the way Emad speaks."[25] Davidi felt strongly that the personal story, delivered by voice-over, would result in a more cogent and artistic film, a sentiment he expresses bluntly: "The Palestinian perception is sabotaged by the national struggle, by the collective struggle, to the point that the personal is sidelined . . . so I came and told him [Burnat] 'Your personal perspective is what we are interested in.' . . . I didn't go to shoot with him but I guided him. 'When there are arrests in the village, instead of going out and shooting, stay home and videotape there. When there's a demonstration, don't go out to shoot the demonstration. Videotape Gibreel or videotape yourself taking him to the demonstration.'"[26] The approach taken by Davidi here is meant to refashion Burnat's initial interest in the collective-political Palestinian *sumud* into a more dramatic and personal tale. The sense that Burnat's activist mission is to bring together the villagers of Bil'in and other villages into the collective struggle despite the political despair is best captured in the scene where he projects clips from his raw footage to the villagers. His voice-over conveys that "people feel that nothing will stop the occupation from its course. So I decide to do something. . . . Screening my footage allows the villagers to gain some distance from [the] events. I think it contributes to the solidarity among us. It encourages them to get more villages to start protesting." It is noteworthy that in this initiative, with its visual emphasis on the villagers' faces and bodies, Burnat as an individual and activist is subsumed within the collective for the greater good of the Palestinian people.

Friedman, who for the purpose of her article conducted interviews with Davidi, Burnat, and others involved in the making of the film, concludes that Burnat reluctantly agreed to opt for the personal angle and would have preferred to focus on the collective story of his community.[27] She quotes Davidi from her interview with him: "Emad's language is the activist language of the political struggle, I tried to bring another language into it . . . a more artistic language . . . the film is not structured as a film that is supposed to show to the world the wrongs in Bil'in, which was how Emad intended it to be . . . if Emad would have written the texts himself, or if it was written in the spirit of Emad's language, it would have been very different."[28] For Friedman, this ultimately resulted in the depoliticization of 5 *Broken Cameras*,[29] and those artistic choices (e.g., the personalization of the story through the first-person narration) advocated by Davidi turned the raw footage shot by the five cameras into a commodity in the market economy of transnational cinema.[30]

We have established that the narrative in 5 *Broken Cameras* is rendered by the context, cohesion, and chronology provided by the combination of the sixth camera, the narration (written by Davidi), and the intertitles. We may ask whether this duality, where we find the linear, purposeful, teleological narrative in contrast to the circular, no-end narrative or even the impossibility of a Palestinian narrative, can be attributed precisely to the play between an Israeli's/Davidi's implied subjectivity (which is narrative-based) and a Palestinian's/Burnat's subjectivity that defies or steers away from a narrative and offers instead an episodic and monadic testimony. At the risk of taking a procrustean position given the diversity within each of the Israeli and Palestinian cinemas and some overlaps and similarities between them, we may nevertheless suggest that it is not only that Palestinian cinema has anti-narrative qualities, as discussed earlier, but that the pressing need for filmic testimonials results in a structurally different cinema than that produced by Israeli filmmakers. In his discussion of 5 *Broken Cameras*, Kamran Rastegar maintains:

> Palestinian filmmakers have indeed been preoccupied—some may say, burdened—by the documentary form, and by the perceived need to offer testimonial evidence to their communal experiences. The channeling of Palestinian experience into the mold of a cause, a just claim, has often led filmmakers to the documentary form so as to offer a witnessing of the conditions of their trauma. And even where Palestinians have engaged in narrative filmmaking, they often have resorted to semidocumentary cinematic techniques or *vérité* style, as if bound by a fidelity to the real even when exploring the imaginary. In this, fiction—or even traditional narrative form—has perhaps failed in its representation of Palestinian experiences, demanding from Palestinian filmmakers as well as from literary figures a rooting within documentary that is irreconcilable with the imaginative resolutions that emerge from the dominant fictional narrative forms. These, it may be argued, all too often lead into the dead-end of the cliché, the metaphorical (or allegorical) construction that often characterizes "political" literary efforts. As Tom Hill (2011, 88) has noted, in the Palestinian context there is a problem of works coming "dangerously close to metaphor," and that "any overly self-conscious attempt at a faithful artistic or creative rendering of Palestinian experience runs the particular risk of cliché, in its broadest sense of failure of mimesis."[31]

Notwithstanding Rastegar's notion of the restricted rhetorical-political possibilities in Palestinian filmmaking and Friedman's suggestion of depoliticization in *5 Broken Cameras*, my claim is that the transnational features of the film and the relations between the five broken cameras and the sixth one highlight the politics of representation, and a close reading of the film augments rather than diminishes its political dimension.

Conclusion: The Real and The Symbolic

The Palestinian filmmakers' commitment to testimonial evidence in the service of their community and the counter-distinction between Burnat's preferred filmic approach with its risk of "failure of mimesis" and the narrative form provided by the metonymic sixth camera conjure up foundational concepts in semiotic and psychoanalytical theory. Specifically, the relations between Burnat's five cameras and the voice-over correspond with the Lacanian distinction between The Real (in this case, Burnat's unarticulated raw footage) on the one hand and, on the other hand, The Symbolic (e.g., language, metonymy, and structure, which in our case constitute the film's voice-over narration). Again, following Jakobson, for Lacan (1970) metonymy in language (and the unconscious) is *ipso facto* predicated on displacement.[32]

In one scene in Jean-Luc Godard's *Notre Musique* (2004), the filmmaker addresses a group of Bosnian students to demonstrate the cinematic technique of "shot and reverse shot,"[33] and he juxtaposes two images: one, in black and white, of Palestinian refugees fleeing their homes by boat in 1948; the other, in color, of Jewish refugees arriving in boats to Palestine/Israel around the same time. Here we may clearly think of displacement in the most literal sense, since many of the new Jewish immigrants were settled in houses and neighborhoods of the former inhabitants—the Palestinian refugees. In the film, Godard comments that in this reversal of images, "The Israelites [Jews] walked in the water to reach the Holy Land [while] the Palestinians walked in the water to drown. Shot and reverse shot. Shot and reverse shot. The Jews become the stuff of fiction; the Palestinians, of documentary."[34]

In Godard's film, this scene is immediately followed by another reflection by the filmmaker: "We say facts speak for themselves. But Céline said: Sadly, not for much longer. And that was in 1936. Because the field of text had already covered the field of vision." The Real (raw materials) and the obfuscation of the field of vision resonate closely with Said's rendering of the Palestinian condition. In his keynote speech from 2003 at the Palestinian Film Festival at Columbia University (and in the preface to *Dreams of a Nation*, 2006), Said asserts that "the relationship of the Palestinians to the visible and the visual was deeply problematic."[35] Yet, in contradistinction to Godard and as suggested earlier, Said does promote "the text"—the narrative that goes with and beyond raw visuality. In "Permission to Narrate," Said claims, "Facts do not at all speak for themselves, but require a socially acceptable narrative to absorb, sustain and circulate them. Such a narrative has to have a beginning and end: in the Palestinian case, a homeland for the resolution of its exile since 1948."[36] Most importantly, though, Said is lamenting more than the lack of Palestinian visibility and cogent narrative; he quotes Hayden White, who notes that "narrative in general, from the folk tale to the novel, from annals to the fully realized 'history,' has to do with the topics of law, legality, legitimacy, or, more generally, authority."[37]

In *5 Broken Cameras*, it is indeed the authority of the Israeli—from travel permits to allow Burnat into Israel proper to the voice-over narration drafted by Israeli filmmaker Davidi and to the place of the metonymic sixth camera in relation to Burnat's cameras—that subtends the Palestinian story. The inclusion of the opening scene (with some modifications) toward the film's end is not simply a circular repeat then, as suggested by Ben-Zvi Morad, but a marking by Davidi and his editor of "a beginning and end" for Burnat and his cameras.[38] The authority of Israel and Israelis in the pro-filmic materials and the extra-diegetic reality amounts to the Lacanian "name of the father"—the occupier who has, inter alia, the power of language and the authority to narrate.

I would like to thank Ariel Sheetrit and Nadia Yaqub for their comments on an early draft of this chapter.

Notes

1. Most, but not all, of these events were documented by Burnat's cameras. Some materials were shot by local villagers and by international and Israeli activists (Skype interviews with Guy Davidi, August 16, 2016; and Emad Burnat, August 18, 2016).

2. For an expansive account of funding and collaborations in the preproduction stages of the film, see Yael Friedman, "Guises of Transnationalism in Israel/Palestine: A Few Notes on *5 Broken Cameras*," *Transnational Cinemas* 6, no. 1 (2015): 17–32. See also Yoad Earon, "Information and Emotion" [in Hebrew], *Cinematheque* 177 (July/August 2012): 4–9; Alon

Hadar, "The Wall: Not One of Us" [in Hebrew], *Yediot Ahronot (Shiv'a Leilot)*, January 25, 2013, 31–34.

3. *Interrupted Streams* (Switzerland and Israel, 2010), codirected with Swiss filmmaker Alexandre Goetschmann.

4. Skype interviews with Guy Davidi, August 16, 2016, and Emad Burnat, August 18, 2016.

5. For more on Israeli pinkwashing and the critique of its strategies, see Sarah Schulman, "Israel and 'Pinkwashing,'" *New York Times*, November 22, 2011, accessed May 18, 2017, http://www.nytimes.com/2011/11/23/opinion/pinkwashing-and-israels-use-of-gays-as-a -messaging-tool.html.

6. See, for example, Hadar 2013.

7. Ibid., 32.

8. Linda Alcoff, "The Problem of Speaking for the Others," *Cultural Critique*, no. 20 (Winter 1991–1992): 20.

9. Ibid.

10. For Mikhail Bakhtin, "The novelistic plot serves to represent speaking persons and their ideological worlds. What is realized in the novel is the process of coming to know one's own language as it is perceived in someone else's language, coming to know one's own horizon within someone else's horizon. There takes place within the novel an ideological translation of another's language, and an overcoming of its otherness." See Mikhail Bakhtin, *The Dialogic Imagination* (Austin: University of Texas Press, 1981), 365. Francesco Casetti's pithy articulation captures astutely the filmic applicability of Bakhtin's theory of utterance: "[When] the film institutes its own destination, it is not expecting to encounter an absolute stranger." See Francesco Casetti, *Inside the Gaze: The Fiction Film and Its Spectator* (Bloomington: Indiana University Press, 1998), 41.

11. Gayatri Chakravorty Spivak, "Can the Subaltern Speak?," in *Marxism and the Interpretation of Culture*, ed. Cary Nelson and Lawrence Grossberg (Urbana: University of Illinois Press, 1988), 271–313.

12. Alcoff 1991–1992.

13. Ibid., 29.

14. Andrew Higson qtd. in Friedman 2015, 18.

15. Ibid., 21. An example Friedman provides of this patronage relationship and "civilized mission" is the Israeli-European culture alliances and, specifically, the training and the professionalization of Palestinian filmmakers that are written into funding agreements.

16. Although toward the end of the film Burnat starts using his sixth camera, in this essay I refer to the sixth camera only in the abovementioned sense.

17. See Jacques Lacan's discussion of metonymy and his rendering of the connection Roman Jakobson makes between metonymy and displacement. Jacques Lacan, "The Insistence of the Letter in the Unconscious," in *Structuralism*, ed. Jacques Ehrmann (New York: Anchor Books, 1970), 114–115, 119–120.

18. Walter Benjamin, "On the Concept of History," in *Walter Benjamin—Selected Writings*, ed. Michael Jennings (Cambridge, MA: Harvard University Press, 2006), 395.

19. Ibid., 396. Benjamin uses these terms in sections XIV and XVII of the essay. Here he draws a distinction between historicism and materialist history. Whereas the former engages with universal history and the mass-additive data is meant to fill the homogeneous and empty chronological time, materialist historiography confronts the monad-like event in

which time comes to a stop and whole history or era bursts through in a single work or event. This messianic-like moment, described in terms of *blast* and *shock*, is impregnated with revolutionary possibilities.

20. Edward Said, "Permission to Narrate," *Journal of Palestine Studies* 13, no. 3 (Spring 1984): 27–48. Said's essay was a response to the 1982 Lebanon War and the lopsided, vilifying, and even demeaning portrayal of Palestinians in Western media.

21. Haim Bresheeth identifies several Palestinian films that attempt to create a narrative (however convoluted or nonlinear it may be). Bresheeth maintains that in these films "the healing process seems to be bound up with storytelling," a statement that is made explicit in Burnat's voice-over toward the end of *5 Broken Cameras*. Echoing Said's "Permission to Narrate," Bresheeth maintains that the films he discusses "deal with the story of Palestine as a strategic defense move, a move designed to recapture ground lost to Zionism and its dominant narrative." For Linda Mokdad, it is not only the embedded impossibility of the Palestinian filmmaker (in her analysis, Elia Suleiman) to narrate, but more importantly, it is his/her "*refusal* to speak as a Palestinian"—indeed, the filmmaker's reluctance to narrate, as the title of Mokdad's essay suggests. In her article on *Paradise Now* (2005), Nadia Yaqub deems Hany Abu-Assad's film an anti-road movie (and possibly, according to her analysis, an "anti-wedding" film) in its refusal to comply with generic conventions. This refusal, although not ipso facto anti-narrational, challenges the viewer assumptions about the way Palestinian stories should be told. Among the various explanations for that phenomenon where "there seems to prevail amongst writers and researchers the idea that the Palestinian story has yet to be told, to be given adequate artistic expression," Nurith Gertz and George Khleifi cite guilt and shame (following Anton Shammas) and the inexorable Zionist narrative that muted its Palestinian rival. But even more importantly for them as a hindrance for the lack of Palestinian narrative is the nature of trauma as a cycle of repetitions where chronological time collapses. See Haim Bresheeth, "Telling the Stories of Heim and Heimat, Home and Exile: Recent Palestinian Films and the Iconic Parable of the Invisible Palestine," *New Cinemas Journal of Contemporary Film* 1, no. 1 (April 2002): 24–39; Linda Mokdad, "The Reluctance to Narrate: Elia Suleiman's *Chronicle of a Disappearance* and *Divine Intervention*," in *Storytelling in World Cinemas: Volume 1—Forms*, ed. Lina Khatib (London: Wallflower, 2012), 192–204; Nadia Yaqub, "*Paradise Now*: Narrating a Failed Politics," in *Films in the Middle East and North Africa: Creative Dissidence*, ed. Josef Gugler (Austin: University of Texas Press, 2011), 218–227; and Nurith Gertz and George Khleifi, "Bleeding Memories," *Palestine-Israel Journal of Politics, Economics, and Culture* 10, no. 4 (2003): 105–112.

22. Yael Ben-Zvi Morad, "Chronicle of Death and the Continuity of Life: A Discussion of the Film *5 Broken Cameras* by Emad Burnet and Guy Davidi" [in Hebrew], *Takriv*, no. 4 (2012).

23. Yet, as Nadia Yaqub pointed out (in personal communication), *5 Broken Cameras* (or, for that matter, many other films about the Palestinian predicament) is hardly a typical film dealing with trauma. If trauma is often perceived as a single event from the past, the narrative of *5 Broken Cameras* makes it patently clear that here one witnesses ongoing traumatic events in the present, including the violence by soldiers and settlers that the villagers experience on a regular basis.

24. The power imbalances between Israel and Palestine and, respectively, between Davidi and Burnat are manifested in various other diegetic and non-diegetic elements of the film.

Informed by a comment Ariel Sheetrit made on an earlier draft of this essay, we can argue that in this film, space should also be taken into consideration in the lopsided access and power play between two political entities and the two filmmakers. Whereas the sixth camera may penetrate the Palestinian space without any obstacles, the five cameras could hardly have entered Israel and operate there unrestricted. The film's sequences in Israel are shot by the Israeli sixth camera (different videographers, according to my Skype interview with Davidi, August 16, 2016). In the scene in the Israeli hospital where Burnat is treated for his wounds, he becomes the object of the gaze of the sixth camera, not the person who explores or penetrates the other's space. Likewise, clearly for Burnat, the collaboration with an Israeli filmmaker is highly precarious; the risks involved are unmatched by those taken by Davidi's decision to collaborate in the making of this film. In turn, this explains Burnat's anxiety about the marking of the film as Israeli.

25. Earon 2012, 6. The translations into English from this interview are mine.

26. Ibid.

27. I should note that what transpired from my interview with Burnat (August 18, 2016) is a sense that for him the political and personal stories have been intertwined from the outset. Burnat emphasized in the interview that the documentation of the events in Bil'in is a testimony reflecting his personal experiences.

28. Friedman 2015, 26.

29. Ibid., 26–27.

30. Friedman is guided by Thomas Elsaesser in her conceptualization of the connection between globalization, transnational cinema, and commodification. For Elsaesser, "the dynamics of globalization affected not only the type of commodity 'world cinema' represents but also what subject matters and styles prevail" (qtd. in ibid., 26).

31. Kamran Rastegar, *Surviving Images: Cinema, War, and Cultural Memory in the Middle East* (Oxford: Oxford University Press, 2015), 94–95.

32. See, for example, a discussion of Lacan's theory in Sean Homer's *Jacques Lacan* (London: Routledge, 2005).

33. In the strict sense, "shot and reverse shot" refers to the cinematic juxtaposition of two opposite images (in terms of content or style). For Godard and other filmmakers informed by Soviet cinema, this technique involves a dialectical process where the first shot is considered a thesis, the second an antithesis, and the juxtaposition creates a synthesis, a new meaning in the mind of the viewer that transcends the individual signification of each of the images.

34. See also Rastegar's analysis of *5 Broken Cameras* in light of Godard's second section in *Notre Musique*—"Purgatorio": "The Palestinian trauma, metaphorically, is a *purgatorio* reflected best in documentary techniques and lacking the narratological depth and completion that is 'the stuff of fiction'" (Rastegar 2015).

35. Edward Said, "Preface," in *Dreams of a Nation: On Palestinian Cinema*, ed. Hamid Dabashi (London: Verso, 2006), 2.

36. Said 1984, 34.

37. Qtd. in ibid.

38. At some point during the editing process, Davidi decided to hire Véronique Lagoarde-Ségot as the film's editor. See Earon 2012.

III

TO SEE WITH FOREIGN EYES: CATERING TO THE EXPECTATIONS OF A TRANSNATIONAL AUDIENCE

8

MOMENTS OF INNOCENCE
AND FRACTURE

Fantasy and Reality in Two Documentary
Visits to Israel

Ohad Landesman

IN THIS CHAPTER, I CONSIDER TWO DOCUMENTARIES, MADE by renowned non-Israeli artists, that focus on Israel: Chris Marker's *Description of a Struggle* (1960) and Susan Sontag's *Promised Lands* (1974). Appearing while the hegemonic narrative still held a powerful sway in Israeli society, these films offer a critical perspective of the Zionist project that appears to be ahead of its time. Today, when filmmaking frequently focuses on exposing the mythic history of the Israeli national narrative, revisiting these documentaries allows us to see a precursor to this contemporary trend. By exploring the gaps between what Marker and Sontag had hoped to see and the reality they encountered, one can reveal the early cracks beginning to appear in the monolithic narrative of Israeli cinema. Thus, in revisiting these films, we not only encounter the gaps created between the initial filmmakers' expectations and what was actually documented in the final projects but also the vast historical changes that Israel has gone through between the original moments of documentation and this contemporary viewing moment.

Even though they are set in Israel and deal with its foundational myths, Marker and Sontag's films have not been discussed as part of studies of Israeli cinema. This may undoubtedly be explained due to the fact that the filmmakers are not Israeli, that their perspective on Israel is inflected by "foreign" concerns that make it incompatible with Israeli national discourses prevalent at the time, and that their films have been made according to some transnational aesthetic influences. While not dismissing these dimensions in this chapter, I do argue, in the spirit of this anthology, that they do not offer sufficient grounds for excluding these works from Israeli cinema. Rather, by enforcing an overly restrictive national paradigm on Israeli cinema, one misses the opportunity of fruitfully exploring the nature of its dialogue with *Description of a Struggle* and *Promised Lands*—and by extension, providing a more nuanced understanding of this cinema's transnational dimension. Redressing this gap, the following chapter will contrastingly profess the importance of these documentaries to Israeli film scholarship on the basis of how they serve as transnational extensions to the cultivation of a national Israeli cinema.

In their manifesto for transnational documentaries, written almost twenty years ago, John Zimmerman and Patricia Hess wanted "to reclaim the term transnational in order to radicalize it"[1] and to begin an investigation "into how the transnational functions within and around concepts of the national, the regional and the local."[2] While addressing more contemporary documentaries than Sontag and Marker's, Hess and Zimmerman's polemical ideas become relevant to the discussion here, as they show how "old theoretical categories linking documentary practice to the nation have changed dramatically in the post-cold war and transnationalized cultural economy; they have been reorganized, reconceptualized, rearranged, remade, rewired."[3] Drawing on this thinking, I explore the problematics of considering the nation in essentialist terms.

Yet the very term *transnationalism* may be viewed as problematic, as Deborah Shaw has argued, since *transnational cinema* has become "a catch-all [that] is inadequate to deal with the complexities of categorising both actual films and industrial practices."[4] One therefore needs to tread lightly in its use, inspecting its various aspects so as to clearly map out its complex operation, as well as its relationship with the national, in the space of certain texts. Using Shaw's typology of "categories of the transnational" as guide, I will show how *Description of a Struggle* and *Promised Lands* are both films that are made by transnational directors "who work and seek funding in a range of national contexts;"[5] these directors display "transnational influences" emerging from filmic traditions in European and American cinema of the 1960s;[6] they use "transnational modes of narration" by employing local and international modes of address;[7] and they expand the notion of "exilic and diasporic filmmaking"[8] by offering the removed gaze of tourists, who have personal stakes in the location they visit.[9]

Utopian Dreams and Daunting Awakenings in *Description of a Struggle*

In 1957, Wim and Lia Van Leer, pioneers of film culture in Israel and founders of the country's cine-club movement, visited the Moscow Film Festival, the first to include Israeli films in its program. One film in the festival stood out among the rest and impressed them deeply: the essayistic travelogue *Letter from Siberia* (1957), made by the French filmmaker Chris Marker. With a little help from his friend, writer and literary critic Yakov Malkin,[10] Wim Van Leer approached Marker directly and asked him if he would be interested in visiting Israel and making a similar travelogue there. Such an essayistic production made by a filmmaker as promising as Marker, so believed the Van Leers, would finally unleash documentary filmmaking in Israel from the propagandistic and didactic shackles that dominated the early heroic period in Israeli cinema during the 1950s. It would also expose it, so they envisioned, to transnational influence in both aesthetic and thematic ways. Marker agreed, but with only one condition: complete artistic freedom. He refused to show the film or consult with anyone else about it before it was done. Marker, who was also a passionate and talented photographer, came to Israel in 1959 for a pre-shooting visit devoted solely to location hunting. Touring Israel on a Vespa given to him by the Van Leers—"following the footsteps of Jesus on a scooter,"[11] as one *Cahiers* critic observed—Marker took between 800 and 1,000 still photographs, which would later form the basis of a future treatment for his film.[12]

Marker returned to Paris after this visit and wrote a script based on both these photos and a short story given to him by the Van Leers, Franz Kafka's first published piece of writing, "Description of a Struggle" (1909).[13] The finished script, the result of a meeting between a written diary, still photography, and a literary piece of writing, accumulates fragmented notes that read as if written by a tourist in a foreign country.[14] A few months later, Marker came back to Israel for a four-week shooting period, an experience that took place while Otto Preminger was there shooting *Exodus* (1960), a film that would later become a monumental Zionist epic. Marker went back to the same places he had visited a few months earlier and looked for the same subjects of which he had previously taken photos. The result, *Description d'un combat* (*Description of a Struggle*), is an essayistic travelogue that evolved and materialized out of those photographs, an assemblage of postcards from the edge.[15] In one particular sequence, for example, Marker revisits a street market where he finds the subjects from his previous trip and hands them their photos. Within a reflexive sequence about photography and its relation to cinema, the subjects' gaze is returned to Marker twice: once in the making of each photo and later in the moment of gratitude.

Description of a Struggle meditates on the circumstances that have led to the establishment of Israel and the different paradoxes that define the state's existence. Watching it, however, one cannot help but wonder about the reasons that made Marker travel all the way to Israel and capture the early stages of a young state barely approaching bar-mitzvah age. What was it in Israel that grabbed his attention and interest at the end of the 1950s? *Description of a Struggle* belongs to what is now considered to be the lost period in Marker's work, "orphaned from the back catalogue if not disowned by its creator"[16]—an era in his oeuvre that is bracketed between *Letter from Siberia* and *La Jetée* in 1962, the year that Marker himself regards as his "year zero" in filmmaking.[17] In much of the work he made during that period, his ideological position remains elusive. Marker's trip to Israel occurred amid an artistic phase in his own life, when he traveled to several countries experiencing important moments of transformation and engaged cinematically in ideological national building, including China under Maoism, explored in his short film *Sunday in Peking* (1956); the Soviet-promoted Five-Year Plan for industrialization and electrification, which served as the background for *Letter from Siberia* (1957); and Cuba's attempt to consolidate Castro's revolution, portrayed in his *¡Cuba Sí!* (1961). These travelogues consider the utopian dream of building a new society, which serves as a recurring theme in his early cinematic work. Israel's inclusion in this series can thus be seen in light of Marker's interest in ideology and utopianism as it crosses through nations. This personal investment in the project adds another layer of meaning that should be considered vis-à-vis the fact that the film was initially recruited by the Van Leers. Providing a cinematic glance at the process of Israel's establishment was also in line with Marker's own political views as a leftist humanist and may have been a gesture of solidarity with the fledgling state. While it is tempting to identify the Orientalist impulse in this film—after all, images of pre-occupation Israel carry the scent of an exotic locale—Marker's conscious decision to employ the epistolary and essayistic narration mode is probably meant to resist such colonial observation of the colorful and primitive. In fact, in all of Marker's early travelogues, which consist of nuanced narration, a collage of postcard imagery, and a good sense of critical distance, one can easily trace the major tropes and strategies of his later essayistic rhetoric in film.

Marker, who worked as an editor in *Les Lettres nouvelles*, the same company that published Roland Barthes's *Mythologies* two years prior to *Description of a Struggle*, embraces semiology as the dominant methodology in the film. It opens with still shots of land and water, after which the first images we see are of rusted and burned tanks in the desert. "This land speaks to you in signs," the voice-over calmly declares, introducing a long enterprise of decrypting dynamic signifiers.[18] Israel becomes a semiotic text that Marker attempts to decode, its identity read as "an accumulation of signs, marks of the multiple conflicts that have carved out its twelve years of existence as a nation."[19] Images of people, places, even animals, sometimes plucked from their original context, speak mutable meanings. The narration, working on the level of unexpected connotation rather than denotation, tries to instigate associations rather than fix meanings. Such a perspective of the semiotician working to invite contemplation rather than to impose didacticism is emblematic of the European essayistic tradition with which Marker was identified. The contrast between this open aesthetic and the simplistic structure of the heroic cinema in Israel at the time may admittedly lead us to define Marker's film as imposing on the Israeli nation a foreign influence. Yet to the extent that it was foreign, the film's rhetoric of intellectual meditation would nevertheless influence the groundbreaking work of Israeli filmmaker David Perlov, especially his essayistic city symphony *In Jerusalem* (1963),[20] as well as help bring about a modernist trend within Israeli cinema. Further complicating its foreignness, Marker decided to produce three versions for the film with a different language of narration in each one: Hebrew, French, and English. Such a multilingual form is important not only because *Description of a Struggle* is one of the few Marker films in which the narration is made in a local language, but also because such a practice was not entirely an anomaly in Israeli cinema at the time. Meir Levin's *The Illegals* (1948), a film about Jewish illegal immigration prior to the establishment of Israel as a state, came out with three versions of narration, as well: English, French, and Hebrew. Larry Frisch's *Amud Ha'Esh* (1959), made eleven years later and dealing with Israel's war for independence, was also released to theaters in both English and Hebrew versions. Considering further these transnational modes may help us re-evaluate the burgeoning film industry in Israel and go beyond the scholarly dominant idea that the heroic cinema of the state's early years was entirely nationalistic in its essence.

There is a tension that Marker constantly builds in the film between a traumatic past and a utopian present. Admiring its process of creation and worrying about its future at the same time, Marker reveals hope that Israel would realize its need to become an unusual and exemplary nation. Such a tension is formally built into the film by using the typical Markerian montage, which French critic André Bazin described, in relation to *Letter from Siberia*, as "horizontal," where "a given image does not refer to the one that preceded it or the one that will follow, but rather it refers laterally, in some way, to what is said . . . montage is made from the ear to the eye."[21] Marker is searching for the signs that show contradictions inherent in the new nation state. He looks, for example, at how ultra-Orthodox Jews live in a religious enclave that is reminiscent of Jewish existence in Europe prior to the establishment of the state—"the sweet little ghosts of the ghettos," the narration recognizes, "who are still present in Mea Shearim, where Jewish destiny is frozen." Later in the film, he shows how the dome shape of the synagogue is shared by Hebrew University's planetarium, indicating how religion lives alongside science. Marker even looks for images that attest to the imminent disruption of nationalistic utopia, like the ruins of a deserted Arab village or the disgraceful conditions of transit camps. Marker's interpretation of objects rests on "a moment of defamiliarization" in which he pulls objects from their everyday context and spotlights their significance from multiple angles, both real and imagined.[22]

Settlements blossom out of the desert, signaling for Marker how Israel is rapidly changing and abandoning its early signs. The early history of pioneer workers makes way for a developing modernity, and socialist utopia is placed next to capitalist development. Marker is fascinated by the kibbutz as a collective experience that fosters an alternative to capitalist economics and devotes a lengthy sequence for observing the members in Manara gathering for collective decision-making. Rachel Rabin, sister of Israel's late prime minister Yitzhak Rabin and a good friend of the Van Leers, is shown here leading a voting process where all decisions are taken by common consent. Marker's empathic look at what he regards as "an absolute form of democracy" is simultaneously worrisome: "Isolated in their own country, isolated from the social states," he asks, "how long will their purity last?"

The kibbutz encapsulates for Marker an essential paradox in the existence of Israel: How will its socialist ideals face the reality of the ever-growing capitalist system?

Marker, who worked with Alain Resnais on *Night and Fog* (1955) five years before visiting Israel and cowrote its script with Holocaust survivor Jean Cayrol, looks for similar signs of the ways in which the past is engraving itself on the surface of things. He wants to capture signs that attest to the tragic trauma of the Holocaust and its pain on the collective psyche of the nation, thus zooming in on numbers tattooed on the young survivors' arms or listening carefully to the different languages heard on the streets (including Yiddish, German, Hungarian). Closer to the end of the film, he decides to include extensive footage from Levin's *The Illegals*, the aforementioned early Zionist film that chronicles the harrowing events of the illegal Jewish immigration during the British Mandate period. It shows how one ship, named *Without Fear*, was violently rerouted to Cyprus and refused entrance to Israel. As these images appear, Marker's tone becomes more didactic and displeased, and the word *we* is carefully used to point a blaming finger toward Europe: "Survivors of the camps, orphans of the camps, born in the camps, crashed by the camps they ran away from us, Germany, with our crimes, France, with our indifference, and when they turned to England, were dragged back to the camps." Unlike Resnais, though, who is looking mostly into the past in *Night and Fog*, Marker is placing the past within the continuous present and offering a realistic challenge for the future.

This penultimate sequence is only a necessary prelude to the final and memorable scene, which questions how the Holocaust trauma is going to shape the country's future struggle for existence, define its character, and justify its legitimacy. Marker visits the painting workshop of Phyllis Malkin and focuses on a twelve-year-old girl, as old as the country itself. The swan-like long-necked girl keeps herself busy drawing on a canvas, never really turning her head away from it. Such innocent and banal activity poses, according to Marker, a big question mark about the imminent future of Israel. That girl, who "would never be Anne Frank" and therefore not a victim, as the voice-over clarifies, belongs to a group of kids who were "born without fear"; thus she becomes "a sign of the miracle of Israel's creation," as Lupton remarks. "We must look at the girl until we lose our sense of what she means, like a word repeated over and over again."[23] "Look at her," the narrator asks us. "There she is. Like Israel . . . A vision that defeats the eye, as words endlessly repeated. Amongst all the wondrous things, most wondrous is her being there, like a cygnet, a signal, a sign." What was the girl drawing on the canvas, wonders Israeli filmmaker Dan Geva in his own film, *Description of a Memory* (2007), a loving homage to Marker's documentary. Perhaps therein may lie the key to understanding why Marker chose her of all the other signs he encountered along the way as an instigator for his prophetic warning. Never mind the fact (or perhaps mind it very much) that this little girl is now a grown woman who decided not to live in Israel but reside as an artist in London, Marker sees her as a sign emblematic not only for conserving the past but also for avoiding the infliction of further injustice, because injustice weighs heavier in the land of Israel than elsewhere. "To become a nation like other nations implies the right to selfishness, to blindness, to vanity," the voice-over concludes, "but the entire history of Israel protests in advance against force that is nothing but force. Force and power are not in themselves anything but signs. The worst injustice weighing on Israel is perhaps its not having the right to be unjust."

Description of a Struggle was screened in Israel in 1961 for four weeks, at the same time as when Adolf Eichmann was being tried in the country. While national attention was mostly focused on the trial, the film was well received as an artistic achievement and attracted a local audience of slightly less than twenty thousand people. There seems to be a common yet unfounded belief that in 1967, following the eruption of the Six-Day War and Israel's invasion of the Occupied Territories, Marker became disillusioned by the situation, viewing his film as no longer relevant and asking for it to be withdrawn from circulation. In fact, while its belated US premiere occurred at the 1982 New York Film Festival, where it was shown as part of a double bill along with its original source of inspiration, *Letter from Siberia*, and generated a hostile reception that was partly due to Israel's invasion of Lebanon that year, Marker did attend two special screenings of the film in both Tel Aviv and London in honor of Wim Van Leer's death in 1992, suggesting that he had not completely disowned the film after all.

Recording the Pain of Others: Political Dissonance and Experimental Sound in *Promised Lands*

While Susan Sontag was mostly known for writing novels, short stories, plays, and especially essays on culture, photography, and film, she worked behind a camera four times during her lifetime. About this rather uneasy experience, which never ceased to outrage many critics, Sontag confessed: "Making movies is accompanied by anxiety, struggle, claustrophobia, exhaustion and euphoria."[24] Her films were not shown to the public very often, and there is hardly anything significant written on them in scholarship. Sontag's first two cinematic endeavors, *Duet for Cannibals* (1969) and *Brother Carl* (1971), were Ingmar-Bergman-type dramas in the Swedish language, while her fourth one, *A Trip Without a Guide* (1983), was based on a short story she wrote that takes place in Venice. *Promised Lands* (1974), her third film and the only documentary she ever made, is a small-scale production that took her to Israel during the immediate aftermath of the Yom Kippur War (1973). Sontag considered it her most personal film, in part because she was emotionally invested in the materials she was looking to find in Israel as a Jewish intellectual and because her immediate family collaborated on the project. *Promised Lands* was produced by the French actress Nicole Stephanie, who was, at the time, Sontag's girlfriend, while David Reif, Sontag's son from an early marriage, served as its assistant director. The film grapples with issues Sontag was intellectually obsessed with around the time she penned her celebrated anthology of essays, *On Photography*, which would be published four years later (1977). The documentary *Promised Lands* marks, I believe, a critical moment in Sontag's thinking about images and power that would later converge into a more full-fledged theory in the book, a monumental scholarly work that stresses the medium's acquisitive, objectifying effects. Such a personal and intellectual interest in filming Israel complicates further the question of national cinema by injecting an internal dimension of the auteur's desires into the template of external characteristics that may define Israeli cinema.

Given the filming's proximity to the Yom Kippur War and the psychic devastation of its events on the Israeli public, Sontag had picked a peculiar time to stroll the streets of Jerusalem and cross the deserts of Sinai: her visit took place twenty days after fighting began, and the conflict was still ongoing. Considering this is the same woman who entered Hanoi in the midst of the Vietnam War in 1968 and directed a play in besieged Sarajevo in 1993, such timing may not appear too surprising and attests, if nothing else, to her intellectual interest in understanding the practice of documenting war. Perhaps she also wanted to use the images from her trip to Israel as a specific case study for a much broader universal reflection about the absurdity of war, of any war. This resonates with what I have outlined earlier as Marker's ongoing interest in exploring the utopian dimension of socialist states and further extends the transnational realm in which both films could be situated.

For seven weeks of shooting, with a small crew and indescribable bravery, Sontag documented a young militarist country confronted by an unexpected crisis and guided by paranoia and fear. She entered the fresh battlefields and drove around the state to closely examine the ways in which Israeli citizens responded to the war. Sontag captured harrowing images of burned tanks and corpses of soldiers surrounded by dried blood and swarming flies in the desert, never shying away from the immediate traces of trauma. Back in 1973, official documentation of the war in Israel was rather clean, censored, and devoid of any catastrophic imagery. Depiction of suffering, pain, or death—of both Israelis and the Arab enemy—was never provided on television or on the radio. Because war in Israel and any other conflict in the Middle East were not covered exhaustively by the media during the 1970s, Sontag could still sneak in as an unprofessional reporter to document the horror. Such a privilege would clearly change dramatically in the years to come, when "the terms for allowing the use of cameras at the front for non-military purposes," as Sontag clarifies in her last published book, "have become much stricter."[25]

The horrific images Sontag captured in Israel now seem closely tied to her developing understanding of photography. Read retrospectively, they illustrate her ongoing struggle with the ethical responsibility a photographer may carry toward horror and suffering in the world and a viewer's relationship toward the abundance of images dealing with it. "Every piece of art made on any war that is not showing the appalling concreteness of destruction and death," she writes, "is a dangerous lie."[26] *Promised Lands* is a film that should also be reevaluated in light of Sontag's late writings, especially *Regarding the Pain of Others* (2003), written thirty years after her visit to Israel. In it, she revisits the similar dilemmas about war photography and arrives at some modified conclusions. About the value of shock photography in war, she writes: "Look, the photographs say, *this* is what it's like. This is what war *does*. And *that*, that is what it does, too. War tears, rends. War rips open, eviscerates. War scorches. War dismembers. War *ruins*."[27]

Sontag takes this obsession with the evidentiary quality of photographs, an essence that derives from their indexical ties with reality, further toward the level of sound in film. She uses two different strategies of sonic representations throughout *Promised Lands*: diegetic sound that provides evidence and an essayistic voice that opens her film for a rhetoric of questioning and contemplation. She aims at once, as Paul Arthur once phrased it, toward concrete facts and inward toward mercurial reflection, where an "argument must proceed from one person's set of assumptions, a particular framework of consciousness, rather than from a transparent, collective 'We.'"[28] Sontag's understanding of film sound as providing indexical evidence correlates with her understanding of photographs as not merely statements about the world but pieces of it, "miniatures of reality that anyone can make or acquire."[29] Accordingly, Sontag builds a sonic landscape that is composed of unrelated audial elements recorded on location (prayers, running footsteps, radar beeps, machine-gun fire, or radio broadcasts) and edited in rhythmic juxtaposition to abstract images of deserted battlefields, graveyards, supermarkets, open landscapes, and clichéd icons of Israeli folklore. The soundtrack is restless and projects anxiety: radio broadcasts are put on top of interviews, explosions and gunshots intrude on mourning ceremonies, Arab singing is contrasted with Western pop music, and Muslim and Jewish prayers are heard simultaneously. Sontag forces us to listen to everything that the unsolvable political conflict constitutes in Israel and creates a synthesis that digs further and deeper; she accumulates audial traces, scars of the painful daily reality after the war: the rituals of mourning, the physical pain of wounded soldiers, and the mental trauma of Israeli citizens. She records the social fracture of a country confronted by its most dreadful nightmare—forces that work toward its destruction.

At the same time, exploiting the film camera's revelatory powers was not the only function of documentary Sontag had in mind. In fact, she chose not to call her film a documentary at all, because she believed it was too narrow a term to accurately reflect its analytical and dialectical rhetoric. She writes about her own film by mentioning instead the poem, the essay, and the lamentation as "possible literary analogues" to it.[30] "To interpret is to impoverish, to deplete the world—in order to set up a shadow world of 'meanings.' It is to turn *the* world into *this* world. ('This world'! This world, as if there were any other)," Sontag writes in her essay "Against Interpretation" (1966).[31] In an attempt to distinguish between a work of fiction and a documentary, Michael Renov uses similar terms to explain that "fiction is oriented towards *a* world," while "non-fiction towards *the* world."[32] Such an epistemological distinction may help us better understand why Sontag's resistance toward the conventional form of documentary took her en route to the meditative essay film, where she was looking for open ruminations and not clear interpretations. It is here that Sontag, like Marker, arrives in Israel with film language tools that derive from her experience with the essayistic in her literary writings; yet the cinematic environment she encountered in Israel over a decade after Marker's visit was one where her foreign aesthetic was no longer foreign (Perlov's *In Jerusalem* being one major precedent of the essayistic in Israeli cinema), subsequently undercutting her film's position as "external influence."[33]

Promised Lands expands on this reluctance toward didacticism and eschews talking heads or any use of expository narration. Since Sontag did not know much about the complex ethnic texture of the young State of Israel and was not really familiar with the subtle differences between economic classes, cultural dialects, and political groups in the country, she cleverly played with the perspective of an outsider. As an American Jew who visits Israel, Sontag refuses to let her Jewishness get in the way and "comes across not so much as a director, but as a tourist in her own subject."[34] While she excludes any explicit reference to her own voice in this travelogue, her poetically insinuated critical outlook, expressed through the prism of a visitor, becomes the existing testament by which her carefully reserved view of Israel can be judged. It is here that Sontag attests quite clearly to her desire not to surrender to an Orientalist impulse and simply enforce a foreigner's viewpoint on Israel but to own up to the fluidity of perspective of a visitor who nevertheless has a vested interest in "knowing" the place she visits and consequently has to negotiate the actual and supposed gaps between foreignness and indigeneity.

Accordingly, such personal confusion is performed through the film's main strategy of sound dialectics, where Sontag's voice is perhaps obfuscated but still elegantly coded into the contrast between two distinct male voices that ruminate thoughtfully from both sides of the political arc: Yuval Ne'eman, an internationally renowned nuclear physicist, speaks about the roots of anti-Semitism and Arab hatred toward the Jewish people, while Yoram Kaniuk, a well-known writer, liberally pontificates about Palestinian rights and the country's dangerous shift from its socialist roots to an American-style commercial culture.[35] The deliberations of those two men run intermittently through the course of the film, underscoring the "deepening divisions within Jewish thought over the very question of Palestinian sovereignty."[36] Sontag, who was influenced by the ideas of Marxist dialectics, surrenders completely to this Hegelian structure of reasoning and produces a rhetorical drama around these opposing voices, each representing a partial truth.

The pairing of those voices together exposes the patriarchal underbelly of *Promised Lands*, as its mode of argumentation remains trapped within a Jewish male perspective. There are no interviews with women, and only a few women appear in the film; this elision resonates with Sontag's subsequent claims, made in 2003, that "war is a man's game" and the "killing machine has a gender, and it is male."[37] Also missing from this documentary is a nuanced representation of Palestinians. Excluding one individual shot, where Palestinians are shown crossing the Allenby intersection through Jordan, and not accounting Kaniuk's vocal explanation of their suffering, their existence in the film remains "shadowy and abstract."[38] For a film that seeks to undermine the young Israeli state's narrative of heroic national liberation and go against the internationally dominant pro-Israeli sentiment during that period, it is odd that it features only Jewish speakers while the Arab enemy remains silent, deprived of a coherent voice and reduced to either exotic scenery (Bedouin herders who become part of a decorative landscape) or nameless bodies torn apart by the atrocities of war.

Where such elements testify to conservativeness, the film's radicalism is felt more strenuously in scenes that deal with Zionist ideology forthright. On one occasion, when she visits the wax museum in Tel Aviv, where a collection of wax sculptures representing famous people from Israeli history are exhibited in lifelike poses, Sontag puts together a montage of bizarre images from the museum that illustrates the Jewish victimhood discourse. By patiently oscillating between various rooms in which establishing moments in Israeli history are represented on wax—the heroic death of famed soldier Yosef Trumpeldor, the Declaration of Independence, the Eichmann trial, or the liberation of the Wailing Wall—Sontag crafts an implied criticism on the official Zionist discourse in Israel and its limitations. What constitutes collective memory is, for Sontag, an artificially restraining narrative that stipulates dogmatically what is important and what is the ideologically dominant version of Israel's history. At other times, Sontag carefully expresses her reservations through edited observation. She repeatedly attends funerals and memorial services held only a few days after the war, when the wound is still open and bleeding. The mourning rituals she is filming are forming historical continuity. They are bookended by the opening shots of the film, which show tombstones and funerals of victims from World War I, and its last sequence, where tanks are making their way to the next future conflict. War begets war, Sontag insinuates, and there is no end in sight to this bludgeoned struggle.

The most memorable—and also most troubling—scene in the film is its penultimate sequence, in which Sontag directs her gaze onto an experimental treatment for shell-shocked war veterans. In a post-combat rehabilitation clinic, we watch a doctor and a male nurse recreating battle noises of shooting and bombing for a drug-induced patient who seems to be in a state of trance. Banging drawers, slamming beds, and shouting orders, they attempt to heal a soldier who suffers from post-traumatic stress disorder (PTSD) using a terrifying treatment of sound reenactment. Sontag, who patiently observes the situation with penetrating and unflinching direct-cinema methods, called the psychiatrist in charge of these therapies (which now seem more torture than therapy) Dr. Strangelove. The scene, which certainly belongs to a very specific time period and to treatment principles that may now seem totally obsolete, functions as a terrifying cinematic allegory to a haunted society and embodies the feeling of claustrophobia a nation experiences in a tragic moment. As viewers trapped in Sontag's silent and merciless gaze on this patient twisting in pain and covering his face with a pillow, we are left with nothing else but his suffering and the sounds that generate it. The artificial audial landscape created for the patient, composed of a tape recorder playing back horrific elements from the battlefield and diegetic sound effects performed by the staff, merges seamlessly with the multilayered soundtrack Sontag uses throughout the rest of the film. Regarding the pain of others, as Sontag would later title her last published book on war photography, means not only watching it in photographs but also listening to it on film.

The hospital scene resonates in many ways with John Huston's *Let There Be Light* (1946), which provided an unprecedented look into the psychological wounds of World War II, specifically PTSD among returning soldiers. While Huston's film was produced by the US Army in 1945, it was first allowed public screenings in December 1980, seven years *after* Sontag returned from Israel. As a penetrating look at a medical procedure, the hospital scene also clearly echoes Frederick Wiseman's *Titicut Follies* (1967), the first direct and merciless documentation of the casually inhuman hospital treatment of the criminally insane. As a frightening testament to masculinity in crisis, the scene was probably also the main reason behind the Israeli government's decision to ban *Promised Lands* in Israel upon its initial release, fearing it would damage the collective national morale. After all, this is a film that was produced ahead of its time. Showing a variety of unresolved complexities, it neither imitated the nationalistic and heroic cinema made in Israel during the immediate post-Independence era nor aligned itself with the worldwide wave of support the country was enjoying after the Six-Day War. Her conservative inclinations notwithstanding, what Sontag captured with her film camera—images of a "beleaguered, paranoid, and terrified nation grappling with the traumas of persecution, war, pain, and death"[39]—was not easy to swallow.

When *Promised Lands* was screened in the United States, it was harshly criticized by Nora Sayre of the *New York Times*, who questioned whether it really "should have been a book instead of a film." *Promised Lands* "won't increase your understanding of Israel," she claimed, failing to understand that Sontag's filmic rumination was not intended primarily for providing information or context.[40] *Variety's* film critic, Gordon Hitchens, was similarly displeased, calling the film "noble, but vaguely misdirected."[41] Sontag, who was rather content with the final result, never resumed her work as a documentarian, perhaps because she was discouraged by the negative reviews. I believe, however, that Sontag more or less anticipated this line of criticism, at least from a political point of view. Sontag belonged at that time to the intellectual and liberal milieu in New York City and tried to undermine its historically sympathetic, yet largely uninformed and one-dimensional, understanding of Israel. She wanted to make clear that Israel is not only a victimized Jewish nation founded on the ashes of the Holocaust and surviving the threats of Arab nations against all odds but also a rather confused and fragmented society, torn apart by "competing values of militarism, consumerism and religious identity."[42] Here, I believe, the national and the transnational become intertwined. Sontag's tourist perspective, looking for traces of a fragmented social fabric in Israel after the Yom Kippur War, aligns quite accurately with the harsh reality of a nation that was indeed left torn apart and fractured after the traumatic experience of the war.

Nowadays, the film seems to be painfully and tragically prescient. It deals with a watershed moment of national rupture in Israeli history, rarely grappled with in both fiction and documentary Israeli cinema (Amos Gitai's *Kippur* [2000] being one striking exception), and provides rare documentation on the outcome of war from the perspective of an outsider. Sontag's film is a pioneering attempt to illustrate the severe moral crisis the country experienced following the war and the resulting sobering-up process from the euphoria of the Six-Day War. As a hybrid of sorts between news reportage and an anthropological essay film, *Promised Lands* documents the sociopolitical catastrophe in Israel, the inevitable collapse of the Zionist dream as it is eaten away by the reality of a continued Jewish-Arab conflict. Caught in an elaborate transnational matrix, this film may seem too conscious of its own liminal standing to impose a dominant meaning on this state of affairs. Rather than dictate a message, it asks its audience members to experience, reminding them that "every image," as Sontag wrote close to the end of her life, is first and foremost "an invitation to look."[43] Taking it a formal step further, *Promised Lands* is an exceptional essayistic struggle that requires not only watching but also listening to the physical and mental pain emerging from an historical moment of national rupture.

Conclusion

Description of a Struggle and *Promised Lands* are not flawless masterpieces. Their creators, trying to document an exotic Levant that they had previously only imagined and conceived in their fantasies and desires, occasionally fell into the trappings of cliché. However, each of these films is still fascinating, challenging, and relevant in its own unique way and should not be dismissed as simply a display of nostalgia. These two documentary efforts dramatize the complex and often turbulent relations between utopia and dystopia, vision and reality, dreaming and awakening. Marker and Sontag came to Israel with different aspirations for observation, different legitimizations for their projects, and separate fantasies about the nature of their object of study. While Marker's vision of Israel as a socialist haven was shattered by the disillusioning traces of capitalism and euphoria he came across during his trip, Sontag's curiosity and vested interest in Israel as an American Jew made her practical findings even more distressing than what she had expected. Their fluidity of perspective, channeled through aesthetics that were formed elsewhere, marked them as outsiders to a nation that still, at that period, attempted to assert its national indigenous exclusivity.

Yet we should be wary of accepting such simple binarism between foreign and local unquestioningly. Considering the nature of their short and singular visits to Israel, Sontag and Marker may have avowedly embraced a tourist's point of view on Israel. Yet this position was taken up in a reflexive manner, exposing the very process by which one acquires knowledge of a place, as well as how a place projects a certain self-image for outsiders to know. Their seeming confusion was thus a result of negotiating the very fluidity that comes to pass when categories of national knowledge are unraveled—a result of their transnational position. Such decentering may not have complemented the dominant ideology of Israeli nationalism (though neither did the dominant tradition of heroic Israeli cinema), and in this sense, it may have foreshadowed the broader process of transnationalism Israel has gone through since the 1990s. Yet one may also say that it clearly resonated with contemporaneous Israeli attempts, albeit marginal, at breaching the national through participation in a fluid transnational sensibility. To the extent that such attempts are apparent in the development of an Israeli high-modernist cinematic style, one could definitely see *Description of a Struggle* and *Promised Lands* as contributors to this evolution. Defining this contribution as a mere importing of modernist aesthetics from without, however, would be to misunderstand the nature of the transnational conversation at play, dictating that Israel belongs solely to Israelis and modernism to Europeans and Americans. Such an argument on belonging, while not without merit, should not be carried too far, for it obfuscates the reality of a transnational project in which Israel is imagined in modernist terms by Israelis and non-Israelis alike, all looking inside and outside simultaneously, attempting to make sense of the very confusion inherent to traversing categories. Marker and Sontag, despite their global prominence, are not foreign instigators of this trend as much as partners within it. Their singular importance is that they exist categorically outside of the border of Israeli national cinema and as such may serve to expose its basic impermeability.

Notes

1. John Hess and Patricia R. Zimmermann, "Transnational Documentaries: A Manifesto," in *Transnational Cinema: The Film Reader*, ed. Elizabeth Ezra and Terry Rowden (New York: Routledge, 2006), 98.
2. Ibid., 100.
3. Ibid., 105.
4. Deborah Shaw, "Deconstructing and Reconstructing Transnational Cinema," in *Contemporary Hispanic Cinema: Interrogating the Transnational in Spanish and Latin American Film*, ed. Stephanie Dennison (Woodbridge, UK: Boydell and Brewer, 2013), 48.
5. Ibid., 60–61.
6. Ibid., 58.
7. Ibid., 54.
8. Ibid., 56.
9. Notably, Marker and Sontag's films are not the only documentaries made by renowned non-Israeli filmmakers as a result of their historical visits to Israel. If we take into account

also Pier Paolo Pasolini's *Scouting for Locations in Palestine* (1964) and Claude Lanzmann's *Pourquoi Israel* (1973)—two other films whose rhetoric should be placed on the thin line between utopia and dystopia, vision and reality—we could possibly trace the contours of a larger group of transnational films that has not been granted appropriate critical reception and has been excluded from the discussion of Israeli cinema throughout the years.

10. Malkin would perform the Hebrew voice-over narration in the film.

11. Qtd. in J. Hoberman, "Postcard from the Edge: Marker's Impression of Israel," *Film Comment* 39, no. 4 (July/August 2003): 48.

12. I am indebted here to Israeli photographer Shuka Glutman, who showed me several of those photographs, which he received as a gift from Lia Van Leer.

13. *Description of a Struggle* would also become the title that Marker gave his film in its English and French versions. The original Hebrew version was called *The Third Side of the Coin (Ha-tzad Hashlishi Shel Ha-matbea)*, attesting perhaps to the ambiguity Marker wanted to keep in his position toward the complexity of the situation in Israel, especially when addressed to an Israeli audience.

14. David Greenberg, "Description of a Struggle: Excerpts from the Script by Chris Marker" [in Hebrew], *Omanut Hakolnoa* (August 1961): 20. Yet while Marker purportedly had full artistic freedom, Lia Van Leer, seeing a copy of the script, encouraged him to edit out the most extreme statements about the State of Israel. See also *Lia* (Taly Goldenberg, 2011), a documentary about Van Leer in which she discusses these editorial changes.

15. The archival recovery of many of these lost photographs would serve to deepen our understanding of this creative process.

16. Chris Darke, "Eyesight: Chris Darke Unearths Marker's 'Lost Works,'" *Film Comment* 39, no. 3 (May/June 2003): 48.

17. Ibid.

18. The word *sign*, it should be noted, appears in the film fifteen times.

19. Catherine Lupton, *Chris Marker: Memories of the Future* (London: Reaktion Books, 2005), 67.

20. For a more thorough attempt to compare *Description of a Struggle* with *In Jerusalem* as two poetic essay films that resist the didactic tone of the propagandistic cinema in Israel during the 1960s, see Shuka Glutman, "Moments of Promise: The Sensitivities of the French New Wave Meeting the Promised Land," *Takriv* 9 (January 2015) [in Hebrew].

21. André Bazin (1958), "Bazin on Marker," *Film Comment* 39, no. 4 (2003): 44.

22. Lupton 2005, 68.

23. Ibid., 68.

24. Yoram Kaniuk, "Susan Sontag Tells How It Feels to Make a Movie," *Vogue*, July 1974.

25. Susan Sontag, *Regarding the Pain of Others* (New York: Farrar, Straus and Giroux, 2003), 66.

26. Kaniuk 1974.

27. Sontag 2003, 8. Emphasis in the original.

28. Paul Arthur, "Essay Questions: From Alain Resnais to Michael Moore," *Film Comment* 39, no. 1 (January/February 2003): 60.

29. Susan Sontag, *On Photography* (New York: Straus and Giroux, 1977), 4.

30. Kaniuk 1974.

31. Susan Sontag, *Against Interpretation and Other Essays* (New York: Penguin, 2009), 7. Emphasis in the original.

32. Michael Renov, *The Subject of Documentary* (Minneapolis: University of Minnesota Press, 2004), 22. Emphasis in the original.

33. See, for example, Miriam Hansen's attempt to track ways in which cinemas from different geopolitical locations and constellations are engaged with the contradictory experience of modernity. Hansen suggests several directions in which the concept of vernacular modernism might provide "a heuristic framework for tracing transnational relations between and within Japanese and Chinese film practices of the 1930s" and thus serve as an example for how national cinema aesthetics can never be truly indigenous. See Miriam Hansen, "Vernacular Modernism: Tracking Cinema on a Global Scale," in *World Cinemas, Transnational Perspectives*, ed. Natasa Durovicova and Kathleen Newman (London: Routledge, 2010).

34. Liam Hoare, "Susan Sontag's Panned and Banned Israel Documentary," *Forward*, January 8, 2015.

35. Remarks of this kind, it should be noted, were pretty rare at that time in Israel, when the debate about Palestinians' rights was practically nonexistent within the public discourse.

36. Taken from the *Fandor* website's description of the film, https://www.fandor.com /films/promised_lands, accessed September 19, 2020.

37. Sontag 2003, 6.

38. Nora Sayre, "Screen: Sontag's 'Promised Lands': Treatment of Israel Is at Screening Room," *New York Times*, July 12, 1974, 44.

39. Hanan Toukan, "Grappling with Israel: From Sontag to Lacan and the Maoists in Between," *Jadaliyya*, September 3, 2012.

40. Sayre 1974, 44.

41. Gordon Hitchens, "Promised Lands," *Variety*, July 10, 1974, 16.

42. Taken from the *Fandor* website, https://www.fandor.com/films/promised_lands, accessed September 19, 2020.

43. Sontag 2003, 45.

9

TWO ISRAELIS IN THE "MECCA OF MOTION PICTURES"

Golan, Globus, and Cannon Film's Transnational Enterprise

Zachary Ingle

A RENEWED INTEREST IN CANNON FILMS HAS RECENTLY TAKEN hold. In early 2016, Cannon Films Ltd., an entirely new corporate entity formed in 2014, announced its intention to revive the legacy of Cannon Films (1967–1994). The time seemed ripe for such a revitalization, which was arguably sparked by the not one, but two documentaries on Cannon Films released in 2014. The first in production was made by Australian director Mark Hartley. After several years shooting short "making-of" documentaries for DVD features, Hartley devoted himself to the history of exploitation cinema, achieving international success with his first feature, *Not Quite Hollywood: The Wild, Untold Story of Ozploitation!* (2008), and inventing the now readily accepted term *Ozploitation* in the process. He followed it with yet another untold story, this time about 1970s genre filmmaking in the Philippines, *Machete Maidens Unleashed!* (2010). After a brief break remaking the Ozploitation film *Patrick* in 2013, he finished his trilogy of exploitation documentaries with *Electric Boogaloo: The Wild, Untold Story of Cannon Films*. As with his previous documentaries, Hartley focused on the more lurid aspects of the Cannon film corpus, and his documentary included copious numbers of clips with nudity and over-the-top violence that were trademarks of Cannon Films. After discovering that Hartley was making this documentary, former Cannon studio heads Menahem Golan and Yoram Globus, who believed that Hartley's documentary would misrepresent them, rushed their own production, *The Go-Go Boys: The Inside Story of Cannon Films*, with the full participation of Golan (who would die later that year) and Globus (whose Globus Productions Films and TV produced the film). Directed by lauded Israeli documentary filmmaker Hilla Medalia, *The Go-Go Boys* even beat *Electric Boogaloo* to the gate and premiered, appropriately enough as will become clear, at the Cannes Film Festival. As one would expect, *The Go-Go Boys* treats the pre-Cannon Israeli work more fully. *Electric Boogaloo* wouldn't debut until August and September at the Melbourne and Toronto international festivals, respectively, although it was generally considered the better of the two Cannon documentaries.

Recent documentaries aside, the only extended work on Golan, Globus, and the Cannon Film enterprise remains Andrew Yule's *Hollywood a Go-Go* (subtitled *The True Story of the Cannon Film Empire* on its cover, *An Account of The [sic] Cannon Phenomenon* according to its title page), an industrial history abundant in budgets, percentages, and other business figures but riddled with Yule's snide remarks concerning what he deemed the poor quality of Cannon's output.[1] Since it was published in 1987 and could only cover events through January of that year, Yule only details the intense financial scrutiny and US Securities and Exchange Commission (SEC) investigation Cannon was under in 1986. Still, even if Yule was able to forecast their uncertain future due to their diminishing returns and the damaging effects of creative accounting, 1987 proved to be a momentous year in Cannon's history (another heavy promotion at Cannes, the disappointing releases of *Superman IV: The Quest for Peace*, *Over the Top*, and *Masters of the Universe*), not to mention one of the final years of the Golan and Globus partnership. Furthermore, its publication by a British publisher seems to have supported its primarily British focus. In light of this continued scarcity of scholarly attention to Cannon, this chapter tenders an investigation into how Cannon became a transnational, vertically integrated operation. Golan and Globus's work with Cannon can also be viewed as an extension of their work in Israel, as they kept a filmmaking base there during the Cannon years, allowing them the ability to return in the aftermath of the company's dissolution. As with many of the other subjects in this volume, the lengthy careers of Golan and Globus have often gone partially or wholly ignored in books grounded in a national cinema paradigm; thus, a transnational approach that situates their Cannon work within the long arc of their Israeli oeuvre points to their international significance, doing justice to these Israeli filmmakers.

First founded in 1967, Cannon's only notable successes were John Avildsen's *Joe* (1970) and the *Happy Hooker* series (1975–1980) before its acquisition by Golan and Globus in 1979. Golan and Globus turned Cannon into a major player, taking it from the burgeoning video store and cable markets that blossomed in the 1980s to the Cannes Film Festival. They maintained a stable of notable stars (Charles Bronson, Chuck Norris) and eventually tackled major franchises (*Superman, Masters of the Universe*), but they were primarily known for specializing in cheap action fare and keeping budgets down. Golan insisted, "If you make an American film with a beginning, a middle and an end and with a budget of less than $5m, you must be an idiot to lose money, a complete unprofessional idiot in today's market. American films have a meaning to the world. They mean professionalism, a professional product. It must have a normal little story, with actors; that's all."[2] They were known for cutting corners, saving as much as possible on their films, and just like Walt and Roy Disney had done in decades previous, they placed all profits into future productions. The average cost of a Cannon film in the 1980s was only between two and five million dollars.[3]

Much of Cannon's success was due to its strategy of preselling the home video, cable, and overseas rights to its films before the films were even completed, with preselling titles remaining unmade if they did not receive adequate advances. Roger Corman, who proudly claims to have never lost a dollar on any of the hundreds of films he has produced, labeled Golan "a master of the pre-sell on the international market."[4] In the early years, Cannon was able to cover most of its entire investment by preselling before a single ticket was sold at the box office. For instance, in 1983, Cannon budgeted $100 million for the eighteen films it was shooting, of which $90 million was already covered in presales.[5] While no Israeli filmmaker has received as much international critical attention as Amos Gitai, it remains safe to say that no Israeli filmmakers have been as commercially successful as Menahem Golan and Yoram Globus. Before their separation and the eventual demise of Cannon, Golan and Globus were inseparable; Golan was the creative force and primary spokesman of the two, while Globus handled financial matters. During the height of their power, they were asked why they still shared a hotel room at the Cannes Film Festival when they were certainly financially able to get their own rooms. Some assumed it was to boost their parsimonious image, but Golan insisted on a better reason: "We do it because we talk about our films until one of us falls asleep."[6]

Born with the surname Globus in 1929 in Tiberias, Palestine, Menahem Golan, after serving as a pilot in the War for Independence, renamed himself after the Golan Heights in a patriotic act. He studied at the Old Vic Theatre School in London and was already considered one of the top theater directors in Israel by the age of twenty-three, before he began transitioning to filmmaking. Wanting to learn filmmaking from one of his idols, Roger Corman, Golan worked as a production assistant on Corman's *The Young Racers* (1963), hoping that Corman would help fund his first feature. Corman instead funded Francis Ford Coppola's first feature (*Dementia 13*, 1963), but Golan still asserted that the famed producer taught him more about filmmaking than anyone else.

Golan's cousin Yoram Globus was born in 1941, also in Tiberias.[7] He grew up in the cinema, working at his father's movie theater from a young age, to which he later attributed his passion for cinema. Golan and Globus formed Noah Films in 1963, releasing the first film directed by Golan, *El Dorado*, which would also star Chaim Topol in his first lead role, along with Israeli heartthrob Arik Einstein and the up-and-coming young actress Gila Almagor. Noah Films would overwhelmingly become the most successful film company in Israel, producing fourteen of Israel's top twenty box office hits between its establishment and 1980.[8] At the top of the list was their production *Lemon Popsicle* (1978), which sold over 1.3 million tickets in a country with a population of only 3.69 million at that time. (It also fared well internationally, especially in West Germany and later Japan.) But from Noah's formation, Golan and Globus were insistent that they make films that were distributed internationally.

Golan had already directed twenty films before directing his first film for Cannon (*The Magician of Lublin*, 1979). All were Israeli or Israeli co-productions, save for the British production *What's Good for the Goose* (1968). *Kazablan* (1973) merited enough international attention to secure a Golden Globe nomination, while *Operation Thunderbolt* (1977) brought Golan's only Oscar nomination (Best Foreign Film) for a film that he directed. Three other films that Golan produced during this era were also nominated for Oscars: *Sallah* (1964), *I Love You Rosa* (1972), and *The House on Chelouche Street* (1973), with *Sallah* winning the Golden Globe. Golan also directed several key Bourekas films during this period, including *Fortuna* (1966), *999 Aliza Mizrahi* (1967), and *The Highway Queen* (also *Queen of the Road*, 1971) based on a story brought to him by Almagor, who starred in the lead role.

Realizing that it would be more cost-effective to buy a preexisting film company than to start their own, in 1979, the cousins bought the Cannon Group Inc. for only $500,000 (some sources say $350,000). From these meager beginnings, Cannon would quickly become the world's most prosperous independent film company of its era. But Golan and Globus struggled early on in their acquisition of Cannon. Their first full year with Cannon, 1980, saw profits of only $8,154.[9] Share prices then were at twenty cents, but they would later peak as high as $44.

After the first two or three years mainly releasing films under the old regime, they drew Hollywood's attention by releasing a more prestigious product, Jason Miller's adaptation of his own Pulitzer Prize–winning play, *That Championship Season* (1982). Although the film received little critical attention and was a box office failure, it showed that Cannon was also interested in films outside of their bread-and-butter, generic fare of action sequels. Still, Cannon was primarily known for their subpar output, so much so that we understand the motivation for the *Mystery Science Theater 3000* characters to scream "Golan and Globus! NO!" when viewing the *Golan-Globus Productions* title card in the opening credits of one of the more wretched Cannon products, *Alien from L.A.* (1988). The descriptor seemingly most used in contemporary commentary to describe Cannon's work continues to be *schlock*.

Admittedly, Golan and Globus focused more on quantity than quality with Cannon's cinematic output. Golan took special pride in boasting about the number of films they were releasing and how it exceeded that of any other studio, not counting the many projects that were little more than a poster with international rights secured, aborted projects that would never reach theaters. Even as early as 1982, Cannon started shooting twelve films that year, more than most of the majors.[10] For instance, Cannon *started* forty-one films in 1986, over twice as many as the next competitor, New World Pictures (eighteen). (That same year, majors like Warners, Universal, Paramount, and 20th Century Fox were apparently more selective, with ten, nine, nine, and seven pictures, respectively.[11]) Nineteen eighty-six was also the year that Golan seemed most satisfied that they had achieved what they had set out to do: "Yoram and me, when we came from Israel and from Europe, we came to Mecca, the Mecca of motion pictures, and we came to pray, and we prayed and prayed. In the beginning nobody listened, but we kept on praying, and finally people began to listen."[12]

But quantity was not their only goal; they sought admiration from their peers by producing films for numerous notable filmmakers, including Liliana Cavani (*The Berlin Affair*, 1985), Jean-Luc Godard (*King Lear*, 1987), Dusan Makavejev (*Manifesto*, 1988), John Frankenheimer (*52 Pick-Up*, 1986), Curtis Harrington (*Mata Hari*, 1985), Michael Winner (four films), Tobe Hooper (three films), Herbert Ross (*Dancers*, 1987), Sidney J. Furie (*Superman IV: The Quest for Peace*, 1987), Bryan Forbes (*The Naked Face*, 1984), Ivan Passer (*Haunted Summer*, 1984, originally to have been directed by John Huston), J. Lee Thompson (eight films), Barbet Schroeder (*Barfly*, 1987), Franco Zeffirelli (*Otello*, 1986), Andrei Konchalovsky (four films), Ruggero Deodato (*The Barbarians*, 1987), Robert Altman (*Fools for Love*, 1985), Raoul Ruiz (*Treasure Island*, 1985), Lina Wertmuller (*Camorra*, 1985), and John Cassavetes (*Love Streams*, 1984). Cannon's desire to add notable, respected international filmmakers merits little attention in Hartley's *Electric Boogaloo*, which, as with his other documentaries, seems more interested in the Cannon films that became bottom-shelf fodder for the video stores. Unrealized projects from other notable directors include Federico Fellini's *Amerika* (based on Franz Kafka's novel), Francis Ford Coppola's *La Brava*, and Bud Yorkin's *Public Enemy*, in addition to planned films with Roman Polanski and Alain Resnais, among others. This desire to balance popular films with more highbrow fare actually resembles the production model of the pre-Cannon Noah Films, evidence of Golan and Globus transferring their Israeli filmmaking experiences to Hollywood.

Few critics drew considerable attention to Cannon's desire to be taken seriously, to employ some of the world's most respected cineastes. Many regarded Cannon as signing top-shelf directors as more of a stunt, such as the legendary story of when Godard signed his contract to make *King Lear* for Cannes at the 1985 Cannes Film Festival on the back of a napkin. One critic who did point to this transition, Roger Ebert, posited, "No other production organization in the world today—certainly not any of the seven Hollywood 'majors'—has taken more chances with serious, marginal films than Cannon."[13] In an archival interview from *The Go-Go Boys*, Golan alleges that he made territories purchase films like *Love Streams* and *A Fool for Love* by dangling *Death Wish 3* (1985) as part of a package deal.

So what drew this type of talent? Some directors were able to get funding for films that no one else would make. In the BBC documentary *The Last Moguls* (1986), Frankenheimer mentions his appreciation for a company that did not mirror the revolving-door situation occurring at other studios in the 1980s: you began and ended your film with Golan and Globus in charge. He echoed the sentiments of many other filmmakers that Golan especially was himself a director, contrasting with most studio heads at that time who had never made a film. And they were more than just talk: "So far, it's been a terrifically happy situation. And I have every reason to believe it's going to continue to be. Unlike England, where everybody talks about making movies but nobody makes them, here these guys make the movies. And they don't talk very much, which I find terribly refreshing."[14] Still other directors appreciated the ability to work without studio interference.

But not everyone had as amiable an experience with Cannon. Golan was so enormously displeased with Godard's *King Lear* ("He's not Godard anymore. He spat into the hand that fed him."[15]) that he refused to give it a proper release. Godard blamed Cannon's inability to market the film correctly and reciprocated Golan's discontentment: "Golan and Globus are just nasty kids. . . . They should have stuck to the Chuck Norris films. . . . I like Golan and Globus all right. A pity they didn't remain just gangsters. They wanted to become noblemen. It's like Al Capone deciding to wear tuxedos."[16] Godard's comments may seem harsh, but when reviewing the list of notable Cannon directors above, few made more than one film for Cannon, including the laudatory Frankenheimer.

After numerous financial disasters and still devoid of achieving the critical success they craved (namely a Palme d'Or or Best Picture Oscar), the Golan and Globus partnership dissolved in 1989. The company had gone bankrupt and was purchased by Italian financier Giancarlo Parretti, who renamed it Pathé Communications. After purchasing MGM the following year, Parretti merged the two to form MGM-Pathé Communications; his fraudulent behavior prompted his ouster within a year. Golan would head 21st Century Film Corporation; that its best-known releases during his tenure were *Captain America* (1990), the 1990 remake of *Night of the Living Dead*, and *Death Wish V: The Face of Death* (1994) is indicative of why it would shut down only a few years later. After this unsuccessful venture, Golan founded yet another production company, this one with the even less original moniker of New Cannon, Inc. Its first release was the Golan-directed *Death Game* (2001), a basketball film with a *Death Wish*–type vigilante narrative. With Minsk attempting to act as a city double for Pittsburgh and what has to be the most unrealistic basketball scenes in the history of cinema, *Death Game* surely marks the nadir in Golan's decades-long work as a director. Later New Cannon films, while still

American productions, were usually just distributed in the theaters Golan owned in Israel.[17]

Globus became president of MGM-Pathé but returned to Israel in 1993 and continued to make Israeli films before forming Rebel Way Entertainment in 2016. Their twenty-six-year partnership would dissolve into a petty rivalry, perhaps reaching its apex on March 16, 1990, when Golan and Globus each released a film about the Lambada dance craze on the same day. Globus beat Golan into production, so he was able to use the word *Lambada* for his title. (Golan was stuck with *The Forbidden Dance*.) In retribution, Golan ensured that Globus would not be able to include Kaoma's global hit song "Lambada." The feuding cousins further retaliated by constantly moving the release date up, to the point that Globus's *Lambada* was released exactly eleven days after shooting had finished, possibly an all-time record. Yet their squabble was for naught—apparently audiences were not ready for two competing Lambada films, as they grossed only $6 million combined. Their time at Cannon may have lasted little more than a decade, but as Winner put it, "In between times Menachem and Yoram were the most wonderful firework display the industry had seen."[18]

Filmmaking was an international venture for Cannon. "American films [had] a meaning for the world" from Golan's perspective, as he also claimed, "There is a great hunger for American motion pictures. And there are thousands of independent distributors who can't satisfy that need in other countries because they're cut off from the American product by the major studios who have their own worldwide networks. So we're here to make American movies to take care of those distributors."[19] Golan would brag that over half of Cannon's box office came through foreign markets; although common today, this was not the norm for most American films in the 1980s. Looking at their 1987 and 1988 slate of films, *American Ninja 2: The Confrontation* was filmed in South Africa; *Dancers* in Bari, Italy; *Business as Usual* and *Superman IV* in the United Kingdom; *Bloodsport* in Hong Kong; *The Barbarians* in Rome, Italy; and *The Kitchen Toto*, *Going Bananas*, *Gor*, and *Gor II* in various African locations. Of course, this is not to ignore the economic incentives of international production; it allowed for numerous cost-saving measures, including the ability to make film prints for about half the industry average by using foreign laboratories.[20] Although Cannon films were distributed throughout the Americas, Africa, Asia, Europe, and Oceania, this chapter will focus more extensively on their presence in six nations: the United Kingdom, France, Italy, Netherlands, West Germany, and Israel.

Cannon may have had its most concentrated presence in Britain. London-Cannon Films Ltd. and Cannon Distributors UK were already established by 1982, with the former producing such notorious failures as *Lady Chatterley's Lover* (1981), *Sahara* (1984), and *Superman IV*, among others. They purchased Elstree Studios (one of England's big three studios, the other two being Pinewood and Shepperton) in order to make about ten films there annually.[21] Knowing that creditors value brick-and-mortar locations as highly as anything else, they had moved into exhibition there as well, purchasing the 130 screens owned by the Classic chain of theaters.[22] They were at 95 theaters and 216 screens by the end of 1985,[23] considered the "biggest single force" in British cinemas, securing 39 percent of all screens.[24] With substantial production, distribution, and exhibition arms in the United Kingdom, Cannon was now vertically integrated. No wonder Golan claimed the United Kingdom was its "international headquarters,"[25] even with its main base still in Hollywood. Even if Golan's statement was not entirely true, the United Kingdom did have the most Cannon employees by 1986, with 1,600 (compared to 400 in Italy, only 250 in the United States, 225 in the Netherlands, 150 in Germany, and 10 in France).[26] Despite neither being British or even really being headquartered there, some called Golan and Globus the most powerful figures in British cinema since the heyday of J. Arthur Rank and his Rank Organisation.

Cannon attempted to acquire an even greater number of UK theaters, but when Thorn-EMI Screen Entertainment put Britain's largest cinema circuit, the ABC chain of theaters, on the market, Cannon was initially blocked in its attempt. Golan blamed it on anti-Cannon sentiment (and sometimes anti-Americanism and antisemitism) in the United Kingdom.[27] Producer David Puttnam (*Chariots of Fire*, *The Killing Fields*), at that time arguably the spokesperson for the British film industry, spared no words in his unequivocal disapproval of Cannon's British ventures:

> We live in a society which is enormously influenced by film and television and we have a responsibility as filmmakers to that society. I've said this before and I sound like a cracked record, but I have a very precise notion of the sort of society that I want to live in—and I've got an idea what the triggers are that create violence and the triggers that create social and decent behaviour. I myself make movies which take a position which is humanist—essentially humanist—and I believe is helpful to society. It's quite clear to me that the majority of their work in the past—and I am talking about the past—has been work which appealed to the lowest common denominator in the audience.[28]

To statements such as this, Golan countered, "We are the biggest investors in the industry in this country since we came here thirty months ago. . . . To claim that this is a threat to the industry in England is a joke. We have injected new blood into the industry in its most difficult days."[29] Whether this argument proved winning is unclear, but Cannon eventually did purchase Thorn EMI and its substantial library for £175 million.

Across the channel over in France, Cannon-France was hoping to eventually rival London-Cannon in production, with plans to produce or coproduce two to five films per annum.[30] The first Cannon production in France was actually a coproduction with Italy, *Salomè* (1986), yet another in the long line of cinematic adaptations of one of the Bible's more lurid stories. Other than that lackluster release, France-Cannon seems to have instead only served as Cannon's French distribution wing.

From the outset of their purchase of Cannon, Golan and Globus insured an increased presence at the Cannes Film Festival, so much so that by 1985, it had been dubbed by many the "Cannon Film Festival." Golan and Globus had been attending Cannes well before they took over Cannon, and Golan bragged about Cannon's success at Cannes: "Cannes is our Christmas. It's where we meet distributors from all over the world who are our friends. And we know how to take care of them because we learned the hard way. What's the hard way? Selling a black-and-white Hebrew film to Japan."[31] Golan even boasted that he knew the international market better than any other American producers, a claim that even if unverifiable does hint at Golan's incomparable attention among his peers at that time to the international market. (Documentary evidence of their wheeling and dealing at the 1986 American Film Market for international distribution can be seen in *The Last Moguls*.)

In his Cannes journal from the 1987 festival, Roger Ebert described the omnipresence of the Cannon Group, with its numerous advertisements, billboards, and parties and with numerous films shown in the Cannes marketplace (including its "family film festival" of fairy tales). Cannon also timed their *Variety* advertisements during Cannes, taking out a fifty-five-page ad in 1985 and increasing it to sixty-five in 1986.[32] Yet even before the publication of Yule's *Hollywood a Go-Go*, Ebert worried that the company may have got a bit too big for its britches in trying to be one of the majors: "Cannon still fights the shabby image of its early days, and this year there were rumblings in the financial pages that the Golan-Globus empire, having bought a studio in England and three of the world's largest theater chains, while financing a bigger production schedule than any other Hollywood studio, might be overextended."[33] Nevertheless, Cannon came back to Cannes in full force. Norman Mailer's *Tough Guys Don't Dance* screened out of competition, and two films competed for that year's Palme d'Or: *Shy People* and *Barfly*. Golan had arrived with *three* Palme d'Or competitors the previous year (*Runaway Train*, *Fool for Love*, and *Otello*, with Roman Polanski's Cannon-distributed *Pirates* acting as opening night selection and *Salome* in Un Certain Regard competition) but came away empty-handed. Yet Ebert decided to make Golan the central figure, featuring him as the hero of his journal.[34] Those who worked with Golan cite how obsessed he was with winning an Academy Award or the Palme d'Or. As Ebert noted, "Golan and Globus are possibly the only producers in the world who enter Cannes every year as if it were a competition, an athletic event. Other producers may enter a film and then not be seen again for a decade. Cannon is back year after year. . . . The festival was like some kind of fundamental obsession with Golan, and I wondered if he sometimes decided to make a movie for the private reason that it might finally win him the prize at Cannes."[35] One can speculate that this desire to receive such a prestigious award as the Palme d'Or burned strongly within Golan because it represented his significance as an artist, not just a financial figure. Furthermore, such accolades would serve as proof in Israel that he had succeeded.

Neither *Shy People* nor *Barfly* won the top award, although *Shy People*'s Barbara Hershey did win Best Actress. Dejected after losing, Golan blamed it on the fact that it was the fortieth anniversary of the festival and that it was set up for a French film to win for the first time in over twenty years: "The French said fuck the world, and gave it to themselves."[36] The next year proved even less fortunate for Cannon, which had no films competing for the top prize, while in 1989, the year of the Golan-Globus split, *A Cry in the Dark* (a Warner Bros. coproduction) was Cannon's lone chance; it claimed another Best Actress winner, this time for Meryl Streep.

Italy had the most Cannon employees outside of the United Kingdom, as Cannon Italia SRL was seemingly more successful than Cannon-France. They acquired the directorial services from Zeffirelli, Wertmuller, Cavani, and Deodato, all of whom actually released films (not always a given for Cannon). They were supposed to produce Francesco Rosi's adaptation of *Saturday, Sunday and Monday* with Sophia Loren and Marcello Mastroianni in the leads; the film would release post-Cannon dissolution in 1990 without Mastroianni and instead with Wertmuller at the helm. Italian productions were filmed across the country, with the majority in Rome but also Naples and other cities;[37] the intent was for half of the productions to be domestic, half foreign.[38] Even before this flurry of Italian productions in the middle of the decade, Cannon Italia SRL had already produced the films starring former "Incredible Hulk" Lou Ferrigno: *I sette magnifici gladiatori* (1983) and *Hercules* (1983) and its sequel (1985). On the exhibition front, they purchased the fifty-three theaters in the Gaumont Italian theater circuit, stretching from Rome to Palermo, for $15 million.[39] But besides owning the largest chain in Italy,[40] Cannon drastically altered exhibition practices in the country by renovating the theaters with air-conditioning so they could stay open in the summer, adding popcorn to the refreshments, and "clean[ing] up every washroom."[41] They also opened the first Italian multiplex in Rome and would soon add one in Milan.[42] Their efforts in Italy were not without labor struggles, however, but Golan responded: "When our Italian theatre face-lift and the multiplex programme is completed, our contribution in bringing back the lost audience will be better appreciated."[43]

Cannon purchased the Tuschinski theaters, the largest chain in the Netherlands with about fifty screens. They also formed Cannon Tuschinski for Dutch distribution and, according to the Internet Movie Database (IMDb), released thirty films in the Netherlands through it, including a handful of Dutch films mixed in with Cannon's American product. This was preceded by Cannon-City Distribution, which distributed solely to the Netherlands, with nine additional films from 1985 to 1986. In West Germany, Cannon bought the Ewert theater group and renamed it the Cannon Theatre Group. More critically, however, through its purchase of United Artists International, Cannon had a 50 percent share in German distributor Scotia Intl-Filmverleih.[44] According to *The Go-Go Boys* documentary, Cannon eventually owned over a thousand theaters, controlling the means of production and exhibition in these European countries to an incredible extent, shaping cinematic culture and defining its tastes.

While both *Electric Boogaloo* and *The Go-Go Boys* both could have discussed Cannon's transnationalism in greater depth, the former documentary at least touches on the antisemitism Golan and Globus faced. The documentary makes an apt comparison to the brashness of Harvey and Bob Weinstein, who have also faced criticism that bordered on antisemitism at times, particularly in how they are often described as shrewd. Even in an industry founded disproportionately by Jews and historically friendly to them, Golan and Globus as Israelis were viewed as "super Jewish." They were sometimes called the "Bagel Boys" and the "Nosh Brothers" (*nosh* is Yiddish for *food*). (Not to mention the body-shaming inherent in calling them the "The Globs," considering Golan's corpulent proportions.) Hartley even includes one talking head who admits that his personal name for them was the "Bad News Jews." But unlike the American Weinsteins, Golan and Globus were perceived as carpetbaggers, foreigners whose films were at times odd and missing that American element. As Cannon quickly became the most powerful independent film company in Hollywood, insiders feared an Israeli invasion. Perhaps Hollywood's fears were exacerbated by Golan and Globus proudly maintaining their Israeli identity, not as much in their actual films as in their personae, their working methods, and the compatriots they brought with them to Cannon. They also preserved their base in Israel through their Noah Films and Cannon-Israel. As another talking head in *Electric Boogaloo* notes, they were Israelis "defined by that culture." But as this chapter articulates, this was surely the intention of Golan and Globus—not to suppress their Israeliness when they came to the "Mecca of motion pictures" but to make an Israeli-influenced cinema that was truly transnational.

These fears of an Israeli invasion may also have been precipitated by some of Cannon's stable of directors who were Israeli, holdovers from Noah Films. Besides directing the first four films in the *Lemon Popsicle* series, Boaz Davidson would direct such Cannon films as *Hospital Massacre* (aka *X-Ray*, 1981), *The Last American Virgin* (1982, the American remake of *Lemon Popsicle*), and the Golan-penned, talking-and-flying-ape film *Going Bananas* (1987). After serving as an assistant director for Golan, Sam Firstenberg also became one of Cannon's most prolific in-house directors, most memorably helming the first two films in *American Ninja* series (1985–1987) but also the film that inspired the title of Hartley's documentary—*Breakin' 2: Electric Boogaloo* (1984). In *The Go-Go Boys*, Globus admits that getting the first *Breakin'* (also 1984) fast-tracked with a three-week shooting schedule before the break-dancing fad fizzled acted as the primary motivation for Cannon employing Israeli director Joel Silberg and an Israeli crew for the film. Silberg would go on to direct *Rappin'* (1985) and *Lambada*.

Itzik Kol headed Cannon-Israel's production; his stated goal was to "make a little Hollywood in the mountains of Jerusalem."[45] Plans even existed to go into the theme park business and build a "Bible Land" in Israel.[46] Although such plans were never realized, Golan was apparently in a Walt Disney state of mind. Cannon-Israel's most lasting work, at least in regard to global impact, was the "Cannon Movie Tales" series, their attempt at breaking into the family market by adapting (public domain) fairy tales. Although sixteen were planned, their lack of popularity meant that only nine were released (between 1986 and 1989); Golan found the Disney market much tougher to crack than he had anticipated. They were filmed in Israel with a mostly Israeli cast, save for Anglo-American stars in the lead roles. Despite their lack of commercial success and variation in quality, the "Cannon Movie Tales" did receive adequate international distribution, unlike some of their Hebrew-language films made primarily for domestic audiences, like *Million Dollar Madness* (1986) and *Prom Queen* (1986). Golan-Globus also produced several more *Lemon Popsicle* films during this time. (Globus produced the ninth and final entry in 2001.) Around the time of shooting *Over the Top*, Golan announced his intention to direct a miniseries based on Moshe Dayan that would also serve as a brief history of the State of Israel, but it never materialized.[47]

Cannon even shot some of its most well-known films in Israel, including the Agatha Christie adaptation *Appointment with Death* (1988), directed by Winner.[48] Israel also served as the home for the anti-PLO treatise *The Ambassador* (J. Lee Thompson, 1984), starring Robert Mitchum, Ellen Burstyn, and Rock Hudson. While often considered one of the most overtly pro-Israeli films ever, it was soon surpassed in notoriety by one of Cannon's biggest hits, *The Delta Force* (1986), also shot entirely in Israel. Directed by Golan, the film feels like a promotional vehicle for US-Israel solidarity, and it remains one of the more memorable Hollywood films about terrorism from its era.[49] Many at the time considered it Golan's cheap exploitation of the 1985 TWA Flight 847 hijacking, as much of the film was based on the events of that particular incident, but it was in fact also a remake of an earlier, pre-Cannon Golan film.

The Delta Force draws from one of Golan's biggest critical successes, the Israeli film *Operation Thunderbolt* (1977), although it was not advertised as a remake. The German freedom fighters and Israeli special forces of *Operation Thunderbolt* were replaced with Arab terrorists and the American Delta Force. Golan's earlier film was considered the more reputable film, with its Academy Award nomination for Best Foreign Language Film. Less an action film than a historical film, *Operation Thunderbolt* was based on Operation Entebbe in 1976, in which over one hundred Israelis and non-Israeli Jewish hostages were rescued at the Entebbe airport in Uganda by an Israel Defense Forces (IDF) task force. Hollywood was immediately interested and quickly developed two made-for-television films about Entebbe: *Victory of Entebbe* (1976, directed by Marvin Chomsky, starring Anthony Hopkins, Elizabeth Taylor, Kirk Douglas, and Burt Lancaster) and *Raid on Entebbe* (1977, directed by Irvin Kershner, starring Peter Finch, Charles Bronson, and Yaphet Kotto).[50] But Golan was selected to offer the official Israeli version of events and gifted with the highest budget yet for an Israeli film: $2.7 million.[51]

Tony Shaw notes *Operation Thunderbolt*'s significance as a "landmark film," one that "brought Israeli cinema to international regard for the first time and significantly boosted international co-production in the country."[52] The film's consistent reputation as a patriotic production can still be seen by perusing its YouTube comments. Furthermore, it spawned other counterterrorist films, many of which were also made in Israel.[53] Golan would return to the formula yet again in his post-Cannon years, directing the straight-to-video *Deadly Heroes* (1993). In that film, Golan again returned to the Athens Airport setting that figured into both *Operation Thunderbolt* and *The Delta Force*, but this time he inserted a group of Navy Sea, Air, and Land (SEALs) teams who save the day instead of IDF commandos and the eponymous Delta Force.

That Golan would effectively remake his own film might seem rather derivative at best and indolent or greedy at worst. But it has since become not uncommon for directors to make English-language remakes from their earlier successes; recall George Sluizer (*The Vanishing*, 1988, 1993), Michael Haneke (*Funny Games*, 1997, 2007), and perhaps most recently, Pablo Larraín (*Gloria*, 2013, and *Gloria Bell*, 2018). As mentioned above, Cannon had already achieved moderate success with Davidson's remake of *Lemon Popsicle*. Despite being based on different historical events a decade apart, the films share many similarities, from character types to a similar structure; the hijackings are initiated at the same point, and the films have almost exactly the same running time (particularly if one ignores the longer credits of the remake). Perhaps the biggest change, however, is in regard to genre: Golan converts the political thriller (based on very recent history) of *Operation Thunderbolt* to the action film *The Delta Force*, whose credentials as an action film became all the more evident considering it spawned two sequels with no basis in history.

Although the film is thoroughly Americanized, with the Israeli heroes replaced with American ones like Chuck Norris and Lee Marvin, Golan inserts his Israeli identity in noticeable ways. For one, *The Delta Force* retains its emphasis on Jewish identity and struggle. The film opens with two middle-aged Jewish American couples. Once the hijacking commences by the Arab terrorists, one of the wives preemptively hides her Hebrew ring, but to no avail; a hijacker unfortunately finds it and assumes that there must be an Israeli passenger onboard. Martin Balsam plays a Holocaust survivor (a character type, like the pregnant woman, recycled from *Operation Thunderbolt*), playing off of Holocaust guilt in the Western world to elicit Zionist sympathy. Head flight attendant Ingrid (Hanna Schygulla) refuses to identify the Jewish names on the passports, explaining that no one should ask a German to perform such a task. Having a German flight attendant may seem like Golan reconciling any anti-German sentiment from the first film, but Ingrid was modeled on her real-life counterpart, German American Uli Derickson (who subsequently received her own made-for-television film, *The Taking of Flight 847: The Uli Derickson Story*, 1988).

Of additional interest is how Golan Christianized his remake, arguably making it more appealing to American sensibilities. Christians and Jews are linked throughout the film in several notable scenes. In one, obvious Jewish names are read off of passports; these passengers are to be segregated from the rest of the flight. After Jewish names like Harry Goldman and Benjamin Kaplan are read, David Rosovsky (played by Israeli actor Yehuda Efroni) is called forward. He explains that he is not Jewish but Russian Orthodox, but he draws no sympathy from the hijackers. *Operation Thunderbolt* also had two nuns on the flight, but here they are accompanied by a character with a much larger role, Father O'Malley (George Kennedy). When the Jewish names are selected, O'Malley chooses to suffer with them: "You called for all the Jews. I'm Jewish, just like Jesus Christ. You take one, you gotta take us all." Furthermore, a Greek Orthodox priest in Beirut, Father Nicholas (notable Israeli actor Shaike Ophir), also appears to be a Mossad agent.

The terrorists on the hijacked plane during the Operation Entebbe mission were a combination of the Popular Front for the Liberation of Palestine and Revolutionary Cells, a German group, but Golan focuses on the Germans (led by Klaus Kinski's Wilfried Boese). They identify themselves as the Che Guevara Force, fighting "imperialist Zionists" as well as "reactionary Germans." The hijack of TWA Flight 847 was allegedly the work of Hezbollah, but lead terrorist Abdul Rafai (Robert Forster, in blackface) identifies himself instead as "a member of the New World Revolutionary Organization" who has "declared war against American imperialists, Zionists, terrorists, and all other anti-socialist atrocities." Thus, Golan's film is implicated in the broader representational pattern, identified by Rachel S. Harris, of "conflating all forms of terrorism, [and] thereby nullifying any meaningful political message."[54]

The Delta Force engages in multiple anti-Palestinian and anti-Arab stereotypes, as delineated in Jack Shaheen's work on the subject *Reel Bad Arabs*.[55] Of course, the film was heavily criticized as one of the most anti-Arab films ever made by Hollywood, with numerous demonstrations held against it. When comparing Israeli films about terrorism to their Hollywood counterparts, Ella Shohat notes that the anti-Arab sentiment is "even magnified in the Hollywood films, resulting in a stereotypical treatment quite unthinkable within current Israeli cinema, in accord with the general, at times hysterical, anti-Arabism of the American mass media."[56] *The Delta Force* further aligns with the "superpatriotic" (per Shohat) films of the Reagan era, concluding with the relieved hostages singing "America the Beautiful" over and over and drinking Budweisers. Despite a few casualties, the release of the hostages at Ben Gurion Airport results in a celebration as they reunite with their families (with the ever-present sea of American and Israeli flags). And as if the US-Israeli codependence was not obvious enough, General Woodbridge (Robert Vaughn) proclaims, "Israel is America's best friend in the Middle East."

While Cannon has primarily been discussed within an Anglo-American context, this chapter points to their transnational enterprise. The "Go-Go Boys" also kept a filmmaking base in Israel during the Cannon years, and both would return to Israel in the post-Cannon aftermath. From his early Israeli blockbusters to Cannon films like *Enter the Ninja* (1981) and *The Delta Force*, Golan has had an immeasurable impact on world cinema that no other Israeli filmmaker (not even Ralph Bakshi, Yoram Gross, nor the award-winning yet frustratingly inconsistent Amos Gitai) rivals. While Golan, Globus, and their Noah Films had an enormous impact on the dissemination of Israeli cinema in the rest of the world, their films with Cannon also arguably attest to the significance of the two Israeli filmmakers to global filmmaking.

In early 2016, announcements were made of the continuation of the Cannon legacy, with CEO Richard Albiston launching Cannon Films Ltd. As he often stated in interviews, this was not a relaunch of the Cannon Group, as the Cannon library was now owned by MGM. Still, with titles like *America Ninja Apprentice*, *Allan Quatermain and the Jewel of the East*, and *Return of the Delta Force*, Albiston's desire to make Golan-esque movies is blatantly obvious.

Even if this new Cannon Films Ltd. doesn't quite make the splash Albiston probably hopes it will, the Cannon legacy continues in the increased internationalization/transnationalism of film, thirty years after the company's heyday. While no film had ever made a billion US dollars worldwide by the time of Cannon's dissolution, forty-six films have done so now (as of April 19, 2020). Unlike the 1980s, most American box office hits now make roughly two-thirds of their grosses internationally.[57] Before Golan and Globus, few American studio heads tried to exploit the foreign markets as systematically or to the degree that they did; today, it is a ubiquitous part of the film industry, one of the many ways that their legacy—and the legacy of Cannon Films—endures.

Notes

1. Andrew Yule, *Hollywood a Go-Go* (London: Sphere, 1987).
2. Ibid., 15. The note about American films is especially interesting, considering the inordinate number of Cannon films with *America* or *American* in the title.
3. Paul Talbot, *Bronson's Loose!: The Making of the Death Wish Films* (New York: iUniverse, 2006), 63.
4. Barry Rehfeld, "Cannon Fathers," *Film Comment* (November/December 1983): 23.
5. Ibid., 24.
6. Yule 1987, 147.
7. This is according to most sources. Yule has his birthplace as Kfar Motzkin, and some sources have him being born in 1943.
8. Robert Friedman, "Will Cannon Boom or Bust?," *American Film* (July/August 1986): 59.
9. Ibid., 57.
10. Rehfeld 1983. 20.
11. Yule 1987, 220.
12. Hilla Medalia, dir., *The Go-Go Boys: The Inside Story of Cannon Films* (Noah Productions, 2014), DVD.
13. Roger Ebert, *Two Weeks in the Midday Sun: A Cannes Notebook* (Kansas City: Andrews and McMeel, 1987), 109.
14. Christopher Sykes, dir., "The Last Moguls," *Omnibus*, season 21, episode 7, aired March 23, 1986, accessed September 22, 2020, https://www.youtube.com/watch?v=2GIZGqlf3AQ.
15. Hector Feliciano, "Jean-Luc Godard the Ill-Fated 'King Lear,'" *Washington Post*, September 4, 1988, accessed April 30, 2019, https://www.washingtonpost.com/archive/lifestyle/style/1988/09/04/jean-luc-godard-and-the-ill-fated-king-lear/046b3f1b-73a9-464c-9400-427dfccdad94/.
16. Ibid.
17. Talbot 2006, 116.
18. Michael Winner, *Winner Takes All: A Life of Sorts* (London: Robson, 2004), 236.

19. Rehfeld 1983, 24.
20. Yule 1987, 149.
21. Alan Stanbrook, "The Boys from Tiberias," *Sight and Sound* 55, no. 4 (1986): 236.
22. Yule 1987, 27.
23. Ibid., 98.
24. Stanbrook 1986, 234.
25. Yule 1987, 99.
26. Ibid., 142.
27. According to Michael Winner, "This produced a furore in the British press including some highly anti-Semitic observations. Menahem and Yoram were painted as vulgar aliens contaminating the purity of British cinema" (242–243). See Winner 2004.
28. Yule 1987, 143.
29. Ibid., 99.
30. Ibid., 121.
31. Rehfeld 1983, 22.
32. Talbot 2006, 75.
33. Ebert 1987, 16.
34. Ibid., 21.
35. Ibid., 179.
36. Ibid., 182.
37. Yule 1987, 78.
38. Ibid., 63–64.
39. Ibid.
40. Stanbrook 1986, 234.
41. Yule 1987, 63–64.
42. Ibid., 209, 216.
43. Ibid., 65 (British spelling in original).
44. Ibid., 64, 66.
45. Sykes, 1986.
46. Yule 1987, 72.
47. Ibid., 128.
48. Michael Winner, a British Jew, later spoke rather harshly about his experiences filming in Israel. Although Israeli crews had a reputation of diligence, Winner "found them rather lazy" and criticized his crew for taking Friday afternoons off to prepare for Shabbat. See Winner 2004, 254.
49. See Helena Vanhala, *The Depiction of Terrorists in Blockbuster Hollywood Films, 1980–2001: An Analytical Study* (Jefferson, NC: McFarland, 2011), 156–168; and Ella Shohat, *Israeli Cinema: East/West and the Politics of Representation* (1989; rev. ed., London: I. B. Tauris, 2010), 95–96.
50. The next major version was the UK-US coproduction *Entebbe* (José Padilha 2018). Since Idi Amin was involved, the incident also figures in *The Last King of Scotland* (2006).
51. Tony Shaw, *Cinematic Terror: A Global History of Terrorism on Film* (New York: Bloomsbury, 2015), 129.
52. Ibid., 137.
53. Ibid.
54. Rachel S. Harris, "No Heroes in a Cycle of Violence: Collaborators, Perpetrators, and the Never Ending Terror of the Arab–Israeli Conflict," in *Terrorism and Literature,* ed. Peter C. Herman (Cambridge: Cambridge University Press, 2018), 320–339.

55. Jack G. Shaheen, *Reel Bad Arabs: How Hollywood Vilifies a People*, rev. ed. (Northampton, MA: Olive Branch, 2009), 173–175. Cannon's output merits special dubious attention in Shaheen's volume, so much so that he includes a special appendix listing Cannon (Golan-Globus) Films.

56. Shohat 2010, 98.

57. See Box Office Mojo website, IMDbPro, accessed July 11, 2020, http://www.boxoffice mojo.com.

10

"A CHANCE TO HEAR SOME HEBREW"

American Jewish Film Festivals and the Transnational Flow of Israeli Film

Josh Beaty

IN 1980, SAN FRANCISCO HOSTED THE FIRST JEWISH film festival in the
world. Forty years later, over one hundred Jewish film festivals exist in
North America alone, with more around the globe. In that time, Israeli
cinema blossomed as well, transforming in the last decade into one of the
world's most acclaimed national cinemas.[1] Israeli films have increasingly
gained theatrical distribution in the United States, but foreign films in the
American market are confined to a limited release of a few hundred urban
art-house screens. Jewish film festivals, on the other hand, attract thousands
of people every year—and not just in major city centers; even Tuscaloosa,
Alabama, has an annual Jewish film festival. For a significant percentage
of the American audience for Israeli film, the viewer's first encounter with
Israeli cinema is at a Jewish festival. For many of these viewers, the first
encounter becomes an annual reunion, with the audience looking to the
festival to gather Israel's most noteworthy films from the year.

Who determines what films are noteworthy? Beyond the Israeli films
bought by American distributors, where the definition of *noteworthy* is
based on a film's commercial prospects, how are certain Israeli films brought
before certain festival audiences?[2] Once the match is made between festival
and film, in what ways do audiences connect with the film? To answer these
questions, I attended a three-day conference among Jewish festival programmers about upcoming Israeli films and the challenges faced by local festivals

at the Jerusalem Film Festival. I interviewed the programmers of many of the leading Jewish film festivals in the world, from Palm Beach to Stockholm, as well as Israeli producers, distributors, exhibitors, and educators. As part of a larger project on Jewish film, I attended JFilm: The Pittsburgh Jewish Film Forum (then known primarily as the Pittsburgh Jewish-Israeli Film Festival) from 2009 to 2011. I adopted the approach of a self-reflexive member of the community rather than the pretense of an objective observer. In this position, I observed and made audio recordings at screenings, festival events, and some planning meetings. I took note in Pittsburgh of the types of people that attended the festival and how they socialized in the lobby, the theater, and at special events like post-screening parties. I also analyzed marketing and publicity material. Finally, and most central to this chapter, I conducted oral history interviews with audience members and festival employees. Some narrators were skeptical of my research and in particular the process of setting apart Jewish audiences from other audiences. "Isn't it a bit . . . segregationist . . . to talk about the Jewish audience as somehow different from other audiences?"[3] This young woman later explained that such examination recalls past discrimination, including, most dramatically, the Holocaust. Such a tension between representation and discrimination complicates both the festival (its perception and purpose) and my own project. These interactions made me aware of my sometimes-problematic presence to members of a culture of which I consider myself a part.

I confined my research primarily to three festivals, from 2009 to 2011, because these years directly precede a transformation in how Jewish American audiences view and interpret Israeli films. During this time, American Jews overwhelmingly supported Democratic candidate Barack Obama in the 2008 presidential election,[4] while Israel elected the Likud's Benjamin Netanyahu as prime minister. The ideological differences of the leaders mirrored the burgeoning divergences of the Jewish communities.[5] Israel's political shift to the right grew more pronounced with the 2016 election of Donald Trump, and the cracks between American and Israeli Jews in 2009 have become fractures in 2019.[6] This paper takes up the decade-long divergence in its infancy so that perhaps this research can provide a useful contrast for future reception studies of Israeli films by American audiences. In addition, these years mark the festivals' first interactions with activist movements like Boycott, Divestment, and Sanctions (BDS) that will grow in awareness and prominence in the ensuing years. This initial encounter usefully draws out the implicit ideology of the festivals and the Israeli films they exhibit.

Most obviously, this period of time marks the beginning of radical changes in home viewing with the rise of subscription video on demand (SVOD): Netflix launched its streaming option in 2007,[7] split off its DVD business in 2011, and by 2012, settled on the streaming model as we know it today;[8] Amazon added Unbox, which would slowly expand into Amazon Prime Video, to its Prime service in 2006;[9] HBO launched its HBO Go app in 2010, creating the model for how cable channels would control viewers' access to their libraries outside the cable on-demand system.[10] In this time before day-and-date releases, theatrical windows were relatively distinct and distant from physical media releases and cable premieres. By looking at a film festival in the infancy of the streaming era, my research can identify the uses and gratifications of a festival experience for a viewer that home viewing was not expected to replicate.[11]

I argue that Israeli films at Jewish festivals serve as a site for the enactment and negotiation of identity and overall community cohesion. At the same time, the festivals use the films as a stage to showcase Jewish and Israeli culture and promote tolerance. My research explicates the strategies by which the festival attempts to fulfill both purposes and the ways in which the audiences understand their experiences. I begin with a look at the Jewish film festival network and how Israeli films tour the various festivals, a success at one yet unconsidered by another. I then turn to the festival itself and analyze the ways in which viewers discuss their festival experiences. I find that audiences attend Israeli films at the festival for two primary reasons: for the exposure to different cultures and as an opportunity for socialization. Finally, I explore how Jewish festivals and audiences carry the ideological weight—often unwittingly and uneasily—of exhibiting Israeli films within a larger, more heterogenous society.

The Jewish Film Festival Network

Film festivals have existed in some form for almost ninety years—from the international festivals designed as showcases for a nation's elite, which persist today with more celebrity than nationalism, to the rise of local festivals intended for a more diverse audience. Early work on film festivals focused on the relationship between them and national cinemas,[12] but film historian Julian Stringer complicates this scholarship by proposing that film festivals embody globalization's collapse of national borders and place increasing importance on the city as an organizing force.[13] SooJeong Ahn and Marijke de Valck have also examined the function of international film festivals (*international* connotes not only geographic location but also the large size of the festival, such as Sundance, Cannes, Berlin, Venice, etc.) within the global economy.[14] Ahn concentrates on the rise of the largest and most recent international festival in the Asian film market, the Pusan International Film Festival, and de Valck uses actor-network theory to examine the circulation of films through the festival circuit (particularly in the international festivals in Europe) and into theaters. Festivals perform a crucial function within the industry: a film's festival run adds value to the work, with the subsequent attention (particularly awards and critical praise) helping to sell it to distributors, exhibitors, and audiences. De Valck also highlights the connection between festival exhibition and production practices, especially the international festival's role in deal-making. Anthropologist Daniel Dayan similarly observed the interactions at an international film festival. He conducted ethnographic research on the Sundance Film Festival and revealed how different groups (journalists, distributors, audiences) negotiate different agendas through behavioral performance and festival materials.[15]

The Jewish film festival network operates in a similar but distinctive manner as this much larger festival network. Given their relatively small number of attendees and scant press attention, Jewish festivals have a very different relationship to global film industries. These festivals often act as an alternative to theatrical distribution and sometimes a supplement to an existing home viewing deal.[16] Of course, sales agents and other industry insiders do not attend cultural festivals, but the films are still being bought and sold—by other festival programmers and by the viewers themselves. As in the international circuit, Jewish festivals look to each other for programming suggestions, so one successful screening can snowball to a successful festival run. This could mean a few thousand viewers are exposed to a film that otherwise would go unseen, and even this tiny word of mouth could make a difference in distinguishing the film from others in ever-expanding streaming libraries. For example, Lin and Sol Toder enjoyed the Israeli film *Noodle* at JFilm (then the Pittsburgh Jewish-Israeli Film Festival) in 2008. They told friends about it and did their best to find a copy:

> SOL: It was funny, it was dramatic, it was well-acted, just one of those great
> films. I was talking to a friend not long ago who rarely goes to the
> movies . . . and I talked to a film buff, I told Tony, I don't know whatever
> happened, but he said he's going to try to get it somehow. At first, it was
> hard to get. We got something from Rosa, saying—

LIN: She found it somewhere, but I don't know. We haven't tried to get it on Netflix.

SOL: We tried at first, and Netflix didn't have it. And I think I called Blockbusters, and they didn't have it. But this was not long after we saw it. We should try again. I would like to buy it and send it to our kids, at least.[17]

For some viewers, the festival serves as a gatekeeper, and the credibility of the festival attaches to the perception of the film, both in forming audience expectations and mediating the film experience. Della attends the festival with her husband with the assurance that the film has passed an approval process: "It seems like a very good opportunity because people have worked to make selections of the best, so I think we're going to be seeing high-quality stuff."[18] The festival partly gains this trust from the community through time but also generally through the cultural capital of the film festival as an institution (not unlike a museum, perhaps).

In an interview with Katriel Schory, the former executive director of the Israel Film Fund, which provides the public financing necessary to the production of most Israeli feature films, I asked if Jewish film festivals serve as an alternative to theatrical distribution for many Israeli films and add value to the films simply by putting them in front of viewers. Schory responded, "I'd say [as late as 2003] what you say is right because the Israeli cinema, Israeli films, found it difficult to get commercial release, exposure, and all of that. But with the success of Israeli films in general festivals, in the leading festivals of the world—this situation has changed really in a dramatic way. And sales agents and people from all over America, they are looking now for Israeli Films . . . it's less, less crucial for Israeli films to take part in a Jewish festival as a launching [pad]."[19]

Documentary distributor Ruth Diskin, on the other hand, still sees Jewish film festivals as an essential part of her business: "I see the Jewish market [as] the natural market for our films—not for all of them; again, there will be films that will not be shown or will not be selected, but I would say that eighty percent of the films in our catalogue are found this way or other relevant [markets]. For me, it's an important market."[20]

Every year, the major Jewish film festival programmers and artistic directors make their pilgrimage to Jerusalem for its international film festival. The Jerusalem Film Festival does not attract international premieres like Cannes, Venice, or Berlin, but it serves as an essential space to exhibit Israeli film to international distributors and programmers. "For feature narrative films, we have two main platforms in Israel: one at the Jerusalem Film Festival, and one at the Haifa Film Festival," Schory told Cineuropa. "Many of the sales agents make it a point to come there."[21] Jewish festival personnel attend in order to determine what films, primarily Israeli, would be of interest to their local audiences. Decisions to book the film for the local Jewish festival are usually not made until later; almost all festivals rely on a committee, at least to some extent, so for available films of interest, the programmer will later request screening copies from the distributor. Jerusalem provides an important opportunity to view Israeli films with an audience, to discover buzzed-about films they might not otherwise consider, and to visit with Israeli distributors and filmmakers.

Over three days, festival personnel gathered at the Jerusalem Film Festival for a Jewish Film Presenters Conference. The meetings took place around a conference-room table a couple of blocks from the Jerusalem Cinematheque, the site of the festival. "There are all these efforts to bring us all together," said conference organizer Isaac Zablocki, the director of Film Programs at the Israel Film Center (NYC), "and this is an effort to bring us all together, on some level, but, as somebody mentioned to me, also keeping our individuality is crucial."[22] Karen Davis, the longtime director of the Palm Beach Jewish Film Festival, went further about the need for individual festival identities: "I do agree that there are different community needs. We do the Palm Beach Jewish Film Festival, down in Miami there's a Jewish film festival, out in Daytona . . . there's a Jewish film festival. Yes, some films do overlap, just as I'm sure we've shown the same two or three large features, but there is a lot of individual difference."[23] Davis then shared a story with her colleagues about a Jewish Community Center (JCC) asking for programming suggestions. "I really find it despicable that people like to take those kinds of shortcuts. You own your own program, and if you own your own program, you better work for your own program."[24]

Pittsburgh's executive director, Kathryn Spitz Cohan, initially learned the job by looking at other festivals, but she began to notice the differences in festivals and the communities they serve: "You realize over time what festivals are going to show films that are more in line [with yours]. I think that Pittsburgh, we're a smaller large festival—you know we're not a large city but we're not a small three-day film festival—we're a large film festival but we take a lot of chances."[25] The North American festivals with the strongest reputations, as both tastemakers and financial successes, can be found in cities with large Jewish communities. San Francisco is unparalleled as both the oldest and most admired among festivals. Boston, Toronto, New York, and Washington, DC, and have arguably accumulated capital in the Jewish Film Presenter Network, evidenced by their abilities to secure regional or even North American premieres of certain Israeli films. Next, the "smaller large" festivals identified by Cohan would include Pittsburgh and also Atlanta, Palm Beach, and San Diego, among others. Like San Francisco and Boston, these festivals can run for as long as two weeks, can sustain year-round programs and can book some films before commercial release. However, their slightly lower profile makes them less desirable for premieres, so they are not often the first or even second stop for an in-demand film. The smaller the festival, the longer it might have to wait to rent a film from a distributor. For example, Israel's 2010 Academy Award–nominee for Best Foreign Language Film, *Ajami*, screened at both New York and Atlanta festivals in January 2010, about six months after its acclaimed premiere at Cannes but two months before its limited theatrical release. Spring festivals, like Seattle and Houston, coordinated events around the film's March release; Pittsburgh screened the film at a hookah bar as part of its young adult program. The film played in the summer at the smaller Rochester film festival, and the three-day Tuscaloosa Jewish Film Festival (mentioned at the beginning of this chapter) screened *Ajami* in March 2011, almost two years after the Cannes screening and a full year after its Oscar nomination, theatrical release, and run of most Jewish festivals.

The Jewish Film Festival Audience

Since 1993, JFilm has taken place every spring between the Jewish holidays of Purim and Passover. The festival screens about twenty films over two weeks, with screenings nearly every day (except Shabbat, i.e., Friday night and during the day on Saturday). Although locations vary across the city and surrounding suburbs, a multiplex theater in the city's South Side hosts the majority of the film program. A Jewish film festival stands apart from other cultural film festivals in three ways. First, Jewish festivals are older and more pervasive than most other festivals. Also, in part, a social imperative lies within the mission of the Jewish festivals that others may lack (despite the importance placed on multiculturalism by every festival)—namely, the prevention of forgetting of the Holocaust and any further Jewish persecution. Finally, another factor that must be considered is the middle- and upper-class position of many Jews, which both coincides with the target audience of film festivals and allows for a large foundation of financial support.[26] Most Jewish film festivals exist as programs within Jewish organizations, often JCCs, but they are rarely independent of community funding, requiring grants from the Israeli government and Jewish Federations, as well as private donations (for example, the United Jewish Federation, a philanthropic fundraising organization).

Film festivals do not attract mass audiences. International festivals generally cater to members of the film industry and press, while cultural film festivals draw cinephiles and those who identify with or are curious about the culture. In other words, film festivals share the same elite audience (typically more affluent and more highly educated) with the foreign and independent films that constitute the "art-house cinema."[27] The Jewish film festival audience perhaps experiences the problem of diversity even more intensely than other festivals. However, the demographic of most concern to Jewish film festivals is young adults. Judaism faces this problem on a broad level as young people who have just graduated from high school and college threaten to catalyze the religion's diffusion into secular society. The median age of adults who consider themselves Jewish by religion is substantially higher than the median age of adults in the general population, partly due to the fewer number of young adults identifying themselves as Jewish by religion. Among all Jews, 22 percent do not identify as Jewish by religion, but the percentage climbs to nearly one-third (32 percent) of adults under thirty.[28] This trend reflects larger trends in American religious affiliation, but Jewish communities are particularly sensitive to issues of assimilation, like geographic mobility and interfaith marriage. Jewish film festivals, under the guidance of their parent organizations and the stipulations of their grants, aim to increase their young adult attendance in order to ensure the sustainability of both Judaism and the festival itself.

Of course, viewer reactions vary by demographics, but audience expectations also influence the reception of a film. Exhibition context not only affects the viewer's experience of the film; the context also functions as an organizing mechanism of expectation. Some contemporary Israeli films might disappoint or frustrate an audience for whom a Jewish film festival, as Diskin put it, consists of Holocaust films, klezmer, and Yiddish. People can find a variety of movies in theaters, and with narrowcasting cable channels and expanding streaming options, home viewing easily accommodates even the most esoteric tastes. Entertainment options abound, so why attend a Jewish film festival? In my interviews with festival participants, I found that people come to the festival for two main reasons—as an encounter with different cultures and as a chance to connect with other members of the community.

Audiences attend the festival in order to engage with new and perhaps unfamiliar cultures. To describe why he liked the film *Gift to Stalin*, set mostly in 1940s Kazakhstan but with flash-forwards to contemporary Israel, an older viewer named Wilbur said, "It brought me to see part of the world I had never seen before. I don't think many people here knew about that era."[29] For other viewers, the films represent a chance to relate to a part of their identities not often represented on screen. Sisters-in-law Mariana and Dana attended an Israeli documentary about Russian immigrants living in a Jerusalem hotel because, as Russian Americans themselves, they could relate to numerous aspects of the story. "It warms your heart, because it was something you grew up with, so it was more enjoyable watching it," Dana explained. "The dialogues, how they were behaving with each other—it was taking you back in time. And you can see similarities with your family and how you experienced immigration."[30] Mariana enjoyed the film as a preview of her near future ("I'm actually going to spend the summer in Israel, this summer") as well as a glimpse into the hidden histories of friends' lives ("and we also have family friends who are Russian Jews who emigrated to Israel back in the early nineties. It was just interesting seeing that we could relate to it in a way").[31] Abby, a young woman who attended a screening of a different Israeli documentary, explained that the film acted as a reminder of a past experience as well as of the world beyond the United States: "I went to Israel many years ago, so a chance to hear some Hebrew and get that cultural perspective is kind of nice."[32]

For Lucille, seeing Israeli films performs the additional task of "support[ing] the Israeli film industry to whatever extent that does it."[33] Richard also believes that the films serve as edification for the audience and that attendance is necessary for the sustainability not only of the culture but of the films themselves. "People are watching because if they don't watch, [the films are] not going to get made anymore."[34] Foreign films often face dim commercial prospects in the United States, with subtitles partly the barrier to entry for some audiences, but for an older Jewish festival audience, there are advantages. Paula works as a librarian for a suburban temple; she orders films to check out to, and sometimes screen for, congregants. "Well, originally, some people said I shouldn't show movies with subtitles, but actually, because a lot of people are older and have hearing problems, subtitles are really good! So, it's not a problem."[35] When the foreign language is Hebrew, a language often studied but rarely spoken among American Jews, the act of seeing a film with a Jewish audience can be a kind of performance: "I thought it was really cool because the people who could speak Hebrew in the audience would laugh at the jokes, and then the normal people who could read would laugh, and then the really slow readers would laugh seconds later."[36]

The opportunity to socialize has an important appeal for many audience members, an attraction perhaps taken for granted by young adults but more valued for its rarity by older attendees. Elderly Lucille, in explaining her lack of exposure to Israeli films, admitted, "I don't go to the movies all that often." When I pointed out that she is attending the festival, she laughed, "Well, I have dear friends who drove."[37] For the elderly, the festival serves as an organizing pretext for friends to make social plans because of the festival's status as a unique community experience. The festival is different from other theatrical engagements because "it's kinda special," Lucille said. "It's scheduled for the community at a given time, at a given place, and I think it's sort of a community event."[38] Audience members who regularly go to the movies, like Israeli film fans Della and Richard, see the festival as an extension of routine socialization at the neighborhood theater. "Well, we see a lot of people we know," Richard explained, "but we also see a lot of people in Squirrel Hill [a heavily Jewish Pittsburgh neighborhood] that we know, so it's simply one more get-together."[39] Paula describes festival screenings in South Hills, a southern suburb of Pittsburgh with a similarly large Jewish population, almost as social gatherings under the pretext of seeing a film: "Oh, it's a social thing. It's like going to an event as opposed to going to a movie. There's just a lot of chitchat, and everybody knows everybody from the two synagogues that are in South Hills. Aside from the fact that usually the movies are good."[40]

The Jewish Film Festival and Its Discontents

For the local attendee of the Jewish film festival, the trust that develops between programmer and audience helps to distinguish the festival event from the myriad ways to view an Israeli film; for the festival network, this curation distinguishes one festival from another, creating festival identities correlated but not restricted to market size. Israeli distributor Diskin views the audience's political attitudes—and the festival's willingness to challenge them—as part of these identities: "There are markets that wouldn't touch political films. I would say that some of the Jewish film festivals would avoid touching political films, and there is still a group—not so little, not so few—of Jewish film festivals that for them a Jewish film festival is a festival about Holocaust films and Jewish themes like klezmer and Yiddish and, you know, I wouldn't say that Boston, Washington, San Francisco, Toronto Jewish are so common. [They] are the unique kind of festivals—not only that [they] are not afraid of controversial films but that [they] are looking for them."[41]

Unsurprisingly, Diskin includes cosmopolitan Jewish communities in Boston, Washington, Toronto, and San Francisco as being more open-minded than other places about controversial content and experimental style. In Diskin's characterization, these Jewish communities tend to be younger and more open to criticism of Israel.

The more adventurous festivals share another important characteristic—a difference in organizational structure that might influence programming decisions and the audience the festival solicits. Among the Boston, Washington, San Francisco, and Toronto festivals, every one but Washington is independent, unaffiliated with a JCC or other Jewish organization. Affiliated festivals make up the vast majority of Jewish film festivals in North America, with involvement and funding varying by festival. Some festivals depend greatly on their affiliation to finance the festival, while others derive only a small amount of funding.[42] Not all affiliated festivals are conservative in content or mainstream in taste—Davis's Palm Beach festival was known for taking risks, and, as mentioned earlier, the Israel Film Center is part of the Manhattan JCC—but the independent festivals have an advantage of fewer stakeholders in the film selection process. All festival programmers claim to make decisions independent of their affiliated organization, and they explain how any consideration of outside opinion is of their audiences' tastes, what they will attend and enjoy. However, the audiences of independent festivals could be very different from the audiences of affiliated festivals, and if so, programming decisions would diverge as well. If affiliated festivals draw a majority of their attendance from members of the Jewish organization and larger Jewish community, then programmers might choose to eschew controversy and select films more favorable to Israel. Cohan noted: "I don't think there's anything we shy away from, although—again, if it's a film that's politically based—there's another film that we did not choose, we chose [title omitted] over this other film called

[title omitted], and [title omitted], to me, just wasn't as, was basically showing one side of the story. . . . If we're going to show a film that pisses people
off, it's got to piss off everybody. It [has to try] to get at something deeper
than what was on the surface."[43]

For example, after a yearlong run of international festivals, including
the Berlinale, Israeli film *Phobidilia* premiered in Los Angeles, the start of
a tour of North American Jewish film festivals. The most popular Israeli
films—but not so popular as to secure a theatrical distribution deal—will
circulate among dozens of Jewish festivals. However, *Phobidilia* centers on
an agoraphobic who shelters himself from the world and uses technology to
mediate all of his experiences, including sex. The film style, comparable to
a Danny Boyle film, employs current mainstream conventions and would
hardly be alienating to most audiences, but the aesthetic, like the content,
pushes boundaries for most Jewish festivals. Cohan is proud that the programming risk distinguishes the Pittsburgh festival from others. "Only Atlanta showed *Phobidilia* besides Pittsburgh," Cohan said. "And then I got
the JCC in Manhattan to show it. That's it."[44]

When JFilm screened *Phobidilia*, the organization also hosted the filmmakers, Doron and Yoav Paz, and the pair made stops at three universities
in Pittsburgh. At the University of Pittsburgh, the brothers participated in
a question and answer session with faculty and students. Questions mostly
concerned the filmmaking process and navigating the film industry. The
film also played at Carnegie Mellon University, which is near the historically
Jewish neighborhood of Squirrel Hill. According to Cohan, this location
worked against the film's reception, as some older members of the community turned out for a Jewish film festival event and found the edgy film
"way too much for [them]," Cohan said as she sifted through a stack of small
papers and comment cards. However, she noted, "One person wrote me,
'Excellent. I thank you, the committee, for having the depth and insight and
courage to choose such an avant-garde and meaningful film.' So you know
you have to save things like that."[45] The film screened again in an auditorium in the student union of Point Park University, located in downtown
Pittsburgh. In the lobby outside the auditorium, the filmmakers mingled
with the audience, discussing cameras with a Point Park film professor and
comic book movies with students. "The young audience at Point Park," Cohan said in a later interview, "when the filmmakers were there, loved it."[46]

After the *Phobidilia* screening at Point Park, the filmmakers stood at the
front of the auditorium before taking questions and gave a few preliminary

remarks. The brothers first wanted to distinguish the film from other Israeli films. Doron started with the example of the protagonist's apartment, which was designed to look like an apartment anywhere in the world, "not like a typical Israeli television [setting]. This story can happen in San Francisco, in Tokyo, in Paris. We wanted it to be very global. Which is quite rare in the Israeli cinema because, if you know, or you don't know, a lot of Israeli movies are very political or [take on] social issues. It's not like that. We wanted to get away from that as much as possible." Their follow-up, the 2015 horror film *JeruZalem*, goes even further in soliciting an international audience, with two American lead characters and mostly English-language dialogue. "There's been enough on the Holocaust, there's been enough on Israelis vs. Palestinians—there were so many movies made on these topics before," Yoav said in an interview to promote the new movie. "The new generation [of Israeli filmmakers] are looking for something new."[47]

Some Israeli filmmakers may wish to move beyond well-trod historical and political subjects, but their films, along with Jewish film festivals, serve as contested sites of meaning simply by existing. For a festival, that existence rests within the context of the local community and the resources available to serve that community. Programmers book a film not only according to their own taste or to their perception of their community's taste but also according to the message(s) they feel obligated to send to the community and/or a larger public. They, to varying degrees, must heed the obligations entailed by the community organizations that provide the resources for a festival. For example, at a JFilm committee meeting of young adults to create an event for other young adults, members wondered whether non-Jews would be allowed to attend. On this point, Cohan explained to the committee:

> I just had to write a grant for the UJF [United Jewish Federation] . . . and they ask you . . . what are the reasons they should give you money. One of the things is engaging young Jews, which I'm doing, but another thing that they say is interfaith relations, showing people in Pittsburgh, in our community. . . . The images that they see in the media of Jews or what's going on in Israel is not always good, so part of what we do, by programming the Israeli films especially. . . it's showing another side, a cultural side of Israel and of Judaism. So that's what it's all about. It's not at all closed, it's completely open to the public.[48]

For Cohan, such a seemingly benign goal aligns with the festival's mission and with the very origin of Jewish film festivals, which, like so many Jewish philanthropic organizations, have sought to promote tolerance through the display of Jewish culture.

However, pro-Palestinian activists argue that some films "showing . . . a cultural side of Israel" can be mobilized as thinly veiled propaganda in order to portray Israel in a positive light. In this view, the rise of Israeli film on the international stage in the last fifteen years coincides with an Israeli government marketing campaign to influence public opinion around the world. In the fall of 2006, the Foreign Ministry conducted a seminar about the launch of Brand Israel and issued a press release stating that "the goal is to improve Israel's image among the different audiences" that might be more likely to travel to Israel, invest in Israeli companies, and buy Israeli products. "Moreover," the press release continues, "strengthening Israel's positive image could improve Israel's political [position]."[49] The Boycott, Divestment, and Sanctions (BDS) movement counters such an objective with a cultural boycott: the Palestinian Campaign for the Academic and Cultural Boycott of Israel (PACBI), which "urges international cultural workers and cultural organizations, including unions and associations, to boycott and/or work towards the cancellation of events, activities, agreements, or projects involving Israel, its lobby groups or its cultural institutions. International venues and festivals are asked to reject funding and any form of sponsorship from the Israeli government."[50]

Activists quickly organized against Brand Israel's attempts to exhibit Israeli culture at film festivals. Toronto's Israeli consulate planned to pilot Brand Israel initiatives, starting with a "significant presence" at the 2009 Toronto International Film Festival.[51] When the festival announced a new annual "City-to-City" program that would begin with Tel Aviv, a group of writers, filmmakers, and activists (including Naomi Klein, Jane Fonda, Noam Chomsky, and Danny Glover) signed a letter of protest, "The Toronto Declaration—No Celebration of Occupation." The letter noted the lack of Palestinian filmmakers among the ten films selected and sought to reframe Israel as an occupying force rather than diverse liberal democracy. *Phobidilia* was part of the Tel Aviv program, though neither *Phobidilia* nor the filmmakers were mentioned in the protest. The drafters of the letter attempted to make clear the target of the protest: "We do not protest the individual Israeli filmmakers included in City to City, nor do we in any way suggest that Israeli films should be unwelcome at TIFF. However, especially in the wake of this year's brutal assault on Gaza, we object to the use of such an important international festival in staging a propaganda campaign on behalf of . . . an apartheid regime."[52] This language mirrors the PACBI position, anticipating charges of antisemitism, that they only seek "boycotts of

Israeli cultural *institutions* not Israeli individuals. BDS targets complicity, not identity."[53] For BDS, complicity takes the form of films and festivals that derive even part of their funding from Israeli government institutions (like the Israeli Film Fund), as well as films or festival programs that seek to promote or normalize the Israeli state.

The Toronto Declaration was a galvanizing moment for BDS because a celebrity-supported petition generated controversy on the grand stage of a famous international festival. Jewish film festivals did not undergo similar scrutiny, despite significant funding from organizations with deep Israeli ties. The Consulate General of Israel to New England has long sponsored the Boston Jewish Film Festival—in 2007, a full-page ad in the festival program boasted of "the new wave of Israeli movies . . . winning acclaimed prizes in the most prestigious international festivals"[54]—and Combined Jewish Philanthropies used to sponsor an annual Boston-Haifa Film Connection program, with selections from the Haifa International Film Festival, in order to "[build] mutual understanding between Boston and Haifa."[55]

The Jewish Federations of North America (JFNA), formerly known as the United Jewish Federation, is one of the largest political and financial advocates for Israel. JFNA also serves as a primary source of funding for associated festivals, with even the most independent Jewish festivals receiving grants and/or sponsorships from a local federation. The financial entanglement can entail constraints on content, implicit limits revealed when festivals push boundaries too far. In the summer of 2009, the San Francisco Jewish Film Festival, the widely acknowledged *avant-garde* of the Jewish film festival network, screened the documentary *Rachel*, about the death of a pro-Palestinian activist, followed by a conversation with BDS supporter Cindy Corrie. The ensuing controversy led the San Francisco Jewish Community Federation (JCF) to pass new guidelines for its funding allocation in February 2010. The policy prohibits funding for organizations that, even in activities or partnerships, appear to undermine the legitimacy of Israel—with the policy specifically calling out BDS support. Perceived violations could result in suspended funding. In addition, "the new policy requires federation grantees to produce documentation demonstrating 'consistency with JCF's core values,' most pertinently an 'abiding commitment to . . . the strong democratic Jewish State of Israel.'"[56] In 2010, the federation is listed as a sponsor of the San Francisco festival but with none of its usual involvement in individual programs. By 2011, the federation had returned not only as sponsor but also as a co-presenter of three films and a workshop, "How to Talk about Controversial Films without Fighting."

Until 2015, Pittsburgh's JFilm (then called the Pittsburgh Jewish-Israeli Film Festival) was an extension of the Pittsburgh Federation. Six months before the Toronto Declaration, in 2009, JFilm was one of many Jewish festivals to show Alan Dershowitz's documentary *A Case for Israel*. After the film, the audience slowly trickled out of the theater, where some people at a table outside sold a DVD of the film, gave away posters, and handed out educational fliers. About a quarter of the audience remained for a mock trial of the State of Israel. "Lawyers" presented common (and perhaps straw man) arguments against Israel, from *Zionism is racism* to *invasion of Gaza as war crime*. The crowd was urged to participate too and put forward their own counterarguments, with the stated intent of giving the audience talking points in their own debates about Israel.

The Pittsburgh chapter of the Zionist Organization of America sponsored a screening of *Ahead of Time* in 2011, a documentary about journalist Ruth Gruber. "ZOA, this chapter, has had a history of trying to help support the film festival when it's possible and when it makes sense," said Stuart Pavilack, the executive director of the Pittsburgh chapter. "When it's possible is when there are dollars specifically to do that, and if it makes sense—we sponsor, in part, a movie that says something about Zionism or supporting a film that has something to do with ZOA or Israel or Zionism, something like that."[57] After looking at the list of films Cohan had booked for the festival, Pavilack decided on *Ahead of Time* partly because he had worked with Gruber to raise money for Israel. ZOA's sponsorship entailed a table outside the theater, where Pavilack distributed information about educational and fundraising events. "That kind of outreach—we're trying to support the Jewish community and efforts of other organizations."[58]

If festivals feel bound to promote Israel—or at least limit the degree of dissent to be programmed—then alternative forums might be more effective than Jewish festivals at giving these marginalized voices entrance to the public and even Jewish community discourse. Zablocki worked with the Manhattan JCC to create The Other Israel Film Festival in New York,[59] the Boston Palestine Film Festival was founded in 2007, and on April 8, 2011, as JFilm entered its final weekend of the festival, a group of University of Pittsburgh students held the inaugural three-day Pittsburgh Palestine Film Festival.

Conclusion

Despite the greater scrutiny of Israeli cultural products, the distribution and exhibition of Israeli films within the Jewish film festival network has so far been unaffected.[60] The network in North America has contracted by as much as a third: I counted over 150 Jewish film festivals in 2009, a number down to about one hundred in 2019. Smaller festivals have disappeared, but for reasons that appear more related to the state of film than the state of Israel. The Tuscaloosa Jewish Film Festival screened its last film in 2012, but its opening night buffet proved so popular that the Tuscaloosa Jewish Food Festival was born in 2014.[61] Between 2009 and 2011, streaming was first beginning to exert pressure, but the library of easily accessible Israeli film and television has expanded exponentially since the period of my research. The most established festivals have adapted in different ways to distinguish the festival experience from home viewing alternatives. Manhattan's JCC established the Israel Film Center in 2011, with the first festival in 2013, and in 2015, San Francisco similarly created a larger project, the Jewish Film Institute, of which its festival could be a part. In 2019, the Washington Jewish Film Festival merged with the Washington Jewish Music Festival to become JxJ, a "multidisciplinary arts project" that offers "original cutting edge hybrid arts programming" in "one massive three-week experience."[62] Israel remains a vital part of these festival expansions, as the Boston Jewish Film Festival spun off the Boston Israeli Film Festival in early 2019. The older, large-market festivals were already inextricable fixtures within the community, but their enhanced event status further differentiates them from the home-viewing competition.

The Pittsburgh festival has perhaps transformed more than any other in the last ten years. In 2011, the old Pittsburgh Jewish-Israeli Film Festival unveiled its new name—JFilm: The Pittsburgh Film Forum. Cohan denied that the name change was intended to remove the word *Israeli*, but JFilm did seek to broaden its appeal: "Jewish culture is a beautiful thing. We're not trying to take a stand between Israelis and Palestinians. We're not trying to solve that conflict. But if we can spread a little Jewish culture, and invite people in—that's our whole marketing plan—to appeal to the masses, not just Jews. And it really worked. People at the theater commented on it."[63]

Like other markets, Pittsburgh seemed more concerned with pivoting away from the *Festival* than the *Israeli* in the name. Cohan explained that the name change was necessitated by qualifications for local funding in which the organization needed to demonstrate year-round programming: "Not just a festival anymore. We do [year-round programs like] Teen Screen, we do Reel to Real, we do Jewcy."[64] In 2015, Cohan established an independent nonprofit, Film Pittsburgh, so that previous JFilm events—ReelAbilities and a program of short films—could become festivals themselves. JFilm, no longer an extension of Pittsburgh's Jewish Federation, was now a part of Film Pittsburgh. The mission of Film Pittsburgh resembles the tradition of Jewish festivals in its aim to strengthen "audiences' understanding of culture, tolerance, and our common humanity."[65] However, with the new festivals no longer limited to Jewish stories and themes, Film Pittsburgh aims to expand its reach within the larger Pittsburgh community. "Our broad range of programming is designed to reach people of all races, religions, ages and abilities, and emphasis is placed on collaboration with other organizations."[66] The expansion has also broadened Cohan's perspective on her work within the Jewish film festival network. "Now that we do other, non-Jewish themed festivals, I can clearly say that Israeli film distributors and others who distribute Israeli films charge more than any other distributors for their content. I don't appreciate this."[67] With these expansions of their programs, the major festivals within the network are leaning into their differentiating features. The uses and gratifications of the festival, identified by audiences in 2009 remained the reasons audiences attended in 2019.

Even as the festivals meet the same needs of the audience in new ways, Israeli film can still serve as a site for community cohesion and cultural exchange. Like Israeli film, Jewish film festivals' existence is a political act in and of itself, and both festivals and films engage in larger ideological discourses, even when striving for the apolitical. Festivals operate at a crossroads between public outreach and artistic display, with mission statements that extend beyond showing the best films; if international festivals strive only to fulfill a gatekeeping function, Jewish festivals proudly nurture the socializing and cultural exploration of their audiences. The tangle of purposes and variety of interactions among films, festivals, and viewers ripple across the festival network and the Israeli film industry and into the everyday lives of American Jews.

Notes

1. Israel earned four Academy Award nominations in five years: two films about the conflict in Lebanon (*Beaufort* and the animated documentary *Waltz with Bashir*), another

film about father-and-son Talmudic scholars (*Footnote*), and a film about the intersecting lives of Israeli Arabs and Jews (*Ajami*). In addition, *Foxtrot* was shortlisted for the 2018 Foreign Language Oscar, and the acclaimed French-Israeli *Gett: The Trial of Viviane Amsalem*, the horror-comedy *Big Bad Wolves*, and the cult comedy *Zero Motivation* all have received significant American theatrical distribution.

2. Similarly, are Israeli films necessarily Jewish films? As part of a larger project on Jewish audiences, I ask every interview subject (including all of the ones included here) how they recognized a film as Jewish. Answers varied from the explicit presence of religious ceremony to mere passing reference to Jewish characters; some people saw a thematic consistency in Jewish films (concern for justice, spiritual struggle), whereas others thought a film could be Jewish with the extratextual knowledge of the Jewish heritage of an actor or filmmaker. In my other work, I am interested in how Jewish audiences organize their experiences of a variety of texts by these shifting definitions of Jewish film. Jewish film festivals must frequently confront the question of what makes a film Jewish, but in my experience, most festivals find the answer of *It's Israeli* to be sufficient. For the purposes of this paper, festivals' conflation of Jewish and Israeli will remain an underlying assumption, but future work should interrogate this assumption more critically.

3. Elaine Bergstrom, interview by author, digital recording, Pittsburgh, PA, March 25, 2009.

4. A Pew Research Center analysis of exit polls found that 78 percent of Jewish voters supported Obama in the 2008 presidential election. See "How the Faithful Voted," Pew Religion and Public Life Project, November 10, 2008, accessed May 22, 2019, https://www .pewforum.org/2008/11/05/how-the-faithful-voted/.

5. Obama's famous 2009 Cairo speech, calling for a cessation of new settlements, may be the first example of strain between the two leaders, but their differences arguably reached the apex with Netanyahu's 2015 speech before Congress to derail Obama's Iran nuclear treaty.

6. Jonathan Weisman, "American Jews and Israeli Jews Are Headed for a Messy Breakup," *New York Times*, January 4, 2019, https://www.nytimes.com/2019/01/04/opinion /sunday/israeli-jews-american-jews-divide.html.

7. Quentin Hardy, "Netflix to Stream Live Movies for Free," *Forbes*, January 16, 2007, accessed May 24, 2019, https://www.forbes.com/2007/01/15/netflix-free-video-streaming-tech -media-cz_qh_0116netflix.html#646b7474c174.

8. William D. Cohan, "Seeing Red," *Vanity Fair*, February 22, 2012.

9. Michael L. Wayne, "Netflix, Amazon, and Branded Television Content in Subscription Video On-Demand Portals," *Media, Culture & Society* 40, no. 5 (2017): 725–741.

10. Greg Sandoval, "HBO Launches Netflix Rival," CNET, February 17, 2010, accessed May 24, 2019, https://www.cnet.com/news/hbo-launches-netflix-rival/.

11. The Jewish film festival proved resilient during Covid-19. Even as cinemas closed down, the festivals moved to specialty platforms online and actually increased attendance, suggesting that the collection and curation of the film festival experience had a significant impact on audience interest.

12. See Liz Czach, "Film Festivals, Programming, and the Building of a National Cinema," *The Moving Image* 4, no. 1 (Spring 2004): 76–88; Bill Nichols, "Discovering Form, Inferring Meaning: New Cinemas and the Film Festival Circuit," *Film Quarterly* 47, no. 3 (1994): 16–30; Jerry White, "National Belonging," *New Review of Film & Television Studies* 2, no. 2 (2004): 211–232.

13. Julian Stringer, "Global Cities and the International Film Festival Economy," in *Cinema and the City*, ed. Mark Shiel and Tony Fitzmaurice (Oxford: Blackwell, 2001), 134–144.

14. Marijke de Valck, *Film Festivals: From European Geopolitics to Global Cinephilia* (Amsterdam: Amsterdam University Press, 2006); SooJeong Ahn, "The Pusan International Film Festival 1996–2005: South Korean Cinema in Local, Regional, and Global Context," PhD diss., University of Nottingham, 2008.

15. Daniel Dayan, "Looking for Sundance: The Social Construction of a Film Festival," in *Moving Images, Culture and the Mind*, ed. Ib Bondebjerg (Luton: University of Luton Press, 2000), 43–52.

16. An increasing number of programmed films are already available on cable television or a streaming service at the time of the festival screening. In 2011, Cohan estimated that four of the twenty films were available for home viewing. The screening for documentary *Client 9*, for example, nearly sold out despite being available for streaming on Netflix (then called Netflix Instant).

17. Lin and Sol Toder, interview by author, digital recording, Pittsburgh, PA, April 25, 2011. At the time of the interview, Netflix was mostly used for disc rentals by mail rather than streaming. In late 2012, the Israel Film Center, part of the Manhattan Jewish Community Center, launched a streaming service of Israeli films. As of early 2019, *Noodle* can be streamed for $4.

18. Della, interview by author, digital recording, Pittsburgh, PA, March 22, 2009. Due to a request for anonymity, this attendee's name has been changed.

19. Katriel Schory, interview by author, digital recording, Jerusalem, Israel, July 13, 2008. Several factors—the introduction of cable television in the late 1980s, the rapid increase in Israeli film schools, the 1999 Cinema Law, the growing availability of transnational financing, and innovations in digital filmmaking—certainly deserve above-the-title billing in the rise of Israeli cinema. Jewish film festivals should be in the credits, but maybe somewhere between the grip and catering.

20. Ruth Diskin, interview by author, digital recording, Jerusalem, Israel, July 2, 2008.

21. Laura Nanchino, "Katriel Schory, Executive Director—Israel Film Fund," *Cineuropa*, June 12, 2014, accessed May 24, 2019, http://cineuropa.org/it.aspx?t=interview&did=258709.

22. Isaac Zablocki, Jewish Film Presenter Network Conference, digital recording, Jerusalem, Israel, July 14, 2008.

23. Karen Davis, Jewish Film Presenter Network Conference, digital recording, Jerusalem, Israel, July 14, 2008.

24. Ibid.

25. Kathryn Spitz Cohan, interview by author, digital recording, Pittsburgh, PA, April 27, 2011.

26. According to a Pew Research Center survey, 25 percent of Jewish households earn an annual income of over $150,000 compared to 8 percent of the population overall. See Luis Lugo, "A Portrait of Jewish Americans: Findings from a Pew Research Center Survey of U.S. Jews," Pew Religion and Public Life Project, October 1, 2013, accessed May 24, 2019, https://www.bjpa.org/jsqb/search-results/survey/144.

27. For a detailed study of the art-house theaters and audience, see Barbara Wilinsky, *Sure Seaters: The Emergence of Art House Cinema* (Minneapolis: Minnesota University Press, 2001).

28. Lugo 2013.

29. Wilbur A. Steger, interview by author, digital recording, Pittsburgh, PA, March 22, 2009.

30. Mariana and Dana Sofman, interview by author, digital recording, Pittsburgh, PA, April 18, 2011.

31. Ibid.

32. Abby Morrison, interview by author, digital recording, Pittsburgh, PA, March 25, 2009.

33. Lucille Katz, interview by author, digital recording, Pittsburgh, PA, March 25, 2009.

34. Richard, interview by author, digital recording, Pittsburgh, PA, March 22, 2009. Due to a request for anonymity, this attendee's name has been changed.

35. Paula Altschul, interview by author, digital recording, Pittsburgh, PA, March 30, 2011.

36. Jerry and Elizabeth Bortman, interview by author, digital recording, Pittsburgh, PA, March 22, 2009.

37. Lucille Katz, interview by author, digital recording, Pittsburgh, PA, March 25, 2009.

38. Ibid.

39. Richard and Della, interview by author, digital recording, Pittsburgh, PA, March 22, 2009. Due to a request for anonymity, this couple's names have been changed.

40. Paula Altschul, interview by author, digital recording, Pittsburgh, PA, March 30, 2011.

41. Ruth Diskin, interview by author, digital recording, Jerusalem, Israel, July 2, 2008.

42. JFilm, before it became part of the independent Film Pittsburgh, falls into the latter category.

43. Kathryn Spitz Cohan, interview by author, digital recording, Pittsburgh, PA, April 27, 2011. Cohan requested that I remove specific titles from the transcript of the interview.

44. Kathryn Spitz Cohan, interview by author, digital recording, Pittsburgh, PA, March 27, 2011.

45. Kathryn Spitz Cohan, interview by author, digital recording, Pittsburgh, PA, April 27, 2011.

46. Ibid.

47. David S. Smith, "Interview with the Paz Brothers on *JeruZalem*," *Horror Cult Films*, September 2, 2015, accessed May 24, 2016, http://horrorcultfilms.co.uk/2015/09/interview-with-the-paz-brothers-on-jeruzalem.

48. Kathryn Sptiz Cohan, Young Adult Advisory Committee meeting, January 25, 2009. I served as a member of this committee and attended meetings between October 2008 and February 2009. All information about this committee comes from observations and recordings made at these meetings. Before recording these meetings, I received permission from all present individuals. Regarding all observations and recordings, I also had the full cooperation of the executive director of JFilm, Kathryn Spitz Cohan.

49. Israel Ministry of Foreign Affairs, "International Brand Israel seminar to be launched by the Foreign Ministry," press release, October 24, 2006, accessed May 24, 2019, https://mfa.gov.il/mfa/pressroom/2006/pages/international%20brand%20israel%20seminar%20to%20be%20launched%20this%20week%20by%20the%20foreign%20ministry%2024-oct-2006.aspx.

50. Palestinian Campaign for the Academic and Cultural Boycott of Israel, "Cultural Boycott Guidelines—A Summary," accessed May 22, 2019, https://bdsmovement.net/cultural-boycott#guidelines.

51. "Toronto Declaration: No Celebration of Occupation," TIFF Open Letter, September 2, 2009, accessed May 24, 2019, http://torontodeclaration.blogspot.co.il/2009/09/toronto-declaration-no-celebration-of.html.

52. Ibid.

53. Palestinian Campaign 2019.

54. Boston Jewish Film Festival, *Program Book: Essays about Festival Films*, November 1–11, 2007, 77.

55. Ibid., 78.

56. Dan Pine, "S.F. Federation: We Won't Fund Anti-Israel Programming," *The Jewish News of Northern California*, February 26, 2010, accessed May 24, 2019, https://www.jweekly.com/2010/02/26/s-f-federation-we-wont-fund-anti-israel-programming.

57. Stuart V. Pavilack, interview by author, digital recording, Pittsburgh, PA, April 18, 2011.

58. Ibid.

59. The Other Israel Film Festival is not without controversy, as a pair of filmmakers pulled their film in response to the escalating Israeli-Arab conflict. The festival's affiliation with the JCC might also suggest that the festival is a mechanism to neutralize criticism by providing a controlled space of dissent. See Paula Bernstein, "Palestinian Film 'Degrade' Withdraws from Other Israel Film Festival," *IndieWire*, November 2, 2015, accessed May 24, 2019, http://www.indiewire.com/article/palestinian-film-degrade-withdraws-from-other-israel-film-festival-20151102.

60. The Boston, Washington, and Pittsburgh festivals, for example, devoted a consistent annual percentage of their programs to Israeli films from 2009 to 2019.

61. "2014 Jewish Food Festival March 9th!," The University of Alabama Hillel, accessed May 25, 2019, http://hillel.ua.edu/2014/02/2014-jewish-food-festival-march-9th/.

62. JxJ website, accessed May 25, 2019, https://www.jxjdc.org/.

63. Kathryn Spitz Cohan, interview by author, digital recording, Pittsburgh, PA, April 27, 2011.

64. Each program targets a different demographic: Teen Screen is an educational program for high school students and teachers; Reel to Real also works with teenagers but instead brings them to senior living facilities for a film screening and intergenerational discussion; and the Jewcy film series was an extension of the Young Adult Advisory Committee, a screening and mixer for adults aged eighteen to thirty.

65. Film Pittsburgh website, "About: Mission," accessed May 25, 2019, https://filmpittsburgh.org/pages/about.

66. Ibid.

67. Kathryn Spitz Cohan, interview by author, email, May 14, 2019.

11

PERPETUATING VICTIMHOOD AS A JEWISH IDENTITY?

The Case of Popular Israeli Cinema Today

Yaron Peleg

UNTIL THE EARLY 1990S, ISRAELI CINEMA FUNCTIONED AS a small and limited national cinema that was not especially popular even at home. But political and economic changes in the 1990s opened up the country's cinema to various cultural and commercial influences that enriched and improved it. As Israeli films became better, they also began to be distributed more widely abroad, taking advantage of a developing global economy and culture and innovations in film distribution that benefited other minor cinemas as well. If the number of nominations for Best Foreign Film at the Oscars is any indication, Israeli cinema today is one of the most popular minor cinemas in the world. With ten nominations to date, though no wins, it comes last among the top ten contenders, far behind cinematic powerhouses like France, Italy, Spain, and Japan but on par with the respectable cinemas of Sweden, Denmark, and Germany. Six out of Israel's ten nominations are films about the Arab-Israeli conflict, underscoring the peculiar fact that the protracted conflict with its Arab neighbors accounts for some of Israel's best artistic exports.

The crossover appeal of a minor cinema film is a tricky affair, especially in a global age of porous borders and an increasingly melded world culture. It needs to be relevant to viewers at home but appeal to viewers abroad as well. Yet it cannot emphasize its crossover appeal too much and lose the artistic integrity that distinguishes it as a minor film.[1] This is where

Israel's conflict with the Arabs comes into play, not only as a major force in the country's life but as one of the most protracted and well-known political conflicts in the last century. It is not surprising, therefore, that a great number of Israeli films that relate to it remain popular abroad. But if the prestige of Israeli cinema continues to rise, the country itself is subjected to growing criticism around the world, particularly through the activism of the Boycott, Divestment, and Sanctions (BDS) movement. While Israel's traditional allies, primarily in the West, remain politically supportive of it in the main, its popularity in some of these countries is eroding, with boycotts of cultural and academic activities resulting in routine disruptions and occasional cancellations.[2] This curious paradox between the appeal of Israeli cinema and the decreasing prestige of Israel itself may be explained by the kinds of films Israelis export—films that present Israelis as victims, albeit of their own aggression.

This chapter examines several Israeli films about the Israel Defense Forces (IDF) that succeeded abroad—that is, they were selected for show at international film festivals, did well at the box office, and attracted positive reviews in the international press. My argument is that films like *Yossi & Jagger* (Eitan Fox, 2002), *Beaufort* (Joseph Cedar, 2007), *Waltz with Bashir* (Ari Folman, 2008), *Lebanon* (Shmulik Ma'oz, 2009), *Rock the Casbah* (Yariv Horowitz, 2013), and *Zero Motivation* (Talya Lavie, 2014) belong to a body of work described in Israel by a phenomenon known as *shooting and weeping*. The phrase describes the problematic relationship with militarism in Israel, which is at once lauded and condemned, at least historically. It encapsulates soldiers' expressions of guilt and remorse for culpability in the enemy's suffering, which in most cases means Palestinians. Early expressions of this confessional style appeared in some of the literary works of S. Yizhar, like his short stories, "Hirbet Khizeh" (1949) and "The Prisoner" (1948), which process the author's military experiences during the 1948 war for Israel's independence. Yizhar was not alone in evincing ambivalence toward Israel's military triumphs. It was also shared by some of his prominent peers.[3]

But it was the publication of *Siach Lochamim* (*Soldiers' Stories*) immediately after the conclusion of the 1967 war that gave rise to the phrase and popularized it. The book contained reflections of soldiers who were traumatized by some of the harsh actions they saw and participated in during the war. It made a profound impression in Israel, went through several printings, and was distributed widely abroad as well. In 2015, the legacy of the seminal book was examined by Mor Loushy in her documentary film *Censored Voices*. Loushy filmed the reactions of the old men, who as young soldiers recorded the original conversations that went into the book, as she played back these recordings to them.[4]

The meaning of the term changed some over the years. As the war for the country's independence in 1948 was long and harsh and its outcome uncertain, remorse over the fate of Palestinian civilians who were caught in it was mitigated by these circumstances. This is the fundamental moral conflict of the soldier-narrator in Yizhar's story "Hirbet Khizeh" who oversees the expulsion of Palestinian civilians from their village at the end of the 1948 war. The conflict is never resolved in the story, which reflects on the connections between the two tragedies, the Jewish and the Palestinian. But with the passage of time and the growth of Israel's might, the balance of power between the two peoples changed as well. At its most cynical, then, *shooting and weeping* also critiques a tendency among Israelis to rely "heavily on the argumentation and rhetoric of a minority struggling for its very existence."[5] As such, contemporary Israeli reality is turned into a narrative that shows how a Jewish history "steeped in suffering" supports a "'fortress mentality' vis-a-vis a largely hostile Arab world."[6]

The ability to switch between the position of conquering hero and impotent victim has informed Israel's worldview as well as the films under review in this chapter, as I argue. Such works seem to feed on Israel's self-identification as victim and reinforce a global tendency that simultaneously wishes to criticize Israel as a powerful military force responsible for the oppression of Palestinians and to see it as a country in peril that requires international support. These films rarely question the inconsistency of a self-righteous complacency that operates within a cultural framework that views the current political reality as untenable and detrimental to the country's image at one and the same time. Instead, a number of Israeli filmmakers play into the postmodern discourse of victimhood and use the trope of Jew-as-victim rather than engage more responsibly with the consequences of Israel's power.

During the 2000s, Israeli films about the IDF began to show a distinct representational shift. In past years, most films about the military considered service in it in relation to a concrete threat, even when they dealt critically with it, as in *The Troupe* (1978), *Paratroopers* (1977), *Avanti Popolo* (1986), *Time for Cherries* (1990), and *Kippur* (2000). Other films, like *Late Summer Blues* (1987), criticized the militarism of Israeli society. The twenty-first century saw a change in such direct cinematic causality and a disengagement of service in the IDF from the political background that informs it. *Yossi & Jagger*, one of the earliest films in this new trend, foregrounds a gay love story in the army, focusing on the civil rights of gay soldiers with little concern for the context of war and military service. Situated in a remote redoubt high in the mountains overlooking Lebanon in the north of Israel, the film follows the relationship between two officers, the post's commander, Yossi (Ohad Knoller), and his handsome deputy, Jagger (Yehuda Levi). Yossi embodies the apotheosis of Israeli manhood. He is a gruff and macho soldier, an exacting officer and a man of few words. His lover, Jagger, on the other hand, is playful and emotionally vulnerable. Although the two are passionately in love—the film opens with a bold picture of them rolling and kissing in the mountain snows outside the base—the secret surrounding their relationship constitutes the film's drama. While Jagger wants to broadcast their love, Yossi is reluctant to do so. As someone who internalized his society's homophobia, he is afraid to lose authority and respect if exposed. Most of the film negotiates this terrain of fear and deception until the climax at the end, when the sight of the mortally wounded Jagger finally elicits an open *I love you* from Yossie. The public kiss they share exposes their relationship and effectively outs them.

As Nir Cohen has shown, the soldiers' heroism and their touching love story legitimate homosexuality for Israeli society.[7] By embodying the masculinity of previously heroic roles, by sharing in the national sacrifice, the gay soldiers earn an honorable place in an Israeli society that valorizes service in its armed forces. But while the film presents war as attractive and homosexuals as patriotic heroes and masculine objects of desire, the film's tragedy lies in Jagger's death and Yossi's personal loss. It avoids any reference to the ongoing conflict in the Middle East; the enemy who kills Jagger remains invisible, and the progressive and problematic militarization of Israel society is left untouched.

The film's central agenda—the positive representation of homosexuality—is accentuated through heightened aestheticism. This is particularly evident in soldiers' physical beauty (both male and female) and often their semi-naked bodies, which are displayed in ways that conjure up a permissive, gay-friendly space rather than the depressing army bunker they occupy. In one scene, soldiers dance to a techno soundtrack as if they were in a Tel-Aviv nightclub. In another unlikely scene, they eat freshly prepared sushi in the bunker's mess. Finally, the bleak and barren surroundings of the ungainly stone hideout is presented in external shots as a magical winter wonderland covered by pristine snow.[8]

The popularity of *Yossi & Jagger* extended far beyond Israel, probably owing to the unusual setting of a gay love story in the military, one of the last frontiers of gay civil rights in the West then.[9] At the same time, the film was also accused of pinkwashing for cynically appealing to LGBT sensibilities as a way to divert attention from Israeli oppression of Palestinians.[10] The film's international reception was viewed through audiences' own ideas about army service (that it should be gay friendly) and about the Israeli-Palestinian conflict (that Israel denies responsibility for its oppression of Palestinians).

The dramatic absence of war in *Yossi & Jagger* recurs in *Beaufort*,[11] the first of three films known as the Lebanon Trilogy together with *Waltz with Bashir* and *Lebanon*. Beaufort is the name of a geographically commanding crusader fortress. Turned into a modern bunker by the IDF after its invasion into Lebanon in 1982, it represents Israeli military supremacy. And yet despite the clear might the mountain, the ancient fortress, and the IDF stronghold stand for, the soldiers who man the bunker deep underground are gradually shown as victims. They are prevented from retaliating against constant attacks on them in order not to undermine the army's imminent withdrawal from Lebanon. And as they languish in wait for their retreat, they also learn of doubts as to the wisdom of capturing the fort in the first place, twenty years earlier, at heavy human cost. The film's central drama is the soldier's frustration about an absurd situation in which they stand armed to their teeth but are not able to use their firepower, at a spot that should never have been taken at all.

The film focuses on the psychological cost of the soldiers' abandonment. But since the military and political context for their neglect is absent, viewers see the soldiers as hapless pawns, victims of some bureaucratic absurdity or, worse still, political machinations. At the same time, the film endears the soldiers to viewers by portraying them as a band of brothers whose friendship is forged by the tests they endure. Using disaster film conventions, *Beaufort* draws viewers close to the soldiers and then subjects them to various dangers. As the characters die, viewers become increasingly empathetic toward them, moved by their senseless deaths.

Beaufort won an impressive array of awards both at home and abroad.[12] Despite the apparent absence of political context, some critics found it in the film's subtext and admired its subtlety: "The political implications of [the] questions [*Beaufort* raises] hover in the background, haunting the action rather than dominating it," wrote A. O. Scott in the *New York Times*. "The film's distance from politics allows it to address the moment-to-moment experiences of its characters with intense, unassuming intimacy."[13] Others chose to view Cedar's soldiers as symbols of the age-old plight of the soldier-as-pawn, sympathetically viewing the young men as victims of history and society: "Cedar has created a movie of tremendous power—nerve-racking, astute, and neutral enough to apply to all soldiers, in all wars, everywhere,"[14] said *Entertainment Weekly*.

European critics were less convinced of this. "A film in which the soldiers are only shot at, and never shoot [back], cannot be the whole truth," wrote Harald Jähner in the *Berliner Zeitung*.[15] Similarly, Elmar Krekeler, of the *Berliner Morgenspost*, wrote that "at the end, the fortress is blown into dust. The boys put down their armor. They have survived. Not more. The killing continues."[16] In their view, the film shirked its political and moral responsibility by not accounting for the continued killing. The French agreed. "Finally," wrote Clément Graminiès, "the limits of Israeli cinema's ability to represent the conflict that never ends should be questioned. . . . *Beaufort* is almost touching in its inability to show the enemy [that the Israeli soldiers] fight against."[17] As with the accusations of pinkwashing in *Yossi & Jagger*, this position exhibits concern about the erasure of Israel's Arab enemies from the narrative.

Ari Folman's award-winning feature, *Waltz with Bashir*, presented this absence as psychological repression.[18] The film is an animated journey into the suppressed memories of the director-protagonist, who suffers recurrent nightmares about his involvement in the massacre that was perpetrated in the Palestinian refugee camps of Sabra and Shatila in Lebanon in 1982, during Israel's invasion into that country. The film follows the protagonist as he visits friends and comrades who served with him in Lebanon in an attempt to understand his complicity in the horrific event. His full realization of the extent of it is conveyed through jarring documentary footage from the aftermath of the bloodbath, which disrupts the aesthetic animation and ends the film abruptly. The howling women filmed on video, relatives of the slaughtered men, are a visually jolting closure that forces the audience to confront the extent of the horror.[19] The documentary clip undermines the trauma of the Israeli soldiers, which occupied center stage up to that point, and establishes a new hierarchy of suffering in which the Palestinians are unquestionably the principal—if not the only—victim.

The film was received extraordinarily well by critics and lay viewers alike. *Bashir* is "not about historical facts but the marks they leave on the soul," wrote Diedrich Diederichsen in *Die Zeit Online*.[20] "Barely grown men, young, unprepared, thrust into brutal, bloody combat," empathized another German blogger, who also saw the film as a meditation on war in general.[21] Even more probing critics, like *The Independent*'s Anthony Quinn, could not avoid the film's powerful confessional allure:

> *Waltz With Bashir* presents its audience with a serious challenge of interpreta-
> tion. Folman stresses the slippery, unreliable nature of memory, but is that ac-
> tually a way of ducking his own responsibility? I began thinking it was, and for
> a long stretch of this film one detects more sympathy for the traumatized Is-
> raeli soldiers than for the massacred civilians of the Sabra and Shatila camps.
> But then one thinks again of those ferocious slavering dogs at the beginning:
> does the image signify a confession of complicity? . . . one wonders why Fol-
> man would include such emotive pictures if they weren't somehow prompted
> by conscience.[22]

Other critics, like Dave Calhoun of *Time Out London*, detected a measure of self-indulgence in the film, a point suggested by various academic
studies of the film.[23] These critics perceived Folman's focus on his own psychological experience as deceptive, a simulation of guilt over his complicity
in the massacre that ultimately presents the solider as victim of a powerful
political-military machine.[24]

Lebanon, the last of the Lebanon Trilogy, is perhaps the best example
of the kind of victimhood dynamics described so far. Based on director
Maoz's personal experience in the 1982 Lebanon War, the entire film is set
inside a tank and follows its four crew members as they negotiate the battlefield, watching the horrors outside through the gunner's sights with growing confusion and fear. The narrative is comprised of an escalating series of
violent encounters, which are repetitious to an extent.

Shortly after the film opens, we see a peaceful lane in the middle of
a lush banana plantation. Through the tank's crosshairs, we see a pickup
truck driving up the lane toward the tank. Suspecting this is a trap, the
tankmen shoot at it from close range and blow it to pieces, sending screaming chickens into the air and literally cutting the innocent driver in half.
The soldiers watch these horrors through their gunner's viewfinder at an
extreme close-up, as if they were watching TV. Thus begins their grim journey into the battlefields of Lebanon. In another scene, which exemplifies
a different kind of terror, they are rushed to aid a Christian family, whose

house was raided by Muslim militia. As they train their gunsight on the house, they realize that an earlier explosion has peeled its exterior wall away, exposing its inside as if it was a dollhouse. The invading forces are now inside the house ready to kill its inhabitants, especially an attractive young woman, who appears to have been snatched out of bed. The gunner is ordered to shoot at the Muslim fighters, but to do so he will have to fire a shell right through the terrified woman, who is held by them. More than any other moment in *Lebanon*, this scene highlights the impossible situation the crew members are thrust into, caught in the middle of a confusing power struggle of social, political, and military forces they do not understand. The soldiers are literally imprisoned in and by the tank, which, after a certain point in the film, becomes a monstrous living creature covered in slime, oozing black oil, filled with excrement and dead bodies—a dirty, ugly, smelly beast whose physical deformity expresses the moral degradation of its inhabitants and the actions they are forced to perform.

Lebanon won the Leone d'Oro Award at the Sixty-Sixth Venice Film Festival in 2009 and was enthusiastically received around the world. The *New York Times* empathized with the director and saw the film as a kind of autobiographical exorcism. "For Mr. Maoz, now 48, the sense of responsibility for killing remains strong. . . . 'There is no escape from it,' [Mr. Maoz] said softly. In the end you were there, and your finger pulled the trigger. That there were no choices makes no difference . . . to make the film was a partial catharsis, Mr. Maoz said. But the war remains the first thing he thinks about in the morning and the last before going to sleep." [25] On the Anglophone *Rotten Tomatoes*, most critics, as well as the lay responses posted on the site, concurred.[26]

Folman and Maoz were not the first to use film as a way to process their personal experiences of war. Both Judd Ne'eman, who served as a medic in the paratroopers during the Six-Day War, the War of Attrition, and the Yom Kippur War, and Amos Gitai, who served in the reserves during the Yom Kippur War, used cinema to comment on their military experiences. But they also used it as a medium for criticizing the political establishment and its cynical use of military force. Ne'eman's *Paratroopers* (1978), for instance, and Gitai's *Kippur* (2000) came out against the growing militarism of Israeli society by showing its devastating effect on individuals.[27]

Israel's wars before 1982, including the War of Independence (1948), the Suez Crisis (1956), the Six-Day War (1967), and the Yom Kippur War (1973), were perceived by a majority of Israelis as necessary defensive wars against blatant Arab aggression. Hence, even when they came at great human and psychological cost, the sacrifices were considered worthy, both by ordinary Israelis as well as by artists, who lauded those sacrifices in their works.[28] That the Lebanon War elicited a very different kind of personal and artistic reaction is therefore significant and explains much of the trauma those films articulate.

In contrast with previous artistic works that dealt with Israel's armed conflicts, the Lebanon films appeared during a time of greater ambivalence about the sanctity of the military in Israel. Questions about the necessity of the campaign in Lebanon have opened up a space for cultural critique. As Rachel S. Harris has argued, "The central position of the army in Israeli society has been weakened from several directions. The opposition to military attacks, maneuvers, and acts of aggression led elements in society to question the position, authority, and purpose of the army."[29] The sheer number of films that were made about that campaign, their proximity in time, and their acceptance and celebration in Israel illustrated this shift. Since then, two recent films, *Rock the Casbah* (Yariv Horowitz, 2013) and *Zero Motivation* (Talya Lavie, 2014), have expanded the conversation about Israeli militarism, moving it from the contested and politically complex situation of the Lebanon War to issues of the Palestinian occupation at home (*Rock the Casbah*) and of gender discrimination in the IDF and the Israeli cult of masculinity (*Zero Motivation*). And while both films deal with these complex issues intelligently, they continue to perpetuate elements of the *shooting and weeping* narrative.

Rock the Casbah is one of only three Israeli films made about the First Intifada (1987–1991) and the first to gain international success.[30] Based, again, on the personal experience of its director, the film follows the difficult situation encountered by a small group of soldiers after they are stationed on the roof of a house and after one of their comrades gets hit and killed during the first riots in the Gaza Strip in December 1987 (the riots came to be known later as the First Intifada). Since the house belongs to a Palestinian family that had nothing to do with the attack, both parties—the Israeli soldiers and the Palestinian civilians—are presented as hostages, victims of a conflict that is bigger than both.

Made more than twenty years after the uprising, the film does not consider the significant milestone that the First Intifada represented, nor the political and historical forces that led to it and were shaped by it. Instead, it seems arrested in time and presents both Palestinians and Israelis equally as victims. Rather than comment on the tragic perpetuation of the conflict, *Rock the Casbah*, as its name suggests, focuses on the innocence of the young soldiers, who just want to have a good time, go on dates, and listen to rock music. Unfortunately, they are inconveniently stationed on a rooftop of a Palestinian house in the middle of a refugee camp and asked to do complicated things they care little about. And since neither the wider context of the conflict nor the narrower connection of the riots themselves are given, viewers are left with both groups, Israeli soldiers and Palestinian civilians, embraced in a kind of enigmatic dance of death.

In one of the most symbolic scenes in the film, we see Tomer (Yon Tumarkin), the most innocent looking and vulnerable of the young soldiers, bringing a young Palestinian suspect for questioning at IDF headquarters. No one knows what the man was arrested for and what he is accused of, including the Palestinian himself. The suspect's hands are handcuffed, and his eyes are covered, and Tomer staggers with him along the empty corridors, looking for somewhere to bring him. At one point, the two stumble into the army's mental health office, and Tomer, with the prisoner in tow, asks the surprised psychologist on duty to help him get a discharge from service in Gaza on mental health grounds. Looking at the odd pair before her, the officer tells Tomer to come back after he has delivered his charge. But when Tomer finally returns, the office is closed and the officer is gone. For a brief moment, he stares blankly at the door and returns dejectedly to his rooftop duty. Tomer may have obtained access to the Castle, but that did not make the System any less arbitrary, surreal, or alienating than it was for Franz Kafka's hero, K. The film thus presents viewers with an innocent young man victimized by obscure, all-powerful forces. Although Palestinians also fall victim to the same cruel and arbitrary forces, their violence against the young Israeli soldiers ultimately makes them part of the powers that work against the young men.

In his review of the film, *Haaretz* film critic Uri Klein commends the director for his direct engagement with the Arab-Israeli conflict. Yet the film itself, writes Klein, "avoids articulating a brave message, lacking political or ideological context and adds nothing to the reality it describes."[31] Moreover, writing about the scene described above, Klein points to its eloquence in "describing the sense of stress and anxiety, the mental isolation and the emotional abandonment the soldiers who serve in the territories feel."[32] Precisely because the violence unites occupier and occupied, he writes, all sense of reality is lost. As a result, the soldiers are thrown on the mercy of viewers, who truly feel sorry for them.

Klein is a sophisticated and exacting critic for whom cinematic considerations often take precedence over more ideological ones. Most Israeli critics of the film were more impressed by the empathy it creates with the soldiers, even as they acknowledged the pro-Israeli bias that inheres in this stance.[33] Their surprise at the empathy the soldiers receive in the film should be viewed against the fierce public debates in Israel concerning the occupation—debates that have escalated precipitously in recent years. As the occupation becomes increasingly normalized, the shrinking voices that call for its end grow louder and more desperate. None of these complexities are visible in the film, an elision that may have elicited critics' surprise in Israel.

As many audiences outside of Israel are unfamiliar with some of these internal debates, the film's favorable reception abroad makes more sense. It won the Confédération Internationale des Cinémas d'Art et d'Essai (CICAE) Award in the 2013 Berlin Film Festival, the Judges Award in the Aubagne International Film Festival in France, and the Audience Award in the Bergamo Film Festival. Otherwise, the film did not raise much interest around the world and attracted very limited critical attention. This is most likely because the film has little new to say about the conflict, rehashes received truths about the complexity of the situation, and is too close to contemporary television reports about it. At the same time, the few critics who did comment on it sympathized with the impossible predicament the soldiers are faced with, marking the soldiers as victims of a situation beyond their control.[34]

The case of *Zero Motivation* is more unusual, as the film is removed from any kind of combat and focuses on female soldiers who serve as clerks in an office at a remote IDF base somewhere in the south of the country. The film is a sardonic comedy about the follies of military service, particularly of the women who are employed in auxiliary roles as aides to the male officers. At the center of the film are Zohar (Dana Ivgy), a profoundly bored office clerk whose greatest ambition is to beat the record on the computer game Minesweeper, and her friend Dafi (Nelly Tagar), who longs to be transferred to a base nearer Tel-Aviv, where the wretchedness of her useless army job would be mitigated by a real life in the city outside the base.

In addition to being an updated critique of the inanity of army service in general, a sort of *Catch-22* or *M*A*S*H*,[35] the film is also a biting satire of the service of women in the IDF, a topic that has not received much attention in Israeli cinema to date.[36] It contains several droll scenes that deal with military chauvinism in refreshingly sophisticated ways, including absurd philosophical comments about the meaning of life in the context of the army, several "masculine" discussions of sex from the perspective of women, and one coffee-serving parody staged as an ironic dance. At the same time—and despite the film's sharp critical agenda—the female soldiers in it remain fundamentally beholden to the IDF behemoth. *Zero Motivation* surely mounts a clever campaign against many of the IDF's problematic attitudes toward women. But it does not examine the role of the army in Israeli culture more generally and instead focuses more narrowly on the service of women in the military, advocating their fuller and more meaningful integration into it.

In one of the film's most critically attuned moments, which exemplifies its acerbic, self-deprecating humor, Dafi initiates a new clerk into the workings of the office. As she walks the newcomer around, Dafi shows her the girls' most prized possession—a staple gun that is kept hidden in one of the drawers. The gun makes several more appearances later on. In a moment of despair, Dafi points the gun at her head and announces her intention to kill herself. Luckily, the gun has no staples in it, and Dafi goes on to leave the base and then return to it after a while as an officer, an elevated role that frees her from some of the office's more tedious chores. In the film's climax, Dafi and Zohar make another use of the staple gun during their bitter fight.

Folded into this story are both rebellion against the army as well as submission to it. Dafi's hatred of the army disappears after she becomes an officer and returns to the base to head the human resources office. Essentially, she is co-opted by the system. This twist in the plot is one in a series of clever ironies that make up the film's humor and sophisticated critique. But the joke is ultimately on Dafi. As I noted in my study about Israeli culture between the two Intifadas (1987–2000), the 1990s generation in Israel showed its alienation from an increasingly jingoistic political establishment by withdrawing from public life and sometimes even from life itself.[37] Some of its most memorable literary protagonists were consummate losers, passive heroes who often hurt themselves deliberately or even killed themselves as an ultimate act of rebellion. Yet, unlike those heroes, whose dispirited rebellion was translated into defiant inaction, Dafi seeks the establishment's embrace. Her clever plan to leave the base only brings her back to it, this time as a much more integrated and invested member of the national community.

In some ways, *Zero Motivation* is a comic version of *Beaufort*. In both films, a group of soldiers is trapped in a remote and isolated military installation, threatened by a menacing and amorphous system. But the two films handle these difficulties very differently. While the soldiers in *Beaufort* are threatened by an external enemy and are generally motivated to serve, the soldiers in *Zero Motivation* hate the army and are a threat to themselves. In both films, however, the soldiers are ultimately presented as victims—a narrative that has been ingrained so deeply into Israeli consciousness that even a mordant comedy like *Zero Motivation* makes use of it.

Such films fail to create a critical distance between their protagonists and the context within which they operate—that is, the IDF. Precisely because *Zero Motivation* is a comedy, it illustrates very clearly the failure of Israeli filmmakers to create truly ironic heroes who would dare to sever the connection between the subject and the nation or, in Israeli-Jewish parlance, between the individual and the group. If irony is the critical difference between an *is* and an *ought*, *Zero Motivation* contains very little of it. Even Zohar, whose actions are sometimes truly subversive, ultimately wishes to be transferred elsewhere, hopefully to a less desolate base. She stops short of actions that would seriously endanger her connection to the group and is reluctantly satisfied with her role as a radical within it. This vacillation between distance and belonging is one of the elements that sustains the victimization discourse in these films. It allows the protagonists to distance themselves from those aspects of Israeli society that are most criticized, especially abroad, without incurring the cost of that critique. By presenting themselves as victims of the same system that victimizes others, they distance themselves from that critique and align themselves, falsely perhaps, with more genuine victims.

This is very likely the reason *Zero Motivation* was such a phenomenal success, both in Israel and abroad. In addition to sweeping all the major prizes of the Israeli Film Academy in 2014 (Ophir Prize), it also won the best narrative feature award at the Tribeca Film Festival in New York City that year. Moreover, the film was a commercial success, attracting more than half a million viewers in Israel alone, and was widely distributed abroad as well.[38] Recently, the rights to it were bought by BBC America for development as a cable TV series.[39] Critical response to the film has also been explosive and overwhelmingly positive. *Rotten Tomatoes* lists 134 of them. Most of them laud the film. Few scold the director for making a loony comedy about a topic as grave as the Israeli military. Nick McCarthy, of *Slant*

Magazine, complained that "the lack of observation on the surrounding political situation is all but washed over in favor of juvenile gags."[40] Manohlda Dargis of the *New York Times* noted how "for the most part, the real world, including Israeli politics, hovers off screen." Although, she added, "if you're inclined, you could read the movie as a vaporous critique of the country's militarization. Or not."[41] To both, Jordan Hoffman of *The Guardian* has this to say: "There are some whose politics have no room for a film like this. 'This is not a laughing matter,' they'll say. This attitude negates reality, and perhaps negates storytelling in general. *Zero Motivation* is a shot of honesty, in which short-term goals are far more important than larger geo-political ones. Perhaps because they are the only ones over which we have any control."[42]

The reactions to the film around the world bear Hoffman's words as the film's reception in Turkey, for instance, illustrates well. Turkey has cooled its relations with Israel significantly after President Recep Tayyip Erdogan's rise to power in the early 2000s, and Turkish public opinion of Israel has soured significantly since then. So when the film was enthusiastically received in Turkey's most important film festival, the IKVS festival in Istanbul in 2015, Israeli diplomats were thrilled. "It was exciting to hear Turkish viewers laugh out loud and appreciate Israeli humor, especially Israeli army humor," said Israel's former vice consul to Turkey, Avidan Kenar. Given the negative opinions about the IDF in Turkey, he considered it a significant achievement.[43] But I think that what the consul and the reporter celebrated was not just the common humanity that all viewers of the film immediately recognize and respond to. Part of the popularity of such films surely comes from the negative portrayal of the IDF. And when the soldiers who serve in it are shown as its hapless victims, viewers who are otherwise critical of Israel naturally empathize with them and perhaps also with the country more generally.

Films do not have an obligation to provide viewers with history lessons or comprehensive cultural and political assessments. But when films about the IDF narrowly focus on the personal lives of Israeli soldiers, without much attention to the greater context that mandates their service in the first place, they undermine their dramatic power and do injustice to their subject matter. To shoot and then weep is not necessarily a bad thing. To feel sorry for a violent action can be a constructive step toward solving a conflict that invited violence in the first place. Weeping for someone is an act of empathy and mercy. This was certainly the sense of the moral anguish in Yizhar's early stories over the plight of Palestinians. In the very real fight for Jewish survival in 1948, the use of force seemed necessary. Yizhar should be commended for agonizing over it rather than celebrating it. To a lesser extent, one can say the same for *Siach Lochamim*, the remorseful confessions of Israeli soldiers in the wake of the 1967 war. But commensurability is an important principle here. As Israel becomes stronger, it loses the ability to cast itself as a David fighting Goliath. Unfortunately, it is a habit the country finds hard to shed. Given the nature of Jewish history and its length, this is understandable. The discourse of victimhood today provides another incentive to continue this narrative. But Israel's participation in this discourse illustrates one of its biggest problems, that vying for victim status contributes little toward eliminating the conditions that made that status possible.

Notes

1. For a useful collection of essays on nation and cinema, see Mette Hjort and Scott Mackenzie, eds., *Cinema and Nation* (New York: Routledge, 2000), especially Philip Schlesinger, "The Sociological Scope of National Cinema"; Anthony Smith, "Images of the Nation, Cinema, Art and National Identity"; and Susan Hayward, "Framing National Cinemas."

2. For specific references to BDS, see Rachel S. Harris and Martin B. Shichtman, "BDS, Credibility, and the Challenge to the Academy," *Shofar* 36, no. 1 (Spring 2018): 161–182. For a more general study on the influence of politics on the academy, see Cary Nelson and Stephen Watt, *Office Hours: Activism and Change in the Academy* (New York: Routledge, 2004).

3. See Rachel S. Harris, "Forgetting the Forgotten Ones: The Case of Haim Gouri's 'Hanishkahim,'" *Journal of Modern Jewish Studies* 8, no. 2 (2009): 199–214; Rachel S. Harris, "Samson's Suicide: Death and the Hebrew Literary Canon," *Israel Studies* 17, no. 3 (2012): 67–91.

4. For a contemporary ethical discussion of the phrase and sensibility, see Oded Na'aman, "The Rise and Fall of the Bleeding Hearts" [in Hebrew], *Theory and Criticism* 33 (2008): 225–238. For an overview about the film's reception, see, Gili Izikovitz, "'Censored Voices': Behind the Great Victory of '67 Hid a Line of War Crimes" [in Hebrew], *Haaretz*, June 6, 2015, accessed May 18, 2017, http://www.haaretz.co.il/gallery/cinema/.premium-1 .2651353#hero__bottom.

5. Hannan Hever and Orin D. Gensler, "Hebrew in an Israeli Arab Hand: Six Miniatures on Anton Shammas's 'Arabesques,'" *Cultural Critique*, no. 7 (Autumn 1987): 48.

6. Ibid.

7. Nir Cohen, *Soldiers, Rebels, and Drifters: Gay Representation in Israeli Cinema* (Detroit: Wayne State University Press, 2012), 104–115.

8. In a private conversation (George Washington University, October 31, 2006), singer Ivri Lider, who sings the title song of the film on the DVD version of it, told me that the snow

was not an original part of the script but a result of a surprise snowstorm that took place a few days before the planned filming. For a critical discussion of the film, see Raz Yosef, "The National Closet: Gay Israel in *Yossi and Jagger*," *GLQ* 11, no. 2 (2005): 283–300.

9. The film received a high rating overall on *Rotten Tomatoes* (88 by critics, 74 by reviewers) and *Metacritic* (70 by critics, 7.9 out of 10 by reviewers). More than a decade after it was first released, it is still widely available for streaming or DVD purchase on Amazon, Amazon Prime, Netflix, and Mubi, as well as many other torrent services. In the gay cinema category, it has become a classic. Neither is very common for Israeli films, as Israeli cinema remains a relatively small and unknown cinema despite its relative success and recognition in the last two decades.

10. For a short introduction to pinkwashing in Israel, see Sarah Schulman, "Israel and 'Pinkwashing,'" *New York Times*, November 22, 2011, accessed May 18, 2017, http://www .nytimes.com/2011/11/23/opinion/pinkwashing-and-israels-use-of-gays-as-a-messaging -tool.html. For two scholarly articles representative of the debate, see Jasbir Puar, "Citation and Censorship: The Politics of Talking about the Sexual Politics of Israel," *Feminist Legal Studies* 19, no. 2 (2011): 133–142; Jason Ritchie, "Pinkwashing, Homonationalism, and Israel–Palestine: The Conceits of Queer Theory and the Politics of the Ordinary," *Antipode* 47, no. 3 (2015): 616–634.

11. The film and the novel by the same name were developed simultaneously by the novelist Ron Leshem and film director Joseph Cedar, who collaborated to some extent. For more on this, see my article, "*Beaufort* the Book, *Beaufort* the Film: Israeli Militarism Under Attack," in *Narratives of Dissent: War in Contemporary Israeli Arts and Culture*, ed. Rachel S. Harris and Ranen Omer-Sherman (Detroit: Wayne State University Press, 2011), 336–345.

12. *Beaufort* received four Israeli Academy (Ophir) Awards, won the Silver Bear award in the 2007 Berlin Film Festival, and competed for Best Foreign Film at the Oscars that year, a rare achievement for an Israeli film.

13. A. O. Scott, "Israeli Soldiers Man a Fortress of Futility," *New York Times*, January 18, 2008, accessed May 18, 2017, http://www.nytimes.com/2008/01/18/movies/18beau.html?ref= movies&_r=0.

14. Lisa Schwartzbaum, "Beaufort," *Entertainment Weekly*, January 16, 2008, accessed May 18, 2017, http://www.ew.com/ew/article/0,,20172267,00.html. A few other critics expressed similar sentiments, with David Edelstein writing that "pro-war audiences on both sides will find Joseph Cedar's vision irresponsible. I think *Beaufort* captures a higher irresponsibility." Ella Taylor commented, "Cedar's understated humanism—passionate but never glib or easy—renders all the more painful the unstated coda that, six years after Israel's retreat from Lebanon, the wounds opened all over again." See David Edelstein, "*Beaufort*," *New York*, January 21, 2008, accessed May 18, 2017, http://nymag.com/listings/movie/beaufort /; and Ella Taylor, "*Beaufort*," *Village Voice*, January 15, 2008, accessed May 18, 2017, http:// web.archive.org/web/20080120094210/http://www.villagevoice.com/film/0803,taylor,78850,- 20.html.

15. Harald Jähner, "*Beaufort*" [in German], *Berliner Zeitung*, February 15, 2007, accessed May 18, 2017; the critique appears with three others at http://www.film-zeit.de/Film/18374 /BEAUFORT/Kritik/.

16. Elmar Krekeler, "Soldiers Despair of the Task" [in German], *Berliner Morgenpost*, February 2, 2007, accessed May 18, 2017, http://www.morgenpost.de/printarchiv/kultur /article103077925/Soldaten-verzweifeln-an-ihrer-Aufgabe.html#.

17. Clément Graminiès, *"Beaufort"* [in French], *Critikat*, March 25, 2008, accessed November 1, 2020, https://www.critikat.com/actualite-cine/critique/beaufort/.

18. *Waltz with Bashir* is one of the most awarded Israeli films to date and one of the most well-known and widely distributed Israeli films abroad. It is probably also the first Israeli film that in some ways mythologized the Arab-Israeli conflict and lent it an artistic quality that transformed its staleness as a ubiquitous news item and transcended its all-too-familiar documentary character.

19. The women are encouraging the filmmakers to record the horror. For a discussion of this scene, see Alison Patterson and Dan Chyutin, "Teaching Trauma in (and out of) Translation: Waltzing with Bashir in English," in *Media and Translation: An Interdisciplinary Approach*, ed. Dror Abend-David (London: Bloomsbury, 2014), 224–226.

20. Diedrich Diederichsen, "War in the Head" [in German], *Die Zeit Online*, December 16, 2008, accessed May 18, 2017, http://www.film-zeit.de/Film/19842/WALTZ-WITH-BASHIR /Kritik/.

21. Rüdiger Suchsland, "West Side Waltz" [in German], *Artechock*, accessed May 18, 2017, http://www.artechock.de/film/text/kritik/w/wesiwa.htm. Most critics agreed. Bettina Spoerri, for example, wrote that the film presents the self-reflection of Israeli soldiers on their pointless and absurd acts of destruction, their total mental overwork, and their fear of death and inability to return to normal life again. See Bettina Spoerri, "Haunted by the Memory of War" [in German], *Neue Zürcher Zeitung*, December 4, 2008, accessed May 18, 2017, http:// www.nzz.ch/aktuell/feuilleton/film/von-der-erinnerung-an-den-krieg-verfolgt-1.1352475.

22. Anthony Quinn, "Fighting for the Truth," *The Independent*, November 21, 2008, accessed May 18, 2017, http://www.independent.co.uk/arts-entertainment/films/reviews /waltz-with-bashir-18-1027847.html.

23. See Patterson and Chyutin 2014; Paul Atkinson and Simon Cooper, "Untimely Animations: Waltz with Bashir and the Incorporation of Historical Difference," *Screening the Past*, no. 34 (2012), accessed May 18, 2017, http://www.screeningthepast.com/2012/08 /untimely-animations-waltz-with-bashir-and-the-incorporation-of-historical-difference/.

24. In Dave Calhoun's words, "Then and now, Folman puts himself centre-stage—which means he's always dancing on the edge of self-indulgence." See Dave Calhoun, "Waltz with Bashir," *Time Out London*, October 1, 2008, accessed May 18, 2017, http://www.timeout.com /london/film/waltz-with-bashir. Academic examinations of the film tend to support its self-indulgence, even if they do not accuse the filmmaker directly of it. Raya Morag's book-length study of what she terms "perpetrator's trauma" is the most substantial exploration of this aspect, which is the subject of other studies as well. These critiques focus on the privatization of war memories. As a result, the mentally scarred soldiers are severed from a national context and become patients in a way, an injured minority. And since the injury was caused by a coercive system they had little control of, their portrayal as victims becomes almost inevitable. See Raya Morag, *Waltzing with Bashir: Perpetrator Trauma and Cinema* (London: I. B. Tauris, 2013); Raz Yosef, "War Fantasies: Memory, Trauma and Ethics in Ari Folman's *Waltz with Bashir*," *Journal of Modern Jewish Studies* 9, no. 3 (2010): 311–326.

25. Steven Erlanger, "A Tank's-Eye View of an Unpopular War," *New York Times*, July 30, 2009, accessed May 18, 2017, http://www.nytimes.com/2010/08/01/movies/01lebanon.html?_r =0. Similarly, Australian critic Leigh Paatsch wrote, "Rarely has a film so intensely conveyed the catastrophic shock to the system a first time on a battlefield must wield. It all comes down to the same conundrum again and again in Lebanon. A mistake made on the spot must

be lived with for the rest of your life." See Leigh Paatsch, "Film Review: Lebanon," *Herald Sun,* December 2, 2010, accessed May 18, 2017, http://www.heraldsun.com.au/entertainment /movies/film-review-lebanon/story-e6frf8r6-1225964663032.

26. Almost all of the critics posted on the site praise the film for similar reasons, and none of the 104 critiques mention the Palestinians. Of the 383 lay comments about the film, four comments only mention the Palestinians. Two of these comments appear twice under two different names and on different dates. One of those harshly decries the image of Israeli soldiers as victims: "This is a hashed and stupid story about poor victimized Jewish soldiers who have to fight monstrous Palestinian terrorists." See Andres V, *Rotten Tomatoes Commentators,* October 24, 2010, accessed May 18, 2017, https://www.rottentomatoes.com/m /lebanon-2010/reviews/?page=11&type=user&sort=; and Andres74varela, *Rotten Tomatoes Commentators,* January 4, 2011, accessed May 18, 2017, https://www.rottentomatoes.com/m /lebanon-2010/reviews/?page=10&type=user&sort=.

27. For more on this, see Nurith Gertz, "The Medium that Mistook Itself for War: *Cherry Season* in Comparison with *Ricochets* and *Cup Final*," *Israel Studies* 4, no. 1 (1999): 153–174.

28. For more on the enthusiastic reaction of various Israeli artists to the country's early wars and military campaigns up to 1973, see the chapter "Jewish and Fanatic: Images of Religious Zionists" in my book *Directed by God: Jewishness in Contemporary Israeli Film and Television* (Austin: University of Texas Press, 2016).

29. Rachel S. Harris, *An Ideological Death: Suicide in Israeli Literature* (Chicago: Northwestern University Press, 2014), 75.

30. The other two, *One of Us* (Uri Barbash, 1989) and *Green Fields* (Isaac Zepel Yeshurun, 1989) were released very close to the actual conflict. Neither film deals directly with the incursion of Israeli soldiers into Palestinians civilian life. Barbash's film focuses on the army's investigation into criminal acts by policing soldiers, while Yeshurun's focuses on a family who is on its way to the son's graduation ceremony from basic training and who are then trapped when their vehicle is caught up in street violence connected to the Palestinian uprising.

31. Uri Klein, "*Rock the Casbah*: Parity above All" [in Hebrew], *Haaretz*, February 24, 2013, accessed May 18, 2017, http://www.haaretz.co.il/gallery/cinema/movie-reviews/1.1936758. This seems to have been the critical consensus in Israel, with one critic, Shmulik Duvdevani, spelling out clearly that by "presenting IDF soldiers as the real victims of the occupation, [the film] creates a distorted picture that eschews self-criticism." Another critic, Adva Lanciano, complained that the film effectively interferes with the victimization of the soldiers by trying to be too balanced and a bit clichéd. See Shmulik Duvdevani, "*Rock the Casbah*: Shooting, Weeping and Clearing One's Conscience" [in Hebrew], *Ynet*, February 22, 2013, May 18, 2017, http://www.ynet.co.il/articles/0,7340,L-4347751,00.html; and Adva Lanciano "*Rock the Casbah*, An Impressive but Disappointing War Movie" [in Hebrew], *City Mouse*, February 27, 2013, accessed August 30, 2020, https://www.haaretz.co.il/gallery/cinema/movie-reviews/1 .3408628.

32. Klein 2013.

33. Shmulik Duvdevani literally labels it a "shooting and weeping" film. A more telling comment is found in Amir Boggen's review of the film: "At the end of one of the film's screenings in the recent Berlin Film Festival, an Arab woman wearing a hijab approached director Yariv Horowitz. 'I am from Gaza, and after watching the film I feel sorry also for the soldiers,' she told him." This response is precisely the kind of reaction this article attempts

to articulate. See Duvdevani 2013; Amir Boggen, "Not All Is Well: Yariv Horowitz on *Rock the Casbah*" [in Hebrew], *Ynet*, March 14, 2013, accessed May 18, 2017, http://www.ynet.co.il /articles/0,7340,L-4356218,00.html.

34. *Rotten Tomatoes* has only two critiques and no lay responses posted; see *Rotten Tomatoes*, accessed May 18, 2017, https://www.rottentomatoes.com/m/rock_ba_casba_2013 /?search=rock%20the%20casbah.

35. *M*A*S*H* was an American 1970s TV series, a dark comedy about the absurdity of war and military service. Although it began as a novel that was then turned into noted a film, it was the TV adaptation of the film that made it famous.

36. Surprisingly, given the frequency of military conflict in the history of Israel and the importance of service in the IDF as a corollary, relatively few Israeli feature films deal with these issues. Out of more than 650 Israeli feature films that were made since 1948, only about seventy deal with Israeli wars and service in the IDF—a little more than 10 percent (numbers based on Wikipedia entries). Out of those films, far fewer deal with the service of women in the IDF, which was never deemed important for the overall war effort or the perpetual state of emergency that has existed in Israel in some form or other since its inception. These films include *The Troupe* (Avi Nesher, 1978), *Girls* (Nadav Livyatan, 1985), *Close to Home* (Dalia Hager and Vidi Bilu, 2005), *Room 514* (Sharon Bar-Ziv, 2012), and *Zero Motivation*.

37. Etgar Keret was the major literary voice of what has been called the dispirited Oslo Generation. His heroes are often so-called losers who express the frustrations they feel about an increasingly incomprehensible world through violence against themselves. For specific examples, see chapter 3 in my book *Israeli Culture between the Two Intifadas: A Brief Romance* (Austin: University of Texas Press, 2013).

38. Avner Shavit, "How *Zero Motivation* Won Out on Hollywood in the Box-Office" [in Hebrew], *Walla*, November 5, 2014, accessed May 18, 2017, http://e.walla.co.il/item/2798587.

39. Nirit Anderman, "Amy Poehler Fell in Love and *Zero Motivation* Will Be Made into a Television Series" [in Hebrew], *Haaretz*, June 1, 2016, accessed May 18, 2017, http://www .haaretz.co.il/gallery/cinema/1.2963205.

40. Nick McCarthy, "Zero Motivation," *Slant*, April 23, 2014, accessed May 18, 2017, http:// www.slantmagazine.com/film/review/zero-motivation.

41. Manohla Dargis, "Where the Biggest Enemy Is Tedium," *New York Times*, December 2, 2014, accessed May 18, 2017, https://www.nytimes.com/2014/12/03/movies /zero-motivation-an-israeli-comedy.html?partner=rss&emc=rss&_r=2.

42. Jordan Hoffman, "Zero Motivation Review: An Off-Kilter Look at Female Soldiers in the IDF," *The Guardian*, December 5, 2014, accessed May 18, 2017, https://www.theguardian .com/film/2014/dec/05/zero-motivation-review-female-soldiers-idf.

43. Itamar Eichner, "*Zero Motivation* Stole the Show in Turkey" [in Hebrew], *Ynet*, April 14, 2015, accessed May 18, 2017, http://www.ynet.co.il/articles/0,7340,L-4646829,00.html.

IV

DENATIONALIZING THE LOCAL AND PROJECTING INTO THE GLOBAL: DISRUPTING ISRAELINESS THROUGH THE TRANSNATIONAL

12

OF NATIONAL HOMES AND DESPOTIC SYMBOLS

Network Narrative Films, Global Cities, and Crossings of Local Paths

Nava Dushi

IN 2007, ISRAELI FILMS RECEIVED UNPRECEDENTED RECOGNITION IN leading international film festivals and among distributors that appeal to niche markets worldwide. At Cannes alone, *Tehilim* (Nadjari 2007, France/Israel/United States)[1] was selected for participation in the festival's main competition; *Jellyfish* (Geffen and Keret 2007, Israel/France) won the prestigious Golden Camera Award, as well as the Young Critics Award; and *The Band's Visit* (Kolirin 2007, Israel/United States/France) won the Un Certain Regard Jury Coup de Cœur Award, the FIPRESCI Prize, and the Award of the Youth, making for a total of thirty-six international awards, including the Tokyo International Film Festival Grand Prix Award, The European Discovery of the Year Award (awarded to Eran Kolirin for best direction), and The European Actor Award (awarded to Sasson Gabai). The Berlin International Film Festival awarded Joseph Cedar the Silver Bear Award for best direction in *Beaufort* (2007, Israel), which later that year received an Academy Award nomination in the Foreign Language Film Category. The Berlin International Film Festival also awarded *Sweet Mud* (Shaul 2006, Israel/Germany/France/Japan) the Generation 14 Plus Crystal Bear Award, this after winning the Grand Jury Prize at the Sundance Film Festival earlier that year. And finally, the Tribeca Film Festival awarded the Jury Best Narrative Film Award to *My Father My Lord* (Volach 2007, Israel).

This trend continued in 2008 with Ari Folman's *Waltz with Bashir* (2008, Israel/France/Germany/United States/Finland/Switzerland/Belgium/ Australia), which won a total of thirty-six international awards, including the Golden Globe Best Foreign Language Film Award and the César Best Foreign Film Award, and was nominated for an Academy Award in the Foreign Language Film category. In 2009, *Lebanon* (Maoz 2009, Israel/France/ Germany/United Kingdom) won the prestigious Venice Film Festival Golden Lion Award, The European Film Awards Discovery of the Year Award (awarded to Maoz), and the European Cinematography Award; the film *Ajami* (Copti and Shani 2009, Germany/Israel) received the Golden Camera Special Mention at Cannes and was nominated for an Academy Award in the Foreign Language Film category. In 2011, the film *Footnote* (Cedar 2011, Israel) garnered its writer-director a second Academy Award nomination and a Best Screenplay Award at Cannes. The international mobility of Israeli films continued to manifest itself in the years that followed; consider *Fill the Void* (Burshtein 2012, Israel), *Bethlehem* (Adler 2013, Israel/Germany/ Belgium), *Youth* (Shoval 2013, Israel/Germany/France), and *Zero Motivation* (Lavie 2014, Israel) and the selection of six Israeli films for screening in the competitive and noncompetitive programs of the 2014 Cannes Film Festival, an achievement that has been dubbed by critics "the Israeli takeover of Cannes."[2] Subsequent to their festival appearances, the films were acquired for distribution in foreign markets and enjoyed varying levels of success at the box office. Thus, the pattern illustrating the dynamic relations between players and forces in the field seems to suggest that global mobility is attainable when the accumulation of prestige (symbolic capital) in leading international festivals creates the conditions for the conversion of cultural capital into economic capital.[3]

Naturally, the successful internationalization of Israeli films on the turn of the millennium coincides with a consistent growth in interest and market openness to emerging cinemas at large. Yet, if historically, international recognition was associated with the formal ingenuity and universal appeal of national film movements such as the Soviet Montage, German Expressionism, Italian Neorealism, and the French New Wave—or, alternately, with the work of celebrated auteurs such as Ingmar Bergman (Sweden), Yasujirō Ozu (Japan), Satyajit Ray (India), and Michelangelo Antonioni (Italy), among others—the output of national films that achieved a state of transnational mobility in the past two decades does not present us with a cohesive unit on the level of style or in respect of its thematic commitments.

On the contrary, what characterizes the global emergence of this new breed of films is their clear tendency for localism in the treatment of internal national issues. How, then, can the increasing recognition of national cinemas that until recently did not attain international visibility be interpreted considering their commitment to the local rather than the universal? Is there a connection, a common feature, if you will, among films originating in Singapore, France, the United Kingdom, Mexico, Norway, and Israel that points to the emergence of an alternative horizon of cinematic production and reception? If the national context remains a factor, as far as the films' conditions of production and local specificity are concerned, does the concept of national cinema continue to be relevant as a critical category of research when the transnational mobility of the films is to be accounted for?

The National, the Global, and the Local

In its early articulation, the concept of national cinema stood as a descriptive category that primarily related to the study of national film movements and their contribution to the development of film style, with the exception of Siegfried Kracauer's seminal work, *From Caligari to Hitler* (1947), in which German cinema is understood as the product of a psychological condition inherent to German nationality. The transition from a preoccupation with style/form to an emphasis on the social/cultural conditions that shape national cinemas was made by scholars in the late 1980s.[4] Henceforth, the body of work dedicated to the study of the national dimension of national cinema habitually invokes Benedict Anderson's definition of the nation as an imagined political community that is limited and sovereign.[5] This working definition brings forth a consideration of the varying social practices and cultural artifacts that produce and sustain national imagination. In turn, the enunciation of culture as a mobilizer of national identity is conceived of as a unifying social practice. Later debates, however, call Anderson's argument into question by suggesting that rather than mirroring a unified or homogeneous national culture, national cinema, among other cultural texts, represents "the loci of debate about a nation's governing principles, goals, heritage and history."[6] Furthermore, concepts developed by scholars vested in the study of globalization in the 1990s expose the limits that the national framework currently presents for the study of cinema. *Globalization from below* and *grassroots globalization* are the processes that led to the formation of new diasporas, genders, and ethnicities in the past three decades.[7] These communities gave rise to the voices of individuals who were historically marginalized and often altogether excluded from the imaginative inscription of the national. The impact of their growing presence in the streets and on the screen has been construed as a counter-movement to the homogenizing forces of the global propelled by corporate capital, the world's leading transnational media conglomerates, and rising technology giants.

Thus, when taken in the context of grassroots globalization, the international visibility of local cinematic texts can be attributed to the formation of a transnational web of themes upon which emergent cinemas thrive and assume their mobility across cultural borders. In this web, the fragmented national foregrounds local particularities that engage global audiences by way of association with similar localities in variable national contexts. One such theme concerns the negotiation of identity and belonging against the backdrop of the global city. Films such as *Code Unknown* (Haneke 2000, France), *Amores Perros* (Iñárritu 2000, Mexico), *Crash* (Haggis 2004, United States), *Be with Me* (Khoo 2005, Singapore), *Hawaii, Oslo* (Poppe 2004, Norway), and *360* (Meirelles 2011, United Kingdom), to name a few, project the city's fractured space with their complex approach to storytelling. Similar to those films, the Israeli films *Year Zero* (Pitchhadze 2004), *What a Wonderful Place* (Halfon 2005), *Jellyfish* (Geffen and Keret 2007), and *Ajami* (Copti and Shani 2009), all located in Tel Aviv-Jaffa, are structured by the interweaving of disparate and fragmented narrative strands in which several unrelated or seemingly unrelated characters randomly intersect on their crossing of local paths. These frequently labeled *fractal, database, mind game, forking-path, puzzle, modular,* or *network* narrative films elicit, a "new and largely uncharted ways of audience address and spectator engagement."[8] Their complex structures typify a recurrent meditation on contingency and determinism, randomness and causality, and in so doing, conjure up a recognition of the ever-increasing complexity of the social and cultural realities of our time.

In a book titled *The New European Cinema: Redrawing the Map*, Rosalind Galt argues that the only way to read cinematic spectacle as politically meaningful in post-wall Europe is to begin with an image from which we can move to the space of the frame and from it to that of geography: "Only by taking seriously contemporary textual practice can we unpick the post-Wall discourses of homelessness and belonging."[9] The growing attentiveness in world cinema to the rapid transformation of the urban space and the muddling of ethnic and migrant communities inhabiting its disparate zones lends itself to the structure of complex narration. In network narrative films, the tension between the cosmopolitan character of the city and its particularity as home is brought into focal awareness by a filmmaking intent on grappling with some of the most acute questions of our time, exploring Fourth World alienation, social disintegration, homelessness, and personal angst. In line with this sensibility, the portrayal of Tel Aviv as a fissured and violated space emerges as a salient thread in an evolving web of transnational themes characterized by a clear tendency for localism and a thematic commitment to minority issues. The disintegration of national sovereignty finds its expression in the proliferation of cinematic texts that explore the experiences of those invisible and voiceless individuals who were left behind in the global race for a prosperous and secure future. How, then, do the films give expression to the city's fractured and alienated space, to the loss of the home and the transience of identity? How is the tension between the global and the local, the public and the private, the urban and the domestic enunciated?

Nation Building and the Negation of the City

In addressing the role played by cinema in the nation building of postrevolutionary Russia, Noël Carroll and Sally Banes argue that unlike other European nation-states for which the idea of the nation has been construed retrospectively, the Soviet Union had to be imagined prospectively—to be invented. To that end, Sergei Eisenstein's *The Old and the New* (1929) sought to emulate Marx and Engles's contention that the rift between town and country, brought about by capitalism, would be reconciled in the advent of communism, thus birthing the imagined community of the Soviet nation.[10] Arjun Appadurai and James Holston point out that "one of the essential projects of nation-building has been to dismantle the historic primacy of urban citizenship and to replace it with the national" by mobilizing an image of the rural as the ultimate manifestation of indigenous authenticity and a rejection of the city—the source of its corruption.[11]

Similarly, from the onset, the place of the city in the historical revival of Jewish life in Palestine was imbued with doubt and contradictions. In the Zionist master narrative, city life was often equated with diasporic existence and stood in opposition to the productive endeavors of rural settlement and agricultural physical labor.[12] Studies of the early Hebrew films of the 1920s and 1930s stress its proximate relation to its formalist contemporaries, insofar as the portrayal of Jewish nation building in Palestine contributed to the invention of the New Jew through the consistent production of Zionist iconography afforded by a "pictorial lexicon" depicting a variety of mostly agricultural activities.[13]

The early cinema of the 1940s, 1950s, and 1960s further sought the reduction of the "dynamism and differences in the Hebrew culture of its time" to a "hierarchy meant to support the homogenous view of the new Hebrew identity" and the negation of its diasporic "other."[14] The unity evoked by the films' commitment to the Zionist master narrative emanated from their male protagonist "who controlled space with his actions and gaze."[15] The early application of these representational standards has often been associated with the universal—or rather, universalizing—coherence that classical storytelling affords, obtained by the seamless crafting of plot-driven films, motivated by the linear progression of events and a space unified by the wants and needs of their protagonists.[16] Over the years, the dominance of these cinematic standards in variable national contexts has been the subject of a searching critique that correlated the films' imaginative unity with the propagation of hegemony.

Despite the concerted effort to undermine the historic primacy of urban citizenship, cities, as Appadurai and Holston suggest, continued to function as a "strategic arena for the development of citizenship."[17] Indeed, the establishment of the garden city suburb of Achuzat Bayit in 1909, later to be known as the first Hebrew city, has been construed as a high point in the realization of Zionism's preoccupation with the question of *home*, namely the reterritorialization of a historically deterritorialized peoples. At the same time, the envisioning of Tel Aviv as a major metropolis was made explicit by the founders of Achuzat Bayit in their 1906 *Founding Prospectus and Declaration of Intentions*: "Just as the city of New York marks the main gateway to America, so we must improve our city so that in the course of time it will be an Eretzyisraeli New York."[18] Today, one is left to wonder whether the realization of its founders' vision surpassed the scope of their intent.

In an essay titled "Whose City Is It? Globalization and the Formation of New Claims," the rise of the global city is linked with the emergence of a new geography of centrality. Its unparalleled concentration of economic power points to the formation of a transnational urban system located on a worldwide grid that overrides the judicial provisions of space-bound continuities.[19] Consequently, the localization of global power in major metropolitan areas has been a driving force in their partitioning to a multiplicity of geographies—the development of high-rise corporate zones and secured residential areas alongside the negligence and decay of minimal-wage housing projects and their multiethnic migrant populace. Thus, old perceptions of the city as the arbiter of a national community sustained by the long-run performances of citizenship are being challenged by the unparalleled growth of economic and social inequalities.[20] In this cartography, spatial disintegration intertwines with the fissuring of an imagined national identity. While scholars of post-unification European cinema discuss its increasing attentiveness to Europe's diasporic and minoritarian communities, the treatment of a waning national solidarity in recent Israeli films can be construed as a *return* to the experience of the minor, an experience that manifests itself in the films' retreat from the enunciation of a national master narrative. This retreat, however, differs from the one advanced by the political cinema of the late 1970s and 1980s in the sense that its concern does not lie with the critique of an existing state of affairs nor with the advancement of an imagined alternative order. That said, a textual sensibility withdrawn from the enunciation of narrative unity or from the establishment of models of representation is not to be equated with meaninglessness. To qualify this claim, one must proceed from an historical contextualization of the emergence of complex narration to an experimentation with the individual text, with what it does, the way it works and affects its viewer. Thus, despite the shared preoccupation with the issue of home and belonging in *What a Wonderful Place, Year Zero, Jellyfish*, and *Ajami*, the appropriation of a networked structure of narration varies from film to film.[21]

Complex Narratives

From its early inception, cinema provided fertile ground for experimentation with nonlinearity and spatiotemporal ambiguity. With the rise of globalization, a portion of contemporary films across distinct cinematic practices has brought to the fore a new narrative and spatial awareness based on multiplicity, simultaneity, and nonlinearity. The grouping of such films by scholars under the predicate *complex narratives* may indeed suggest that such films present us with a new tendency or phenomenon that cannot be reduced to an all-inclusive generic categorization. Thus, the study of complex narratives generates a variety of approaches, correlating its emergence with the introduction of new technologies such as hyperlinking, new media, and computer games, the changing geopolitical landscape, and the proliferation of scientific theories of complexity such as chaos, small world, and the science of networks.[22] And while each scholar theorizes their complexity with different films and different aspects of film narrative in mind, what seems to be consistent across a significant number of films is that they all take place against the backdrop of the global city. In an essay titled "Fractal Films and the Architecture of Complexity," Wendy Everett suggests that the ability of such films to animate the "chaotic patterns of action and reaction, of chance and outcome" are best suited to "articulate the challenges of postmodern cinema."[23] Indeed, the films' experimentation with unrestricted narration and their conflation of a multiplicity of life experiences contour the city's fractured spaces and the impossibility of obtaining a broad and totalizing perspective. The incipience of this fragmentation can be traced to the experience of the labyrinthian metropolis of Walter Benjamin's Flâneur: "We observe bits of the 'stories' men and women carry with them, but never learn their conclusions; life ceases to form itself into epic or narrative."[24] In like manner, the films' multiplicity of perspectives, ambiguous causality, and loose plots confront the viewer with a reality out of hinge. Yet, to what extent do complex narrative films exhibit new and uncharted ways of spectator engagement? What kind of epistemic effect do they evoke?

David Bordwell's cognitivist interpretation finds that whatever new forms complex narratives may take, by and large they "remain coherent and comprehensible, thanks to principles of causality, temporal sequence and duration, character wants and needs, and motivic harmony that have characterized mainstream storytelling for the last century."[25] Indeed, in some cases the binding of the films' narratives to degrees-of-separation plots typify their implicit commitment to a causality that seeks coherence where there is none. Those instances display, yet again, the successful assimilation of formal and stylistic innovation into mainstream production and its propagated standards of representation. In other cases, the employment of a complex structure of narration cannot be dissociated from the film's minor sensibility. The minor in the context of Gilles Deleuze and Felix Guattari's theorization draws its inspiration from Franz Kafka's meditative diary entry dated December 25, 1911, concerning the social and cultural dimensions of the literatures of small nations.[26] While the concept of the minor has been taken up by film scholars in several important studies, the aim of the present discussion is to move beyond its metaphoric appropriation. To that end, the appeal to the term veers from its exclusive association with the cinema of numerically small nations and/or with the thematic representation of numerically small and oppressed minorities. For, the minor, when read in the broader context of Deleuze and Guattari's writing, circles around three entwined tendencies that touch upon the minor use of language, the political action of the text, and the collective assemblages of enunciation that it effects—qualities that inform the reading of the affective and epistemic qualities of the film rather than its cultural or folkloric commitments.

Studies of contemporary European cinema are particularly attuned to the articulation of new perceptions of urban geometry and the inherent connection between their alternative configuration of filmic space and the fragmentation of narrative form.[27] Unlike the unified world that continuity editing affords, complex narratives open up film language and "remind audiences that what we see in the frame is always relational, linked to presences beyond the immediate field of visibility."[28] Hence, it is the films' treatment of the city's space and their focused articulation of its lived experiences that form the subject of our concern.

If the employment of a complex narrative structure can be construed as the films' minor use of a major language, in what sense can it be said to subvert the major from within? If indeed complex narrative films remain coherent thanks to principles of causality that characterized mainstream storytelling for the last century, then how are we to account for their minor disposition? To begin, let us consider the interlocking of the films' thematic occupation and its formal treatment. The four Israeli features mentioned at the opening of this discussion attend to the waning of the national and the increasing significance of the local for the enunciation of identity. To this end, the networking of multiple narrative strands is generative of a broad perspective necessary for a consideration of the social implications of Israel's burgeoning global economy: the reduction of the public sphere to the fiscal value of human transactions, the services provided by foreign workers substituting familial responsibilities, the plight of the displaced migrant worker, the oppressed Palestinian *other*, and the inevitable alienation experienced by all. In this context, the unity once evoked by a national master narrative is superseded by minute attention to those moments that otherwise would have been omitted, taken as details that bear no consequence to the progression of the plot. And yet, the multiplicity of perspectives in *Year Zero, What a Wonderful Place,* and *Ajami* present the viewer with a tapestry whose threads are joined by story events that ultimately weave the causal connections among the characters that populate the film. In that respect, their formal logic, as Bordwell suggests, is consistent with the structure of classical narration. That is, ultimately, all characters and events are connected and somehow form a unified whole. In certain respects, the films' morbid illustration of Tel Aviv's social reality gravitates toward an apocalyptic climactic resolution reminiscent of the political cinema of the 1980s and early 1990s.[29] Consider the shooting spree in the hotel's lobby at the end of *Year Zero*, the violent clash with the police and the shooting of the film's lead protagonist and narrator in the underground parking lot at the end *Ajami*, and the all-hell-breaks-loose montage sequence at the end of *What a Wonderful Place*. Thus, the films' initial presentation of a meditative social commentary turns into a full-fledged political critique of an existing state of affairs. The question is whether the novelty of complex narration can be interrogated vis-à-vis the possibilities that it opens for a move beyond the principle of causality, a move toward experimentation with what the text does, the way it performs and bears the potential for the production of a textual encounter that is creative rather than reflective of identity.

Jellyfish

Jellyfish follows the lives of three women in the course of several days. One of its narrative strands revolves around a reclusive young waitress who works for a company that caters weddings. The first shot of the film presents the last moments of her separation from her boyfriend as he moves out of their shared apartment. The separation triggers her encounter with a mute girl who emerges from the sea, the gradual decay and ultimate flooding of her apartment, the loss of her job, a nearly fatal accident, and the beginning of a new friendship. Another narrative strand tells the story of a bride who breaks her ankle on her wedding night and is forced to abandon her honeymoon plans for a romantic cruise in the Caribbean and settle for a stay in a shabby beachfront Tel Aviv hotel. And a third narrative strand follows a Filipino nurse who works on short-term jobs as a caregiver to elderly women. Each of these narrative strands is linked to an additional set of characters, such as an actress who hires the Filipino nurse to care for her estranged elderly mother, a mysterious woman who is the sole occupant of the hotel's only suite, and a photographer who shoots weddings for the same business that employs the waitress.

The film opens with an event frame in which the mingling of several of its characters in the same locale, a wedding hall, hints at the invisible threads that form a relation between their disparate storylines. The wedding scene opens with a traveling shot that follows the entrance of the waitress into the kitchen and toward the wedding hall. Her hurried steps motivate the movement of the camera leading to the newlywed bride, who further leads the camera to her grandmother and her Filipino nurse. The shot's reflexive continuity is interrupted by the flash of a camera, which motivates the cut and with it, a transition to a multiplicity of spaces and storylines. As the film progresses, we learn that each of its narrative strands presents a variation on the unfulfilled promise entailed by the collective space of the wedding ritual and the symbolic act of marriage—the establishment of a home. The photographer who serves as the catalyst of this break ignores the demands of her manager to focus her attention on the wedding's dance floor. Her fascination lies with the ability to preserve the presences that remain excluded from the wedding's restrictive network of meaning or, if you will, of its coded representation—a beautiful bride, an embracing groom, and the promise of happiness ever after. That is, the break in the continuity that the flash of the camera introduces also serves as the film's break with the idea of representation by means of which the establishment of a home is interrogated against its substantive core—relationships. In Hebrew, the word *bayit* (*house/home*) stands for two different kinds of signifiers; the former stands for a signified recognized as a physical place of dwelling, whereas the latter stands for an abstraction that totalizes the field of meaning, particularly in the case of Israel's historical narrative.

Though neither of the film's disparate plot lines has priority over the others, we can begin with the newlyweds, who find themselves on the first day of their honeymoon in a hotel room infested by the smell of sewage. The bride's complaints about the smell motivate their move to a room penetrated by the oppressive noise of Tel Aviv's bustling traffic, a loud air-conditioning unit, and cement structures that block their view of the sea. Furthermore, the bride's incapacitated leg and the hotel's out-of-order elevator restrict her to the room while her husband persistently looks for a satisfying solution. Their move from one hotel room to another is emblematic of the impossibility of their relationship beyond its fantasy plane.

In the caregiver's narrative strand, a different detachment is sensed. Away from her home and from her son, the nurse attends to the daily needs of strangers in a foreign land. Her relationship with the new client, for whom she works, further emphasizes the detachment and inability of family members to care for their loved ones. The elderly woman, bitter and frustrated by the fact that her daughter did not find the time to pick her up from the hospital on the day of her discharge, refuses to communicate with her in English. The daughter, a professional actress who hired the nurse for the job, cannot cope with her mother's stern disposition and inability to show any sign of affection toward her. The only moment of tenderness between the two occurs when the daughter notices the presence of her mother among the viewers in the theater while she performs the role of Ophelia on stage. In this moment, it is not only the physical distance that allows the mother to see her daughter; it is the divide between the space of the observer and the site of the observed that produces the possibility for this moment of mutual recognition.

In the waitress's story, the division between these spaces does not yield the same results. On the morning that follows the departure of her boyfriend, the waitress awakens in her disintegrating empty apartment; a caterpillar is found crawling on its crumbling walls, and the ceiling is leaking. Her mother calls to make sure that she received the invitation to a fundraising event that she organizes for the homeless. The fundraiser is marketed by the slogan *Everyone deserves a roof over their heads*, presented in its televised campaign by the mother, who concludes her speech with the formation of a triangle with her hands. Her universal pledge is ridiculed by its juxtaposition with the impending homeless state of her only daughter. The intergenerational rift between the waitress and her mother reflects the mindset of a generation for whom the promise of a home has been reduced to a logo and succeeded by a reality of loneliness, emotional resignation, and a rootlessness hinted by the film's title.

The jellyfish is alluded to by the waitress's character, whose emotional paralysis stems from a repressed childhood experience. At the age of five, while spending a day on the beach with her parents, she is approached by an ice-cream man and offered a Popsicle. Her mother turns him down with the pretense that the man will return. The father's questioning of her reaction instigates a fight between the two concerning his infidelity; during the argument, the child is placed in the water by her father, who promises to return shortly. But the ice-cream man and her father never return. On that day, her witnessing of her parents' violent quarrel constituted a traumatic event that left her at the sea, locked up in the pre-symbolic phase of her mental development. Her encounter with a little mute girl who emerges naked from the sea—and for whom she assumes responsibility—draws her attention to the fact that her childhood photo album is empty, and the memory of her past is a void. Hence, the enunciation of the minor in *Jellyfish* is encapsulated in its noncharacter protagonist. Unlike the heroes of the past, who controlled the unified space of the nation with their actions and gaze,[30] the waitress lacks the symbolic network necessary to navigate her life. Her role as a blank slate constitutes the film's vanishing point at which the characters take on the image of the drifting jellyfish. As such, lack of identity, loss of identity, or refusal to be "second generation of something" become inseparable from the question of space and place.[31]

By the film's end, the hotel's suite is generously offered to the newly-wed couple by its sole occupant, who is determined to put an end to her life and struggles with the writing of her suicide letter. Ultimately, it is a poem that was written by the bride that gives her the words to articulate her death; it is the Filipino nurse who gives the estranged elderly woman the unconditional affection denied by her daughter; and it is the photographer who saves the waitress from drowning and losing herself to the sea. In forging these unlikely connections, the film imagines the possibility of another consciousness and another collectivity envisioned by two suicide attempts, one of which concludes with the death of the woman who waited to be saved by a man and the other with the rebirth of a woman as an act of absolute freedom.

This duality raises the question of "whether everything that happens or that one can do is determined in advance by a kind of a monolithic big Other" or whether an act can assume a truly subversive move that breaks "with the code in a more radical or fundamental, or even an absolute way."[32] The former is engendered by the so-called subversive practices that critique and dispute the dominant code but in fact "turn out to be determined and in a sense even authorized by the code and thus fail in their subversive aim."[33] While the political stance enunciated by *Year Zero*, *What a Wonderful Place*, and *Ajami* advances a break from the false unity of classical narration, the causal logic regulating the links between their disparate narrative strands points to their reactive pursuit of unified cohesiveness. Yet, what is most relevant to the affect that is induced by our encounter with the political action of the minor film is the shock that comes in response to the collapse of the symbolic structure (i.e., the collapse of the idea of a stable world and the socially affirming meaning that follows from it). Gilles

Deleuze and Felix Guattari name the process of the bestowal of meaning "despotism" and state that in despotic representation "signs become signifying under the action of a despotic symbol that totalizes them in the absence of its withdrawal."[34] Unlike the apocalyptic undertone and frontal critique of the global condition that often characterize the network narrative film, *Jellyfish* dismantles the function of the despotic symbol *home* and ends on a hopeful note. By the film's end, an alternative collectivity emerges, one that is transient and porous, formless and open on all sides—a collectivity that does not make claims, assume ownership, or promote the rise of a new regime of signs.

Fortification and Homelessness

The prime occupation of Michael Haneke's *Code Unknown* can be conceptualized as a study of the transformation of urban space in the era of global migration and the treatment of private space as a defensive shell against the outside world.[35] And if the private sphere metonymically connotes the security that accompanies cultural and social fluency, Haneke's film forces a recognition of Western civilization's present encounter "with the unwanted presence of its colonial others, be these the old Arab immigrants of its recent past, the diasporic subjects of second generation, or new immigrants from Eastern Europe."[36] Beyond the private realm, the public in *Code Unknown* is figured as a leftover space, the stage of random and solitary crossings of paths, a space of failed encounters "precipitated by the characters' own inability or refusal to see the other."[37] Thus, the notion of an unknown code addresses the pervasiveness of failed communication between strangers, friends, family, and lovers. It is this sense of failed communication that seems to eradicate the protective shell that the private realm presumably affords. In *Code Unknown*, as in the Israeli films, the fortification of space can fail at any moment and turn against those who seek refuge. This failure is portrayed either by the unavoidable penetration of the outside world or by the creation of impenetrable "bourgeois entrapments."[38] Both construe a sense of isolation and the impossibility of belonging. Thus, much like the fate of the colonial immigrant, the work migrant, and the member of an ethnic minority, in the Paris of *Code Unknown* and the Tel Aviv of *Jellyfish*, *Year Zero*, *What a Wonderful Place*, and *Ajami*, all characters experience displacement, marginalization, and homelessness. And yet, unlike *Code Unknown*, in which the sidewalk is figured as a site of ethnic clashing; *Amores*

Perros, Crash, and *Year Zero,* in which the street is the site of a fatal accident waiting to happen; or *Ajami, Year Zero,* and *Hawaii Oslo,* in which a restaurant or a hotel lobby becomes the site of tragic shootings, *Jellyfish* positions the beach, the street, the hospital, and the hotel emergency stairwell as bearing the potentiality and the possibility of the unforeseeable and the new.

Thus, the open structure of complex narration has proven adept at thematizing the disruptive and destabilizing condition of the global city's racially, ethnically, and culturally mixed crowds. It is this sense of frail stability that contemporary cinema brings into focal awareness—the rise of transnationalism, hybrid identities, and loss of identity. Hence, our understanding of the concept of national cinema in the context of globalization should be attuned to its "changeable and non-permanent notion, as a transboundary process rather than a set of fixed attributes."[39] If indeed that is the case, should the films' transcendence of national borders be read as the undermining of the national? If contemporary films no longer mirror an imagined national unity and homogeneity, does the enunciation of the national reside in the films' negotiation of civic and social inclusion, which counters the historical nationalist exclusion of all *others*?

Luisa Rivi contends that "only by accounting for its own multiplicity and contradiction can Europe de-Eurocentrize itself and can its new hybridized interlocutors speak their voices." This perspective is of particular relevance in view of the emerging trends in European cinema. Rivi's attention is directed toward those films that emulate an image of a Europe capable of inclusion and of being constituted through otherness.[40] At the same time, the films' loose plots and ambiguous open-ended conclusions stress the notion that the prime function of contemporary cinema is to ask the questions without, as Haneke insists, the lie of a forced answer.[41]

The imagining of the national is thus reconfigured by a filmmaking intent on the narrow study of local particularity. Interestingly, one of the effects of this so-called elevated locality, as Thomas Elsaesser points out, is that filmmakers of various national origins, such as Paul Thomas Anderson, Alejandro González Iñárritu, Michael Haneke, Tom Tykwer, Fatih Akin, Wong Kar-Wai, Kim Ki-Duk, or Abbas Kiarostami, seem to have "more in common with each other than with directors of their respective national cinemas, which paradoxically, gives a new meaning to regional or local attributes."[42] In their work, the multiplicity of identity, cultural complexity, and difference advance an overturning of a unifying sense of the national by exposing the very thing that nationalism, for many years, sought to deny. It then follows that in the global context, the paradox of national cinema is that "the parochial and ultimately/eventually the periphery find a new relevance and importance within discourses of nationalism."[43] Thus, Susan Hayward suggests, it is the inverted center/periphery configuration that gave national cinema its renewed purpose and direction—to interrogate and problematize the nation's pretense of unity. Notice, however, that in her revised assessment, Hayward insists on focusing her discussion on what she continues to term *national cinema*.

In that respect, revisited accounts of the national insist on problematizing this very point by challenging the often-unquestioned application of new terminology that seeks to bypass the national framework. Terms such as *cross-cultural* and *transnational* already contain within them an assumed primary existence of bounded national zones or the existence of distinct cultural zones within countries, and these very zones are separated by borders that can be crossed.[44] Paul Willemen's critical search seeks to rescue the notion of what he terms *subjective individuality* from the hijacked national identity figured by industrialized cultural practices such as cinema. The former, he argues, can escape and surpass any such identity straitjackets.[45] The question that persists is whether such subjectivity is in fact reliant upon the national framework as a condition for its very subjectivity, and if so, how can it be articulated vis-à-vis the channels that a theoretical discussion of national cinema in the age of globalism may currently afford?

Notes

1. In the context of this chapter, the listing of a film's multiple countries of origin is necessary, as it points to the transnational basis of its production. While binational and regional production agreements are as old as cinema, the larger scale and scope of transnational cooperations as far as financing is concerned have become more prevalent since the turn of the millennium. Despite the significant increase in the allocation of state funding subsequent to the installment of the New Cinema Law in 2000, the Israeli film industry continues to rely on multinational coproduction agreements. On these grounds, Israeli films are often criticized at home as post-Zionist, anti-Israeli, or simply lacking in national solidarity.

2. Avner Shavit, "Cannes Film Festival 2014: Ronit Elkabetz and Menachem Golan Provoked a Stir and Garnered Applause," *Walla News*, May 17, 2014, https://e.walla.co.il/item /2747009 (in Hebrew, my translation).

3. David Swartz, *Culture and Power: The Sociology of Pierre Bourdieu* (Chicago: University of Chicago Press, 1997), 80. Pierre Bourdieu's theory of action extends the

Marxian notion of capital to all forms of power relations, whether material, cultural, social, or symbolic. To this end, Bourdieu adopts a conception of labor that models the struggle for the accumulation of three additional kinds of capital: *cultural capital*, which encompasses all forms of accumulated cultural knowledge, competence, and education; *social capital* corresponding with the value accorded to acquaintances and social networking; and *symbolic capital*, which stands for the accumulation of prestige and institutional legitimization. Under certain conditions, each of these accumulated kinds of capital can be converted into another.

4. See, for example, the work of Andrew Higson, "The Concept of National Cinema," *Screen* 30 (1989): 36–46; of Susan Hayward in the early 1990s, including *French National Cinema* (London: Routledge, 1993); of Paul Willemen, "The National," in *Fields of Vision: Essays in Film Studies, Visual Anthropology, and Photography*, ed. Leslie Devereaux and Roger Hillman (Los Angeles: University of California Press, 1995), 21–34; and of Mette Hjort, "Danish Cinema and the Politics of Recognition," in *Post-Theory: Reconstructing Film Studies*, ed. David Bordwell and Noël Carroll (Madison: The University of Wisconsin Press, 1996), 520–532. Also see Ella Shohat, *Israeli Cinema: East/West and the Politics of Representation* (Austin: University of Texas Press, 1989).

5. Benedict Anderson, *Imagined Communities* (London: Verso, 1983), 6.

6. Mette Hjort and Scott Mackenzie, "Introduction," in *Cinema and Nation*, ed. Mette Hjort and Scott Mackenzie (London: Routledge, 2000), 4.

7. Arjun Appadurai, "Grassroots Globalization and the Research Imagination," in *Globalization*, ed. Arjun Appadurai (Minneapolis: University of Minnesota Press, 2001), 1–21. See also Stuart Hall, "The Local and the Global: Globalization and Ethnicity," in *Culture, Globalization and the World System: Contemporary Conditions for the Representation of Identity*, ed. Anthony King (Minneapolis: University of Minnesota Press, 1997), 19–40.

8. Jan Simon, "Complex Narratives," *New Review of Film and Television Studies* 6, no. 2 (Summer 2008): 111.

9. Rosalind Galt, *The New European Cinema: Redrawing the Map* (New York: Columbia University Press, 2006), 231.

10. Sally Banes and Noël Carroll, "Cinematic Nation-Building: Eisenstein's *The Old and the New*," in *Cinema and Nation*, ed. Mette Hjort and Scott Mackenzie (London: Routledge, 2000), 121–138.

11. Arjun Appadurai and James Holston, "Cities and Citizenship," *Public Culture* 8 (Fall 1996): 188–189.

12. Hizky Shoham, "Of Other Cinematic Spaces: Urban Zionism in Early Hebrew Cinema," *Israel Studies Review* 26, no. 2 (2011): 110–111. It is important to note that in this work, Shoham directs our attention to two Jewish films from 1932 and 1935 that stage a more complex and nuanced imagination of the Zionist space and its urban enactment.

13. Judd Ne'eman, "The Death Mask of the Moderns: A Genealogy of New Sensibility Cinema in Israel," *Israel Studies* 4, no. 1 (Spring 1999): 102.

14. Nurith Gertz, "Gender and Space in the New Israeli Cinema," *Shofar: An Interdisciplinary Journal of Jewish Studies* 22, no. 1 (Fall 2003): 110.

15. Ibid.

16. David Bordwell, *The Way Hollywood Tells It: Story and Style in Modern Movies* (Berkeley: University of California Press, 2006), 30.

17. Appadurai and Holston 1996, 188.

18. Barbara E. Mann, *A Place in History: Modernism, Tel Aviv, and the Creation of Urban Jewish Space* (Stanford: Stanford University Press, 2006), 17.

19. Saskia Sassen, "Whose City Is It? Globalization and the Formation of New Claims," in *The Globalization Reader*, ed. Frank Lechner and John Boli (Oxford: Blackwell, 2000), 70–76.

20. Appadurai and Holston 1996, 196. The writers associate the tumult of citizenship in cities with the sprouting of shanties of migrants alongside the mansions and corporate zones of industrial-state capitalism, a parity that births "struggles over the nature of belonging to the national society."

21. To this end, this chapter proposes a focused reading of the film *Jellyfish* with references to other relevant network narrative films.

22. Wendy Everett, "Fractal Films and the Architecture of Complexity," *Studies in European Cinema* 2, no. 3 (Spring 2005): 159. See also Simon 2008 and Bordwell 2006, 72–103.

23. Everett 2005, 167.

24. Elizabeth Wilson, "The Invisible Flâneur," in *Postmodern Cities and Spaces*, ed. Sophie Watson and Katherine Gibson (Cambridge: Blackwell, 1995), 59–79.

25. Bordwell 2006, 100.

26. Gilles Deleuze and Felix Guattari, *Kafka: Toward a Minor Literature* (Minneapolis: University of Minnesota Press, 1986).

27. Everett 2005.

28. Michael Cowan, "Between the Street and the Apartment: Disturbing the Space of Fortress Europe in Michael Haneke," *Studies in European Cinema* 5, no. 2 (Winter 2008): 117–129.

29. Ilan Avisar, "The National and the Popular in Israeli Cinema," *Shofar: An Interdisciplinary Journal of Jewish Studies* 24, no. 1 (Fall 2005): 125–143. Consider especially Avisar's contention that "beginning in the eighties, there has been a growing radicalization of the political messages, and the themes of solidarity or cooperation eventually have given way to skeptical attitudes and apocalyptic visions" (134).

30. Gertz 2003, 110.

31. A statement made by the photographer in the film who is a second generation to Holocaust survivors.

32. Russell Grigg, *Lacan, Language, and Philosophy* (Albany: State University of New York Press, 2008), 120–121.

33. Ibid., 120–121. Here Grigg addresses the Lacanian act via Slavoj Žižek's theorization of its varied manifestations and outcomes for the subject.

34. Gilles Deleuze and Felix Guattari, *Anti-Oedipus: Capitalism and Schizophrenia* (Minneapolis: University of Minnesota Press, 1983), 310. Also qtd. in Joe Hughes, *Deleuze and the Genesis of Representation* (London: Continuum, 2008), 56.

35. Cowan 2008.

36. Luisa Rivi, *European Cinema After 1989: Cultural Identity and Transnational Production* (New York: Palgrave MacMillan, 2007), 125.

37. Cowan 2008.

38. Ibid., 123. In *Code Unknown*, it is the crying of the neighbor's abused child that penetrates the protagonist's apartment, in *Jellyfish*, the leaking ceiling that floods the apartment, and so on.

39. Ulf Hedetoft, "Contemporary Cinema: Between Cultural Globalization and National Interpretation," in *Cinema and Nation*, ed. Mette Hjort and Scott MacKanzie (London: Routledge, 2000), 282.

40. Rivi 2007, 114.

41. Everett 2005. In an interview with Scott Foundas for Indiewire in 2001 Haneke stated that "the only thing that you can do is put the question strongly . . . if you give the answer, you lie. Whatever kind of security you try to feed somebody is an illusion. . . . I think every art form today can put out only questions, not answers. It's the fundamental condition."

42. Thomas Elsaesser, *European Cinema Face to Face with Hollywood* (Amsterdam: Amsterdam University Press, 2005), 18.

43. Susan Hayward, "Framing National Cinemas," in *Cinema and Nation*, ed. Mette Hjort and Scott MacKanzie (London: Routledge, 2000), 88–102.

44. Paul Willemen, "The National Revisited," in *Theorising National Cinema*, ed. Valentina Vitali and Paul Willemen (London: British Film Institute, 2006), 29–43.

45. Ibid.

13

FANTASIES OF OTHER DESIRES

Homonationalism and Self-Othering in Contemporary Israeli Queer Cinema

Boaz Hagin

Raz Yosef

T HE INTERNATIONAL TRIUMPH OF ISRAELI CINEMA IN THIS millennium has included numerous films that feature queer representations. In this chapter, we argue that the recent success of these Israeli films can be understood not only in relation to the historical junctures in our region—as they are frequently described in scholarship on the topic—but also in relation to two wider transnational contexts. One is that of gay and queer identities and rights and particularly their coupling with a teleological concept of unidirectional historical progress from tradition to modernity understood as Western, individualist, and neoliberal. The second is that of transnational film production, distribution, and consumption, such as the global trade in pornography on the web and the global filmmaking network in which many of the highest profile films from our region are funded and distributed, complicating their belonging to the very region they supposedly represent. We suggest that these contexts can offer a fruitful framework for analyzing queer representations in Israeli cinema and can complement the existing work that usually places the films within the context of Israel and Palestine.

As we have noted in a previous essay,[1] many of the best-known films from Israel and Palestine—the ones with the highest visibility outside of the region, that garner nominations and prizes in international competitions and the Academy Awards, and that receive substantial attention from Israeli studies and film studies scholars—can be viewed as instances of *world cinema*. As Thomas Elsaesser writes, these world cinema films, in many cases, and certainly in the Israeli one, rely on a modification of the way European national cinemas of the 1970s and 1980s were financed by state-funded support schemes and cultural subsidies. In contemporary world cinema, by contrast, this model extends beyond nationally representative cinema, and it now facilitates film production and distribution across the globe.[2] Like other examples in world cinema, many Israeli films are in fact transnational coproductions relying not only on local film funds and investments by Israeli television channels but also on European coproduction funds and presales to television channels like the Franco German ARTE.

The success of these films depends on a global distribution system that is closely tied to the network of international film festivals, where many world cinema films find an audience.[3] Some festivals offer production funds, development money, or a talent campus with workshops and platforms for collaborations. The festivals hold a "clearing house function" for distributors of minority interest films that have attracted critical plaudits or have won prizes;[4] they also "act collectively as a distribution system . . . effectively select[ing] each year which films will fill the few slots that art-house cinemas or the dedicated screens of the multiplexes keep open for the minority interest cinema."[5] In festivals, films can gather the cultural capital and critical prowess necessary for further exhibition so that "no poster of an independent film can do without the logo of one of the world's prime festivals, as prominently displayed as Hollywood productions carry their studio logo."[6] Some of these Israeli films can become relatively successful at the Israeli box office, sometimes following their success in international festivals. Other films do poorly in the domestic market; some are derided by local critics for being simplistic and superficial "festival films" that are made for foreign consumption.[7]

World cinema, according to Elsaesser, is often driven by an "ethnographic outlook," a "self-othering" or "self-exoticization" in which "the ethnic, the local or the regional expose themselves, under the guise of self-expression, to the gaze of the benevolent other" so that like the participant observer of anthropology, world cinema might be presenting "the mirror of what the 'native' thinks the other, the observer wants to see."[8] Considered from the Israeli perspective, we might claim that what the films ultimately show is the beliefs that the native Israeli harbors about what the Western *other* wants Israelis to display. The films, in other words, are Israeli fantasies about what the festival-going *other* desires Israelis to desire.

In this chapter, we look beyond these festival films and also consider lesser-known films and videos, but we use Elsaesser's formula of self-exoticization as the starting point. All of the texts reflect or consider a fantasy of Israelis about the Western other and what the other wants from Israel. We will suggest three different formulas that can be discerned in contemporary queer-themed moving-image texts:

1. A homonational fantasy that depicts Israel/Palestine as flawed and the Western other as being able to fill in the lack that often has to do with sexuality across a tradition-modernity divide.
2. A homonational fantasy presenting Israel as an Oriental sexual utopia embodying the *other's* desire in which the promise of the future has already been fulfilled and any troubling differences that might characterize premodern or non-Western locals are defanged.
3. Queer images and logics that undo the assumptions underlying these fantasies while very much acknowledging their existence in an image-saturated world. These texts upset a trajectory of development from repressive Oriental tradition to enlightened Western modernity.[9]

Speaking the Same Language: A Homonational Trajectory from Tradition to Modernity

World cinema films, Elsaesser claims, cater to the needs of the festival circuit and foreign viewers, a fact that influences and is even reflected in their subject matter. Elsaesser notes world cinema's attention to globalization and to national and subnational identities. Questions of "underdevelopment, exclusion, racism, genocide, poverty, and of the clash between traditional ways of life and the impact of globalization, modernity, and Western habits or lifestyles" play a major role in world cinema, as do "the constructions of gender and ethnicity, family values and religion, concepts of good and evil, state authority and censorship, and the role/oppression of women in traditional societies."[10] In addition, Elsaesser discerns the festivals' interest in topical areas and international hot spots—two positions that Israel/Palestine has been filling for many years—as well as their receptivity to various groups and causes, including queer issues.[11]

The Israeli films that have achieved significant success in world markets seem to bear out Elsaesser's account. They deal with topical and political issues in the region or in Israeli society—such as the Israeli-Palestinian conflict, wars, and the Holocaust and its aftermath (which seem to be perennially topical in the Academy Awards and in European film festivals). They self-exoticize conflicts around ethnic and familial identities (such as Georgian Jews in Dover Koshashvili's *Late Marriage*, 2001, and *Gift from Above*, 2003) or communities that resist Westernization, such as ultra-Orthodox Jews in *Ushpizin* (Giddi Dar, 2004) and *My Father, My Lord* (David Volach, 2007).[12]

Festivals are receptive to queer content, and numerous international lesbian and gay film festivals are entirely devoted to queer films. In the competition over coproduction funds and the attention of festival programmers, a film can gain points by offering a combination of Israeli self-othering and gay characters, thus adding a gay twist to the familiar Israeli formula or providing an exotic locale to revitalize otherwise worn-out gay narratives. For example, *Walk on Water* (Eytan Fox, 2004), an Israeli Swedish coproduction boasting the logos of major film festivals such as Berlin and Toronto on its DVD cover, features a bromance between a macho and heterosexual Israeli Mossad assassin whose parents were Holocaust survivors and a gay German who is the grandson of a Nazi criminal whom the Israeli assassin is sent to kill.[13] *The Bubble* (Eytan Fox, 2006), which won multiple prizes, including at the Berlin International Film Festival and many gay and lesbian film festivals, focuses on a gay love story between an Israeli reserve soldier and a Palestinian who becomes a suicide bomber after struggling with being gay in a traditional society.[14] *The Secrets* (Avi Nesher, 2007), an Israeli-French coproduction and an official selection at the Toronto Film Festival, tells of two young religious women who fall in love, while they and the viewers discover the joys of ritual bathing in the nude in a mikvah.[15] *Eyes Wide Open* (Haim Tabakman, 2009), an Israeli, German, and French coproduction and an official selection at the Karlovy Vary, Toronto, and Cannes film festivals, tells of two men in an ultra-Orthodox Jewish community in Jerusalem who have an affair while they and the viewers discover the joys of ritual bathing in the nude in a spring outside the city.[16] And *Out in the Dark* (Michael Mayer, 2012), an Israeli-US coproduction, which premiered at the Toronto International Film Festival and won numerous awards, such as at the Berlin Jewish Film Festival, the Haifa International Film Festival, the Long Island Gay and Lesbian Film Festival, and the Miami Gay and Lesbian Film Festival, deals with the relationship between an Israeli Jewish lawyer and Palestinian student whose brother happens to be a leading militant leader in the West Bank.[17] The two gay men keep their briefs on when they break into a pool at night and go for a swim.

In the case of the double exoticization of queer characters in Israeli films, we can spot a tendency to view the societies depicted through the lens of Western neoliberal individualism and, in particular, gay liberation. That other societies might have or combine other forms of nonheterosexual desires and conducts remains unimaginable in many of these films. Thus, as Elsaesser argues, self-othering can "stand in the way of encountering the otherness of the other."[18] When the individualist gay liberation discourse is combined with Israeli self-othering—notably ultra-Orthodox communities, wars, and the Israeli-Palestinian conflict—the result can be a story of self-realization and liberation of Westernized and Westernizing gays that is often contrasted with the tragedy of others who are unable to break away from their repressive society and achieve Western neoliberal gay identity. Palestinian and religious Jewish communities are viewed as atavistic and homophobic. The only possible solution, for those who are fortunate enough to have chosen it, is to embrace Western individualist neoliberalism—including certain gay identities.

These films, then, have managed to secure funding and international distribution not only by means of double exoticization but also by reducing the otherness of the other for a neoliberal Western audience. Some films even bundle this turn away from tradition with an actual encounter with a benevolent Western non-Israeli: the gay German teaches the macho Mossad agent in *Walk on Water* to become more tolerant and ultimately a better Israeli; the love story in *The Secrets* is triangulated through an empowering encounter with a non-Jewish French woman; and the temptation of leaving the conflict behind and seeking a better future in Europe, especially for gay Palestinians, is embraced in *Out in the Dark* as well as in the documentary *The Invisible Men* (Yariv Mozer, 2012) and considered in the documentary *Oriented* (Jake Witzenfeld, 2015).

Moreover, insofar as these films represent Israel in world cinema, they are ipso facto cases of homonationalism, the convivial relation that Jasbir Puar has explored between queerness and normative nationalism at a time in which liberal queer and gay rights have emerged within "the bountiful market and the interstices of state benevolence."[19] This neoliberal acceptance of some homonormative bodies within the state coincides, according to Puar, with a construction that couples nonwhite terrorism with sexual pathologies as well as homophobia and justifies military interventions.

Several scholars have shown that Fox's work, in particular, has adhered to this positive view of gay neoliberal identity and has displayed a tendency to eliminate all those who deviate from it.[20] Fox's internationally successful *Yossi and Jagger* (2002), for example, tells of two gay officers serving near the Lebanese-Israeli border. It promotes an image of gay men as handsome, straight-acting army officers who can be incorporated into a military framework as "respectable homosexuals" and is careful to avoid any lingering ideas or images that might offend a Western liberal audience or in any way question the view that homosexuality can and should be assimilated into mainstream normalcy. The film is particularly careful to fend off the possibility that the boundaries between homosexuality and heterosexuality are permeable, especially in the army, and downplays anal penetrative sex between men. Moreover, the officer who comes closest to challenging the film's sexual conformist politics—by an uncompromising demand that he and his lover come out of the closet—is killed during a military operation at the end of the film, burying his potentially subversive identity in a heroic death and dismissing his troubling presence in the film.[21]

Similarly, Avi Nesher's *The Secrets* seems unable to imagine any alternatives to a Western individualist gay identity. Its protagonist is the precocious and reserved young daughter of a rabbi who falls in love with another young woman at a Jewish women's seminary. In the film, the option of a gay identity in secular society is never shown, and the *L word* is never uttered. Moreover, the protagonist claims that she never even dreamed that such a love or attraction was possible. Nevertheless, she seems to discover and embrace gay liberation quickly and all on her own: she refuses to marry her fiancé, leaves her father's house, suggests to the woman she loves that they move in together and create a home, resents the latter's implication that they or she might not be "normal" or is violating Jewish laws (she decides that only men are forbidden by Jewish law to have sex with a member of their own gender)—all but directly demanding ultra-Orthodox Judaism to endorse and perform lesbian marriage.

The formula is taken to an extreme in the stylistically artificial and colorful *Cupcakes* (Eytan Fox, 2013). The film depicts a journey of six Tel Aviv neighbors to represent their country in a Eurovision-like song contest in Paris, which magically ends up resolving all of their (or their significant others') personal problems, particularly, as the *Variety* review notes, by enabling them to come out in various ways and learn to dare "to be yourself."[22] However, in a curious twist, it turns out that while liberal Israelis believe in being themselves and, inter alia, celebrating their gay identity openly, the flamboyant Russian singer in the Paris contest manages to represent his country by staying in the closet and "performing" together with his "lovely wife," as he refers to her. The Israeli contestants mock his presumably faux heterosexuality, but in the contest it is the blatantly performed heterosexuality of the Russian couple that ends up defeating the true-to-themselves Tel Avivians and winning first place. When apparently flirting with the gay Israeli man on the team, the Russian comments that he thinks that they speak the same language. Perhaps he is implying not only that both are men who are attracted to other men and extravagant song contexts but also that the neoliberal Western agenda adopted by the Israelis is not that different from his, and both are ultimately serving their nations and shutting out other sexual options and traditions.

Pinkwashing Pornography: Israel as a Sexual Utopia

One of the realms in which queer characters transcend local borders in Israeli moving images is the recent wave of pornographic videos made in Israel, such as the work of Russian-born Israeli American filmmaker Michael Lucas. In 2009, his Manhattan-based Lucas Entertainment announced that it was releasing the first gay adult production shot entirely on location in Israel with an all-Israeli cast, *Men of Israel* (Michael Lucas and Mr. Pam). The film's website explains that this "groundbreaking event" and "landmark in the history of Israel and in the evolution of adult entertainment" has two aims: to represent the "sexually arousing" and "tanned and chiseled muscle hunks" of Israel for whom "it came naturally to perform with such raw sexual passionate [*sic*]" and also to allow Israel to "play a lead visual character as a country with rich history and a wide range of natural beauty." It assures us that "Israel has a number of sites and destinations to lure any tourist to book a flight."[23] According to the website, the film's codirector, Michael Lucas, hopes that through the film's dual adulation of the raw attractiveness of the men "in their remarkable natural environment" and of Israel itself—which not only offers an Orientalist fantasy of passionate rawness but is also, according to him, "a truly progressive, multicultural society"[24]—he will be able to parlay the film's success into a tourist boom for Israel, as the Eastern European gay pornography company Bel Ami did for that region.

The film's double role as gay pornography and tourist advertisement is hard to miss. At times, the roles harmonize and resonate. In one segment, the camera tilts up from the groin of an aroused man on a balcony overlooking Tel Aviv–Jaffa to the erect skyscrapers of the city's skyline. In another, the men discuss in Hebrew their decision to switch sexual position (because of one of the men's discomfort), adding a local, authentic ingredient to the film while also making sure the non–Hebrew-speaking potential tourists are less likely to suspect that the Israeli men's performance is not quite raw and natural.

The two functions cohere less smoothly at other moments—for example, when some of the men insist on announcing their imminent ejaculation in English, with a heavy Israeli accent. The filmmakers sometimes prefer extreme long shots that are better at highlighting the scenic vistas than the attractiveness of the men, or they include both the men and sprawling beaches in the same frame, resulting in awkward compositions. Furthermore, no lighting arrangement seems to capture both Israel's exotic scenery and the men together, resulting either in overexposed backgrounds or low-key illumination schemes that form bizarre chiaroscuro effects, underexposing the men's bodies or leaving them as mere silhouettes.

Assuming that the film's point is indeed to lure tourists to the region, we can view it as exposing what its filmmakers believe these potential tourists want from Israel—that is, the filmmakers' fantasy about what the Western other wants Israel to be: a Middle Eastern utopia that proffers to its tourists/viewers both Oriental rawness (the untamed beaches and deserts and the ancient archeological sites) and a gay neoliberal Western lifestyle that extends not only to tolerant urban Tel Aviv and its modern skyscrapers but also seems to have modernized the entire land, as in these films there is no trace of non-Western cultures; there are no Palestinian or traditional Jewish lifestyles that might possess different sexual mores. There is particularly none of the homophobia or the difficulties encountered in the festival films dealt with in the previous section. Every locale and person are part of the liberal lifestyle; no matter how "ancient" or "natural," the multicultural progressiveness of Israel is never in doubt. The views of Israel, selected and deliberately engineered for foreign viewers, are a mélange of an Orientalist paradise for tourism and a progressive Western haven in the Middle East.

Not relying only on pornography, Lucas also made the documentary *Undressing Israel: Gay Men in The Promised Land* (Michael Lucas and Yariv Mozer, 2012). The film makes no pretense of being natural self-expression but is rather clearly a polemical piece intended to educate foreign viewers. It begins in Times Square, with interviewees from all over the world responding to the question of whether they think homosexuality is legal in Israel. Many believe it is not and think that that is wrong while admitting that they do not really know that much about Israel at all. The film then goes on to disprove their false beliefs through rapidly edited gay Israeli talking heads and segments in which Lucas meets several prominent Israelis, such as an openly gay member of Israel's parliament, a gay Arab journalist, and Eytan Fox (often confounding Israel in general with Tel Aviv). The film leaves no doubt as to the legality of homosexuality in Israel and repeatedly compares gay rights in Israel with their poor state in other Middle Eastern countries as well as with US legislation. Lucas, ostentatiously wearing a Star of David pendant, meets a gym trainer who explains that he was out of the closet during his military service, gay rights activists, and a gay couple who had children through surrogacy, and he attends the Tel Aviv Pride Parade and a gay wedding. Whereas the festival films discussed in the previous section portrayed Israel as flawed and underdeveloped due to some of its subcultures still adhering to traditional patriarchy and homophobia and Western neoliberal individual rights as the progressive solution for its denizens' suffering, for Lucas, Israel is already a triumphant haven of gay rights. Not only is homosexuality legal, but, as he claims, in terms of gay rights, it "is much more progressive than the United States."[25] An Arab journalist admits that he loves Tel Aviv and how brutal traditional Arab families can be to their gay sons, implying that Israel is the solution to the travails of gay Palestinians. As in the festival films, here, too, the film's gay participants and its viewers get to enjoy scenes of same-sex joint bathing (see fig. 13.1)— this time, however, in a local swimming pool with their children and husbands (and not, as in the festival films, in clandestine liminal zones that allow them a rare retreat from the suppression of their sexuality in traditional societies).

In *Undressing Israel*, the future promised by the West has already happened in the Israeli utopia. Homonormativity and homonationalism have already been achieved, and it is the West that needs to correct its misperceptions about Israel and catch up with it in terms of progressive rights. Lucas's work can and has been accused of taking part in Israeli *pinkwashing*—that is, as Sarah Schulman explains, "a deliberate strategy to conceal the continuing violations of Palestinians' human rights behind an image of modernity signified by Israeli gay life."[26] Journalist and author Max Blumenthal has described Lucas as "one of the world's wealthiest gay porn producers," who "leveraged his fortune to found a company promoting gay tourism to

Figure 13.1. Itai Pinkas (*left*), Michael Lucas (*center*), Yoav Arad (*right*), and Pinkas's and Arad's children demonstrate Israeli progressiveness through gay marriage and attractive fatherhood in *Undressing Israel: Gay Men in The Promised Land* (Lucas and Mozer 2012).

Israel."[27] According to Blumenthal, one of the scenes in *Men of Israel* "featured two actors having sex inside a Palestinian village that was ethnically cleansed by Zionist militias in 1948," while Lucas incorrectly claimed that "the village had been depopulated hundreds of years before."[28]

The notion of *pinkwashing* describes an important aspect of Israeli government policies in which gay rights in Israel are used as a propaganda point and compared with the violations of gay rights in other parts of the Middle East. While we do not doubt that this is indeed the intention of the Israeli government and is very clearly stated by Lucas in *Undressing Israel*, we do believe that it is not always necessarily successful and that the notion might at times be used in a way that assumes a simplistic view of the media as mimesis and posits an unmediated reality that can subsequently be either correctly or incorrectly represented.[29] This idea in fact mirrors Lucas's own critique of the way Israel is misrepresented in world media and the common right-wing Israeli refrain that the Israeli-Palestinian conflict receives disproportionate attention when many much worse human rights violations in the region and the world are underreported or ignored. All of these believe that the suffering in the region could be remedied by striving for more perfect and complete representation of a supposedly unmediated reality. They ascribe immense power to the manufacturers of representations and sometimes even presume that nefarious forces with the supposedly infinite power to manipulate the media are at work behind the scenes (wealthy well-connected Jews, mysterious Muslims willing to invest their petrodollars in an organized effort to demonize Israel, or grassroots antisemites). Such notions ascribe little agency and sophistication to media consumers and leave little room for the more complex role of the media as part of the reality of the world and a cause of change. Couldn't we, for example, let reality simulate its representation and use pinkwashing to alter the conditions it purports to represent—to buttress gay rights in Israel and perhaps extend them, notably to queer Palestinians both with and without Israeli citizenship?

Queer Balagan: Beyond Homonational Fantasies

A third and final formula that we would like to present in this brief chapter is that of queer films or moments within films that subvert the underlying premises of the other formulas, especially any notion of predefined progress and simple representation of reality or self-expression. Whether their audiences are domestic or foreign, these texts acknowledge the significance of transcending the borders of the local and the tangle of transnational fantasies in a media-inundated world. These are not ideal queer utopias beyond identities and nations and make no claim to undo homonationalism. As Puar explains, homonationalism should not be thought of as "as an accusation, an identity, a bad politics," another way of "distinguishing good queers from bad queers," but rather as a historical moment—a convergence of state practices, neoliberal capitalism, the "human rights industrial complex," and Islamophobia. We "must engage it in the first place as the condition of possibility for national and transnational politics."[30]

Acknowledging these conditions, the option for moving images discussed in this section makes no claim to proffer either answers or even a compelling diagnosis of the problem. It brings together elements that within a progressive teleology might be viewed as contradictory, gives us not even a glimpse of any already-known utopias, and clarifies little about its own desires or those of *others*. It meanders in queer times and places, is fully aware that it is toying with images and not trying to better represent any reality, and nihilistically laughs as it refuses to fall in line with mainstream politics or pretend there is any deeper truth in colonial masquerades. If it had a core, it would be queer.

For example, *Joe + Belle* (Veronica Kedar, 2011) is a dark Israeli indie comedy about two women—Joe, a Tel Aviv drug dealer who, at the beginning of the film, declares her indifference toward Israel in English, and Belle, a young woman who comes out of a psychiatric institute and speaks French with her mother.[31] The two meet when Belle tries to commit suicide in Joe's bathtub. They fall in love, kill a man, flee from the police, and end up in Sderot, a "development town," with many immigrants and high unemployment. Due to its proximity to the Gaza strip, Sderot is frequently the target of Qassam rocket attacks, which are constantly mentioned on the radio throughout the film. Joe and Belle even make love in the bathroom in Sderot's cinematheque during one such attack. They later borrow an electric cart. When a policeman spots them, Belle asks Joe whether they should stop or keep on driving. Alluding to *Thelma & Louise* (Ridley Scott, 1991), Joe responds that there is no cliff there; if they keep on driving, they will reach Netivot, another godforsaken development town, and they do not want their ending to be there. They stay in Sderot—the policeman just wanted to invite them to a local talent show—where Belle works at a local food plant, and Joe waits for her to come out of the plant on Paris Street. They romantically walk into the sunset as rockets explode around them, and they complain that they hate it when that happens at dusk but remain unfazed.

This queer love story begins by stating that its protagonist does not belong in Israel. Yet, it continues with the realization of both women that they are in Israel. But far from embracing Israeli reality, they end up in a cliché of Israel as a war-torn region in a city that is repeatedly on the news throughout the movie, and the film's ending appears to be shot on scratched black-and-white film (although *Joe + Belle* was shot on video), as the title song's lyrics enigmatically declare that all of the movies in the world are tinted in black and white. Far from seeking to correct a misrepresentation of Israeli reality, *Joe + Belle* acknowledges the intensely mediated world, inundated with screens and media, that is our reality today and merely notes that the images that they live with and in are not those of high-concept Ridley Scott movies but of deteriorated art-house films and news reports. Nor does it seem possible to organize the film's plot in any familiar narrative. Both of the women seem to lack any drive (or a driver's license, for that matter) and seem to land in various situations by chance. Their flight following the murder they commit is resolved by chance without their involvement when the police believe someone else is responsible. The film constructs Sderot as an emblem of stasis at the end of the world, and it halts whatever narrative there was up to that point (or slows it down to the speed of an electric cart), creating a meandering plot that might be considered as akin to the queer refusal to be subjected to the trajectory of heterosexual families and reproductive futurism as well as to the hectic busyness that a war zone might prompt.[32] Particularly, there is no trajectory from tradition (and homophobia) to modernity (and gay rights). The film's protagonists move from supposedly modern urban Tel Aviv to the peripheral "development town" of Sderot, characterized by lower-income immigrants and, one might assume, more traditional societies. It is there that they can express their love freely and, moreover, that there are signs of supposedly urban culture, notably the local cinematheque and a Paris Street.

An additional example that disturbs the assumptions of the formulas described in the previous two sections is thriving on YouTube. The Arisa line of monthly Tel Aviv parties that has also toured globally and performed in South America, Asia, and Europe presents itself as the first line for gays with Mizrahi music in Israel. It thus from the very start does not seem to find any problem with being both gay and non-Western.

In Israeli culture, Mizrahi Jews (Jews from Arab and Muslim countries) are stereotypically constructed as being associated with the working class, right-wing politics, and a stronger attachment to religion. The Mizrahi Jews are contrasted with the European Ashkenazi ethnicities, which dominated Israeli society in its first decades and still hold many privileged socioeconomic and cultural positions in the country. Ashkenazi Jews are often associated with economic privilege, left-wing politics, secularization, and Westernized cosmopolitanism.[33] Like whites in North America and Europe, Ashkenazi ethnicity is often unmarked and viewed as universal or simply as Israeli. Many of the gay images and struggles in Israel have been dominated by an Ashkenazi middle-class sexual politics and views that adopted the Western Eurocentric gay identity while disavowing ethnicity in the formation of sexual identity. Israeli gay media has often reduced the repertoire of gay Mizrahi men to two types that alarmingly match colonial fantasies about savage Oriental male bodies—the hypersexual virile "stud" and the feminine delicate "boy"—while gay political advocacy has frequently remained silent about the racism that Mizrahi queers confronted within and without the gay community.[34] When gay activists advocated coming out as a universal rite of passage within a narrative of growing up and leaving the family, there was little consideration of the role the attachment to the family can have as a source of strength against discrimination for Mizrahi people, the possible economic role of young working-class gays and lesbians in supporting their families, and other characteristics besides sexual orientation that factor into the identities of working-class Mizrahi queers and might be more significant to them.

Arisa has been using short humorous online videos to promote its parties that have gone viral and have frequently toyed with the Mizrahi gender stereotypes, notably a "masculine" Mizrahi man portrayed by the muscular, hirsute model Eliad Cohen, for whom a golden bling Chai (the Jewish symbol spelling *life*) pendant no doubt makes wearing a shirt redundant and who often just stands stoically and refrains from expressing any emotion, and an energetic Mizrahi drag queen played by Uriel Yekutiel, who lip-synchs to women singers while wearing high heels and dresses that expose his hairy chest and never seems to be concerned about shaving off his mustache.

Their two characters maintain a passionate relationship across many of the videos that often aligns well with the emotionally powerful torch songs Yekutiel lip-synchs to (known as *depression songs* in Mizrahi music). In one of their more notorious productions, Yekutiel sings doe-eyed to Cohen, who flexes his muscles and beats Yekutiel to a pulp in a camp take on the Mizrahi stereotype of violent men and submissive women who continue to love them (see fig. 13.2).

The video mixes realistic makeup to reflect the injuries with cartoonish logic that includes the magical appearance of bandages. It flaunts its stereotypes with no narrative logic: Cohen as the abuser calmly stares at the camera as he beats Yekutiel up or displays his muscular physique with no apparent reason or motivation besides realizing a stereotype. In a later video, perhaps in response to those who did not find a video about battered women amusing, Yekutiel strikes Cohen with a skillet and kidnaps him.[35]

Arisa's videos construct playful (and somewhat adolescent) spaces for experimentation with identities, cultural attachments, and affects involving Jews, Arab culture, Israeli patriotism and nationality, Arab belonging, religion, queer bodies, and same-sex attractions. They do not seem to fear being stereotypical or offensive (particularly misogynist, homophobic, and racist toward Eastern cultures) or bringing together illogical and incongruent elements. They maintain an irresponsible, juvenile sense of humor that might be thought of in relation to the extended adolescence of queer subcultures, which, as Judith Halberstam has suggested, could indicate a

Figure 13.2. Eliad Cohen parodies stereotypes of masculine Mizrahi violence to Nivin's "What Have You Done to Me?" [*Mah 'aśita li*] in a provocative 2011 Arisa video. Uriel Yekutiel, as the adoring battered woman, is dancing in the background. Not all viewers were amused by the clip's arch attitude to gender violence.

refusal to supposedly grow up by entering the heteronormative adulthoods implied by the concepts of progress and maturity.[36] In the ethnic Israeli context, this would be a refusal to accept the *coming out as growing up* narrative that leads to a neoliberal Western gay identity. The Arisa videos and parties have been tremendously successful, attracting an avid fan base that includes Palestinians and obviously has no problem enjoying both Eastern and gay cultures. It has hosted mainstream Mizrahi stars who identify as straight and are happy to perform at the parties and take part in the promotional videos.[37]

Cohen has since become an international entrepreneur and model; he is notably involved in Gay-ville, a vacation rental service of gay-friendly accommodations, and Papa Party, a global event, marketing, and swimwear brand; he has appeared on the cover of the 2011/2012 *Spartacus* international gay travel guidebook; and he is interviewed in Lucas's *Undressing Israel*, where he proudly talks about his military service as a gay man. Isolated from the context of the Arisa videos and gay Mizrahi subculture, without any clear trace of parody or exposure of the performative aspect of identities, the stereotype that Cohen embodies in these other texts could be seen as a simple case of self-exoticization. The Mizrahi male body is presented as a sensual exotic object for the Western gay tourist in a way that duplicates the Western ethnographic white gaze on the Oriental other and continues the Israeli tradition of objectifying and effacing Mizrahi gay identity.[38]

One of Arisa's best-known productions is a video for the official song for the 2013 Gay Pride Parade, which strives to attract international gay tourists. The song was written especially for the event and performed by the popular, openly heterosexual Mizrahi male singer Omer Adam.[39] It immediately upsets any easy dichotomies by featuring a Mizrahi song celebrating Tel Aviv (the most Westernized, progressive city in the country, if Michael Lucas is to be trusted) and making use of gay slang, some of which was derived from Arabic. The song, mostly about the divine hotness of guys in Tel Aviv, tells of a meeting with a masculine man and the desire to have him take the singer "on the camel," followed by lyrics in English embracing a beauty-and-the-beast fantasy in the Middle East. It thus ridicules touristic Orientalist views of the region and of the Mizrahi hypersexual savage. The accompanying video features not only the requisite camel (with remote central locking, true to the production's disregard for the supposed tension between the East and progressiveness) but also Yekutiel competing with another drag queen (Netanel Atias) for the manly Cohen, who enjoys watching the contest. The two drag queens then go up to Cohen, push him aside, and begin kissing. They seem to have decided that they would rather be with each other, after having enjoyed and perhaps exhausted the pleasures of performing, observing, and seducing the straight-acting gay man and playing with the Orientalist beauty-and-the-beast fantasy of gender divisions, which has served their pleasure and not that of the tourist. Neither the song nor the video seems to be very interested in unscrambling the copresence of Arab culture, Jews, modernity, the Orient as fantasized in English, and an assortment of masculine, feminine, gay, and straight elements. By sending up ethnic and gender stereotypes and presenting Arab Jewish queer and gay men who require no Western savior, haven, or progress and who do not perform for a Western gaze, the Arisa videos and songs address the assumptions behind the transnational aspects of Israeli gay moving images discussed earlier in this chapter.

Perhaps Arisa's most irreverent video features an original song performed by Margalit Tzan'ani,[40] a famous Mizrahi singer, and confronts young Israeli "hipsters" who try to pose as Western and European. Three years prior to the release of the video, in 2011, Tzan'ani publicly condemned the protesters against economic inequality in Israel,[41] claiming that they were spoiled Ashkenazi youngsters who complained simply because they had not inherited apartments from their grandmothers in the more fashionable and expensive areas in Tel Aviv. She said she felt Schadenfreude because they had called her a "professional whiner" and "professional Mizrahi" when she had taken part in "authentic" protests in the periphery in the past and accused them of really wanting to replace the government and right-wing prime minister, Benjamin Netanyahu.[42] The Arisa song attacks a Mrs. Rothschild (reference to the street in Tel Aviv that symbolized the protest) and a Mrs. Hipster, who had gone to Paris and Berlin and should realize that they have come back to Israel, where it is "not Europe" but rather chaos (*balagan*), "the Old Middle East" (a reference to Shimon Peres's left-wing dream of a peaceful "New Middle East"). The song insists that even those who try to leave Israel are still easily recognized, as their face (using the Arabic term *wedj*) is from Bat Yam, a satellite city South of Tel Aviv. The song and video were accused of being a conservative Mizrahi text posing as subversive. They were said to be anti-protest, conformist, right-wing propaganda by the populist hegemonic mainstream that reconfirmed the reigning order and supported the right-wing neoliberal Netanyahu and his Likud party and justified their economic policies.[43] In fact, the video is far less coherent.[44] It features Yekutiel in an elaborate dress and neck ruff surrounded by scantily clad olive-skinned (and presumably Mizrahi) young men donning aristocratic *ancien régime* white wigs in a less-than-glamorous industrial area in Southern Tel Aviv, thus incongruously bringing together ludicrous stereotypes of the European nobility of centuries past with male Mizrahi bodies in Israel. Yet both Europe and Israel are not presented as having any essential identity or ethnicity. When the song mentions Amsterdam, we see one of the men with dreadlocks, wearing a Rasta cap and smoking a joint, representing the Netherlands through a Jamaican-Ethiopian religion. In the scenes that depict Israel (apparently South Tel Aviv), Yekutiel interacts exclusively with black men and a black child (see figs. 13.3 and 13.4).

These, at the time the video came out, would have been associated in Israel with the community of African asylum seekers whose presence in the southern neighborhoods of Tel Aviv was not well received by the local population and, fueled by inflammatory comments by ultranationalist right-wing politicians, particularly Interior Minister Eli Yishai of the Mizrahi religious party Shas and Miri Regev of the Likud, was accompanied by xenophobic protests and violence.[45] Israelis are represented singularly by these African asylum seekers. The Arisa video, then, ends up mixing

Figures 13.3 and 13.4. Arisa's promotional video for "This Is Not Europe" (2014) presents both Israel (fig. 13.3) and Europe (fig. 13.4) as already hybrid, thus challenging any notion of ethnic purity alongside the song's mocking of a cosmopolitanism that attempts to ignore the local and any sense of belonging.

right-wing propaganda (a notion of an inability to escape Israeli identity and a belittling attitude toward those who seek a better personal or collective Israeli future through European standards) together with a radical anti-essentialist depiction of national identities—surely enough to offend everyone. Thumbing its nose both at the left-wing protests and at right-wing racism, this queer text refuses any easy notion of a fluid cosmopolitan identity as well as of a pure or non-hybrid national local identity. It could perhaps be characterized, following Homi K. Bhabha, as exploring "vernacular cosmopolitanism,"[46] a concept through which he calls for us to assume a more "global" responsibility without taking on an abstract universal identity in an attempt to harmonize the local and the general; this approach emphasizes the mediated nature of identity and event. It designates an attempt to deal with an era in which problems and coalitions cross borders without resorting to a humanist universal or to the myopic assumption that all migrants and refugees today can enjoy the privileged status of "citizens of the world." On the other hand, it does not accept national, racial, or class differences as fixed essences and presents them as performative articulations. Whereas Bhabha, inspired by Adrienne Rich, finds the key to this position in transformative dissatisfaction, Arisa's videos opt for giddy and gay adolescence as they manage to evade the festival film's favorite trajectory of supposedly universal progress from tradition to Western modernity as well as a promotion of Israel as utopia found.

In this chapter, we explored three permutations among the possibilities of configuring the crossing of local borders in terms of moving images and queer sexualities: a world cinema formula that in the guise of self-expression presents a rescue fantasy of homophobic underdeveloped Israeli subcultures by the West; a utopian fantasy that presents a harmless "East" for tourists that has already been successfully Westernized and strives to educate the misinformed Western other about the progressiveness of Israel; and a vernacular cosmopolitanism queer formula that acknowledges the homonationalist moment in which we currently must act but tries to jolt the images of the previous formulas and particularly rejects the unidirectional trajectory of Enlightenment modernity, replacing it with a meandering camp sensibility as it exhibits a knowing recognition of living in an image-saturated, new media world in which consumers are also producers and which has made the guise of self-representation impossible. It is for future research to translate the meanings of these irreverent texts into a new politics and seek other formulas of Israeli queer moving images in a border-crossing age.

Notes

1. Boaz Hagin and Raz Yosef, "Festival Exoticism: The Israeli Queer Film in a Global Context," *GLQ* 18, no. 1 (2012): 161–178.

2. Thomas Elsaesser, *European Cinema: Face to Face with Hollywood* (Amsterdam: Amsterdam University Press, 2005), 502–503.

3. For more on the global film festival network, see Kenneth Turan, *Sundance to Sarajevo: Film Festivals and the World They Made* (Berkeley: University of California Press, 2002); and Marijke de Valck, *Film Festivals: From European Geopolitics to Global Cinephilia* (Amsterdam: Amsterdam University Press, 2007).

4. Elsaesser 2005, 88, 504.

5. Ibid., 91.

6. Ibid., 87.

7. For more on the negative reception in Israel of one such film, see Boaz Hagin, "Male Weeping as Performative: The Crying Mossad Assassin in *Walk on Water*," *Camera Obscura*, no. 68 (2008): esp. 105–107.

8. Elsaesser 2005, 510.

9. While the examples we will be giving of each possibility will be from different texts, we do not in principle rule out the possibility that the same text will include different moments or be amenable to different readings. Indeed, one of the films dealt with in detail in the second category, a documentary that includes numerous interviews, features figures involved in films from the other two categories. Furthermore, our goal is to give examples of each formula and not an exhaustive survey of all gay, lesbian, bisexual, transgender, and queer representations in Israeli moving images, which would need to take into account television and countless web videos (including dramas, sitcoms, reality shows, and commercials that feature non-heteronormative characters), documentaries, and texts of varying lengths (that might furthermore be packaged together, so that several short films might be distributed in a feature-length collection). We are committed to a queer outlook and are not interested in trying to set up borders and precise definitions, and we will not be excluding texts that blur boundaries, for example, between the homosocial and homoerotic and between friendship and sexual attraction.

10. Elsaesser 2005, 509.

11. Ibid., 504, 100.

12. Examples of Israeli films that received a nomination for an Academy Award in the Best Foreign Language Film category include *Ajami* (Scandar Copti and Yaron Shani; nominated in the 2010 awards), which depicts Jewish-Arab violence and conflicts; *Waltz with Bashir* (Ari Folman; nominated in the 2009 awards), which deals with the traumatic memories of Israeli soldiers during the first Lebanon War, including the massacre in the Sabra and Shatila Palestinian refugee camps and a reference to the Holocaust; *Beaufort* (Joseph Cedar; nominated in the 2008 awards), which tells of the evacuation of an Israeli post at the end of the first Lebanon War; and *Footnote* (Joseph Cedar; nominated in the 2011 awards), which deals with Talmud scholars. For further discussion of contemporary Israeli cinema, see Raz Yosef, *The Politics of Loss and Trauma in Contemporary Israeli Cinema* (New York: Routledge, 2011). The situation with Israeli nominees for Best Documentary Feature is similar. For one case study, see Yael Friedman, "Guises of Transnationalism in Israel/ Palestine: A Few Notes on *5 Broken Cameras*," *Transnational Cinemas* 6, no. 1 (2015): 17–32.

13. It was also screened at the Boston Jewish Film Festival and Outfest.

14. The film won prizes at the Dublin Gay and Lesbian Film Festival, Durban International Film Festival, the GLAAD Media Awards, Outfest in Los Angeles, Miami Gay and Lesbian Film Festival, Torino International Gay and Lesbian Film Festival, and the

Inside Out Lesbian and Gay Film and Video Festival in Toronto. See IMDb website, accessed July 17, 2020, http://www.imdb.com/title/tt0476643/awards.

15. It was additionally an official selection at the Stony Brook Film Festival and won best feature at the Jackson Hole Film Festival and Audience Choice Award at the Los Angeles and New York Israeli Film Festival. See the film's official website (no longer online, archive site provided), https://web.archive.org/web/20191006052445/www.montereymedia.com/theatrical /films/secrets_the.html.

16. It was also awarded the best first feature prize at the Palm Springs International Film Festival. See the film's official website (no longer online, archive site provided), https://web .archive.org/web/20130105022328/http://www.eyeswideopenfilm.com.

17. See the film's official website for a list of awards and festivals (no longer online, archive site provided), https://web.archive.org/web/20161220184957/http://outinthedarkthemovie.com /festivals-awards.

18. Elsaesser 2005, 509. Gay liberation discourse has been dominant in substantial portions of Israeli Hebrew-language secular media. It is even possible to construct a triumphalist local history from invisibility (or *symbolic annihilation*) to the growing visibility and normalcy of gay, lesbian, and queer representations in the Hebrew-language secular media in Israel. See Amit Kama, "From *Terra Incognita* to *Terra Firma*: The Logbook of the Voyage of Gay Men's Community into the Israeli Public Sphere," *Journal of Homosexuality* 38, no. 4 (2000): 133–162.

19. Jasbir K. Puar, *Terrorist Assemblages: Homonationalism in Queer Times* (Durham, NC: Duke University Press, 2007), xxvii.

20. This has frequently been read in light of Israeli society's mainstream gay politics, which might help contextualize Fox's point of view but does little to explain the astounding success of his films abroad and their accessibility to audiences who know little about internal Israeli politics.

21. Raz Yosef, "The National Closet: Gay Israel in *Yossi and Jagger*," *GLQ* 11, no. 2 (2005): 283–300. Similarly, Fox's later film, *The Bubble*, seems unable to break out of the confines of a gay Western liberal point of view. As Raya Morag shows, employing a critical reading of Joseph Massad's work, this tragic gay romance between an Israeli and a Palestinian contains absolutely no representation of the gay Palestinian man's process of sexual maturity within his own society. The only viable alternative to the Palestinian conservative heterosexual lifestyle, as far as the film shows us, is passing as a Jewish Westernized gay Israeli in Tel Aviv under the supervision and guidance of gay Israelis. Moreover, the suicide terrorist attack at the end of the film is presented as an act not of a radical fundamentalist Muslim as it is commonly perceived in Israeli society but, according to Morag, of a person who despairs of ever being able to live as a proud gay in his own Arab society. There seems to be no alternative to Western gay liberation. See Raya Morag, "Queering Terror: Trauma, Race, and Nationalism in Palestinian and Israeli Gay Cinema during the Second Intifada," in *Deeper Than Oblivion: Trauma and Memory in Israeli Cinema*, ed. Raz Yosef and Boaz Hagin (New York: Bloomsbury, 2013), 167–198. For more on *The Bubble* and Fox's conservative gay politics in his other works, see also Rebecca L. Stein, "Explosive: Scenes from Israel's Gay Occupation," *GLQ* 16, no. 4 (2010): 517–536.

22. Ronnie Scheib, "Film Review: 'Cupcakes,'" *Variety*, February 12, 2014, accessed May 18, 2017, http://variety.com/2014/film/festivals/film-review-cupcakes-1201100763/.

23. *Men of Israel* home page, Lucas Entertainment (no longer online, archive site provided), https://web.archive.org/web/20100208034044/http://menofisraelxxx.com/.

24. Ibid.

25. This was not entirely a fatuous claim in 2012, when the film came out. In the United States, "Don't Ask, Don't Tell" had only recently been repealed, and the speed with which the US Supreme Court would require states to allow gay marriage could not have been easily foreseen. Israel, at the time, recognized gay marriages conducted in other countries; its military had been indifferent to the sexual orientation of its soldiers since the 1990s; and Tel Aviv funded and supported a LGBT center and the annual gay pride parade. This argument would probably have been less compelling today, as many Western countries now allow same-sex marriage, whereas in Israel, Jews can only wed through a religious Orthodox ceremony (that does not permit same-sex marriage), and the Israeli Knesset has explicitly rejected a proposal to extend surrogacy to same-sex couples and single men, who often turn to surrogate mothers in other countries, underlining the legal discrimination against gay men in Israel (see *Knesset News*, October 31, 2018, accessed January 27 2019, https://main .knesset.gov.il/News/PressReleases/Pages/press31.10.18y.aspx).

26. Sarah Schulman, "Israel and 'Pinkwashing,'" *New York Times*, November 23, 2011, accessed May 18, 2017, http://nyti.ms/19uZ60D.

27. Max Blumenthal, "Israel Cranks Up the PR Machine," *The Nation*, October 16, 2013, accessed July 17, 2020, http://www.thenation.com/article/israel-cranks-pr-machine/.

28. Ibid. On his blog, Blumenthal notes that Lucas never actually mentions the name of the village, but, he adds, "my guess is it was Lifta, which was attacked by Zionist militias in December 1947 (five months before any Arab armies entered Palestine), bombed, and ethnically cleansed" ("Money Talks, Desecration Walks: Nakba Porn Kingpin Michael Lucas Bullies LGBT Center Against Anti-Apartheid Party," *Max Blumenthal* (blog), February 24, 2011 (no longer online, archive site provided), https://web.archive.org/web/20110228200108/http://maxblumenthal.com/2011/02 /money-talks-nakba-porn-kingpin-michael-lucas-bullies-the-lgbt-center. On the film's website, the scene is described as taking place in "ancient edifice in Jerusalem" ("Men of Israel," Scene 2, "Avi Dar and Jonathan Agassi").

29. Perhaps the best-known challenge to the relevance of this logic in recent decades has been in the work of Jean Baudrillard, such as his *Simulacra and Simulation*, trans. Sheila Faria Glaser (Ann Arbor: University of Michigan Press, 1995).

30. Jasbir Puar, "Rethinking Homonationalism," *International Journal of Middle East Studies* 45 (2013): 337.

31. In addition to Veronica Kedar, in recent years, numerous women film directors, including lesbian and queer filmmakers such as Tali Shalom Ezer and Michal Vinik, have made narrative feature films in Israel. For more on the recent rise of women filmmakers in Israel and their views on changing the masculine outlook that characterizes many of the feature films made in the country, see Nirit Anderman, "The Women Who Will Revolutionize Israeli Cinema" [in Hebrew], *Haaretz*, September 19, 2013, accessed May 18, 2017, http://www.haaretz.co.il/gallery/cinema/.premium-1.2120655. For a survey of Lesbian representations in Israeli films, see Nirit Anderman, "Can Israeli Cinema Already Tolerate Lesbians Having Onscreen Sex?" [in Hebrew], *Haaretz*, November 5, 2015, accessed May 18, 2017, http://www.haaretz.co.il/gallery/cinema/.premium-1.2767593.

32. See Lee Edelman, *No Future: Queer Theory and the Death Drive* (Durham, NC: Duke University Press, 2004); Judith Halberstam, *In a Queer Time and Place: Transgender Bodies, Subcultural Lives* (New York: New York Press, 2005); Damon R. Young, "The Living End, or Love without a Future," in *Queer Love in Film and Television*, ed. Pamela Demory and Christopher Pullen (New York: Palgrave Macmillan, 2013), 13–22.

33. For more on the current popularity and mainstream status of Mizrahi music in Israel, including the Arisa productions, see Matti Friedman, "Israel's Happiness Revolution," *Tablet*, August 31, 2015, accessed May 18, 2017, http://www.tabletmag.com /jewish-arts-and-culture/music/193162/israels-happiness-revolution.

34. Raz Yosef, *Beyond Flesh: Queer Masculinities and Nationalism in Israeli Cinema* (New Brunswick: Rutgers University Press, 2004), esp. chap. 5.

35. Arisa, "Ma Asita Li," for January 27, 2011 party, accessed May 18, 2017, https://www .youtube.com/watch?v=UNeJyrU6hYQ; and Arisa, "Le Téléphone d'Amour—Zehava Ben," for July 21, 2011 party, accessed May 18, 2017, https://www.youtube.com/watch?v=RqcjCrbft5g.

36. Halberstam 2005, 175.

37. See "Omer Tobi, Yotam Pappo, Uriel Yekutiel, and Eliad Cohen" [in Hebrew], *Mako*, December 26, 2011, accessed May 18, 2017, http://www.mako.co.il/pride-culture/cultura-hall -of-fame/Article-737e240f81f6431006.htm; Shachar Atwan, "Arisa, the Mizrahi Gay Party Line Started Five Years Ago as a Hipster Prank and Has Caused a Cultural Revolution" [in Hebrew], *Haaretz*, December 31, 2016, accessed May 18, 2017, http://www.haaretz.co.il /.premium-1.2809662. Tobi is credited as the videos' director.

38. The meaning these texts convey, of course, depends on specific readings. Cohen's presence in these other texts might serve as a *punctum* and associate them with Arisa's self-conscious playfulness. Conversely, his work as a self-objectifying model might further complicate Arisa's videos, reminding us that they engage with a complex reality that often requires compromises and collaborations. The videos promote a commercial line of parties (where financial necessities and desires are at work). Cohen has been less active in Arisa's videos since launching his independent international career. Yekutiel has also enjoyed success beyond Arisa and has appeared for example in the mainstream, high-ratings Israeli version of *The Amazing Race*.

39. Arisa, "Tel Aviv Pride 2013—Arisa feat. Omer Adam," for the parade on June 7, 2013, accessed May 18, 2017, https://www.youtube.com/watch?v=srOFki9PGM0. Words and lyrics by Doron Medalie. The song tells of someone referred to as *she*, presumably a gay man using the female pronoun as part of the gay slang employed throughout the song, but is not entirely explicit in its same-sex male attraction. As it was part of the gay pride events and accompanied by the queer Arisa video, this did not seem to be a deliberate attempt to obfuscate its potentially gay content.

40. Arisa, "This Is Not Europe," for October 24, 2014 party, accessed May 18, 2017, https:// www.youtube.com/watch?v=OFZmcSVHnxs. Words and lyrics by Doron Medalie.

41. The Israeli protests were contemporaneous with Occupy movements in other countries and the Arab Spring.

42. Sefi Katzav, "Margol: It Is a Protest of Spoiled Rich Youngsters from Northern Tel Aviv [*tsfonbonim*]" [in Hebrew], *Mako*, August 1, 2011, accessed May 18, 2017, http://www.mako.co .il/news-specials/social-protest/Article-18d1b712f358131006.htm; Avi Shushan, "Margol: 'The Protest Is Political, My Heart Is Not with Them'" [in Hebrew], *Ynet*, August 1, 2011, accessed May 18, 2017, http://www.ynet.co.il/articles/0,7340,L-4102829,00.html.

43. Yoav Lifshitz, "Margol's New 'Protest' Song Can Be a Likud Party Advertising Jingle" [in Hebrew], *Haaretz*, October 30, 2014, accessed May 18, 2017, http://www.haaretz.co.il /magazine/the-edge/.premium-1.2471166.

44. The song includes additional stanzas, which are not featured in the truncated version used in the video clip and refer to a Spanish passport (which Mizrahi people with ties to Spanish culture can issue) and start-ups relying on a "Jewish brain" and assert that we are "nuts" and Americans with Arab honor.

45. Bureau of Democracy, Human Rights and Labor, the US Department of State, "Israel and The Occupied Territories," *Country Reports on Human Rights Practices for 2012*, accessed May 18, 2017, http://www.state.gov/j/drl/rls/hrrpt/humanrightsreport/index.htm?year=2012 &dlid=204363; Hila Shamir and Guy Mundiak, "Spheres of Migration: Political, Economic and Universal Imperatives in Israel's Migration Regime," *Middle East Law & Governance* 5 (2013): 112–172; Yoav H. Duman, "*Infiltrators Go Home!* Explaining Xenophobic Mobilization Against Asylum Seekers in Israel," *Journal of International Migration and Integration* 16 (2015): 1231–1254.

46. Homi K. Bhabha, "Unsatisfied: Notes on Vernacular Cosmopolitanism," in *Postcolonial Discourses: An Anthology*, ed. Gregory Castle (Oxford: Blackwell, 2001), 39–52.

14

HAGAR BEN-ASHER'S *THE SLUT* AS THE FIRST ISRAELI TRANSNATIONAL FEMINIST FILM TEXT

Yael Munk

Since the beginning of the new millennium, Israeli cinema has undergone a radical change for the better. It has succeeded in producing award-winning fiction dramas and documentaries and is often presented as an interesting example of world cinema.[1] While some would contend that this radical change in Israeli cinema's nature has to do with its wish to relate to Western or international intellectual spheres, I propose here to read this metamorphosis as an expression of the benefits of adopting the transnational cinema mode. In this chapter, I shall seek to demonstrate that Israeli cinema's transnational shift is first and foremost an attempt to resist the political dominant discourse and that what might seem to be an ideological detachment is in fact a rebellion against the hegemony. In cinematic terms, if the sovereign discourse is that of the Hollywood film industry, an industry that dictates the norms and measures to all other cinemas, during the last decade, a world cinema has appeared, revealing new forms and new discourses and thus challenging the traditional Hollywood forms and calling for nontraditional interpretations. As Ella Shohat and Robert Stam have described it, in the critical discourse of transnational cinema, "Hollywood' functions as a term meant not to convey a kneejerk rejection of all commercial cinema, but rather as a kind of shorthand for a massively industrial, ideologically-reactionary, and stylistically-conservative form of 'dominant cinema.'"[2]

For a Definition of Transnational Cinema

Born out of the weakening of nationalism and national cinemas in general, transnational cinema is first and foremost an issue of collaborative production as expressed, in its most basic form, in an exchange of ideas. However, it differs from international productions in the sense that it provides little space for creative interactions between the involved sides or for the foreign coproduction partner to interfere in its contents. Hamid Naficy argues that the transnational exchanges enabled by the vast global, economic, and structural changes since World War II have given a voice to diasporic filmmakers in the West while transforming the national by framing their difference or accent within the discursive of the national cinema and traditional genre. "Transnational filmmakers not only have given expression to their own worlds but also have enriched the cinemas of their home and adopted land."[3] Therefore, Naficy proposes the category of "independent transnational cinema," a genre that combines that of cine-writing and self-narrativization and that "considers the relationship of the transnational filmmakers to their subjects to be a relationship that is filtered through narratives and iconographies of memory, desire, loss, longing, and nostalgia."[4] What is reflected in transnational cinema is a world apart, a world in which the sovereign power has declined and left unsupervised spaces in which transnational themes can surface. Therefore, what transnationalism reflects is not only a mode of production but also a series of themes that together can be considered, in European terms, as the new post-wall world. As such, it relates to many contemporary issues, including immigration and border crossing, as well as the need to adapt culturally to a new world, to changes of government, and to the imposition of new rules that threaten to change the traditions. No less important is the building of a borderless world in which people—men and women alike—live confined lives away from all laws and prescriptions.

This idea is reflected in Rosalind Galt's quotation of Philip Rosen, who refers to the problematics of national cinema in order to define and revise the transnational one. For European cinemas, writes Galt, "a series of transnational-themed films in Europe in the 1990s have addressed questions of immigration, ethnicity, and nation. Examples include *Beautiful People* (Dizdar, 1999) and *Steam: The Turkish Bath* (Ozpetek, 1977). However, these films are overwhelmingly contemporary in their setting and narrative, seeking to document recent cultural changes rather than to reread the past."[5]

Transnational cinema appears against a background of the changes that have taken place in our postmodern multicultural word, a world in which technological devices have reduced the distances between nation-states and created new and unpredicted bridges between those that once were rivals or enemies. As a result of this blurring of distance and boundaries, world cinema has distanced itself from Hollywood's dictatorship and created additional micro-centers in which practices are reviewed and criticized. At the same time, it has also redefined our understanding of film. Mitsuhiro Yoshimoto described this tendency in relation to Asian cinema: "In a market increasingly controlled by multinational conglomerates, so-called local film production is extremely difficult to sustain. Films are bifurcated into two categories: Hollywood and 'international productions.' The location of cinematic production and reception can no longer be discussed in terms of 'inside' and 'outside' the national boundaries. Independent and national cinemas try to survive either by producing films for the international film festival circuits or by targeting Hollywood producers."[6] Thus, films that are bounded by national frameworks for production (funding, technical work) may exist thematically as transnational cinema.

Above all, and independently of the concepts of exile and diaspora, "the concept of transnationalism enables us to better understand the changing ways in which the contemporary world is being imagined by an increasing number of filmmakers across genres as a global system rather than a collection of more or less autonomous nations."[7] This is exactly the point in the new Israeli forms of transnationalism: to speak beyond the evident traces of the Israeli-Palestinian political conflict that throughout the world has become synonymous with Israeli existence. In other words, transnational Israeli cinema claims the right to live beyond the ongoing Israeli issues of war and surrounding enemies and experience the individual's universal privilege of a trivial life. But since no life is really trivial, transnational cinema reveals the multilayered complexity behind seemingly common places and actions—or, in Naficy's words, "narratives and iconographies of memory, desire, loss, longing, and nostalgia."[8] In the present case, it is not the case of longing but rather of repressed memory. *The Slut* achieves this goal through the use of less identifiable spaces—the same spaces that Gilles Deleuze named as "spaces we no longer ascribe any certainty to, spaces inhabited by a new race of characters, who see rather than act."[9]

The Slut, or a Feminist Transnational Israeli Voice

The film that is at the focus of this article has indeed earned its credentials at world film festivals. By the time that it reached the Israeli screen, it already enjoyed international appeal, but paradoxically, it did not become a box office success. One of the aims of this article is to understand the ways in which filmic distancing from the national meta-narrative in order to convey a transnational experience can be considered a kind of betrayal of the founding conventions of the nation. I relate here to a specific case of feminist Israeli transnational cinema[10] and, more particularly, to an Israeli feature film that I believe did not receive the attention it deserved, perhaps because of its provocative title: Hagar Ben-Asher's *The Slut* (2012).[11] Co-produced by the Israeli production company Transfax Films in Tel-Aviv and the German company Rohfilm in Berlin and Leipzig, *The Slut* depicts the routine life of Tamar (played by the filmmaker Ben-Asher, who also wrote the script), a thirty-five-year-old woman who lives in an unspecified countryside space with her two daughters, Mika and Noa. In an interview with *Judaicine,* Ben-Asher comments on the importance of isolated space in *The Slut*: "I wanted this place to look like an undefined space for many reasons. I believe that these kinds of stories do not have a particular time or space. The brutality of human nature is an integral part of the soul and not only of the physical location. I think that the abstraction of a space abandoned by everyone draws the attention to the essence of its characters and not to their social motivations. My intention was to present the story like a fairytale."[12]

Indeed, just like in a fairy tale, the film opens with an enigmatic scene: A static camera reveals an open field in daylight; the only movement is a horse's tail swishing slowly and sensually from side to side. This almost immobile frame is interrupted violently when the horse snaps its tether, leaps over the fence, and begins to gallop freely along the road, among cars and trucks, until it is eventually hit by a speeding truck. The driver gets out of the car and looks at the wounded horse lying on the road. In retrospect, the viewer will understand that the driver is no other than Shay, the man with whom Tamar will get emotionally involved for the first time. This opening scene can be read as establishing the symbolic analogy between the horse running away from the meadow and Tamar running away from all conventional frames of life.

The following sequence introduces the protagonist Tamar, who is giving oral sex to one of her neighbors in the open air, against the background of a deserted barn. The dissonance between the location and the act illuminates the protagonist's relationship to sex and intimacy, which can be understood as one of complete alienation. The narrative continues in the same mode. Tamar makes her living by selling the eggs of the chickens she raises on her poultry farm, which is also where she meets with various male neighbors for sexual purposes. Is she trading her casual sexual relationships in order to feed her daughters? The dialogue does not seem to indicate this. Nonetheless, that she is isolated, with no female friends and only casual lovers who do not seem to care too much about her, is a painful premise. Tamar is indeed alone in a world with no boundaries, since no one comes and goes from this place, except her casual male lovers.

Using a technique that she had already employed in her short *Pathways*, Ben-Asher uses high-angle shots that formulate anew the relationship between women and space in *The Slut*. These choices, along with decisions made over the shaping of mise-en-scène, also serve to inform our reading of the discrepancy between what is known and what is unknown with regard to the sexual trauma. Indeed, in the film's first part, Tamar is often seen partly concealed behind an object. Later, as she wanders randomly among haystacks, only the high-angle camera informs the viewer of what she herself cannot know: she is trapped in a labyrinth, unable to exit from the path she has chosen. The same camera angles can be found in the sexual scenes. While the plot ostensibly deals with a woman's sexual promiscuity and her environment's response to it, the cinematic representation of these sexual encounters is not intended to satisfy the pornographic gaze, as can be deduced from the cinematography used to depict them.[13] On the contrary, it gives a realistic perception of the protagonist's alienated existence while depicting sexual intercourse as one of the routine acts taking place in this rural environment.

On one occasion, Tamar is walking with her bike through the fields and is viewed through a tracking shot from inside a car. The car window with its windshield wipers provides a framing for Tamar's back as she walks. When the car stops, we see that the driver is Shay (actor Ishai Golan), an old acquaintance from the village who has become a veterinarian and returned after his mother's death to pack up her apartment. Tamar begins a relationship with him and soon comes to realize that this one differs completely from her previous relationships. When they make love for the first time,

Figure 14.1. Tamar standing by the window. From *The Slut* (Ben-Asher 2011), image by Vered Adir, courtesy of Transfax Film Productions.

Tamar offers him oral sex, as she does to all her other lovers; he refuses and draws her into a genuine lovemaking scene, accompanied for the first time by a dramatic soundtrack—a somewhat forgotten old Israeli song whose title (translated from the original Spanish) is "Itrag'ut" ("Relaxing"). Their relationship develops, and he invites her to move with her daughters to his mother's house. They do so, and as a result of the normal relationship she develops with Shay, they begin a normal family life. When she becomes pregnant, however, she refuses to keep the baby, and from this point on, her past in the little rural settlement comes back to haunt her new love story. At a school party, she encounters her past lovers and suddenly cannot justify to them or to herself the change that has taken place in her relationship with men. Gradually she returns to her old behavior, and Shay finds himself taking care of her daughters in her absence. The alienation between the two intensifies until the film's climax, which I consider to be the key to understanding Tamar's nonconventional behavior.

Comprising three consecutive scenes, *The Slut*'s final sequence begins as Tamar walks along an empty path at night and reaches home. Suddenly, the camera position changes and reveals her inside the backyard from a

Figure 14.2. A happy family life. From *The Slut* (Ben-Asher 2011), image by Vered Adir, courtesy of Transfax Film Productions.

high-angle shot. She realizes that the door is locked, turns back to the back-yard, and comes across Shay's wounded horse standing motionless in the garden. She begins to caress the horse but then suddenly recognizes inti-mate sounds of moaning and groaning coming from inside the house. She turns her gaze to the window, but the camera does not provide the expected reverse shot; rather, it focuses on her still face in a close-up that now fills the entire frame, as if seen from the inside of the house.

This relatively long shot, devoid of any extra-diegetic soundtrack or re-verse shot that could inform the viewer about what Tamar is witnessing, reveals a woman's emotional metamorphosis from happy and satisfied to horrified. It is followed by a reaction shot, from a high angle, where she is seen running to the neighbors' houses, knocking at their doors and enter-ing one after the other. The distant camera does not reveal the content of these encounters and in a way resists the spectator's expectations. It thus achieves a defamiliarization that forces the spectator to reconsider its origi-nal positions regarding Tamar, the promiscuous woman who now reacts and behaves like any other mother whose children are endangered. Does she really deserve the title she has been assigned by her neighborhood?

This sequence's third and final scene should perhaps have closed this drama, but instead, it just added one more layer of ambiguity. Again, the camera is situated at a distance, showing Shay grooming his wounded horse in the middle of an empty field. The silence that accompanies the shot is suddenly interrupted by the eruption of three men, who violently shove him to the ground, beating and kicking his entire body, until the camera rests on his convulsed face. The horse begins to flee, a scene that recalls the opening sequence, and the camera follows it for just a moment, revealing the beauty of its movements. After the horse has gone, Tamar comes out from behind the trees and walks toward the injured man, who is curled up in an embryonic position. She touches his face and takes him into her arms. She remains seated in the mud, and for one last time, the camera moves upward to the sky, emphasizing the enigmatic Pietà-like composition in the empty space. Then, still from a high but steady angle, the song "Relaxing," which had been heard on the soundtrack during the first lovemaking scene, is played again. Just as in the first true lovemaking scene, in which it was used to differentiate that specific episode of lovemaking from all the previous ones, here too it reveals the understanding of a new kind of emotion—in this case, forgiveness.

This last scene provides an explanation for Tamar's promiscuous behavior and for her desperate search for physical love as the only expression of love she has ever known. Suddenly her distanced and silent behavior becomes the clear expression of a traumatic childhood event she may have long sought to forget. In this sense, Tamar is a survivor of the sort defined by Judith Lewis Herman in her *Trauma and Recovery* (1992):

> As the survivor struggles with the tasks of adult life, the legacy of her child-hood becomes increasingly burdensome. Eventually, often in the fourth or fifth decade of life, the defensive structure may begin to break down. Often the precipitant is a change in the equilibrium of close relationships: The failure of a marriage, the illness or death of a parent. The facade can hold no longer, and the underlying fragmentation becomes manifest. When and if a break-down occurs, it can take symptomatic forms that mimic virtually every form of psychiatric disorder. Survivors fear that they are going insane or that they will have to die.[14]

The final sequence offers a closure to Tamar's promiscuous existence. The questions remain open, but the viewer understands that, for some, "to love," as defined by Jacques Lacan, "is essentially, to wish to be loved."[15] Though we do not know anything about Tamar's past, her behavior offers a positive reflection of her longing for love, a longing she had sought to sat- isfy through casual sexual encounters. Moreover, because we do not have any knowledge about her childhood or her past in general, we are able to imagine various possible scenarios of what might have damaged this strong woman's soul. What finally confirms the nature of this injury, however, is her reaction to what she sees behind the window. Hiding more than it re- veals, the cinematic language prefers merely to hint rather than to follow visually a consecutive series of events. The viewer knows that shortly before, Shay had put her younger daughter to bed, and the camera had shown him standing in front of her bed and undressing. The following action does not have to be shown on screen in order to be understood. In his wish to take revenge on Tamar's promiscuous behavior, Shay may have committed the most terrible crime by sexually abusing her little daughter, with whom he seems to have had a special relationship from their very first encounter. Has the sexual act been consummated, or did it stop at the last moment? And, importantly, can it be forgiven? Tamar's final reaction in the last high-angle shot, where she is seen cradling the injured Shay as if he were her baby, reminds us that throughout her entire life, Tamar has always been a giver of love, of compassion, and of empathy. Yet, there may be something more: when Tamar realizes that Shay has been beaten and injured, she consid- ers that he has paid the price for his sin(s) and now they are both, equally, sinners. They will both seek redemption and will perhaps attempt to build their future there.

A Survivor of Childhood Sexual Abuse

As noted above, the spectator knows nothing about Tamar's previous life, about the fathers of her two daughters, about her childhood.[16] She pretends to be part of the place, being polite toward everyone and offering herself to some of them without any clear distinction. However, the identity of those who refer to Tamar as *the slut*, as eponymously indicated in the film title, remains vague, and the film's perspective limits itself to her subjectivity and tells no more. She is present in most of the frames almost until toward the end, when her daughters start to develop a relationship with Shay, who begins to act like a loving stepfather to them. Surprisingly, it is from this point on that she stops being aware of what is becoming of her two daugh- ters. Convinced that Shay has unconditionally taken upon himself the role of the father, she feels secure enough to leave him with her daughters; but it is exactly at this moment that her trust is betrayed. The film text does not provide a graphic depiction of the nature of this betrayal, but Tamar's reaction, the frozen expression on her face, seems to translate something she had once known and successfully repressed until this moment. Whether child abuse and/or incest, the vision of what may have been taking place behind the closed window pushes her to react violently. For the first time, she rejects passiveness and reacts as we can only presume she should have done then, in her childhood, during the traumatic events that had forever marked her life as a victim.

She alerts her neighbors and seeks revenge both for her daughter and for the child she herself had once been. Only after witnessing the attack on Shay by the male neighbors can she relax, as again indicated through the extra-diegetic reappearance of the song "Relaxing." Tamar looks at him differently. The issue of child abuse is thus the hidden secret behind *The Slut*. Conforming to Naficy's definition of a transnational genre where "narratives and iconographies they produce . . . are palimpsestical, inscribing ruptures, fantasies and embellishment, as well as ellipses, elisions and repressions,"[17] everything in the film's confined world hints that something had gone very wrong in the past but has apparently left no visible trace—until being evoked once more by the traumatic repetition, this time on her own daughter. This may explain her tendency to have become a victim once more in her vicarious sexual encounters with the men around her, a tendency that is suddenly revealed to her own eyes when she sees her daughter similarly endangered. In other words, while, from the ego-psychological perspective, trauma repetition can be considered as an attempt to master traumatic experience,[18] revictimization is explained as being caused by the traumatic influence incorporated in one's own psyche. Through her daughter's victimization, Tamar has reexperienced her repressed past and finally reacted to it.

The French Influence

As noted above, one of the most remarkable features of Ben-Asher's film lies in its disconnection from any form of Israeliness. This artistic and ideological tendency, which appeared for the first time in the *New Sensibility* Israeli cinema in the 1960s, serves a different function here. While the New Sensibility wished to express its affinity with new European cinema—and particularly the French New Wave—*The Slut* wishes to convey another message, a message hinting at the universal fragility of women's condition in a so-called liberated world.[19] Since the feminist revolution, women may have acquired various privileges, but some issues are still unspoken and continue to haunt women's private sphere. This is not particular to Israel or to any specific country. It is the discursive taboo of sexual abuse that still cannot cross the threshold of normative lives. Thus, though the filmmaker declared in her many public interviews that she had aspired to reconstruct a European setting in the violent Middle East and in practice succeeded quite well in her mission, the film remains deeply rooted in a feminist way of thinking according to which the transnational feminist project has to do with uncovering the palimpsest of women's trauma anywhere in the world.[20] This explains the filmmaker's decision to locate the film's plot in the moshav,[21] a rural setting reminiscent of Tuscany or southern France that by definition is ideologically disconnected from the state's main social and political issues, which are preoccupied with the occupation and the religious/secular divide; whereas once the moshav was a central tenet in the construction of Zionist ideology, it now holds a marginal place both physically and ideologically. Amit Yasur's cinematography defamiliarizes the well-known Israeli spaces, decoupling the setting from the association with the state. In turning to an ideologically unmarked space, the filmmaker succeeds in pointing at the transnational relevance of the issue of sexual abuse as if to say that sexual abuse appears everywhere, independently of class and origin. And hegemonic women subjects that appear to be an integral part of their native landscape do not escape the curse of victimhood.

This unusual standpoint is deeply rooted in director Ben-Asher's professional trajectory. After winning the prestigious Cinéfondation Residency scholarship for her debut short *Pathways* at the Cannes Film Festival,[22] Ben-Asher spent several months in France in order to write the script for her first full-length feature film. This may explain the accentuation of certain usually taboo themes, which were only hinted at in *Pathways* and have become the main issue in *The Slut*.

Film scholar Carrie Tarr contends that a certain contemporary French cinema, which she calls "extreme French cinema,"[23] has developed a new thematic approach that focuses on women in a context of violence and/or pornography: "Women filmmakers' embedding of visceral imagery within narratives relating to female desire and female violence may still have the potential to disrupt and destabilize normative constructions of sexual difference, including the taken-for-granted understanding of violence as 'normal' when associated with masculinity but traumatic and perverse when associated with femininity."[24] She continues: "These films, or particular moments in these films, require a different kind of analysis than that posited classic feminist gaze theory, one based on embodied spectatorship and the masochistic pleasure of self-abnegation and abjection . . . rather than the sadistic power dynamics of the 'male gaze.'"[25] Moreover, Tarr claims that this new tendency arises "when ideology fails [in France] and strictly defined gender roles break down."[26] Ben-Asher adopts this concept and creates a transnational contention regarding women and space in Israel, countering the decay of the dominant ideology. The French influence in Ben-Asher's film is therefore more than just circumstantial; it is followed by a similar ideological claim that has become dominant in Israeli cinema. Indeed, *The Slut* follows this path and reveals, against highly spectacular Israeli landscape representations, the failure of Zionist ideology, first and foremost by her representation of a woman as holder of the space-controlling gaze.

Besides the universal issue of sexual abuse, the film's narrative reveals a number of key issues in our postmodern, gendered world, none of which are particularly Israeli. Although the protagonists' names—Tamar and Shay—are Hebrew names, and the language spoken is Hebrew, the film relies only very slightly on the national ethos and its derivations.[27] Moreover, the landscape that was carefully chosen does not refer to a specifically Israeli geography but rather to a vast Mediterranean one.[28] The narrative could have taken place in any other Mediterranean country or similar configuration. In other words, the interchangeability of the nature of the space provides the film with a feminist message that extends beyond any national interpretation. In the case of Israeli cinema, which has always entertained a conflictual relationship with its history, this is a tour de force.

Between Honor and Shame: *The Slut* as a Mediterranean Tale

Finally, the transnational aspect of the film is achieved through the use of Ben-Asher's construction of the narrative around two major forces: honor and shame. She invokes these as symbolic of the Mediterranean world, addressing an exoticization that evokes violence and sexuality. The film's power lies in the dissonance between the repressed expressions of these primal conditions and the veneer of calm that pervades the landscape and movements within the film. Thus, she creates a sense that nature is good and man is evil—that the appearance of kindness is merely a social veneer that is disrupted by man and woman's true passions—which can be both elevating and destructive.

The Slut succeeds in reviving the forgotten transnational Mediterranean option, an option that was rejected a long time ago by the forefathers of Zionism. Dissimulated by the course of the plot, this option emerges during the film text, especially in its relationship to the undefined landscape that recalls other rural environments of the Mediterranean. There is another element here, however, that also orients the spectator toward this option: that of the honor and shame dichotomy. According to anthropologists such as Jean G. Peristiany, the Mediterranean concept of honor is attributed to men, whereas shame is provoked—and endured—by women. Honor is gained through careful adherence to the norms defined by the relevant honor code, and a meticulous adherence to this code entitles a person to honor. A failure to adhere to it bestows shame. Thus honor is ceaselessly sought, enhanced, accrued, and inevitably lost, while shame is dreaded and avoided at all cost.[29]

In light of the provocative theme with which it ostensibly deals—sexual promiscuity—honor and shame are interwoven throughout the film's text, indicated in its very title. Referring to the heroine as a slut is certainly implying shameful behavior. Considering that it is unlikely that she gave herself this title, one can only presume that this is the general attitude toward Tamar, an attitude that is certainly reinforced by her social isolation. According to the honor and shame paradigm, Tamar is the shameful woman who cannot achieve redemption in her natural surroundings. The appearance of Shay after so many years may resemble the theatrical deus ex machina, but matters continue to evolve in a shameful way, as noted above, leaving little hope for the matching of Tamar and Shay. And yet, in the closing scene, with the couple viewed from above in a Pietà composition, it becomes clear that they have succeeded in overcoming the primary values of honor and shame; with both now designated as shameful people, they can cradle and support one another, on their way to a better world.

Just like the lovers who succeed in escaping the small-minded concepts of honor and shame, the film's Mediterranean aspect succeeds in transgressing the Israeli national borders and acknowledging its belonging to another place, beyond the political borders of the State of Israel. Moreover, rather than linking these themes to a Jewish tradition, the dislocation of the characters universalizes the film's thematics. This landscape enables the filmmaker to speak in the name of numerous voiceless women whose un-explained feelings of guilt have condemned them to silence. To speak in the name of those women who could not tell their stories in real time and may still be persecuted by feelings of guilt regarding the sexual promiscuity they are accused of by those around them—this is the film's true transnational achievement.

Against Ideology: Transnational Cinema as Another Kind of Political Cinema

As this chapter has attempted to demonstrate, *The Slut* is in many ways a pioneering film; it addresses some of the most controversial and universal feminist issues while also challenging the history of Israeli cinema. In an interview for the French journal *Liberation*, Ben-Asher related to the politi-cal issue that is so crucial to Israeli cinema, stating:

> I know all the political implications of my film and I gave them great attention. This is because politics is inevitable but also because it is meaningless. It is true that a woman who refuses to have sex with the man she loves but chooses to have sex with the others in the outdoors, is more reminiscent of a male fantasy. Indeed, if you read this film as a large symbol, it can be read as a political ges-ture. Although I do not say this officially, I hope that knowing that the film has political implications, it will remain free of political interpretations.[30]

Against the background of the always-political Israeli cinema, *The Slut* represents a unique transnational film text in the sense that it dares to go beyond the familiar Israeli themes and to adopt global feminist subjects—namely female promiscuity and the trauma of child abuse. These two themes are subtly interwoven in the plot and enable the viewer to read the film beyond its national context. In her interview with Nirit Anderman, Ben-Asher admitted that she had made some conscious choices but, at the same time, that some others had come to her intuitively, as a natural con-tinuation of a well-recognizable pattern. She was particularly interested in the paths Tamar chose. "Tamar," says Ben-Asher, is examining

> the story she tells herself about herself, what she thinks others see in her, and her functioning as a mother, both real and imagined.... There is something in her complexity that interests me, because in my eyes she does not fit into the categories of either the victim or the one who makes the sacrifice, the one who satisfies or the one who is satisfied. I want to hope that she moves inside her own specific sphere and that she is not representative of anything else. But I'm still looking for her; she is still moving from scene to scene.[31]

Her main character's aspirations for freedom seem to go beyond the film's plot, in the sense that they seem to disconnect her expected ties from the national context. As Elizabeth Ezra and Terry Rowden have described it, "Each film requires a particular . . . referential framework in order to be fully readable [but] increasingly these frameworks are losing the national and cultural particularity they once had."[32] Therefore, they conclude, transnational cinema is not a utopian state of universal human experiences and of universally accessible creative endeavors. Rather than being immediately accessible to any and all viewers, they claim, "Transnational cinema imagines its audiences as consisting of viewers who have expectations and types of cinematic literacy that go beyond the desire for a mindlessly appreciative consumption of national narratives that audiences can identify as their 'own.'"[33] Here lies the true achievement of Hagar Ben-Asher's *The Slut*: choosing ambivalence in order to go beyond the national boundaries and conventions.

I would like to thank the Hadassah-Brandeis Institute at Brandeis University for its hospitality, generosity, and support and especially for the privilege of being a Helen Gartner Hammer scholar-in-residence in the summer of 2015. In addition, I would like to thank the anonymous reviewers and the editors for their valuable comments.

Notes

1. This contention does not take into account the numerous television dramas that have appeared over the last decade, some of which have been adapted for foreign television (the most famous being Hagai Levi's *In Treatment*, 2005–2008).

2. Ella Shohat and Robert Stam, *Unthinking Eurocentrism: Multiculturalism and the Media* (London: Routledge, 1994), 7.

3. Hamid Naficy, "Phobic Spaces and Liminal Panics: Independent Transnational Film Genres," in *Global-Local: Cultural Production and Transnational Imaginary*, ed. Rob Wilson and Wimal Dissanayake (Durham, NC: Duke University Press, 1996), 120.

4. Ibid., 121.

5. Rosalind Galt, *The New European Cinema: Redrawing the Map* (New York: Columbia University Press, 2006), 105.

6. Mitsuhiro Yoshimoto, "National/International/Transnational: The Concept of Trans-Asian Cinema and the Cultural Politics of Film Criticism," in *Theorizing National Cinema*, ed. Valentina Vitali and Paul Willemen (London: BFI, 2006), 255.

7. Elizabeth Ezra and Terry Rowden, "General Introduction: What Is Transnational Cinema?," in *Transnational Cinema: The Film Reader*, ed. Elizabeth Ezra and Terry Rowden (New York: Routledge, 2006), 1.

8. Naficy 1996, 121.

9. Gilles Deleuze, *Cinema 1: The Movement-Image*, trans. Hugh Tomlinson and Barbara Habberjam (Minneapolis: University of Minnesota Press, 1986), xi.

10. In the course of the last decade, a large number of Israeli women directors' films have been coproduced, extensively but not exclusively, with Germany. For example, the young Israeli director Yaelle Kayam recently produced her debut film, *Mountain* (2016), in collaboration with a Danish company, thus marking the first Danish-Israeli coproduction.

11. The film's Hebrew title *HaNotenet* literally means *The Giver*, hinting at the protagonist's sexual promiscuity. However, as Shmulik Duvdevani notes, she gives more than just sexual services to her male neighbors—she gives them friendship and attention, and this attention stops suddenly when she begins her relationship with Shay. See Shmulik Duvdevani, "The Slut: Hagar Ben-Asher Rules" [in Hebrew], *Ynet*, May 22, 2012, accessed May 18, 2017, http://www.ynet.co.il/articles/0,7340,L-4231982,00.html. It should be mentioned that the French chose the easy way and titled Ben-Asher's film, upon its presentation at the 2011 Cannes Film Festival, *La Femme qui aimait les hommes* (*The Woman Who Loved Men*) as a kind of distorted homage to Francois Truffaut's *The Man Who Loved Women* (1978), though, of course, there are no similarities between the two films.

12. See "Hagar Ben-Asher: A Filmmaker on the Edge" [in French], *Judaicine*, June 21, 2012. In this and all other non-English sources, the translation is mine.

13. Pornographic cinematography is a kind of filming that presumes that the viewer is a heterosexual male, and it therefore follows the lines of his fantasies. It victimizes women and objectifies them so as to provide the male viewer with "the image of the sexually ecstatic woman so important to the genre, [which is] a celebration of female victimization and prelude to female victimization in real life" (10) See Linda Williams, "Film Bodies: Gender, Genre, and Excess," *Film Quarterly* 44, no. 4 (Summer, 1991).

14. Judith Lewis Herman, *Trauma and Recovery: The Aftermath of Violence—From Domestic Abuse to Political Terror* (New York: Basic Books, 1992), 114.

15. Jacques Lacan, *The Seminar. Book XI. The Four Fundamental Concepts of Psychoanalysis, 1964*, trans. Alan Sheridan (London: Hogarth Press and Institute of Psycho-Analysis, 1977), 253.

16. I would like to thank my friend, psychoanalyst Shmuel Berenstein, for helping me elaborate on this interpretation.

17. Naficy 1996, 121.

18. Sigmund Freud, "Beyond the Pleasure Principle," in *On Metapsychology* (New York: Pacific, 2010).

19. According to Judd Ne'eman, the New Sensibility cinema serves as a direct reaction to the 1948 generation's ethos despite the evident European influence. Furthermore, Ne'eman describes it as the pinnacle of a radical critique on this ethos. See Judd Ne'eman, "The Moderns: A Genealogy of the New Sensibility," in *Fictive Looks—On Israeli Cinema*, ed. Nurith Gertz, Orly Lubin, and Judd Ne'eman (Tel Aviv: Open University Press, 1998), 30.

20. Such films often include explicit and violent depictions of sexuality. Notable examples include Israeli director Keren Yedaya's cerebral description of prostitution in *Or, My Treasure* (2004) and French director Catherine Breillat's portrayal of adolescent sex in *Fat Girl* (2001). According to film scholar Ginette Vincendeau, the brutal precision characterizing *Fat Girl* serves to disengage the audience and to deny eroticism. Vincendeau sees the film as a "merciless critique" of male romantic discourse and its hidden violence. See Ginette

Vincendeau, "Fat Girl: Sisters, Sex, and Sitcom," The Criterion Collection, May 4, 2011, accessed January 8, 2019, https://www.criterion.com/current/posts/495-fat-girl-sisters-sex-and-sitcom.

21. The moshav is a type of Israeli settlement, in particular a type of agricultural community of individual farms pioneered by the Zionist Labor movement during the second wave of Aliyah (immigration). Its particularity is that, in contrast to the kibbutz, it retains the family as the center of social life.

22. Ben-Asher's short film *Pathways* (*Misholim*), which she created as her thesis project, was screened in 2007. According to Nirit Anderman, "*Pathways* is a daring, blunt protest movie about a young woman from a moshav in the countryside who seeks consolation by having occasional sex with men and who falls victim to rape." See Nirit Anderman, "Sex and the Farm Girl" [in Hebrew], *Haaretz*, July 5, 2010, accessed May 18, 2017, http://www.mouse.co.il/gallery/1.3318824.

23. It should be noted that this tendency can be seen in both men and women directors' French filmmaking—in radically controversial films such as Gaspar Noé's sensational *Irreversible* (2002) and, more recently, *Love* (2015).

24. Carrie Tarr, "Mutilating and Mutilated Bodies: Women's Takes on 'Extreme' French Cinema," in *Visions of Struggle in Women's Filmmaking in the Mediterranean*, ed. Flavia Laviosa (New York: Palgrave Macmillan, 2010), 64–65.

25. Ibid., 64.

26. Ibid., 64–65.

27. The most striking example is the complete absence of the military in the plot. Whereas realistic depictions of Israeli male existence are always interspersed with depictions of compulsory military reserve duty, the men in *The Slut* seem to be exempted from this obligation, a feature that certainly contributes to the plot's transnational accessibility.

28. According to Shmulik Duvdevani, even the rural landscapes do not necessarily refer to Israeli landscapes but rather bear a certain European appeal. See Duvdevani 2012.

29. See Jean G. Peristiany, ed., *Honor and Shame: The Values of Mediterranean Society* (Chicago: Chicago University Press, 1966).

30. Eric Loret, "Hagar Ben-Asher, and Tender Flesh" [in French], *Liberation*, May 21, 2011, accessed May 18, 2017, http://next.liberation.fr/cinema/2011/05/12/hagar-ben-asher-chair-et-tendre_735138.

31. Anderman 2010.

32. Ezra and Rowden 2006, 4.

33. Ibid., 3.

V

BRINGING THE GLOBAL INTO THE LOCAL: TRANSNATIONAL ENCOUNTERS IN CONTEMPORARY NARRATIVE AND FORM

15

ENCOUNTERS AND INTERSPACES

The Place of Germany and Germans in Israeli Cinema

Tobias Ebbrecht-Hartmann

IN 1965, AFTER YEARS OF MUTUAL RAPPROCHEMENT, West Germany and Israel established diplomatic relations. Beyond these official ties based on not always convergent political interests, personal encounters between Israeli and German citizens had paved the way for this relationship.[1] Besides West German initiatives for reconciliation with the Jewish people (and despite skepticism regarding Germany among large parts of Israeli society), representatives of both countries had already developed a cooperation in soft power sectors, such as science, youth exchange, and culture. Film, cinema, and television played a small but important—and until today, mainly overlooked—role in this process.[2]

But most notably, in recent years, an increasing number of films began to investigate the transitions between Germany and Israel. Such transitions include journeys from one country to the other, both in terms of the narrative and the production context of the films. Filmmakers started to travel back and forth and collaborated with colleagues from the other country, while the films depict Israeli and German protagonists transforming them into a cinematic space of encounter. What became a popular motif in movies—confronting the ghosts of the past that were repeatedly haunting Israeli cinema, such as *Made in Israel* (2001) and *The Debt* (2007)—turned into entangled journeys between both countries in *Walk on Water* (2004) and *Metallic Blues* (2004) and finally cinematic spaces of mutual encounters and transitions in *Strangers* (2007), *Playoff* (2011), *Hanna's Journey* (*Hannas Reise*, 2013), and *Anywhere Else* (*Anderswo*, 2014). Germany then became a central trope in several films negotiating Israeli memories and identities, most notably *Past Life* (2016) and *The Cakemaker* (2017). Also, mostly autobiographical documentary films by Israeli directors, such as *The Flat* (*Ha-dira*, 2011), *Farewell Herr Schwarz* (2013), and *Cafe Nagler* (2016), received increased attention by audiences in both countries. Eight of these films were coproduced with German partners, three were predominantly German productions, eight introduced actors from both countries, at least ten were shot on location in Germany, and twelve films include dialogue in German.[3]

This chapter intends to explore these cinematic journeys between Germany and Israel, not only in their most recent shape but also related to earlier decades in film history. Therefore, I attempt to conceptualize these films as part of a specific German-Israeli *Cinema of Encounters*, which is characterized by exploring a specific geo-cinematographic interzone between both nations.[4] In his seminal book, *The Europeanization of Cinema*, Randall Halle has defined the interzone as a "tentative communication that can double space and shift time, bind distant places, and give separated individuals a sense of possible community."[5] Cinema is a privileged place for establishing such interzones, because, as Halle states, it "repeatedly and uniquely proves capable of imagining collectivities and of acting as a bridge to bring people together in new ways."[6]

Accordingly, German-Israeli films adopt elements from transnational cinema, such as an aesthetic of interspaces that reflect the notion of borders that need to be transgressed, as well as non-places, seemingly ahistorical transit places. However, the German-Israeli interzone is significantly marked by shared and still-conflicting memories. Hence, I attempt to conceptualize German-Israeli cinema as being not only constituted by transnational but also transtemporal encounters.

As interzone cinema, the films discussed in this article create an ensemble of interspaces that refer to different cinematic dimensions: a spatial dimension, a visual dimension, and a figurative dimension. Regarding the spatial dimension, many German-Israeli films establish a room for encounter that is often characterized by non-places and points of transit. These preliminary places are mostly constituted through acts of looking and through various gazes, which include mostly unstable and shifting gazes of the traveler, the immigrant, the foreigner, and the *other* (visual dimension). Such acts of looking then constitute specific subject positions that are significantly embodied by various fictional and sometimes even allegorical characters that are mutually engaging each other at these places (figurative dimension). The interplay of this figurative dimension with the spatial and visual dimensions, then, negotiates the complex German-Israeli relationship in such encounter films but often also evokes the respective counterpart as reflection of particular self-perceptions. This also refers to a specific, often uncanny and persisting past, because the relations between Israel and Germany are obviously foremost and deeply shaped by the impact of the Holocaust, the expulsion and systematic murder of millions of German and European Jews in the course of World War II. But this fundamental disruption is otherwise also related to the prehistory of the catastrophe, which includes Jewish participation within Germany's society and culture, as well as to its post-history, the stepwise rapprochement with West Germany and especially contemporary passages between both countries.

Since the end of the 1970s, Germany's image in the Israeli public has become more and more positive.[7] In 2012, 88.9 percent of Israelis regarded German-Israeli relations as "normal." Compared with 54.7 percent in 1998, this is a significant increase, mirroring also the changing general perception of Germany.[8] Thus, 82.8 percent stated that contemporary Germany is a "different" Germany, which is also illustrated by the significant number of Israelis that moved to Berlin in the last few years. It is estimated that twenty-five thousand Israelis are temporarily or permanently living in the German capital. In 2012, six times more Israeli citizens visited Berlin than in the year 2000.[9] As Tel Aviv–based historian Galili Shahar stated, Berlin became part of the "Israeli Diaspora."[10] Thus, complex historic layers as well as central tenets of Israeli identity, such as immigration and the Holocaust experience, significantly merge in the *German topic*. Within Israeli cinema, this is expressed in a depiction of Germans and Germany that serves as a complex imaginary space for Israeli self-perception and its negotiation within the parameters of cinema. I start by exploring the significance of references to the Holocaust and the Nazi past in the representation of Germans and Germany in Israeli films. The second part of this chapter will then review German-Israeli encounters related to the topic of journeys and border crossings. The third part discusses the intertwining of both aspects in the cinematic treatment of a "return to the place of trauma."[11] In the conclusion, I discuss German-Israeli encounters in cinema as a transnational and transtemporal entanglement.

The Impact of the Nazi Past and the German as *Other*

For many years, Germany's main personification in Israeli cinema was that of the Nazi who vividly reappears in the present and challenges the new Israeli self-perception as a painful reminder of weakness and persecution. Israeli films were and are inhabited by such ambiguous ghostly tenants, the character of the last remaining Nazi who repeatedly haunted Israeli cinema. The prototype of this character was introduced by *Hill 24 Doesn't Answer* (1955), directed by Thorold Dickinson. Starting from a hard-fought hill in the war of independence, the narrative unfolds as a series of flashbacks telling the stories of soldiers from different backgrounds.[12] One of the episodes depicts a young Israeli who was born in the country. Lost in the desert, the soldier captures an Egyptian army officer. He carries the wounded enemy into a cave, where he recognizes that the Egyptian is in fact a German, a former Nazi and member of the Schutzstaffel (SS). When the German starts to verbally attack the Israeli, the young soldier "transforms for a brief moment into an Orthodox Jew."[13] Hilla Lavie indicated that it "remains unclear, however, from whose of the two characters' minds this image arises: Does the German imagine the Israeli as a Jewish victim from his Nazi past, or does the Israeli construct himself as a Jewish victim of the Holocaust?"[14] Encapsulated in the cave in the midst of the desert, the film creates an opaque space of intertwining time, memories, anxieties, and nightmarish fantasies. The cave thus evokes "cataracts of time," once described by Siegfried Kracauer as being marked by a rupture in the temporal flow.[15] Kracauer correspondingly defines them as places where past and present meet, as small holes, "'pockets' and voids," that are embedded in the present but contain traces toward the past.[16] The cave in *Hill 24 Doesn't Answer* resembles these cataracts that, as cinematic spaces, can function like an emigrant's transit place that preserves the past within a different world or as a place of a sudden and uncanny encounter with the ghosts of a traumatic past.

In this case, the cave transforms into a container of hidden, suppressed, even adopted memories; it preserves the Diaspora experience as the reverse side of the Israeli hero, expressed by the intercut image of the Orthodox Jew with an attached yellow star. A shadow play on the wall on the other hand revives the brutal Nazi past within the Israeli present. Finally, the shadows of the past are overcome—not by revenge but by laughter. The Israeli soldier thus transforms into the prototype of a "victorious victim,"[17] while the German character is intended to symbolize "transhistorical enemies personified by the Nazis."[18]

Consequently, the Nazi character appears in the following years in Israeli films in different shapes and with various faces. In Natan Gross's *The Cellar* (1963), the young Jewish survivor Emmanuel returns to his family's home, now occupied by Hans, a former Nazi who once was a childhood friend. Most of the film is set in the basement of the house, again an entangled transhistorical space that serves also as a storeroom of lost childhood memories and hidden traumas.[19] The final encounter between the protagonist with the shadowy inhabitant of the house, who killed his father and took his family home as well as his former girlfriend, is envisioned as an encounter between the revenging Jew and the ghostly Nazi shadow that is "represented as a reflection of Emmanuel's traumatized consciousness."[20] In Moshe Mizrahi's *The Traveller* (1969), the former Nazi is living with a false identity in the Jewish state and is running a lonely hotel at the shore of the Red Sea close to Eilat. When one day a stranger shows up, he fears being exposed. In an act of repeating the cruel and brutal deeds from his past, he kills the stranger, obviously a survivor of the Nazi crimes. In this case, the positions are reversed. The last remaining Nazi appears as Israeli, while the Jewish victim is a stranger to the country.

These early depictions of Germans illustrate that such characters mirror the complex search for an Israeli identity, which on the one hand rejected the Diaspora experience and on the other hand preserved a self-perception as victims. The German character expresses this ambivalence and also serves as a transhistorical symbol for the constant repetition and reappearance of the traumatic past. Such a transhistorical symbol is also signified by the German terrorist, played by the German actor Klaus Kinski in Menahem Golan's *Operation Thunderbolt* (1977). Relating to the real-life Entebbe Operation (1976), the film depicts the hijacking of a French airplane that had originated in Tel Aviv by Palestinian terrorists and two German left-wing extremists.[21] Since the hijackers decided to divide the passengers into Israeli and non-Israeli groups after landing the plane in Entebbe Airport (Uganda), the memory of the Entebbe hijacking was directly related to the repercussions of the Nazi past. In *Operation Thunderbolt*, the multilingual dialogue is interrupted by German expressions related to the selection process in death camps, such as "Schnell, schnell" ("Faster, faster").[22] Here, the *German topic* relates the horrors of the past to the threats of the present.[23] In this case, the place of encounter is not a cave in the desert but an aircraft hangar at Entebbe airport, and the Israelis no longer face a German dressed as an Egyptian soldier, a faceless shadow, or a murderer hiding behind a false Jewish identity but the German children of the Nazi generation.[24] Nevertheless, and although the film was completely shot in Israel, transforming Tel Aviv's exhibition center into the Entebbe airport where the hostages were kept,[25] *Operation Thunderbolt* also creates a transnational space of encounters. Hidden behind the spectacles of action cinema, the film clearly adopts motifs referring to traveling and interspaces through the appearance of German actors and its depiction of transit places such as airports and planes, the international composition of the hostages, and the collaboration between German and Palestinian activists.[26]

A more complex—and thus transnational—approach toward the ambiguous character of the last remaining or returning Nazi didn't appear in Israeli films until after 2000, when several directors actually adopted this motif into their narratives. All these films are clearly influenced by transnational aesthetics of traveling and border crossings or set in spatial or cinematic interspaces. Ari Folman's *Made in Israel*, for example, is situated at the Golan borderland in between Israel and Syria and takes as a starting point a future peace treaty between both countries that binds Syria to hand over the last remaining German war criminal to Israel. From this evolves a complex and often grotesque road movie on the quest of finding and finally getting the remaining "last Nazi," Egon Schulz, portrayed by the well-known (East) German actor Jürgen Holtz. In a film that was obviously inspired by the transcultural cinematic clashes of Serbian director Emir Kusturica, the Golan Mountains serve as a landscape of anxieties and memories, an imaginary space for an expedition into disturbing psychological effects and the aftermath of the past. The German Nazi is primarily an artificial character that triggers conflicting aspects of Israeli self-perception. The artificiality of the character is already obvious in the very first sequence of the film. "When he crosses the border, he is wearing a heavy coat that gives him the look of a dangerous shadow emerging from the fog."[27] Thus, on the one hand, the black coat evokes classical stereotypical features of portraying a Nazi. But on the other hand, the film identifies him as an unreal and ghostly outline that suddenly appears from a different time and space, similar to the shadow plays in *Hill 24 Doesn't Answer* and *The Cellar*. As the film's protagonist, who was assigned with catching and killing Schulz, finally rejects this task, it becomes obvious that the film does not intend to cure but to transcend the Israeli preoccupation with the Holocaust and the ambivalent place of Germany and the Germans within this traumatic past. Folman indeed had stated that he wanted to address the inhibited handling of the Nazi topic by young Israelis.[28] Consequently, the film caused controversial reactions and unsettled feelings among his Israeli audience.[29] But *Made in Israel* is rather a transfiguration of a transnational interspace in favor of retreating to an internal Israeli perspective than a film about Israeli-German encounters or the impact of a shared but divided past. The last remaining Nazi serves as a trigger but finally remains an obstacle. At the end, the film's protagonist Eddie understands, as Ido Ramati has convincingly demonstrated, "that this particular man has nothing to do with the Israeli remembrance, which is an internal issue. Killing him would mean nothing for the collective internalization and processing of the Holocaust."[30]

By contrast, *The Debt*, by Assaf Bernstein, is a multilayered interplay of two different time levels and three geographic spaces in which the fateful events of a never-ending past unfold. Germany is the site of a series of flashbacks that establishes the primal scene of the film's conflict. A group of young Israeli agents is assigned to hijack a former Nazi physician who had served in a Nazi concentration camp. The storyline depicts his hijacking and the disturbing face-to-face encounter with the former Nazi at the hiding place as well as the tensions among the agents and the failure of the mission after the physician manages to escape. On this spatial and temporal level, Germany is presented as a strange and disturbing place. The dark hiding place recalls the encounters with the former Nazi or his revenants in the desert cave in *Hill 24 Doesn't Answer* as well as in the basement in *The Cellar* or the aircraft hangar in *Operation Thunderbolt*. But in contrast to these earlier depictions of the last remaining Nazi, the Nazi past in *The Debt* emerges not only as repetition but also as a suppressed and disturbing traumatic remnant that significantly affects the heroic Israeli generation.

The plot focuses on the story of the female agent, flashing back between past and present. The choice of Gila Almagor as lead actress in the present timeframe of the plot creates a resonating intertext. She also played her mother, a traumatized Holocaust survivor, in *Aviva's Summer* (1988), an adaptation of her own autobiography, as well as one of the Israeli hostages in *Operation Thunderbolt*. Her participation in *The Debt* serves to resonate beyond the filmic text, heightening the sense of trauma and the significance of the Nazi hunt. Yet when the protagonist fails in her mission, she allows the Nazi to continue, thereby failing to exorcise the ghost of the Nazi past as her cinematic forebears had. When the old Nazi reappears in an elderly home in Ukraine, he creates a professional and personal crisis of the female agent, because the three agents had never reported the real course of events and were publicly celebrated for successfully eliminating the Nazi physician. He also creates an existential crisis for the nation, which has failed to destroy and to avenge the Holocaust trauma. Almagor has to travel to Ukraine to deal with the past in a double sense: the suppressed embarrassing memory of the failed hijacking and the hidden traumatic memories of the Nazi past.

Thus, a third space comes into play. Besides Germany as an uncanny place of the traumatic past's aftermath and Israel as its counter-place of Jewish self-defense, Ukraine becomes a deserted space for struggling with the ghosts of the past. Accordingly, traveling in *The Debt* is related to a journey into the suppressed past that is revived in strange and deserted countries, such as an evocative 1960s Germany painted in monochromatic colors or the post-socialist Ukraine. But therapeutic hope is rejected. The "film does not offer a real chance to work-through the trauma by confronting its effects in the present, but only to repress it deeper into the past."[31] The foreign countries will not cure the trauma. In fact, it at first returns in a renewed way in Germany and then is reenacted in the elderly home in Ukraine, whose bright corridors mirror the places of German-Israeli encounter in earlier films. Moreover, the rejection of the traumatic past through killing the last remaining Nazi does not offer relief. The final sequences show the female protagonist wounded and falling down close to the tracks of a local train station. The Ukrainian landscape as a place of traumatic memory as well as the train tracks as an iconic sign of the Holocaust illustrate that the struggle with the past will remain even beyond the German-Israeli encounter.

The Debt refers to the traumatic Israeli-German memories by combining a transtemporal narrative with a transnational cinematic geography. In a similar way, Avi Nesher's *Past Life* entangles an Israeli family history with Polish-Jewish memories while referring to Germany as an uncanny third place that oscillates between the potential of new mutual relationships and recurrences of the traumatic past. In this film, a young Israeli singer and composer encounters a family secret during a concert trip to Germany, which triggers a journey into a silenced past that leads her to different places in Israel, to Poland, and then back to Germany. *Past Life* interrelates elements from films that depict Germany as a spatial or figurative reference to the Holocaust with narrative structures of a search or a journey.

In Eran Riklis's film *Playoff*, the protagonist, a successful Israeli basketball coach who accepts an appointment to coach the mediocre West German national team, confronts his own suppressed past when moving to Frankfurt. However, other people have left their marks and traces on the streets that once were his home. Now mainly migrant workers from Turkey or North Africa are living in Max Stoller's former neighborhood. Supported by tracking shots and slow panning, the camera explores Stoller's familiar but extrinsic world as he constantly negates his personal affection. However, when he accidentally meets Sema, a young Turkish girl now living in his old flat, his memories return. On the night after the accidental visit, Stoller leaves for a restless journey through the abandoned and altered city back to the places of his childhood. His journey leads to a pastry shop, a place that bears a secret. This pastry shop appears like a void, a place of suspended time. It is constituted through the interference of inside and outside. Stoller stands, illuminated only by the light of the street lanterns, in front of the shop's window, which thus likens itself to a display case in a museum exhibition. In a spectral and disembodied reverse shot, the pastry shop then looks back on Stoller. In the background are luminous advertisements for a Turkish kebab restaurant. Stoller himself is placed exactly in the space in between the relic of his childhood, the pastry shop, and the insignia of the new city of migrants and immigrants. When he then looks up to his old flat, he sees Deniz, Sema's mother. Finally, the experience of the new German immigrants helps Stoller to face his own suppressed memories and the hidden secrets of his childhood. Like in *Playoff*, many films depicting German-Israeli encounters create such a paradoxical mode of spatial and temporal existence, of being at one place and at the other at the same time, structured by constant transitions that will never create a state of arrival, of belonging, and of contingency.

Travelers and Border-Crossers

Playoff, Past Life, and *The Debt* significantly adopt the transnational narratives of traveling and border crossing, which are paradigmatic for the German-Israeli cinema of encounter. As Michel de Certeau has stated, the border creates an ambiguous space that separates and at the same time creates communication. Thus, as a narrative element, "the frontier functions as a third element. It is an 'in-between'—a 'space between,' *Zwischenraum.*"[32] This interspace is the place in which identity and belonging are debated, defined, and challenged. Thus, it is a "middle place, composed of interactions and inter-views, the frontier [as] a sort of void, a narrative symbol of exchanges and encounters."[33]

Israeli-German films are indeed built around visible and invisible borders. The transgressing of these borders, which sometimes only appear as a cinematic cut between two images, is crucial and significant in these films. Accordingly, de Certeau's understanding of the border as a point of entanglement is particularly useful to describe the German-Israeli Cinema of Encounters because its films are similarly characterized by such points of entanglement, which are dividing and connecting at the same time. Another recent example of such temporal as well as geographical border crossing, this time from the documentary genre, would be Arnon Goldfinger's autobiographical quest to discover his family's past in *The Flat*. The topographic and mnemonic center of the film's narrative is the orphaned flat of the filmmaker's grandmother in Tel Aviv, which, similar to the cave, the cellar, and the airport hangar, functions like a cataract of times in which numerous remnants of the past could tell a compelling but also disturbing story of German-Israeli relations, disruption, and coexistence. These transhistorical places in Israeli cinema are spaces that encapsulate time. They remind of the past, but often they also refer to the experience of exile and immigration and thus provide a space that, in a nostalgic or traumatized way, preserves the remnants of lost lives. Thus, they can transform into a closed space of reencountering the trauma of the past.

In *The Flat*, the apartment as a time capsule reveals the background of the director's grandparents, their life in prewar Germany, their immigration to Palestine, and their friendship with a high-ranking Nazi officer. On the second level, which is situated in the present, the film encounters today's Germany and the remaining traces and memories of the past on the director's journey together with his mother to Berlin and Wuppertal. The film's preservation of the flat transforms the private place into a transhistorical interspace in which the traces of Jewish German self-perception remained. While those traces—along with the disturbing reality of a continuing friendship between Zionist Jewish Israeli immigrants and a former Nazi's family in postwar Germany, another return of the Nazi ghost in Israeli cinema—are hidden in this transit space, Goldfinger, a representative of the third generation of Jewish Israelis after the Shoah, seems to be obsessively preoccupied with the German question. But the changing perspective on Germany as a historical space of return dominates his perspective in the same manner in which his parents once rejected the suppressed pre-history of his grandparents and their origin from the Diaspora.[34]

References to Germany resonate in many Israeli films that depict the issue of immigration and exile as a successful or failing transition, although references to the experiences of Jewish German emigrants in Israel only had a subliminal place in most Israeli films. Ilan Moshenson expressed this in the atmospheric design of his film *The Wooden Gun* (1979), which depicts the situation of immigrants and survivors in the early fifties who are facing a young generation that was already born in the country and strongly identifies with the role model of the New Hebrew. Reenacting the heroism of the young state and its wars in their children's games, a group of kids unwittingly are on the verge of repeating the outrage of a past that is suppressed in everyday life but nevertheless had an impact on the next generation. In a significant scene, the particular German experience of loss and emigration among the various other emigrants who appear as grownups in the film is expressed on an aural level. In the background of the children's war games, vague voices can be heard speaking in German and transforming the Jewish German experience into a sense of aural unsettledness and hidden vocal traces.[35]

The Wooden Gun thus represents a subliminal turning point followed by a slow-moving opening toward the Jewish German immigrant perspective in Israeli cinema. "Only at the end of the 1970s did Israeli culture gradually start to accept the presence of the German culture in its sphere."[36] A year after *The Wooden Gun*, Daniel Wachsmann directed *Transit* (1980), the first of a series of films during the 1980s that "transformed the image of the refugees from Olim (new immigrants) with hopeful national aspirations to desperate immigrants who display open longings for the German past."[37] Although *Transit* has to be seen foremost in the context of an allegorical depiction of a disputed national narrative, it not only reverses the notions, transforming Germany from a rejected place to a place of longing, it also inverts the stylistic patterns of the early Zionist films. Already, the opening situates the film within the modes of traveling by depicting a plane and an empty street by dawn. Thereby *Transit* expresses its critical stand toward the "representation of Israel as safe haven" and instead tells about the "life of an alienated immigrant in Israel."[38] This is the starting point of a journey through empty streets and transit spaces such as a hotel, in the sense of French anthropologist Marc Augé, "a world thus surrendered to [the] solitary and ephemeral."[39] Although centered on such *non-places*, meaning spaces that are not "defined as relational, historical and concerned with identity,"[40] flashbacks are constantly evolving and recalling the past's interspersing of the narrative. Thus, according to Augé's assumptions, "places reconstitute themselves in it; relations are restored and resumed in it."[41] Here and there, German dialogues disrupt the already-sparse conversation. Although the social environment of the lonesome and lost protagonist, an emigrant from Germany, includes people who speak mostly Hebrew, suddenly German words and expressions interrupt the flow and highlight the discrepancy between desire and reality.[42] In this film, the origin of displacement, Germany, becomes the projection screen of nostalgia. The immigrant transmutes back into the homeless Diaspora Jew, even in his "promised" land.

In later films, episodic narration and references to the topic of migration and displacement became a typical element in films that touch the *German topic*. Similar elements and references were also used in Tzipi Trope's *Tel Aviv-Berlin* (1986), a film that likewise portrays the problems a German immigrant faces when attempting to integrate into Israeli society, although the persisting and traumatic memories of the Holocaust are much more emphasized than in *Transit*. *Tel Aviv-Berlin*, however, still presents the lost home as an irretrievable place that only continues to persist because the past, in this case similar to the constellation in *The Traveller*, is still haunting the present.

In contrast, *Berlin-Jerusalem* (1989) by Amos Gitai, filmed in a very theatrical and sometimes even surrealistic style, creates interspaces and passages between different worlds and times. Two stories—that of Jewish German poetry writer Else Lasker-Schüler and Russian Zionist Manya Shohat—are intertwined. Berlin and Jerusalem are both mythic places. Permanently moving from one to the other, the film creates an opaque space in which both places merge. While Jerusalem is a place built on various sediments of identity layers and histories, Berlin of the 1920s appears as a place of revolution, excess, and violence but also of lost or unrealized utopia.[43] Therefore, the film "uses Expressionist techniques associated with German cinema of the late 1920's and early 30's" and thus integrates a particular tradition of German film history into Israeli cinema.[44]

Only in recent years has an explicit transnational aesthetic shaped Israeli filmmaking and brought up narratives that are constantly traveling back and forth between different geographic places and identity spaces. The topic of Israeli migration thus became especially vivid and also controversial with regard to the rising numbers of Israelis traveling and moving to Berlin over the last decade. One of these immigrants is Israeli filmmaker Ester Amrami. Her film *Anywhere Else* (2014) depicts the feeling of a place in between both poles, Israel and Berlin/Germany, as a fleeting narrative of a road movie involving travel from the German capital to Israel and a longing for the notion of home. The film's protagonist, Noa, decides to visit her family in Israel and leaves behind her German boyfriend and her stagnant dissertation project on untranslatable words. However, Israel is still not the perfect home she was longing for, although her grandmother's disease and her boyfriend's sudden arrival provoke new encounters and a different perspective on the country, her family, and everyday life. The plot is interrupted by short video sequences about language and identity, labeled as Noa's PhD research material, which adds another layer to the discourse about migration and home. In the final interview sequence, Noa's grandmother is talking about her understanding of language and home. Embedded into the film after her death, this final video sequence on the one hand demonstrates the potential of cinema to bridge time and space. On the other hand, Noa's grandmother, who spoke Yiddish, Hebrew, and English, was born in Eastern Europe, was educated in several Eastern European languages, and was expelled to and resettled in Israel, becomes the personification of an in-between identity space that is communicated through the mediating potential of audiovisual media. Thus, *Anywhere Else* combines a transnational production background with an explicit discourse about migration and identity conflicts and creates a cinematic interspace between the two conflicting but nevertheless connected worlds of Israel and Germany. Similarly, *The Cakemaker* discovers German-Israeli encounters as a plot element that helps address questions of identity and belonging. In this film, a young German who had a relationship with a married Israeli man in Berlin travels to Israel after his lover's sudden death in an accident and begins working for his recently widowed wife. *The Cakemaker* thereby represents a more universalized attempt to address and utilize the *German topic* within the motivational conflicts recently negotiated by Israeli films.

Toward an Imaginary Germany

Most contemporary Israeli films depict Germany as the destination of a journey that intertwines transnational elements, the motif of traveling, and the persistence of a haunting past. These films thus combine elements from both traditions of German-Israeli encounters in and through cinema. Eytan Fox's *Walk on Water*, for instance, explores possible German-Israeli encounters and interspaces and adopts transnational production modes as well as related narratives and stylistic devices that combine traveling between both countries with an exploration of transgressing identities. The film's story is centered on Eyal, a Mossad agent who works as a professional hit man abroad. After returning home, he encounters the suicide of his wife, which fractures and ultimately destabilizes his tough and arrogant self-conceptualization. His deserted flat transforms into a non-place of solitude and suppressed trauma similar to that of the emigrant in *Transit*. Likewise, it becomes the starting point of a journey, which, in contrast to the one depicted in *Transit*, finally leads to Germany and—in a utopian move—to an imagined revision of Israeli identity.

To rebalance Eyal, his fatherly boss, Menachem, decides to put him on a mission to find and execute the former Nazi officer Alfred Himmelmann, who is supposedly hiding in South America. Eyal takes on the guise of a guide driving Himmelmann's grandson Axel around the holy land on behest of the latter's sister, who has joined a kibbutz. Axel, a liberal and openly gay third-generation German, confuses Eyal's self-perception and ultimately prompts him to travel to Berlin. Once there, Eyal is able to resituate himself and thereby create a private utopian interspace at the film's ending.[45]

Boaz Hagin has pointed toward the splitting of Eyal's character into three different parts: "It is thus possible for Eyal in *Walk on Water* to appropriate three different languages (English, Hebrew, and German), three different 'I's' that can communicate with three different (but not necessarily mutually exclusive) groups of other subjects; in other words, to belong to three different 'we's.'"[46] These three identity spaces, which are related to three different languages spoken in the film, also correspond with differing aspects of the film's narrative. While Hebrew is linked to the Israeli sphere (inhabited primarily by the Mossad agency), English defines a space in between, which is primarily linked to a touristic gaze. Most parts of the film introduce the well-known landmarks of Israel and Berlin and comply with the modes of traveling known from the road movie genre. Some of these landmarks even connect both places, such as Berlin's television tower, which marks the Alexanderplatz and appears already in the Israel episode of the film as a small replica and hiding place for a surveillance microphone in Axel's sister's flat.

Listening to the German siblings' conversation evokes the third but mainly suppressed aspect of Eyal's tripartite identity position. The German language denotes his parents' German origin and characterizes him as the heir of an experience of displacement and expulsion from Germany.[47] This scene implicitly also marks Eyal's connection to German tradition and cultural heritage and is clearly linked to another key sequence within the second part of the film, which is situated at the subway station of the Alexanderplatz.[48] When Axel and Eyal witness violent neo-Nazis attack a group of gays and drag queens, both interfere, and Eyal finally yells in German toward one of the attackers and threatens him with a gun. In this scene, "Eyal marks himself as a member of the German-Jewish diaspora by revealing his linguistic and affective ties to Germany."[49] At the same time, he changes the historical roles, this time expelling the Nazis' revenants and replacing himself within the German frame on the side of an identity position that is opposed to German as well as Israeli exclusiveness, as Nicholas Baer has observed: "Jews, queers, and drag queens are here linked by association with the transgression and obscuration of boundaries of gender and nationality."[50] Thus, in the subway station, the transit place of transnational and transcultural encounter and the transtemporal interspace of encountering the ghosts of the past, the revenant of the cave and the aircraft hangar are superimposed: "The return of a descendant of Holocaust survivors to Germany initiates a working-through process that allows Eyal to solve some of his emotional inhibitions. His journey highlights the tensions between the surviving parents and their disaffected son."[51]

The revealing and entangled encounter in the subway station becomes the starting point for the final journey of Eyal via the Avus highway to the Himmelmann villa at the Wannsee Lake, both historically determined places from German history. Here he finally encounters the ghost of the past in the shape of Axel's grandfather. As he was in *Made in Israel* and *The Debt*, this last remaining Nazi is also clearly marked as an unreal and imaginary character. Face-to-face with the perpetrator, Eyal loses the ability to kill. At the end, Axel fulfills this mission. The last sequence shows Eyal, who is now married to Axel's sister, caring about his newborn son, reflecting the idealized utopia of a harmonized German-Israeli interspace.

Reviewing the film's concept of German-Israeli encounters, *Walk on Water* uses Germany and Germans mostly as a projection screen for dealing with the conflicting identities and unsettled past and present within the Israeli context. Fox's interest in investigating and questioning the Israeli concept of masculinity makes the film foremost a reversed coming-of-age story in which the hero displaces himself by splitting up his fixed identity into different parts. The motif of journey and traveling mirrors this dissolution. In return, his German counterpart symbolizes an imaginary Germany. The character serves a "therapeutic approach" to "confront" Israeli society with its "alleged enemy."[52] Thus, the film shows Germany mainly as a place where ghosts of the past haunt dark holes or the underground, while above, a new colorful and liberal German capital devotes itself to everything that is different. In this way, *Walk on Water* adopts the *German topic* as an allusive mirror for a conflicted Israeli self-perception.[53]

The depiction of Germans and Germany in contemporary Israeli cinema oscillates between Germany as an uncanny place of a persisting history and as an idealized space of encounters beyond the trauma of the past and the conflicts of the present. This entanglement of two conflicting perceptions of Germany is explicitly explored in *Metallic Blues*, which takes its starting point from a garage in Israel. Its main protagonist is a Lincoln Continental Limousine that triggers a net of transnational encounters. Imported to Israel by an exiled Israeli Arab from Canada, the car is sold to two Israeli car dealers, one from German-Ashkenazi origins (Shmuel) and the other from Sephardic ones (Siso). They decide to sell the car in Germany, expecting to get a fortune in return. At first symbolizing inaccessible wealth—"it's no car, it's America," proclaims Siso when he initially enters the car—the limousine later transforms into a shelter within an inhospitable environment. While at the beginning Germany is a place of aspiration and promise, it soon transforms into an uncanny landscape. Mainly set in Germany, the film evolves through several encounters with the country and its people in such transit spaces as the harbor and hotels. The tragicomic tone of the film creates an ambivalent mood, introducing the presence of the past parenthetically but with an increasing intensity. Shmuel is confronted with the impact of a traumatic past that he never personally experienced. "*Metallic Blues* takes the protagonist through a trip in Germany in which he encounters, for the first time in his life, his own demons—the heritage of his parents' trauma."[54] As a child of Holocaust survivors, he finds that Germany, for him, becomes an affected space of imaginative memories that suddenly appear out of nowhere. In a crucial sequence, Shmuel looks from a balcony of his hotel down to the harbor—a significant non-place and transit space—when suddenly the people down on the street transform into a group of Jews marked with yellow stars and led forcibly by German policemen. "Only when he realizes that his trip to Germany was motivated by the wrong reasons (mainly greed) is he able to disconnect himself from his parents' past and see the present as it is. This is also the point where the twisted delirium stops."[55]

Director Danny Verete clearly transforms the German landscape—roads, streets, and highways—into an imaginary interspace in which past and present collide. Thus, Germany again becomes a projection screen for the Israeli condition, but in a far more complex way than in *Made in Israel*, *The Debt*, and even *Walk on Water*. *Metallic Blues* not only merges elements of a road movie with unrelated cinematic strategies so as to juxtapose different time levels; it creates a multi-occupied interspace merging Israeli-German with imaginary post-memory encounters, conflicting Israeli identities (between Ashkenazi and Sephardic Jews), and social differences. As such, Germany in *Metallic Blues* functions as an externalized landscape of projected Israeli anxieties and aspirations.[56]

Hanna's Journey, by director Julia von Heinz, can be seen as a German complement to this approach. In this film, a young German woman is traveling to Israel. Against her original intention, she starts to engage with the land and the people and begins to discover her own family past. Likewise set in a temporal and spatial interzone, *Hanna's Journey* opens in a plane. Hanna, on her way to Israel, where she is supposed to work in a center for disabled people in order to enhance social activities on her curriculum vitae, is thus placed in a mode of *not yet there* and *not there anymore*. This mirrors the general notion of the film, which oscillates between the two poles, Germany and Israel. Following the opening shot, the narrative flashes back and presents the pre-story of what happened to Hanna in Berlin before she arrived in Israel. Such transition of past and present, memories and new encounters, is typical for German-Israeli films. Through her encounters with Israel and Israelis, especially with Itay, a coworker at the center for disabled people, and her increasing irritations, miscommunications, and surprising discoveries, the cold carrier-related interspace slowly fills with new experiences and people who reconnect her with her own unknown history.

At the end of the film, Hanna stays in Israel as a result of a spontaneous decision. Something holds her back from returning to Berlin. The film's ending marks a moment of respite, of dynamic asynchrony. While Hanna stays in Tel Aviv, Itay decides to travel to Berlin. German-Israeli relations are still determined by such asynchrony, a history that divides and at the same time creates points of entanglement defined by encounters that lead to misunderstanding and nevertheless enable transitions and exchange. Cinema is a significant place for such encounters. It is creating interspaces that evoke relations while also proving distance. It trespasses borders but also withholds final closure. Accordingly, in a movement of unforeseen transition, the final shots of *Hanna's Journey* interweave Berlin and Tel Aviv into one cinematic space. Here the film transforms into a utopian place—an imaginary Tel Aviv-Berlin, a transitory space, a meeting place for travelers, an imaginative site in constant transformation.

Conclusion

The German-Israeli Cinema of Encounters can be described as an increasingly mobile, unstable, and provisional interspace between both national cinemas. Through the adoption of significant elements from transnational cinema, such as transnational production modes and aesthetics, German-Israeli encounters in and through cinema significantly refer to the motifs of journeys, traveling, and migration. Transit points, points of entanglement, and non-places play a crucial role for the films' narratives and visual style. Temporal, spatial, and visual layers intertwine and create new, sometimes unforeseen, sometimes unsettling, but also sometimes utopian constellations. As a result, German-Israeli films generate particular rooms for encounters that establish relations between protagonists from both countries without negating or successfully healing the wounds from the past. Hence, the connecting but still dividing past is an important factor in these films, often disrupting the narratives and thus emphasizing the significant asynchrony of German-Israeli relations. Thus, eventually the German-Israeli interzone is also a highly mediated space. Its constant interplay of cinematic operations, places, gazes, and encounters finally constitutes the significant interspaces that turn into meeting places for the negotiation of the German-Israeli past and present in and through film and cinema.

As pointed out, Germany is a multi-occupied space in Israeli cinema that connects different historical layers as well as identity conflicts. As a projection screen for inner Israeli tensions and the externalization of a conflicting Israeli self-perception, these narratives largely adopt the motif of a journey in order to culminate in particular interspaces or places of transit. Furthermore, beyond the transnational encounters within the films' narratives, the encounter of audiences with the films may also constitute interspaces that tie together different time layers and identity positions without necessarily harmonizing conflicting perspectives and memories. Thus, the cinema itself becomes an interzone of German-Israeli encounters that is mirrored in the stories of border-crossing journeys and traveling narratives.

Notes

1. For more on the early rapprochement between both countries and the "'schizophrenic' state in which the [Israeli] government's promotion of economic and cultural ties with Germany exists alongside intense rhetoric, most notably in the media, calling for the 'negation of Germany,'" see Hilla Lavie, "An Ambivalent Relationship: Representations of Germany and Germans in Israeli Cinema, 1950–1990," in *Simon Dubnow Institute Yearbook XIV*, ed. Raphael Gross (Göttingen: Vandenhoeck & Ruprecht, 2015), 219. Dan Diner recently coined the term *ritual distance* to describe the early stages of German-Israeli rapprochement in *Rituelle Distanz: Israels Deutsche Frage* [in German] (München: DTV, 2015). Individual and social initiatives toward German-Israeli reconciliation are explored in Hannfried von Hindenburg, *Demonstrating Reconciliation: State and Society in West German Foreign Policy toward Israel, 1952–1965* (New York: Berghahn, 2007). I analyzed and discussed the impact of Rolf Vogel, a postwar German pioneer of German-Israeli encounters in and through cinema, in Tobias Ebbrecht-Hartmann, "Projected Encounters: Rolf Vogel and the Beginnings of Cinematic Relations between Germany and Israel," *Leo Baeck Institute Year Book* 63, no. 1 2018): 11–33.

2. Parts of such a German-Israeli film history are delineated in my German-language book *Übergänge: Filmische Passagen durch eine deutsch-israelische Filmgeschichte* (Berlin: Neofelis, 2014), on which this chapter is mainly based.

3. Despite an often-distorted view of Israel in the German public, which is mainly a result of the dominant focus on the Israeli-Palestinian conflict and its unbalanced presentation in the media, Israeli films have gained increasing interest in recent years. They are regularly present at all important international German film festivals, including Berlin, Leipzig, Hamburg, and Munich, and are often also awarded prizes. Joseph Cedar won the Silver Bear for Best Director for *Beaufort* (2007) at the Berlinale, *Anywhere Else* received the DIALOGUE award at the Berlin Film Festival in 2014, and *Farewell Herr Schwarz* was given awards in Leipzig and Cottbus. At least four Jewish film festivals are screening Israeli movies on a regular basis. The oldest and biggest of them is the Jewish Film Festival Berlin-Brandenburg. Israel also became a popular destination in many German television dramas, such as *Die Seele eines Mörders* (2009) and *Mörderischer Besuch* (2010) with the popular German actor Heiner Lauterbach as Israeli detective, *Das Jerusalem Syndrom* (2013) and *Herbe Mischung* (2015) by the Israeli German director Dror Zahavi, and most recently in the TV series *Der Tel-Aviv-Krimi* (2016–), which is produced by the main German public broadcasting station ARD.

4. The term *interzone* is taken from Randal Halle's analysis of interzones in European cinema in Randal Halle, *The Europeanization of Cinema: Interzones and Imaginative Communities* (Urbana: University of Illinois Press, 2014).

5. Halle 2014, 13.

6. Ibid., 14.

7. Moshe Zimmermann, "Facelift—Das Image der Deutschen in Israel seit der Wiedervereinigung" [in German], in *Deutsche(s) in Palästina und Israel: Tel Aviver Jahrbuch für deutsche Geschichte*, ed. Jose Brunner (Göttingen: Wallstein Verlag, 2013), 288.

8. Ibid., 201.

9. Gisela Dachs, "Berlin, Diaspora der Israelis" [in German], *ZEIT ONLINE*, October 28, 2013, accessed May 19, 2014, http://www.zeit.de/politik/ausland/2013-10/israel-emigration -berlin-yair-lapid.

10. Ibid.

11. Ido Ramati, "Between Israel and Germany: Therapeutic Return to the Place of Trauma in Contemporary Israeli Cinema," *New German Critique* 4, no. 3 (Fall 2014): 179.

12. Uri S. Cohen, "From Hill to Hill: A Brief History of the Representation of War in the Israeli Cinema," in *Israeli Cinema: Identities in Motion*, ed. Miri Talmon and Yaron Peleg (Austin: University of Texas Press, 2011), 44.

13. Ilan Avisar, "The Holocaust in Israeli Cinema as a Conflict between Survival and Morality," in *Israeli Cinema: Identities in Motion*, ed. Miri Talmon and Yaron Peleg (Austin: University of Texas Press, 2011), 154.

14. Lavie 2015, 222.

15. Siegfried Kracauer, *History: The Last Things Before the Last* (Princeton, NJ: Wiener, 2013), 199.

16. Ibid.

17. Lavie 2015, 223.

18. Avisar 2011, 154.

19. Hilla Lavie describes the film as "the first film to portray the story of a Holocaust survivor suffering from post-traumatic nightmares." Lavie 2015, 231.

20. Ibid., 232.

21. Tobias Ebbrecht-Hartmann, "Resonating Trauma: Framing Conflicting Memories of the Entebbe Hostage Crisis," *New German Critique* 46, no. 2 (2019): 91–116.

22. Avisar 2011, 156.

23. Hilla Lavie emphasizes that this resonance between past and present in the depiction of Germany and German characters can also be found in two other films by Menahem Golan, *Eight against One* (1964) and *Trunk to Cairo* (also *Operation Cairo*, 1965). Lavie 2015, 226.

24. The danger of repeating the errors of the past, especially through taking specific lessons from the Nazi era, fundamentally shaped the German postwar left and produced a puzzling return of antisemitic resentments that were covered by anti-Zionist or pro-Palestinian attitudes. The events of Entebbe played a crucial role in this chapter of postwar German history. See Hans Kundani, *Utopia or Auschwitz: Germany's 1968 Generation and the Holocaust* (New York: Columbia University Press, 2009), 133–136.

25. Shraga Har-Gil, "Eine Schlacht wird ausgeschlachtet" [in German], *Hannoversche Allgemeine*, January 6, 1977.

26. Besides the two German terrorists, the film also contains another German character, a medical doctor among the hostages who "embodies the 'good German.'" Lavie 2015, 229.

27. Ido Ramati, *Images in Transformation. Representations of Germany and Germans in Contemporary Israeli Fiction Cinema*, accessed September 21, 2020, https://www.academia

.edu/1755992/Images_in_Transformation_Representations_of_Germany_and_Germans_in
_Contemporary_Israeli_Fiction_Cinema, 23.

28. Rolf-Rüdiger Hamacher, "Made in Israel" [in German], *Film-Dienst* 56 (2001): 23.

29. Hans Dieter-Schmidt, "Letzter Nazi, letztgültige Gerechtigkeit?" [in German], *Neues Deutschland*, March 28, 2003.

30. Ramati, *Images in Transformation*, 29.

31. Ibid., 16.

32. Michael de Certeau, *The Practice of Everyday Life*, 3rd ed., trans. Steven Rendall (Berkeley: University of California Press, 2011), 127.

33. Ibid.

34. Another Israeli documentary film that explored such an entangled family past between Germany and Israel is Yael Reuveny's *Farewell Herr Schwarz*. The documentary *Café Nagler* by Mor Kaplansky portrays a similar German-Israeli family past in a more nostalgic way.

35. In this regard, *The Wooden Gun* complements the use of the German language in *Operation Thunderbolt*; whereas in the latter, German serves as an indicator of the continuing Nazi past, in the former, its artistic use instead refers to the suppressed origin and memories of the new immigrants. *Jellyfish* (2007) by Shira Geffen and Etgar Keret uses German words in a similar way. In this film, an old immigrant from Germany refuses the help of a Filipino migrant worker hired by her daughter by yelling, "Geh, geh!" ("Go, go!"). The utilization of the German language, which the migrant does not understand, tacitly connects both women through a shared experience of migration and immigration.

36. Ramati, *Images in Transformation*, 5.

37. Avisar 2011, 159.

38. Lavie 2015, 236.

39. Marc Augé, *Non-Places: Introduction to an Anthropology of Supermodernity*, trans. John How (New York: Verso, 1995), 78.

40. Ibid., 77.

41. Ibid., 78.

42. Volker Baer, "Transit" [in German], *Der Tagesspiegel*, February 21, 1980.

43. The film also expands the German-Israeli perspective so as to create a German-Israeli-Palestinian triangle. "In the . . . final scene, the film shifts from the reality of Jerusalem in the 1930s to the violence in the 1980s. . . . The film thus leaves the viewers in the midst of the unresolved Israeli-Palestinian conflict. In so doing, it suggests that even the return to Germany (represented by the direction in which Else is walking) does not bear a solution and can exist only in utopia. The film offers a symbolic return to Germany as an answer to the Israeli-Palestinian conflict while reflecting on the unfeasibility of this return." Ramati, "Between Israel and Germany," 188. The German-Israeli-Palestinian entanglement is also explored in two films by Judd Ne'eman, *Fellow Travelers* (1984) and *Streets of Yesterday* (1989). See Lavie 2015, 237–241.

44. Vincent Canby, "Two Movies Examine Israel," *New York Times*, March 8, 1991.

45. Ido Ramati interprets this journey as reversion of the German concept of Bildung (and respectively the Bildungsroman), as it is expressed in Theodor Herzl's iconic Zionist novel *Altneuland* (Old New Land): "When Eyal learns that expressing emotions does not compromise his masculinity—a consequence of his encounter with the German past and with a contemporary German—he allows himself to become vulnerable." Ramati, "Between Israel and Germany," 191.

46. Boaz Hagin, "Male Weeping as Performative: The Crying Mossad Assassin in *Walk in Water*," *Camera Obscura* 23, no. 2 (2008): 111.

47. Raz Yosef, "Homonational Desires. Masculinity, Sexuality, and Trauma in the Cinema of Eytan Fox," in *Israeli Cinema: Identities in Motion*, ed. Miri Talmon and Yaron Peleg (Austin: University of Texas Press, 2011), 189.

48. Uta Larkey, "Mehrsprachigkeit in neueren israelischen Spielfilmen" [in German], *Medaon* 13 (2013): 10.

49. Nicholas Baer, "Points of Entanglement: The Overdetermination of German Space and Identity in *Lola + Bilidikid* and *Walk on Water*," *Transit* 4, no. 1 (2008): 17.

50. Ibid.

51. Ramati, "Between Israel and Germany," 189.

52. Daniela Pogade, "In Israel war 'Schindlers Liste' ein Flop. Der israelische Regisseur Eytan Fox über, 'Walk on Water'" [in German], *Berliner Zeitung*, May 13, 2005.

53. Hagin 2008, 126–127.

54. Ramati, "Between Israel and Germany," 192.

55. Ramati, *Images in Transformation*, 11.

56. Another, more recent example of the combination of transnational aesthetics, the motif of migration and traveling, and the persistence of memories from the past in the context of German-Israeli cinema would be *Playoff*. In contrast, the multicultural new Germany in a film like *Strangers* (2003), by Erez Tadmor and Guy Nativ, becomes a kind of third place for the encounter of an Israeli-Palestinian couple during the 2006 World Cup.

16

BLOOD, SWEAT, AND TEARS

The Rise of Israel's New Extremism

Neta Alexander

WHEN ASKED WHY THEIR HIGHLY SUCCESSFUL SECOND FEATURE, *Big Bad Wolves* (2013), focuses on pedophilia and violence directed against children, Israeli filmmakers Aharon Keshales and Navot Papushado explained, "For us, childhood essentially reflects a state of innocence and naïveté. At the same time, the world to which we are born is saturated with violence and brutality. No matter what you do, you will always be exposed to violence. Every time violence breaks out, you soak it up like a passive smoker. You cannot escape it, and it informs your personality in myriad, mostly unrecognized, ways."[1]

This claustrophobic, pessimistic, and morbid description of everyday reality, which equates violence with the suffocating smell of cigarettes refusing to evaporate from human bodies and clothes, can be found in a surprising number of Israeli features made between 2010 and 2016. These films—many of which have become headliners of festivals such as Cannes, Berlin, Venice, or Tribeca—depict a reality characterized by persistent, ubiquitous, and quotidian violence. Contrary to the most recent wave of conflict films that take place on the battlefield, such as *Beaufort* (Joseph Cedar, 2007), *Waltz with Bashir* (Ari Folman, 2008), *Lebanon* (Samuel Maoz, 2009), or *Rock the Casbah* (Yariv Horowitz, 2012), the tormenting stories of what I will term the *New Violence* movement emerge and play out within the claustrophobic confines of the domestic sphere. Instead of a distant, faraway frontline, the new combat zones are to be found everywhere: between the living room and the kitchen, the streets of Tel Aviv, and the luxury villas of the wealthy beachfront district Herzliya Pituah.

As in *Big Bad Wolves*, violence is present in almost every scene in films such as Keshales and Papushado's *Rabies* (2010), Hagar Ben-Asher's *The Slut* (2011), Michal Aviad's *Invisible* (2011), Dana Goldberg's *Alice* (2012), Johnathan Gurfinkel and Rona Segal's *S#x Acts* (2012), Tom Shoval's *Youth* (2013), Maya Dreifuss's *She Is Coming Home* (2013), Eitan Gafny's *Cannon Fodder* (2013), Tali Shalom-Ezer's *Princess* (2014), Keren Yedaya's *That Lovely Girl* (2014), Roni Keidar's *The World's End* (2014), Doron and Yoav Paz's *JeruZalem* (2015), and Yaelle Kayam's *Mountain* (2015), along with other recent works. Whereas these films confront their viewers with disturbing taboos, including pedophilia, incest, rape, and torture, other young filmmakers focus their attention on social violence and economic inequalities. This group includes Nadav Lapid's *Policeman* (2011), Idan Hubel's *The Cutoff Man* (2012), Amir Manor's *Epilogue* (2012), Noam Kaplan's *Manpower* (2014), Meny Yaesh's *Avinu* (2016), and Ben-Asher's *The Burglar* (2016), all of which are dark indie dramas protesting the waning of the Israeli middle class and the growing gap between the haves and have-nots.

This essay considers the recurring themes, concerns, and confrontational aesthetics these films share. The challenge of mapping out a new cultural wave, genre, or movement requires evidence for at least three different claims: first, that the works grouped together are substantially different from the works that preceded them; second, that despite the many differences between the works, they share similar styles, themes, plotlines, or concerns; and third, that these similarities correlate with a specific national, cultural, economic, or political context in which the films have been made. The emergence of the New Violence movement in Israeli cinema draws inspiration from New Extremism trends in European cinema. While the filmmakers share no specific manifesto or official name, their group identity is based on generational, social, and political affinities explored throughout this essay. Their works share a particular understanding of the engagement between cinema and society that demonstrates an urgent need for political activism. This is enacted through the use of extreme violence that subversively directs attention to the horrors of Israel's ongoing militarism, wars, and occupation. It is this central theme that stands in contrast to the ways in which violence is deployed within recent European cinema.

European cinema turned to extreme violence for various reasons, one of which is shock value—as evident, for example, in the works of French filmmakers Bruno Dumont, Gaspar Noé, Catherine Breillat, and Philippe Grandrieux. Relating to these filmmakers as the "New French Extremity," film critic James Quandt highlighted their shared use of "shock tactics," associated with earlier artistic movements such as Surrealism and the French New Wave, and decried such choice as a superficial attempt to respond to the cultural crisis that led to "the death of the ineluctable (French identity, language, ideology, aesthetic forms)."[2] According to this reading, the urge to break every taboo is a modern-day version of anti-bourgeois art that originated in postwar France, and its purpose is to awaken audiences from their apathy, as Dumont proclaimed to the press when discussing his use of violence in *Twentynine Palms* (2003): "People are way too set in their ways, they are asleep. They have to be woken up."[3]

Throughout his essay, Quandt denies the possibility of New French Extremity being a movement, rather than a trend, arguing that these French provocateurs use violence to different ends: they do not share an artistic vision and have no common purpose. In the past decade, numerous international filmmakers have used the visual and thematic tropes associated with the French New Extremity, suggesting that this trend has had the broad impact of an artistic movement. In *Screening the Unwatchable*, for example, Asbjørn Grønstad distinguishes between the graphic violence portrayed in films such as *A Clockwork Orange* (Stanley Kubrick, 1971), *Reservoir Dogs* (Quentin Tarantino, 1992), and *Fight Club* (David Fincher, 1999) and the new and unique manifestations of violence in the films of Lars von Trier, Michael Haneke, and other representatives of the European Cinema of Extremity. Coining the term *razorblade gestures*, Grønstad writes that "in the earlier tradition, the unpleasant and the provocative were carefully contained within the fictional universe . . . but in the new controversial film epidemic it is as if their violent energy has burst through the membrane of the work to target the spectators themselves."[4] This distinction between old and new violence can also be seen in Israeli cinema, whereby the new films offer different models of violence than their traditional war-film predecessors, known as the "shooting and weeping genre."[5]

Tanya Horeck and Tina Kendall list the global trends that are often included under the umbrella of New Extremism, such as "torture porn," "Asia Extreme," and "the new brutality film."[6] They then stress the drawbacks of using the word *new* in relation to a cinematic style: "In using this term, we do not wish to suggest that the extremism of these films is unprecedented; nor do we intend to enumerate a comprehensive catalogue of new, or newly extreme, practices or representations. Graphic representation and the tradition of artistic transgression have complex histories, and the definition of what one takes to constitute extreme is notoriously subjective, slippery, and bound by historical and social pressures."[7]

Alongside the difficulty in clearly distinguishing between old and new violence, we should also bear in mind that any discussion of a work of art as representative of a national cinema or an ideological metanarrative is problematic at best. When it comes to the cinematic work, the production and distribution require significant funds that often rely on the support of national agencies. Hence, the fact that most of the Israeli films considered in this essay were partly funded by the Israeli Film Fund, a governmental agency that has been supporting Israeli cinema since 1979, is noteworthy when we read the films as ideological or political acts, as is the fact that many of the films in question are also coproductions that were made with the support of European funds.[8]

While this chapter traces the cultural specificity of the Israeli New Violence, it is important to bear in mind that these works—much like the works of the New Extremism—make use of the prominent global currency of on-screen violence. That films such as *S#x Acts*, *The Slut*, or *Big Bad Wolves* challenge Israelis to move away from the old politics of shooting and weeping and offer a more complex and ambiguous understanding of the Israeli "existential disease"[9] does not negate an understanding of their overseas success as testament to the international power of extreme art cinema as a "highly lucrative global commodity, marketed to consumers in a range of different national contexts."[10] In a world saturated by an endless stream of images, shock gains new relevance. Ironically, mounting an attack on the viewer can prove to be a highly efficient way to attract audiences who know nothing about the Israeli-Palestinian conflict. Violence is an international language, and Israeli filmmakers turn out to be eloquent and skillful speakers of this idiom.

Moving between national and transnational frameworks, this study is also informed by the debate regarding the "problem of generations," a debate that can be traced back to Karl Mannheim's formative discussion (1927).[11] As described by Sofia Aboim and Pedro Vasconcelos, the term *generation* implies "either a degree of shared collective subjectivity often consciously perceived, or mere birth cohorts which entail a common historical location and experience but not necessarily self-conscious agency."[12] As I will later show, the New Violence movement exemplifies both categories.[13]

Instead of coming up with a formula that can help future scholars decide whether or not an Israeli film should be classified under the rubric of the New Violence movement, I offer an overview of contemporary Israeli cinema and its discontents. By so doing, I will shed a light on the ways in which recent features made by young Israeli filmmakers can to some extent be read as national allegories in a Jamesonian sense of being symptoms of deep national anxieties and concerns,[14] even as they use transnational aesthetic elements that make them relevant to a global sphere of consumption.

Generation War: The Rise of a New Cinematic Movement

As noted by such Israeli film scholars as Ella Shohat, Raz Yosef, and Judd Ne'eman, Israeli cinema and the Zionist state emerged at the same time.[15] The historical circumstances under which the State of Israel was established—from the Holocaust to the 1948 War of Independence and the numerous wars that followed—called for an allegorical framework in which the "micro-individual is doubled by the macro-nation."[16]

The New Sensibility filmmakers of the 1960s and the 1970s, for example, translated their critique of the Zionist metanarrative into open-ended, dark, and nonlinear narratives deliberately lacking cathartic closure.[17] By focusing on interiors, the films strived to create "an effect of universality" and to operate in a "social and historical vacuum."[18] This tendency resulted in an individualism that replaced national concerns. Adopting what Shohat calls "ideology-of-no-ideology," the personal cinema movement expressed a cultural necessity according to which "it was a political act to be apolitical . . . because you did not manifest bombastic Zionism, and therefore you did the right thing."[19]

This penchant for personal stories concerning relationships, lust, parenthood, or loss, rather than military conquest dramas or Bourekas comedies about the cultural tensions between immigrants and native-born Israelis (Sabras), can be read in two contradictory and revealing ways: On the one hand, Shohat sees it as "narcissistic self-contemplation" presenting young Ashkenazi Sabras as victims while ignoring the suffering of, and discrimination against, minorities such as Sephardic/Mizrahi Jews, Arab Israelis, and Palestinians.[20] On the other hand, Ne'eman argues that these films are, in fact, subversive manifestations of "cultural critique" committed to exploring and articulating political alternatives to the Zionist hegemony.[21] The tension between these two possible readings will prove productive in my discussion of the New Violence movement, which has many similarities to the personal cinema created decades before.

While personal cinema filmmakers were the first generation to challenge and complicate the humanistic image of "beautiful Israel" as a melting-pot "miracle," the New Violence movement represents a different generation.[22] Its members are Israeli men and women who were born during the late 1970s and the early 1980s, when the occupation of Gaza and the West Bank had already become established facts. This group of filmmakers grew up during the First Lebanon War (1982–1985), the First Intifada (1987–1993), the First Gulf War (1990–1991), and the social and political rupture caused by the assassination of the Israeli prime minister, Yitzhak Rabin, in November 1995. After graduating high school, many of them served in the military during the Second Intifada (2000–2005) and its aftermath. Hence, their identities and perceptions were shaped in a generational crucible of violence, producing feelings of frustration, helplessness, and "spatial anxiety."[23]

Apart from the ongoing conflict between Israelis and Palestinians, Israel is a nation built on a set of tensions or divisions: first, the inherent tension between *democratic* and *religious*; second, the gap between Israel's unique status in the Jewish world as a light unto the nations and its insistence on occupying another nation and ruling its habitants through military force; and third, the often unrecognized tension between the goals of the Israeli ethos of egalitarian socialism (as epitomized, for example, in the idea of the kibbutz) and the realities of an ever-growing disparity between rich and poor in Israel's contemporary neoliberal climate. Taken together, these different aspects of the Israeli existence germinate what I wish to call *perpetual violence*—the notion that violence is the rule rather than the exception and that daily existence takes place inside a precarious bubble that might burst at any given moment. The violence can therefore never be fully eliminated or controlled; it forever moves in circles, creating an endless loop of anxiety and fear in which the encounter with a violent act can, ironically, be perceived as a form of relief from the endless anticipation of an unknown and uncontrollable danger or threat.

This loop echoes official policies enforced by the Israel Defense Forces (IDF) in the Occupied Territories, designed to germinate and sustain a constant fear of invasion, violence, and arrest. Breaking the Silence, an Israeli non-governmental organization (NGO) established in 2004 by veterans of the IDF in order to provide serving and discharged Israeli personnel and reservists a means to confidentially recount their experiences in the Occupied Territories, documents these tactics and their official and unofficial names. According to a 2012 collection of testimonies by IDF soldiers, one such policy is to "demonstrate a presence" by means such as recurring night patrols in Palestinian villages, shooting into the air, conducting random house arrests, and destroying property.[24] As the report stresses, these policies are meant to intimidate the civilian population rather than to prevent terror or punish those who break the law.[25] While this has become a daily horrific reality for Palestinians, the New Violence films explore how the logic of intimidation and random acts of violence has pervaded the Israeli existence, albeit in less direct, brutal, and deadly ways.

The various profilmic manifestations of perpetual violence are very much in dialogue with the global proliferation of the New Extremism since the late 1990s. Works such as Noé's *Irreversible* (2002), Breillat's *Anatomy of Hell* (2004), or von Trier's *Antichrist* (2009), to name but a few examples, all portray contemporary society "as isolating, unpredictably horrific and threatening, a nightmarish series of encounters in which personal relationships—families, couples, friendships, partnerships—disintegrate and fail, violently."[26] As Quandt demonstrated, this obsession with the cinematic depiction of taboo subjects such as rape, incest, mutilation, and bodily fluids draws its inspiration from a long line of anti-bourgeois filmmakers, artists, and writers, including the Marquis de Sade, Luis Bunuel, George Bataille, Jean Genet, and Samuel Beckett. The New Extremism could therefore be read as a cinematic interpretation of previous literary and theatrical movements.

The young Israeli filmmakers, however, refer less to these cultural antecedents as to their recent cinematic and televisual renderings. While the notion of perpetual violence has deepened during the past decade, the Israeli economic and cultural infrastructures have progressively transformed Israel from a country with a modest local film industry into one with a significant foothold in the international cinema and television markets. With the benefits of technological and economic development, those born in the 1970s and the 1980s became the first Israeli generation to live in a truly globalized cultural sphere. This means that unlike the New Sensibility directors, who were highly influenced by theater and literature,[27] the New Violence filmmakers grew up watching commercial-saturated, multichannel television. When this group—which, for the first time in the history of Israeli cinema, included a significant number of women—entered film schools during the first decade of the twenty-first century, they were thus already fluent in the visual language of mainstream Western media and especially the confrontational aesthetic of New Extremism.

Much like the films of European New Extremism, Israeli films made in the past few years often confront their viewers with shocking, provocative, and "unwatchable" images and plotlines. These tendencies can be traced back to Yedaya's *Or* (2004), an award-winning drama about an abused prostitute and her teenage daughter, and to two dark family melodramas made by the siblings Ronit and Shlomi Elkabetz—*To Take a Wife* (2004) and *Seven Days* (2008). Yet such articulations pale in comparison to the level of disturbing imagery offered by recent films, which include a girl's body beheaded by a serial pedophile (*Big Bad Wolves*), two boys locking a girl in their bomb shelter in an attempt to blackmail her rich father (*Youth*), and a high-school student suffering from repeated sexual assaults at the hands of her classmates (*S#x Acts*).[28] Yet while this unwatchable quality of perpetual violence is the major distinguishing element of these and other films, it also acts as the axis around which other shared strategies of story, style, and theme revolve. The following serves as an attempt to explore the common features that make these films stand apart from earlier works and to trace their transnational lineage as it is adapted toward a specific national-social critique.

Watching with Your Entire Body: Israel's New Extremism

The New Violence filmmakers subscribe to the call for awakening contemporary audiences, as phrased by Dumont, and utilize much of the aesthetic and thematic strategies of New Extremism to achieve this result—most specifically, the reliance on dysfunctional families, mutilated bodies, sexual taboos, and endless acts of aggression. Yet their overall purpose differs from that of their European counterparts, in the sense that they do not wish to criticize the capitalist and bourgeois obsession with consumption but rather to identify the specters haunting and shaping the Israeli bubble.

Despite the almost complete absence of Arab characters (other than one secondary character in *Big Bad Wolves*), and even though the words *occupation* or *Palestinians* are never uttered, the reality these films depict is one in which the street has become a battlefield and violence is the quintessential definer of Israel's unstable existence. Militarism enters the characters' lives indirectly, as a backdrop or prop rather than the central motif; but precisely because of this recurring thematic choice, the feeling is that its presence is all-pervasive. There is the army weapon that makes it possible for the twin brothers in *Youth* to kidnap the girl and imprison her in a bomb shelter; the uniform that Ze'ev wears in his first meeting with Michal (when he is on his way back from reserve duty) in *She Is Coming Home*; the military experience of the protagonists of *Big Bad Wolves*, which enables them to kidnap and torture an alleged pedophile; and the mundane exchanges of the boys in *S#x Acts* about their motivation to serve in a combat unit. To use the words of *Youth*'s screenwriter-director, Tom Shoval (born 1980), "The occupation has a constant presence in all of the recent Israeli movies made by my generation. It always exists in the background, in one way or another."[29]

These works resemble the European New Extremism in their visceral storytelling techniques and their eschewal of the overtly political. In their essay "Traces of the Modern: An Alternative History of French Cinema," Martine Beugnet and Elizabeth Ezra argue that the "emphasis on the corporeal and the visceral" in the works of the French New Extremism serves to resist "explicit interpretations and overt political messages."[30] This, however, does not mean that these works are apolitical; in fact, this aesthetic of excess offers a new, radical way to think about the interrelation between aesthetics and politics by invoking a bodily—rather than an intellectual, rational, or cognitive—experience. This approach, which can also be found in Adam Lowenstein's study of horror films and in Asbjørn Grønstad's analysis of the New Extremism, suggests an epistemology based on corporal affects and reactions.[31] Citing Roland Barthes, Grønstad summarizes this notion by stating, "The most painful wounds are inflicted more often by what one sees than by what one knows."[32] In applying a new aesthetics of razorblade gestures, with its shocking depiction of violent acts and sexual provocations, the young filmmakers of New Violence Cinema flirt with this notion of wounding. They avoid the classic narrative conventions or didactic moral tales in the *mea culpa* tradition of shooting and weeping films, refusing to comfort their audience via cathartic closures. Their aim is rather to drive shock across an open narrative structure that leaves no safe refuge but only room for the viewer's imagination. It is in this sense that New Violence also creates a new radical form of politics.

To that extent, these films stand apart not only from New Sensibility but also from the recent wave of politically charged documentaries. By including interviews with politicians, retired combat soldiers, and policy makers, renowned documentaries like Ra'anan Alexandrowicz's *The Law in These Parts* (2011), Dror Moreh's *The Gatekeepers* (2012), or Mor Louchy's *Censored Voices* (2015) all aimed to reveal and explore the underbelly of the occupation and its devastating, ongoing impact. Using talking heads, infographics, digital maps, and interviews with experts, these films offer the Israeli viewer a cerebral engagement that can shed new light on the state violence aimed against Palestinians. Yet at the same time, they also carry the risk of preaching to the choir. The hidden assumption such works seem to share is that a well-researched historical overview—as long as it is condensed into a tight ninety-minute narrative with compelling soundtrack, digital effects, and cinematography—can awaken the sleeping Israelis and possibly change their political affiliations. New Violence Cinema, in many ways, positions itself as an alternative to this approach; rather than cerebral engagement or emotional identification (tears, empathy, forgiveness), this movement likes to punch its audience in the gut, establishing reality as an ongoing and unavoidable nightmare.

The Home Is the Battlefield

To fully understand the contours of this cinematic horror, we should take a closer look at how these works translate the notion of contingency and helplessness into on-screen depictions of perpetual violence. Whereas Israeli cinema has always contained scenes of violence, they were generally confined to the battlefield. From *Hill 24 Doesn't Answer* (Thorold Dickenson, 1955) to *Rock the Casbah* (2012), violence was mostly associated with the Israeli-Arab conflict and the ongoing occupation. Even when violence penetrated Israel's home front, as in films like *Ajami* (Scandar Copti and Yaron Shani, 2009) or the more recent *Bethlehem* (Yuval Adler, 2013), its overarching frame of reference remained the conflict, and its resolution was still seen as contingent on a resolution of the political situation. In this pattern of representation, the enemy was identifiable and could therefore be fought against (even at the price of losing one's moral bearings). Concordantly, violence used conventional military weapons that connote traditional ideas of warfare: rifles, tanks, bulldozers, pistols, fists.

The New Violence films, however, offer a new formulation of the battleground and of the border between the war zone and the allegedly protected urban existence. As seen throughout these works, the battlefield is the domestic sphere, the body (mainly the male body) is the weapon, and violence is repetitive, omnipresent, and circular, rather than cathartic as in the climactic battle scene of an American Western or war movie. This change dictates a thoroughgoing fragmentation of spatiality. Within the movement's aesthetic language, the inner contradictions and tensions between Jews and Arabs, rich and poor, left and right, and religious and secular manifest themselves as a psycho-spatial split between a normative, seemingly happy, domestic world above and a disturbed, psychotic, and violent world below. The brothers in *Youth*, for example, imprison their victim in the empty basement of their building. Upon returning to their parents' apartment, they are presented as two teenagers who obsess over American action films and tease each other. However, whenever they are forced to enter the world below and make sure that their hostage is still alive, the siblings wear a different face and abruptly transform into violent criminals.

This psycho-spatial fragmentation is influenced by a rich cinematic tradition of contemporary psychological thrillers or dark indie dramas—for example, the American drama *Hard Candy* (David Slade, 2005) or Noé's most recent feature, *Love* (2015)—but it has a unique significance within the Israeli context. We can read it as an expansion of a psychological split that preoccupies the protagonists of shooting and weeping films, men who served in the IDF: a duality of fulfilling their roles as model citizens, husbands, and fathers on the one hand and recognizing that their actions directly or indirectly facilitated various atrocities against innocent people on the other. This split is negotiated in complex ways in recent manifestations of the genre, such as *Waltz with Bashir, Lebanon,* and *Bethlehem,* which operate squarely within the landscape of the conflict.[33] With their domestic emphasis, the New Violence films bypass a need to resolve the problematic through a provocative role reversal: instead of occupying the point of view of the perpetrator, as was done in the shooting and weeping cinema, these works ask the spectator to *embody* the place of the victim.

Sadistic Men, Masochistic Women

Whereas the men project outwardly as pedophiles, rapists, or simply confused adolescents who vent their anger on random girls, the female characters tend to undergo processes of internalization: their bodies are a source of constant pain while generally not inflicting pain on others. Thus, in most of these films, sexual relations are experienced by the woman as a trauma involving humiliation and violence, even if she has been their initiating party. Although the lion's share of New Violence films were made by first-time directors in their late twenties or early thirties, their depiction of lust and love is strikingly gloomy. There are no sex scenes reflecting love and reciprocated passion. In fact, the line between consensual sex and rape is blurred to the point of nonexistence.

In *S#x Acts*, for example, a sixteen-year-old girl named Gilli (Sivan Levi), who recently transferred into a new high school, tries desperately to gain popularity in a suburban community inhabited by rich adolescents. After she falls for and makes out with one of her classmates, he introduces her to his friends, who pressure Gilli into taking part in various sexual activities that become increasingly abusive and—from the viewer's perspective—challenging to watch. As the story unfolds, one cannot help but define sexual relations in the terms of coercion, especially after one of the seventeen-year-old boys decides to document the sexual act and use it to humiliate Gilli and brag about his masculinity.

In various female-centered New Violence films, rape is thus experienced as a continuing nightmarish reality rather than a singular, one-time event. In *Or*, for example, the teenage daughter who failed to convince her mother to stop selling her body eventually decides to follow in the path of her destructive behavior. In the shocking climax of the film, we see her as she arrives at a bachelor party and sits on a king-size bed on the upper floor of a suburban villa; she is waiting for the young, mostly drunken men who "bought" her services to come up and rape her. Similarly, *S#x Acts* ends when Gilli is offered a ride home by the father of one of the boys, who ogles her awkwardly while driving his car. Although the film ends while they are in the car and nothing has yet happened, we are left with a disturbing feeling that something terrible and violent may occur.

Taken together, these dark endings paint a disturbing picture of the state of Israeli womanhood. If women are often seen as the source of Israeli society's continuity through reproduction and its imperatives, their masochism and lack of proper support systems suggest at some level the impossibility of perseverance under such circumstances. In New Violence Cinema, sex is a signifier of power and domination; not only is it not a part of building relationships, but it also denies the possibility of a future.[34]

The Violence Is New

In the past few years, as Israeli cinema has become more dependent on special effects, digital cameras, and higher production values, it has been able to feature violent spectacles of unparalleled intensity, at least by its own industry standards. Unlike the war movies that depicted their violent subject matter from a safe distance by using animation or discreet camerawork (such as in exclusive soldiers' point-of-view shots that render the enemy distant and invisible), *Big Bad Wolves* and Keshales and Papushado's previous film, *Rabies*, depict graphic violence that aesthetically references contemporary Asian (mainly South Korean) cinema and European New Extremism. Contrastingly, low-budget experimental films, like Yuval Mendelson and Nadav Hollander's *Cats on a Pedal Boat* (2011) and Gafny's *Cannon Fodder*, use special effects and makeup to present more comic depictions of graphic violence, including amputated limbs, close-ups of internal organs, and rivers of blood. In addition, the films directed by female cineastes follow the stylistics of European filmmakers such as Breillat, Noé, and Cristian Mungiu, showing visceral and aggressive sex scenes that are difficult to watch and involve acts of physical and mental violence that provoke different physical responses—from erotic arousal to horror and repulsion—with both the on-screen characters and the audience.

Once again, the result is an attack on the body—whether it is the body of the (mostly female) characters or the body of the spectator. Much like in New Extremism, the source of attraction is sensory endurance, and the challenges it poses on commonplace perceptions of entertainment and pleasure. By forcing the Israeli viewer to *feel* the film rather than simply watch it, New Violence filmmakers expose the extent to which helplessness and violence have become our familiar and unending routine. The audience becomes as much a victim of the violent act as the character upon which this act is perpetrated; and even when the tension is broken with comic scenes, the viewing experience creates a cumulative uneasiness that stays with us long after we have left the theater.

This form of confrontational aesthetics distinguishes New Violence Cinema from earlier traditions of Israeli filmmaking. It also attests to the influence of the New Extremism movement. According to Michael Haneke, one of the movement's leading figures, his intention has always been "to rape the spectator into independence," a statement that echoes Bruno Dumont's description of his works as "terrorist attacks" aimed at the audience.[35] To this end, the sense of perpetual violence that appears local in the most intimate sense of the word becomes a bridge that connects Israel—epistemically as much as affectively—to the greater West.

Conclusion

Despite its similarities to New Sensibility, the New Violence movement marks a substantive shift in the development of Israeli cinema. True, its members do not share a catchy manifesto, support an influential cinema journal, or even sport an official and recognizable name. Yet they all seem to emerge out of a singular background—a generation of thirty-somethings born into the violent reality of an ongoing occupation, as well as myriad other socioeconomic tensions. And from these shared conditions, there arrived a corpus of almost twenty features made between 2010 and 2016 that can be grouped along a common set of traits.

Undoubtedly, the films I mentioned do not all display these traits in the same way and to the same degree.[36] Nevertheless, despite stylistic divergences, the investment in these characteristics—drawn largely from the vocabulary of New Extremism—serves to evince that most young filmmakers in Israel today harbor powerful feelings of outrage, claustrophobia, instability, and temporariness. Whether through more conventional dramas or genre-bending films like *Big Bad Wolves*, these directors deliberately challenge and even dissolve the boundaries between battlefield and home front, consensual and forced sex, sadism and masochism, victim and assailant. Their films do not always make for pleasant viewing. Hardly ever does a happy ending await us; indeed, there is an inordinate number of suicides, whether metaphoric or literal, in New Violence Cinema (for example, the suicides in *Youth* and *Epilogue* or the self-destructive behavior in *Or* and *She Is Coming Home*).

While these works are often inhabited by isolated and helpless characters, some of their creators came together in a short-lived and ultimately futile attempt at political engagement and activism. This collaborative effort emerged during the military (IDF) operation Protective Edge in the summer of 2014. In early July, Israel issued a large-scale attack on the Gaza Strip in response to escalating fire on Israel from within the Gaza Strip and following the kidnapping and murder of three Israeli teenagers by Hamas members.[37] In response to the mounting number of civilian casualties in Gaza, the directors participating in the Israeli feature competition of the Jerusalem Film Festival held a joint press conference and called for a cease-fire. They read a statement released later in Hebrew, English, and Arabic:

> We believe that in these violent days, it is impossible to talk only about cinema while ignoring the killing and horrifying events around us. . . . In these terrible

days, we as artists and creators expect ourselves, the festival's administration, the spectators, and the media to use this event to issue a clear, loud cry for change. We call on the Israeli government to cease fire; we urge it not to send our troops to be killed again, in another pointless, cruel military campaign; we call on it to engage in meaningful dialogue with the Palestinian people and its leaders, to achieve a viable peace for both sides.[38]

This unprecedented press conference, which took place at the height of the operation in Gaza, foregrounds the complex interrelation between art and activism within a conflict zone. The solidarity among mostly young filmmakers competing for one of the most prestigious awards in Israel indicates that many members of the New Violence movement see themselves as part of a politically engaged local community, brought together by the particular generational and national traumatic experience of perpetual violence. It is important to stress that this was a unique and exceptional event that did not include all the filmmakers mentioned throughout this article,[39] but the 2014 press conference suggested that they may be a potential for social solidarity. At the same time, it points to the futility of radical change under the prevailing conditions of perpetual violence.

Still, this brief moment of solidarity sets these Israeli filmmakers apart from their European contemporaries. As Quandt argued with regard to its French inflection, New Extremity could not be described as a "movement" due to its lack of a unified "purpose and vision."[40] Noé, Dumont, Breillat, and others do not share a similar political agenda or even an agreed-upon worldview (in fact, it is possible to argue that Breillat's oeuvre goes against everything that Noé's films stand for). Contrastingly, and in spite of the many differences between the Israeli films explored in this piece, there seems to be an underlying concern for Israel's possible future that binds these works together. The decision to portray multiple violent acts takes numerous shapes and forms, but it seems to stem from a common cry for urgent action. As is made painfully evident in all of these films, things cannot simply stay as they are.

Whether the violence is overt or implied, it never ceases to define the existence of both Palestinians and Israelis and effect not just the fictional space and the cultural imagination but actual bodies and communities. The Israeli bubble is therefore destined to burst, a scenario these films are committed to exploring with various degrees of urgency, brutality, and pain.

This chapter is a revised version of an article originally published in *Jewish Film & New Media* under the title "A Body in Every Cellar: The 'New

Violence' Movement in Israeli Cinema" (spring 2016). I wish to thank the journal editors and Wayne State University Press for their permission to use this material.

Notes

1. Qtd. in Pablo Utin, *Lessons in Cinema: Conversations with Israeli Filmmakers* [in Hebrew] (Tel Aviv: Asia Press, 2017), 310 [my translation]. I wish to thank Utin for his many useful comments and observations on earlier drafts of this essay.

2. James Quandt, "Flesh and Blood: Sex and Violence in Recent French Cinema," in *The New Extremism in Cinema: From France to Europe*, ed. Tanya Horeck and Tina Kendall (Edinburgh: Edinburgh University Press, 2011), 19.

3. Ibid., 24.

4. Asbjørn Grønstad, *Screening the Unwatchable: Spaces of Negation in Post-Millennial Art Cinema* (London: Palgrave Macmillan, 2012), 2.

5. For more on the *shooting and weeping* genre, see Yaron Peleg's chapter in this volume.

6. Tanya Horeck and Tina Kendall, "Introduction," in *The New Extremism in Cinema: From France to Europe*, ed. Tanya Horeck and Tina Kendall (Edinburgh: Edinburgh University Press, 2011), 1.

7. Ibid, 5.

8. *Youth*, for example, is a coproduction of Israel, Germany, and France, while *Mountain* mostly received funding from Denmark.

9. I borrow this term from J. Hoberman's celebratory review of *The Kindergarten Teacher* (2015). See J. Hoberman, "Nadav Lapid's Genius Sees Israeli-ness as an Existential Disease," *Tablet*, July 30, 2015, accessed August 15, 2015, www.tabletmag.com /jewish-arts-and-culture/192409/nadav-lapid-2.

10. Tanya Horeck and Tina Kendall, "The New Extremisms: Rethinking Extreme Cinema," *Cinephile* 8, no. 2 (Fall 2012): 7.

11. Karl Mannheim, "The Problem of Generations," in *Essays on the Sociology of Knowledge*, ed. Paul Kecskemeti (London: Routledge, 1952), 276–320.

12. Sofia Aboim and Pedro Vasconcelos, "From Political to Social Generations: A Critical Reappraisal of Mannheim's Classical Approach," *European Journal of Social Theory* 17, no. 2 (May 2014): 165–183.

13. In Israel, the terms *first generation*, *second generation*, and *third generation* refer to the historical distance from the trauma of the Holocaust and are thus understood as a well-defined set of specific behaviors, speech patterns, and PTSD symptoms. While this is beyond the scope of this essay, it is interesting to note this additional understanding of the Israeli generational divide.

14. According to Fredric Jameson, "The aesthetic act is itself ideological, and the production of aesthetic or narrative form is to be seen as an ideological act in its own right, with the function of inventing imaginary or formal 'solutions' to irresolvable social contradiction" (79). Fredric Jameson, *The Political Unconscious: Narrative as a Socially Symbolic Act* (Ithaca, NY: Cornell University Press, 1981).

15. For an overview of pre-state cinematic works made in Palestine between the 1920s and 1948, see Ella Shohat, *Israeli Cinema: East/West and the Politics of Representation* (Austin: University of Texas Press, 1989), 13–52.

16. Ibid., 164.

17. Shohat isolates several factors that led to the emergence and proliferation of the Israeli personal cinema: the approval of a new tax-return policy for local filmmakers in 1960; the emergence of "an alternative production scheme" consisting of small crews and micro-budgets; the founding of the first Israeli filmmakers' consortium, called Kayitz (the Hebrew acronym for *Young Israeli Cinema*), in 1977; and the proliferation of international film festivals in Israel, such as the Jerusalem Film Festival.

18. Shohat 1989, 183.

19. Israeli filmmaker and film scholar Igal Bursztyn, quoted in Shohat 1989, 185.

20. A similar position, which sees personal cinema as yet another handmaiden to Israeli hegemony that excludes women, Holocaust survivors, and Arabs from the public discourse, can be found in the works of Israeli film scholar Nurith Gertz. See, for example, Nurith Gertz, "The 'Other' in Israeli Cinema" [in Hebrew], in *Fictive Looks—On Israeli Cinema*, ed. Nurith Gertz, Orly Lubin, and Judd Ne'eman (Tel Aviv: Open University of Israel Press, 1998), 381–403.

21. Judd Ne'eman, "The Moderns: The 'New Sensibility' in Israeli Cinema" [in Hebrew], in *Fictive Looks—On Israeli Cinema*, ed. Nurith Gertz, Orly Lubin, and Judd Ne'eman (Tel Aviv: Open University of Israel Press, 1998), 29–30.

22. See, for example, Gertz, Lubin, Ne'eman 1998, 381–403.

23. Ella Shohat, "Postscript," in *Israeli Cinema: East/West and the Politics of Representation*, rev. ed. (London: I. B. Tauris, 2010), 287.

24. See Breaking the Silence, *Our Harsh Logic: Israeli Soldiers' Testimonies from the Occupied Territories, 2000–2010* (New York: Macmillan, 2012).

25. Ibid., 10–11.

26. Tim Palmer, "Style and Sensation in the Contemporary French Cinema of the Body," *Journal of Film and Video* 58, no. 3 (2006): 22.

27. Shohat 1989, 164.

28. Due to its limited scope, this chapter only explores full-length fiction films and cannot include a discussion of recent trends in documentary and experimental cinema. For an overview of "the personal turn" in Israeli nonfiction films since the early 2000s, see Shmulik Duvdevani, "The Agonies of an Eternal Victim: Zionist Guilt in Avi Mograbi's *Happy Birthday, Mr. Mograbi*," in *Deeper than Oblivion: Trauma and Memory in Israeli Cinema*, ed. Boaz Hagin and Raz Yosef (London: Bloomsbury Academic, 2013), 93–116.

29. Neta Alexander, "New Directors/New Films Interview: Tom Shoval," *Film Comment*, March 24, 2014, accessed May 20, 2015, www.filmcomment.com/blog/interview-tom-shoval.

30. Martine Beugnet and Elizabeth Ezra, "Traces of the Modern: An Alternative History of French Cinema," *Studies in French Cinema* 10, no. 1 (2010): 11–36.

31. See Adam Lowenstein, *Shocking Representation: Historical Trauma, National Cinema, and the Modern Horror* (New York: Columbia University Press, 2005).

32. Grønstad 2012, 4.

33. For a useful overview of Israeli conflict films and in-depth interviews with several of their directors, see Pablo Utin, *The New Israeli Cinema: Conversations with Filmmakers* [in Hebrew] (Tel Aviv: Resling, 2008).

34. This connection between the depiction of sexual violence and the inability to imagine a future became apparent through conversations with Faye Ginsburg. I also wish to thank her for many invaluable comments on earlier versions of this article.

35. Qtd. in Horeck and Kendall 2011, 6.

36. There are also other films that do not operate squarely within this movement (and thus are excluded from this essay) but still are very much in dialogue with its themes and concerns. One such film is Talya Lavie's *Zero Motivation* (2014), which broadly deals with the relationship between sexism and militarism in Israel and which specifically includes a scene where a male combat soldier sexually assaults a female IDF solider. While Lavie's debut feature deals with many of the themes I identified with New Violence Cinema, it takes place on a military base and is therefore more in dialogue with earlier conflict films than with the movement's domestic claustrophobia. Additional examples that depict extreme violence and share some elements and themes with New Violence are Lapid's *The Kindergarten Teacher*, Eliav Lilti's *Urban Tale* (2012), and Joseph Pitchhadze's *Sweets* (2013).

37. As is often the case with IDF operations, the events of summer 2014 have been given different names: Israel officially named the military operation it launched on July 8, 2014, Operation Protective Edge (Hebrew: Miv'tza Tzuk Eitan). However, it is sometimes referred to as the 2014 Gaza war.

38. Wendy Mitchell, "Israeli Filmmakers Call for Ceasefire," *ScreenDaily*, July 14, 2014, accessed June 15, 2015, www.screendaily.com/news/israeli-filmmakers-call-for-ceasefire /5075171.article.

39. The filmmakers who signed this declaration were Keren Yedaya, Tali Shalom-Ezer, Nadav Lapid, Efrat Corem, Shira Geffen, Bazi Gete, and Shlomi and Ronit Elkabetz.

40. Quandt 2011, 24.

17

THE EXCHANGE

Reinventing Israeliness through Koreanness

Pablo Utin

IN MAKING HIS SAMURAI FILMS, KUROSAWA AKIRA WAS inspired by John
Ford's Westerns. Drawing elements from the American Wild West, he
translated and adapted them into Shogunate Japan. His films were further enriched through the redeployment of character arcs and symbolic
narratives cannibalized from the works of Maxim Gorky, Fyodor Dosto-
evsky, and William Shakespeare. In turn, Italian director Sergio Leone was
inspired by Kurosawa's style and themes in his creation of the spaghetti
Western. His *A Fistful of Dollars* (1964) is an unauthorized and unofficial
remake of *Yojimbo* (Kurosawa, 1961). This Italian Western reimagines and
translates Japanese samurai films' influences and American Westerns into
a violent political European form. Simultaneously, Hollywood reappropri-
ated Kurosawa through the making of *The Magnificent Seven* (John Sturges,
1960), a remake of *Seven Samurai* (Kurosawa, 1954).[1] This film would shape
a new form of action narrative in the West, create professional killers as
heroic anti-heroes, lead to the comingling of comedic and serious characters within a band of brothers, and influence cinematography and musical
scores that would shape Leone's Westerns. This network of influences is
encountered again in the films of Quentin Tarantino, such as *Inglourious
Basterds* (2009), *Django Unchained* (2012), and *The Hateful Eight* (2015), and
Korean filmmaker Kim Jee-woon's *The Good, the Bad, the Weird* (2008),
which draw from all of the above. Thus, the political landscape of a historical and feudal Japan becomes a symbolic marker in cinema's cycle of creative

engagement, revealing an exchange between East and West in a search for inspiration—one where each side appropriates the other's cinema, translating it into personal, regional, and often (trans)national particularity.[2]

This interplay of translations, interpretations, influences, and appropriations should not be viewed as a singular trajectory but as a wide net that shapes and reshapes through transnational artistic contact;[3] it is a global, transnational game of influences that is essential to cinema and to national and transnational dynamics of identities. It demonstrates an ongoing dialogue between artists that translate, sometimes consciously and sometimes unconsciously, into a dialogue between (trans)national cultures. This dialogue, in turn, creates a constant process of national self-definition through translation, interpretation, and appropriation.

The purpose of this chapter is to investigate the ways in which a transnational dialogue is articulated through the encounters between Israeli and South Korean national cinemas. Instead of approaching the topic through the familiar strategy of textual and comparative analysis, I will discuss how Israeli directors process their transnational identities and consciously and purposefully adopt foreign Korean influences. Through interviews with Israeli directors who have expressed an interest in South Korean cinema, this article traces the kinds of dialogue that occur in a game of cultural contact that has, as I will argue, definitive influence on constructing a (trans) national cinema and a (trans)national identity. More specifically, it raises questions about the characteristics Israeli directors interpret as *Korean, specifically Korean,* or *uniquely Korean* when they watch a Korean film and the ways in which this interpretation of Koreanness is adopted, transformed, and translated into their own Israeli work. Rather than establishing essentialist boundaries that demarcate an authentic Korean style or an authentic Israeli style, these interactions expose how Israeli directors' encounter with Korean cinema is filtered through their personal inclinations and tastes. This imagined and interpreted Korean style conveys an intercultural dialogue that invents Korean national identity as perceived through Western or specifically Middle Eastern eyes; concurrently, it directs our attention to the process by which Israeli national identity also becomes an invented form, always already transnational, a mongrel that is a result and a participant of an ongoing transnational dialogue.[4]

The aim of this chapter is not just to understand how Koreanness is imagined or invented by Israeli directors but primarily to stress how certain imagined (Korean) national elements are transformed and translated by artists, thus acquiring a new (Israeli) national identity. Namely, it is crucial to understand that when the influences present themselves in the new product—the Israeli film—they are rendered in it as authentically Israeli. This way, without the cultures having a profound or continuous contact and cultural interchange, one nationality is able to nevertheless enrich and influence the other, thus expanding and helping to define its national style and its national culture, even without being knowingly or deliberately noted. This kind of process allows for an understanding of national authenticity not as an original, exclusive, or essential characteristic of a national cinema or culture but as a hybrid construct that exposes national identities to be fundamentally transnational.

Consumption of South Korean Cinema in Israel

That South Korean cinema has any impact on Israeli filmmakers may seem extremely unlikely given that there has been almost no commercial distribution of South Korean films in Israel. Aside from several of Kim Ki-duk's films,[5] Im Sang-soo's *The Housemaid* (2010), and Park Chan-wook's *Oldboy* (2003), Israeli audiences' encounters with South Korean cinema are scarce and in alternative venues. By virtue of this lacuna, mainstream Israeli media does not devote much space to the discussion of South Korean cinema, and a general debate about Korean films has been rare in Israel.

The main exposure of Israeli audiences to films coming from South Korea has been through specialized DVD stores like The Third Ear, which opened a section dedicated to Korean cinema. Cable channels have also showcased several South Korean films during a recurring special framework Asian Cinema Month[6] and international film festivals in Israel have included some globally recognized South Korean films in their programs.[7]

Because South Korean cinema is featured in Israel mainly through ancillary markets that are relatively marginal or target-specific, ultimately only audiences with great interest in world cinema—and especially in Asian cinema—are likely to discover Korean cinema in an effective way. Following patterns developed in Europe, Israeli audiences associate South Korean cinema with violent, extreme revenge thrillers and horror movies.[8] One of the reasons for this trend is the promotion and distribution of Korean cinema in different platforms through the British label Tartan Asia Extreme. Although the label is devoted to the promotion of Asian cinema in the West, it also reinforces the Orientalist perception of Asian films, and among them Korean films, as exotic and dangerous and thus leads to wrongly identifying the Korean film industry as one dominated by extremely violent genres.[9] Given that Korean films in Israel are consumed mainly after they are filtered via international English DVD labels (such as Tartan Asia Extreme) and European international film festivals, this European tendency to classify Korean films under the headings of *extreme*, *exotic*, and *violent* is imported into Israel.

Jinhee Choi notices two institutionalized practices in contemporary Asian cinema that are prominent in international film markets and international film festivals: the above-mentioned Asia Extreme and Asian Minimalism. South Korean films that are consumed in the West tend to adapt to one of these categories or practices and in Choi's view sometimes even attempt to transcend them.[10] Both practices tend to preserve the Orientalist perception of the East as exotic, mysterious, violent, and dangerous in one case or as exotic, mysterious, restrained, and spiritual in the other.[11] By analyzing two films by Kim Ki-duk, *The Isle* (a film marketed under the label of Asia Extreme) and *Spring, Summer, Winter, Autumn . . . and Spring* (a film that didn't suit the categorization of *Asia extreme* and thus was marketed as *world cinema*),[12] Choi stresses that "the notions of 'primitivism' and 'transcendentalism,' as manifested in these two films, are in fact two sides of the same coin, and both satisfy the western desire for 'otherness.'"[13]

The research on South Korean cinema in the academy in the West has been very prolific since the early 2000s, following the emergence of New Korean Cinema and the Hallyu phenomenon.[14] During the 1990s, the Korean film industry grew into one of the most powerful, prominent, and present film industries in the global market, especially in Asia, though it also penetrated the Western market. This was followed by extensive academic attention that tried to define and characterize South Korean national cinema and its role in the international film distribution arena.[15] Notably, some extensive research focused on the causes that led to the success of an industry that only a few years before had zero presence in Western film discourse.[16] In this context, a lot of attention was paid to the rapid process of modernization in South Korean society and how it influenced the film industry's growth and the movies' style, where the recurring concept of hybridity would be key for understanding Korean cinema, culture, and society.[17] Serious research focused on the emergent Korean blockbuster and in the way Korean cinema mixed, blended, and challenged genres, structures, and conventions,[18] and some scholars began trying to disseminate the ways in which Korean cinema was creating new, original, and authentic forms and content versus the ways in which it was just copying Hollywood models.[19] The scope of this chapter is already too broad to go into detail about all the ways Western academia took interest in Korean cinema. But eventually this growing interest in Korea and its culture crystalized with the growing popularity of Korean media products in the global market. In other words, academic interest in Korea and specifically in Korean cinema emerged as a part of—or one could even say a reaction to—a more general cultural global interest in South Korea. Thus, the main concerns of academic research on South Korea were in a way a reflection, prolongation, and continuation of the main concerns that could be found in the popular, global, nonacademic discourse about South Korea and its cinema.[20] This correlation is noticeable also regarding Israeli consumption of Korean cinema and specifically in the way the Israeli directors discussed in this chapter perceived Korean cinema. The Israeli directors' intuitive reactions and thoughts on Korean cinema and culture have a visible correspondence with the international academic discourse on the films.

In Israel, distribution and marketing of Korean cinema developed in the main along the two aforementioned practices of minimalism and extreme cinema: on the one hand, through film festivals and art-house commercial distribution of films by Kim Ki-duk and Hong Sang-soo that feature more minimalistic or spiritual tendencies;[21] and on the other, through the ancillary distribution markets cited above, the consumption of extreme cinema in the works of Park Chan-wook, Kim Jee-woon, and Bong Joon-ho. It must be said that both kinds of Korean cinema are consumed primarily by film connoisseurs. In addition, there is also a separate Israeli audience that consumes South Korean romantic and historical films, which complement in genre and tone the Korean dramas it watches on TV.[22] The exposure to this latter group of films is apparently achieved through (illegal) downloading via the internet. Since it is not the objective of this chapter to interrogate the reception patterns of South Korean films in Israel, the data presented here is at best speculative. What is attempted in the following is to understand the ways in which, given the relative lack of general exposure to Korean cinema in Israel, some Israeli filmmakers managed to discover Korean films and become influenced by them. While watching Korean films, Israeli filmmakers interpret and thus imagine a cinematic attribute as related to a Korean identity, which is then filtered through their limited cultural understanding of Korea and Korean culture and further refined by being considered in relation to their own conceptions of cinema in general and national cinema in particular. Finally, they adopt this interpreted and translated trait into their own work, creating a new feature of the local that can again be rendered and understood as authentically Israeli, even if it never was. In this fashion, national cinema emerges as authentic and artificial, created and interpreted, presenting an artificiality that doesn't cease to be authentic and a nationality that is at the same time also trans-nationality.

Israeli Directors and South Korean Influences

Israeli directors who acknowledge the influence of Korean films on their work encounter them in the forms of extreme cinema and Asian minimalism through the two connoisseur markets described above (DVDs and art house). My case studies focus on three such directors: Navot Papushado and Aharon Keshales, the filmmakers who are behind such Israeli genre hits as *Rabies* (2010) and *Big Bad Wolves* (2013) and are influenced by the former form, and art-house favorite Eran Kolirin, who directed the award-winning internationally successful films *The Band's Visit* (2007) and *The Exchange* (2011) and has been influenced by the latter form.[23]

The interview questions I posed to these directors were focused on five main topics. First, how were they exposed to South Korean films—that is, where did they see the films and how did they hear about them, taking into account that, as previously noted, commercial release and mainstream exposure of South Korean films is scarce in Israel? Second, what are the main aesthetic and narrative features they recognize in these films and the features that specially caught their attention? Third, what are the ways in which they interpret these features as specifically Korean? Did they recognize any Koreanness in the features? Fourth, did they have any contact with Korean culture and traditions other than through the films they watched? Fifth and finally, how did they translate and adapt these features into their own artistic work?

These questions offer us an opportunity to understand the ways in which Israeli artists reinterpret Koreanness, thereby creating a certain image of Korean culture that can function as a double mirror. Firstly, Israeli directors become translators and communicators of the foreign culture to local Israeli audiences, transforming it through their particular understanding of its features. This way, the Israeli film directors construct an idea of Korean national identity that is by definition different from—though perhaps not exclusive of—an indigenous Korean understanding of this identity but at the same time find its inspiration in films that are read as Korean national products and reinterpreted as such. And secondly, this re-interpretation functions as a way to reflect on their own culture and identity. Thus, by adapting what they devise as Korean features into their own work, Israeli directors are actually redefining, questioning, and expanding what is commonly understood as Israeliness through its cinematic rendering or otherwise. As a result, the concepts of national identity and national cinema are confirmed and at the same time deconstructed and dismantled through a trans/national dialogue. This kind of dialogue could be better explained through Thomas Elsaesser's concept of *double occupancy*, an alternative formation to exclusive national, cultural, and even personal identity, which stipulates that identity is always already occupied, influenced, and constructed by the interaction with so-called *other* nationalities, cultures, and so on.[24] My use of the term will extend the notion of occupancy from *double* to *multiple*. In this sense, what is perceived as Israeli national culture or national cinema emerges as a construct that is always already occupied by what are usually considered as its various *others*. In the following section, we will look at the ways the Israeli filmmakers' encounter with South Korean films led to the creation of new categories and new pre/occupations for a multiply-occupied Israeli cinema.[25]

Rabies and *Big Bad Wolves*

In *Rabies*, Papushado and Keshales tell the story of a brother and sister who escape their family and get lost in the woods. They are hunted down by a serial killer, while other characters also enter the woods, thereby making it difficult for us to differentiate who is the prey and who is the perpetrator, who are the "good guys" and who are the "bad guys." The two directors stated in the media that the brother and sister were inspired by the Korean movies they saw.[26] Although these characters are not Korean, the two directors created them as larger-than-life figures reminiscent of the characters they discovered in Korean cinema. They are, in their words, "cinematic" characters—not just people you meet in everyday life, as usually portrayed through the more realistic mode of Israeli cinema, but some hyperbolic version of a human being.[27]

Big Bad Wolves, the second feature film by the filmmaker duo, was inspired by South Korean revenge thrillers and more specifically by Kim

Ji-woon's *I Saw the Devil* (2010), which the two saw while presenting *Rabies* at the Fantasporto Film Festival in Portugal. The film tells the story of the father of a murdered little girl who teams up with a rogue cop to capture, imprison, and torture the main suspect of the murder (and rape). The ultraviolent quality and bleak atmosphere of *Big Bad Wolves* are mixed with black humor and several plot twists.

When asked how he discovered and was exposed to South Korean cinema, Papushado explained that the first South Korean film he ever watched was Park Chan-wook's 2003 revenge thriller *Oldboy*:

> I took it from a video store, probably The Third Ear. . . . The film won an award in Cannes that Tarantino gave, and it was from South Korea. I saw it on DVD with a friend and it blew our minds. It wasn't like anything else we had seen before in our lives. . . . We said to ourselves that there should probably be more films like this one, and that's how we went and rented *JSA* and *Sympathy for Mr. Vengeance*. From there we continued our exploration and watched *Save the Green Planet!* and later we also discovered the films by Bong Joon-ho. I saw most of the films on home video formats, DVD or Blu-Ray. But films like *The Yellow Sea* and *I Saw the Devil* I could catch at film theaters during film festivals around the world.[28]

Papushado's words reveal several important points regarding the exposure of South Korean cinema in Israel. First of all, the "discovery" of Korean cinema was made possible as a result of the attention a film got by winning an award at Cannes. Most importantly, the film was marked out by Quentin Tarantino, a director admired by young filmmakers. So, in other words, this discovery was filtered through the sensibilities of American and European film industries and festival circuits. Secondly, the Korean films were mostly discovered through home-video formats. Even if *Oldboy* did eventually receive a theatrical release in Israel, it was possible to watch the film months before on DVD through the specialized video store The Third Ear. This kind of home-video market was essential in the early 2000s for film buffs who wanted to be up-to-date with world cinema. Finally—and most importantly—the reaction to the discovery is profoundly emotional and visceral, hyperbolic and accentuated with phrases like *It blew our minds* or *It wasn't like anything else we had seen before in our lives*. This excessive reaction is integral to the extreme genre, which generates heightened physical and affective reactions. This kind of response would be expected from future encounters with Korean cinema and would become, as we shall see, a characteristic very much associated with Koreanness.

When asked about specific features that he admired in these films, Papushado emphasized their grandeur, where "everything is big, powerful, so intense." The exaggerated and over-the-top style that impressed him so was something that was recognized as a feature of his own subsequent creations. "This is why a lot of people said that *Big Bad Wolves* is a Korean movie, because there is something there that is bigger than life. The association of vengeance films with such 'smart aesthetics' created the impression that they can achieve 'iconic, unforgettable' effects without having to rely on the extravagance (and huge budgets) of large-scale Hollywood films." What Papushado admiringly viewed as smart was also extended into his own reading of actor direction: "You believe them when they act out those strong feelings. There's something there that is very exaggerated but at the same time very convincing." Moreover, he compared this acting style to that of other cultures including his own, claiming that it was unusual for global cinema. Thus, in his understanding, "Americans try to balance the acting, Europeans try to lower the volume of it, here in Israel we try to make the volume non-existent, to turn the acting volume off and leave it between zero to one." But rather than creating an unwieldy melodramatic effect, Korean acting is believed to be in tune with the overall style of that cinema: thus, "in Korea the acting is full volume, level fifteen. They don't hold back. A film like *Save the Green Planet!* is two hundred kph, its volume level is fifteen, over the top, and the acting is in accordance with that."[29]

Papushado maps out different cinemas by their level of intensity, placing Korean cinema as a cinema of exaggeration and opulence that renders it more cinematic, in his view. Following that observation, he laments the West's loss of this idea of cinema as bigger than life, especially noticeable in European and Israeli cinema. This perspective could be perceived as Orientalizing Korean cinema, situating it in opposition to Western trends and projecting onto it an exoticism mixed in with nostalgia for a lost Western cinematic history.

Papushado's own admission that his and Keshales's film is considered by some to be a Korean film is not something to be dismissed as a fallacy or just placed under the heading of spectatorial negotiation that is somehow founded on a misguided appropriation. Rather, this case study reveals that in a broad sense, these films are also Korean, even as they operate as Israeli—and that, in a deeper sense, these national categories should not be overemphasized to the extent that they lose their explanatory power and flexibility in encountering social realities.

Nevertheless, Papushado recognizes the limits of his point of view and tries not to fall into an Orientalist perception of the Korean otherness, even as he simultaneously celebrates the larger-than-life quality of Korean films and thus participates in the broader tendency of seeing the Orient as exciting, exotic, and dangerous.[30] In this, he bases his admiration of the grandiose film style on the grounds that it allows for moral complexity that has by now disappeared from Western cinema.[31] Accordingly, for him, "another thing that is very Korean [. . .] would be the shades of gray. When you see a Korean film even the bad guys have a sensitive side." Here the filmmaker draws a link of character complexity between contemporary South Korean cinema and American "New Hollywood" films of the 1970s: "Scorsese, De Palma, and all the guys who made you very involved with the movie, always prompting guesses as to where they are taking you. In *Scarface* I am rooting for the bad guys. In *The Untouchables* things shift all the time." This transnational analogy further draws out Korean cinema as a site of global cultural exchange.

When asked whether anything essentially Korean remained in his films that connected them to an authentic Korean culture or tradition, Papushado, acknowledging his own Western perspective, replied: "I only see these films through foreign eyes, so to me the mixture of all those things is perceived as Korean." The emphasis on physical violence (kicks) is identified by him as characteristic of Korean cinema, testifying to this cinema's preference to establish power dynamics without relying on firepower; thus, in Papushado's words, "guns are very rarely seen in Korean movies, and this is something that actually makes the films very interesting because they have to be creative and invent things." Without giving examples, he presupposes the influence of the West on Koreanness but emphasizes the films' determination to represent something he deems Korean identity, attributing a quality of authenticity that also highlights a sense of inadequacy: "It is very important for them to show their Koreanness. Americans don't need to show they are American because they are *Americans*, they don't have the need to show it to the world. But there is something about Koreans that they still have the need to do it."

Papushado characterizes national identity in much the same way some scholars present the concept of national cinema as opposed to Hollywood cinema.[32] In fact, Hollywood cinema could be also interpreted as a national US cinema, defining and expressing American national identity. The constant use of the American flag and nationalistic speeches in Hollywood blockbusters and the constant debates about American values and the American dream would contradict Papushado's assumption that Hollywood is not focused on stressing American national identity. Interpreting American cinema as a nationally transparent or denationalized cinema while understanding South Korean blockbusters as fundamentally national not only ignores the national charge of Hollywood cinema and the way it is a priori perceived as natural, it also over-nationalizes South Korean cinema, rendering it as a preconceived exotic otherness. Trapped in the binary conception of world versus Hollywood cinema, Papushado reproduces here a problematic understanding of national cinemas that still exists in academia,[33] ignoring the ways in which both categories are implicated in one another. Hollywood and American cinema in general tend to appropriate foreign influences and adopt international filmmakers into its industries in order to maintain its relevance and look for fresh, diverse styles and talented directors. This practice, with all its complexities, blurs the lines between films that are considered national or Hollywood, as seen very clearly in the cases of the "American" films directed by cineastes such as Alfonso Cuarón, Alejandro Gonzales Iñiarritu, or Bong Joon-ho. Are they just professionals working in the Hollywood industry (in a broad sense) and making American films, or are they bringing their national and cultural sensitivities into these films, thus making, in a sense, Mexican- or Korean-Hollywood cinema? Do we need a component of the film to be expressly transnational, such as a foreign director or funding body, or can *Big Bad Wolves*, for example, be considered, from a heuristic perspective, an Israeli-Hollywood-Korean film? Even if the film was made entirely with Israeli funding and an Israeli crew, I would endorse this latter definition because of the aesthetic influences being filtered into the filmmaking process. This definition may still prove accurate, even when it becomes impossible to dissect the particular elements and ascribe them to a specific national culture.

Papushado states no knowledge of Korean national identity, culture, or history apart from what he has learned from films. He does stress, however, how invitations from film festivals afforded him the opportunity to visit South Korea on a couple of occasions. On these visits, he met with Koreans and came to the conclusion that "they are very different from what you see in the movies. Actually, Koreans don't even like violence. They prefer dramas and melodramas. When I talked to Korean people and told them what films influenced us, they understood our kind of cinema, but they covered their eyes, because it's too extreme for them. I think they identify violence as something more Western. Even if Busan is a city of gangsters, people there don't identify with violence, they don't want to be seen as a violent nation."

Ironically, even as Korean cinema has gained a reputation for being extreme, to Koreans, these films are deemed Western, just as Kim Ki-duk's spiritual fantasies are viewed as European. In Papushado's experience, a distinction is made between the films the public seemed to disavow and their directors, whose international celebrity has meant that they have gained a prominent place in the hearts of Koreans. Filmmakers such as "Bong Joon-ho and Park Chan-wook are like gods there. They are very honored and respected, I didn't see anything like that."

Through his encounter with Koreans, Papushado inverts the common notion of violence as associated with Korean culture, associating it with Western culture instead. Thus, he implicitly suggests that the label Asia Extreme is rather a product of Western cultural perceptions more than an innate characteristic of the East. Yet his descriptions of the celebrity culture surrounding Korean directors, which bears remarkable resemblance to that of other cultures, is Orientalized by Papushado. The appraisal in the West of a prominent artist is seen as normative and not out of the ordinary, while the appraisal in the East of a prominent artist could be interpreted as extravagant verging on religious worship.

The problematics of a world cinema economy can be seen in the necessity of performing national cinema with a particular set of attributes or a clearly defined style.[34] Failing to do so or acknowledging influences by another national cinema—or worse, Hollywood—undermines national authenticity and suggests a derivative (and therefore debased) cultural production. This struggle for authenticity and autochthony can create challenges for filmmakers from countries with less influential or internationally recognized film history and culture. These cineastes find themselves in a position of weakness vis-à-vis more powerful foreign industries. This becomes even more blatant for those who want to make genre films that by definition are based on repetition and have to adhere to cross-cultural generic and aesthetic conventions.[35] In this context, Papushado, who wishes to be recognized as a filmmaker specializing in genre films and is a director coming from a country that is weak on the global cinema stage, must balance the (local and international) industrial demand for a nationalized or localized variation with the conventions of his chosen genre. As such, he notes that Korean cinema is already interculturally shaped: "When you see a film by Park Chan-wook you understand that he saw all the same movies you saw from the US and from Japan." Yet at the same time, he views this cinema as a local rendition in the sense that "their films are very personal and very Korean." Through this example, it becomes clear that an Israeli film that is influenced by Korean filmmaking must acknowledge the influences of both Korean cinema and Hollywood on Korean cinema while still asserting an essentialist local/national quality that makes it appear personal rather than imitation.

The larger-than-life quality of Korean cinema that Papushado identifies is difficult to achieve in Israeli cinema, which is a small industry with low budgets that accordingly tends to make modest, realist films—or low-volume works, in Papushado's terminology. Rather than see this local condition as a handicap, Papushado and Keshales emphasize the need to respect it: "It is OK to be influenced by different cultures around the world, but we still have to externalize and express our mentality, the Israeli mentality, for otherwise it will feel fake." Yet in keeping with the genre expectations, they also wanted to capture the qualities of a film such as *Oldboy*, as described by Papushado: "The music is very bombastic, bigger than life, dramatic. They don't hold back. They go at two hundred kph and say 'eat it.' It is as if they say 'you are the ones with the problem, you got used to an anemic cinema, poor, without emotions, that's realistic. It is your fault. We are the ones who were right all the time.' Two hundred kph with punches and knives and kicks and jumps and feelings of vengeance and sadness and love . . . that's cinema." Drawing on these qualities, in *Big Bad Wolves*, the two filmmakers tried to capture the magnitude of emotions by creating a powerful revenge drama modeled after Korean vengeance cinema, "a film about these kinds of basic and over-the-top emotions: 'They did something to me so I will take revenge. They took something from me so I will take something too.'"

Papushado defines the influences of Korean cinema on his work as the impact of a national culture that is different from his own. The Korean traits penetrate or are adapted and translated into the new national or personal style. Having stated the differences, Papushado nevertheless also tries to find some common ground between the cultures. In order to do so, he uses the Hebrew words *arsiut* and *arsim*, which can't be literally translated into English. Their pejorative associations with male Mizrahi low-class thugs contain a racist charge, but Papushado attempts to reclaim these terms and have them refer more broadly to the shared street-thug quality that connects Korean films with certain works in Israeli cinema. Thus, he notes that "there is something very similar between Israelis and Koreans, specifically in the simplicity, I mean the 'arsiut.' They are punks just like us. In the movies, they are just a bunch of 'arsim.' They are like Moshe Ivgy and Tzahi Grad,[36] slapping each other on the neck.[37] They are very human, very down to earth and there is something very Israeli in that—they are anti-heroes." This similarity is nevertheless offered with a particular caveat. While in Papushado's view, Israeli cinema never has bad-guy characters, Korean cinema, as he interprets it, is dominated by such figures, to the point that even the good guys are essentially bad guys: "The good guys are scum. If you look at the character who is supposed to be the good guy in *Bittersweet Life*—he's a piece of s——t. Or the good guys in *Memories of Murder*, they are supposed to be the cops, but they are torturers, they are scum too. In *Oldboy* you have the same thing. So even your heroes are actually villains."

In this sense, one of the main influences of Korean cinema on Keshales and Papushado's work is in the way they relate to good versus evil. Rather than mutually exclusive characterizations, good and evil coexist in every character. This moral complexity is conveyed by shifting the tone in a single scene or even in a single shot. Thus, the spectator copes with mixed and contradictory emotions, laughing and crying as the film progresses from drama to comedy and then to horror. This can be seen, for example, in *The Host* (2006), a Korean film about a dysfunctional family confronting a monster that mysteriously appears out of the Han River, where director Bong Joon-ho juxtaposes the father's death with a comedic touch.[38] These sudden switches of emotional tone are a key characteristic of *Rabies*, most noticeably in the scene where the macho cop (Danny Geva) dies. In that sequence, the spectator is led at first to identify with its dramatic thrust, supporting the death of the cop who tried to rape and kill the two lead female characters. But while he is dying, his telephone sounds off with a vivacious ringtone, creating a comic, ironic, disaffecting effect. The mood then immediately shifts again and turns into a sad, tragic one when we identify the caller as the cop's estranged and angry father and understand that the son will be unable to say goodbye properly to him before he dies. Suddenly, the monster of the movie is transformed into a comedic character and then immediately into a tragic figure with whom the spectator can identify. These sudden shifts of mood and identification are inspired by South Korean films, as the directors explicitly acknowledge.[39]

This example shows a complex dynamic where foreign elements are indigenized and perform as local so as to protect the national purity demanded in Israeli and international distribution circuits, while at the same time the indigenous is made international so as to allow its acceptance across broader transnational networks. Such maneuverings reveal the complex relationship that filmmakers have with their (in)voluntary classification as ambassadors of their particular nationality. They have to create a work that performs authenticity as perceived by foreign markets, thereby leading to self-exoticization,[40] but they must simultaneously present their authenticity as sufficiently foreign for the international audiences. This paradoxical expectation from national cinemas and national filmmakers disguises the power relations between strong film industries and weaker ones, presenting the powerful as accepting of other cinemas while conditioning this acceptance on these filmmakers' acquiescence to the power structures and expectations of the international film industries.

To be fair, Papushado might be very conscious of the futility of national cinema as a thematic and/or aesthetic category. Indeed, he emphasizes that the question of Israeliness is not necessarily a determining factor in his filmic choices: "We never stop to think what is 'Israeli' and what is not. Is a tennis uniform Israeli? Who cares, it looks good, it's cool and it goes well with the genre. [. . .] You are Israeli, so the Israeliness will come out of you anyway, you can't deny it."[41] In this sense, national identity can be understood not as an essence of a particular group but as a presence that is unsystematic, arbitrary, singular, and constantly changing.

The Exchange

By contrast, *The Exchange* by Eran Kolirin, who is associated with the art cinema mode rather than with genre,[42] shows influences from Kim Ki-duk's *3-Iron* (2004). Kolirin is inspired by the idea of the empty spaces and the strange relationship between space, objects, and characters in Kim's film. *The Exchange* deals with a university professor who returns home at an irregular hour and starts to see his house, his wife, and his life from a different angle. Absorbed by this discovery, he starts making small changes in his lifestyle, challenging routine and predetermined, expected behaviors. More abstract than narrative driven, the film explores the ways by which the main character inhabits spaces and moves through them.

Much like Papushado, Kolirin discovered Korean cinema through home-video viewing. He explains: "A friend recommended some South Korean films to me. He said I should watch *Sympathy for Mr. Vengeance* and some films by Kim Ki-duk, such as *Bad Guy* and *Samaritan Girl*. I'm not the kind of enthusiast that watched every Korean film, but it was fun to discover some of them. I watched the films on DVDs rented from The Third Ear video store."[43]

Kolirin identified a general feeling of freedom and liberation from Western narrative conventions in the Korean films: "It is difficult for me to explain what I found in the films, but they are totally different from the Western perception of what a story is or how to tell it. The films start their journey through images, through the eroticism of the images and the violence of the images. [...] There is a lack of psychological justification for the actions of the characters and there isn't an attempt to explain the 'why'—why the character did this or that. The question of 'why' is almost never asked."[44] The move away from a linear narrative form substitutes an explicated storyline with general moods. But Kolirin's interpretation of Korean art films also suggests an Orientalist reading, both through exoticization (eroticism, violence, difference) and through the notion that rational logic is absent here. He finds in these characteristics a positive influence that is liberating: "I feel that the films are free from things I am bound by, maybe because of the culture I come from." This association of the film's primal qualities with Kolirin's own liberation from cinematic conventions feeds into an Orientalist narrative of spiritual growth away from culture and offers the East as a site of projection.

As for the question of whether he interprets these kinds of features as typically or characteristically Korean, Kolirin's answer is ambiguous. He claims he didn't really have any contact with Korean culture, tradition, or history. All the same, he does identify a "different way of approaching narrative and cinema" that is related to a different mentality, fashioned by different cultural conditions. Kolirin reinterprets this essentialized different way into his own filmmaking by attempting to incorporate an aesthetic that creates the sense of liberation; as he explains it, "In *The Exchange* I tried to follow that freedom, a freedom from narrative that allows you to start your journey from a different place that is not bound to a narrative device or a plot. I don't think my films are 'Korean' in any way, but this idea of freedom from the conventions of narrative was adopted into my work."

Yet what Kolirin defines as Korean may instead be traced to the art cinema mode, which was largely formed in a European context during the

1950s and 1960s and whose signature characteristic was nonlinear, non-causal, narrative structures that create a sense of ambiguity.[45] Indeed, Kim Ki-duk's films themselves could actually be seen as an example of the appropriation of European modes by a Korean filmmaker. And accordingly, when Kolirin appropriates them, he discovers an element in South Korean cinema that had already influenced Israeli cinema during its 1960s encounter with modernist European cinema.[46] This network of influences again points to the existence of global cinematic interchange, as well as to a concomitant and constant need to reinterpret global thematics in light of a local national context.

Kolirin mentions another influence he got from a Korean film, specifically from *3-Iron* by Kim Ki-duk—the theme of empty spaces, "a sense of being in spaces as if you were a trespasser. The film can be seen as a variation on a feeling of intimacy that can emerge in alien spaces, or a feeling of alienation that can materialize while in familiar spaces or at home. [. . .] This is something I saw specifically in *3-Iron* but haven't seen in other Korean films, so I wouldn't say it is characteristically Korean."

Kolirin does not arrive at the conclusion that the features he identifies in the Korean films are specifically or typically Korean. He does not imagine any specific Koreanness that produces a particular kind of cinematic freedom or anti-narrative approach. Even if he can generalize that Korean films are more liberated in their approach to narrative and produce images that are more erotic and violent, the concept of Koreanness remains very vague, inaccessible even to him. In that sense, national identity remains essentially disconnected from the films that are supposed to express it. It is the need to reconnect the two by way of specialized interpretation that produces the concept of a national cinema.[47]

Conclusion

The Korean influences on Israeli filmmakers are not found within the films in the form of citations, quotes, or an homage to a specific moment within a Korean film. These influences are instead reworkings, restagings, and reimaginings of a certain characteristic that the filmmakers found in one or several Korean films. Nationality—or in this case Koreanness—functions as an empty or floating signifier that can be filled with a signified according to the interpreters' needs.[48] Koreanness would signify what they need it to signify for the sake of defining their own identity and cinematic forms.

When certain characteristics appear in a film or recur in various films coming from Korea (exemplars of Korean cinema), these become for Israeli filmmakers prototypical of nationality in Korean films and are categorized as Korean.[49] Subsequently, these "prototypically Korean" traits are translated by the filmmakers into the personal style of their own films. Once those reinterpreted and later translated features are part of an Israeli film, they appear as an exemplar of Israeli cinema and start functioning as potentially prototypical Israeli national features for others to interpret them as such. As a result, something that was always already interpreted and signified as typically Korean becomes a characteristic of a different national filmic identity and is expanded and re-created as an image of national (Israeli) authenticity that was never authentic but is nevertheless signified as such. The most recent and relevant example for this dynamic can be found in Neta Alexander's definition of a new national movement in Israeli cinema—what she labels *The New Violence*—of which *Big Bad Wolves* and *Rabies* form a part.[50] Characteristics that were inspired by Korean cinema and appear in the films of Keshales and Papushado (like a specific approach to depicting violence and its ethics) become Israeli through their inclusion in the New Violence Israeli cinema movement.

This kind of transnational dialogue allows for cultures to impact each other even when the cultures have come into minimal contact, because this contact is mediated through agents whose influence shapes the formation of national culture. By way of this strategy, directors manage to elude power structures and the cultural dominance of one culture over others and develop both a personal and a national cinema not by copying or surrendering to imposed forms and styles but by appropriating, translating, reinterpreting, and even cannibalizing.[51] Thus, they construct an ever-imaginary and almost invisible transnational dialogue. This means that every national identity is always already a mongrel, a transnational construct. In that sense, this is not a dialogue between two national cinemas or cultures but a transnational dialogue between two interlocutors that are themselves, consciously or not, always already transnational.

Notes

1. Joseph L. Anderson, "When the Twain Meet: Hollywood's Remake of *The Seven Samurai*," *Film Quarterly* 15, no. 3 (Spring 1962): 55–58.

2. Rachael Hutchinson, "Orientalism or Occidentalism?: Dynamics of Appropriation in Akira Kurosawa," in *Remapping World Cinema: Identity, Culture and Politics in Film*, ed. Song Hwee Lim and Stephanie Dennison (London: Wallflower, 2006), 173–187.

3. Israeli directors Aharon Keshales and Navot Papushado announced they are working on an Israeli Western, keeping this kind of interplay in constant development. For details, see Ken W. Hanley, "Exclusive Q&A: Directors Keshales & Papushado on 'BIG BAD WOLVES,'" *Fangoria*, April 22, 2014, accessed May 22, 2017, http://www.fangoria.com/new/exclusive-qa -directors-keshales-papushado-on-big-bad-wolves.

4. JungBong Choi, "National Cinema: An Anachronistic Delirium?" *Journal of Korean Studies* 16, no. 2 (Fall 2011): 173–191.

5. Kim Ki-duk has become a household name for local distributor Lev Cinema, which purchased virtually all of his films since *Spring, Summer, Fall, Winter . . . and Spring* (2003) but didn't distribute all of them.

6. I covered this event through several journalistic articles in different publications. The Asian Cinema Month was held in 2004, 2005, and 2006 on the Hot Cinema cable channel. I covered it for the Israeli newspaper *Globes* in 2004 and 2005: Pablo Utin, "Hollywood Wasn't Conquered" [in Hebrew], *Globes*, May 3, 2005, accessed September 10, 2016, http://www .globes.co.il/news/article.aspx?did=910187.

7. There is a need to also take into account the audience's exposure to South Korean cinema through illegal download sites, where Israeli fans have amateurishly translated into Hebrew some of the main Korean films of the last years. I don't go into this category because this chapter is not a study of fandom and general consumption of Korean cultural products in Israel but is focused specifically on the expressions of artistic dialogue between artists and films.

8. See, for example, Tomer Kamerling, "The Cinema of South Korea: Violence for the Sake of Art" [in Hebrew], *Ynet*, February 1, 2012, accessed September 10, 2016, http://www .ynet.co.il/articles/0,7340,L-4183386,00.html.

9. Chi-Yun Shin, "The Art of Branding," in *Horror to the Extreme*, ed. Jinhee Choi and Mitsuyo Wada-Marciano (Hong Kong: Hong Kong University Press, 2009), 85–100; Robert L. Cagle, "The Good, the Bad, and the South Korean," in *Horror to the Extreme*, Jinhee Choi and Mitsuyo Wada-Marciano, eds. (Hong Kong: Hong Kong University Press, 2009), 123–143; and Jinhee Choi and Mitsuyo Wada-Marciano, "Introduction," in *Horror to the Extreme*. ed. Jinhee Choi and Mitsuyo Wada-Marciano (Hong Kong: Hong Kong University Press, 2009), 1–12.

10. Jinhee Choi, *The South Korean Film Renaissance: Local Hitmakers, Global Provocateurs* (Middletown, CO: Wesleyan University Press, 2010), 14.

11. Israeli cinema tends to suffer from this kind of categorization—if not a stylistic, then surely a thematic one—by the West. Israeli films that deal with issues of religion and the Orthodox community or the Israeli-Palestinian conflict are more prone to generate interest in the festival and art-house cinema circuits.

12. Shin 2009, 99.

13. Choi 2010, 180.

14. Do Kyun Kim and Se-Jin Kim, "*Hallyu* from its Origin to Present: A Historical Overview," in *Hallyu: Influence of Korean Popular Culture in Asia and Beyond*, ed. Do Kyun Kim and Min Sun Kim (Seoul: Seoul National University Press, 2011), 13–34.

15. Christina Klein, "Why American Studies Needs to Think about Korean Cinema, or, Transnational Genres in the Films of Bong Joon-ho," *American Quarterly* 60, no. 4

(December 2008): 871–898; and Nikki J. Y. Lee, "Localized Globalization and a Monster National: The Host and the South Korean Film Industry," *Cinema Journal* 50, no. 3 (Spring 2011): 45–61.

16. Doobo Shim, "South Korean Media Industry in the 1990s and the Economic Crisis," *Prometheus* 20, no. 4 (2002): 337–350; Kwang Woo Noh, "Compressed Transformation of Korean Film Industry from Old to New Regime," *Asian Cinema* 20, no. 1 (March 2009): 137–154; and Darcy Paquet, "The Korean Film Industry: 1992 to the Present," in *New Korean Cinema*, ed. Shin Chi-Yun and Julian Stringer (New York: Edinburgh University Press, 2005), 32–50.

17. Doobo Shim, "Hybridity and the Rise of Korean Popular Culture in Asia," *Media, Culture & Society* 28, no. 1 (January 2006): 25–44.

18. Choi 2010, 31–59; David Scott Diffrient, "South Korean Film Genres and Art-House Anti-Poetics: Erasure and Negation in the Power of Kangwon Province," *CineAction* 60 (February 2003): 60–71; and Julian Stringer, "Putting Korean Cinema in its Place: Genre Classifications and the Contexts of Reception," in *New Korean Cinema*, ed. Chi-Yun Shin and Julian Stringer (New York: New York University Press, 2005), 95–105.

19. Suh HaeLim, "South Korea's Film Dilemma in the U.S. Market: 'Copywood' or Asian New Wave?—Case Study of *Dragon Wars* and *The Host*," *Asian Cinema* 19, no. 2, (September 2008): 270–280; Jeeyoung Shin, "Globalization and New Korean Cinema," in *New Korean Cinema*, ed. Shin Chi-Yun and Julian Stringer (New York: Edinburgh University Press, 2005), 51–62; Chi Yun Shin and Julian Stringer, "Storming the Big Screen: The Shiri Syndrome," in *Seoul Searching: Culture and Identity in Contemporary Korean Cinema*, ed. F. K. Gateward (Albany: State University of New York Press, 2007), 55–72; and Chris Berry, "'What's Big About the Big Film?': 'De-Westernizing' the Blockbuster in Korea and China," in *Movie Blockbusters*, ed. Julian Stringer (London: Routledge, 2003), 217–225.

20. See, for example, Darcy Paquet, "Genrebending in Contemporary Korean Cinema," *Koreanfilm.org*, July 6, 2000, accessed October 13, 2015, http://www.koreanfilm.org /genrebending.html; Anthony Leong, *Korean Cinema: The New Hong Kong* (Victoria: Trafford, 2006); and Jin Kim, "'Copywood' Pix Pay Unwanted Homage," *Variety.com*, July 13, 2003, accessed June 15, 2019, https://variety.com/2003/film/news/copywood-pix-pay -unwanted-hommage-1117889185/.

21. Achieving far less exposure, other art-house/minimalist films from directors such as Hong Sang-soo and Lee Chang Dong were shown to the Israeli public in local film festivals rather than through commercial release. The exposure to this kind of films was extremely limited and thoroughly unnoticed by the media.

22. Irina Lyan and Alon Levkowitz, "From Holy Land to 'Hallyu Land': The Symbolic Journey following the Korean Wave in Israel," *The Journal of Fandom Studies* 3, no. 1 (2015): 7–21; and Nissim Otmazgin and Irina Lyan, "Hallyu across the Desert: K-Pop Fandom in Israel and Palestine," *Cross-Currents: East Asian History and Culture Review* 3, no. 1 (2014): 32–55.

23. A third case could have been that of Yosef Pitchhadze, a lesser-known director in the international arena but one of the leading and most important and praised filmmakers in Israel, who is responsible for the eccentric and impressive film *Sweets* (2013). Pitchhadze also expressed his appreciation of South Korean cinema. On this, see Pablo Utin, *The New Israeli Cinema: Conversations with Filmmakers* [in Hebrew] (Tel Aviv: Resling, 2008). An interesting

fourth case in point would be Yaelle Kayam, whose film *Mountain* (2015) was influenced by Bong Joon-ho's *Mother* (2008), as expressed during a personal conversation with me.

24. Thomas Elsaesser, "Real Location, Fantasy Space, Performative Place: Double Occupancy and Mutual Interference in European Cinema," in *European Film Theory*, ed. Temenuga Trifonova (New York: Routledge, 2008), 47–61.

25. In my view, to use *occupation* with regard to Israeli cinema only makes the political meaning of this concept more interesting and complex.

26. Pablo Utin, "The Right Disproportions" [in Hebrew], *Cinematheque* 169 (April 28, 2011): 28–33.

27. Ibid., 30.

28. Navot Papushado interview with the author, conducted on April 13, 2014. The English translation is mine.

29. Ibid. Subsequent quotations in the text are from this interview unless/until otherwise noted.

30. Edward Said, *Orientalism* (New York: Vintage Books, 1978).

31. It may be useful to point out that Papushado's ideas coincide with Robert L. Cagle's arguments. See Cagle 2009.

32. Thomas Elsaesser, *European Cinema: Face to Face with Hollywood* (Amsterdam: Amsterdam University Press, 2005).

33. Lúcia Nagib, "Towards a Positive Definition of World Cinema," in *Remapping World Cinema: Identity, Culture and Politics in Film*, ed. Stephanie Dennison and Song Hwee Lim (London: Wallflower, 2006), 26–33.

34. Elsaesser 2005, 57–107; and Jinhee Choi, "National Cinema, the Very Idea," in *Philosophy of Film and Motion Pictures: An Anthology*, ed. Noël Carroll and Jinhee Choi (Oxford: Blackwell, 2006), 310–319.

35. Raphaelle Moine, *Cinema Genre* (Oxford: Blackwell, 2008).

36. Two prominent Israeli movie actors.

37. Originally, Papushado uses the word *kafa*, which is slang for a slap on the neck with an ambivalent meaning of punishment and degradation but also caring and sympathy all at the same time.

38. Pablo Utin, "Sliding through Genres: The Slippery Structure in South Korean Films," *Journal of Japanese and Korean Cinema* 8, no. 1 (2016): 45–58.

39. Utin 2011, 31.

40. Boaz Hagin and Raz Yosef, "Festival Exoticism: The Israeli Queer Film in a Global Context," *GLQ* 18, no. 1 (2012): 161–178.

41. Pablo Utin, *Lessons in Cinema: Conversations with Israeli Filmmakers* [in Hebrew] (Tel Aviv: Asia Publishers, 2017), 328–329.

42. David Bordwell, "The Art Cinema as a Mode of Film Practice," *Film Criticism* 4, no. 1 (Fall 1979): 56–64.

43. Eran Kolirin phone interview with the author, Tel Aviv, conducted on April 26, 2014.

44. Ibid. Subsequent quotations in the text are from this interview unless/until otherwise noted.

45. Bordwell 1979.

46. For more on these modernist influences, read the chapter by Shmulik Duvdevani and Anat Dan in this volume.

47. Hutchinson 2006, 174–175.

48. Claude Levi-Strauss, *Introduction to the Work of Marcel Mauss* (London: Routledge, 1987), 63–64.

49. Choi 2006.

50. See Neta Alexander's chapter in this volume, as well as Neta Alexander, "A Body in Every Cellar: The 'New Violence' Movement in Israeli Cinema," *Jewish Film & New Media* 4, no. 1 (2016): 4–24.

51. Oswald De Andrade, "Cannibalist Manifesto," *Latin American Literary Review* 19, no. 38 (July–December, 1991): 38–47.

LIST OF CONTRIBUTORS

Editors

RACHEL S. HARRIS is Associate Professor of Israeli Literature and Culture at the University of Illinois, Urbana–Champaign. Her books include *An Ideological Death: Suicide in Israeli Literature* (2014) and *Warriors, Witches, Whores: Women in Israeli Cinema* (2017). She is coeditor of *Narratives of Dissent: War in Contemporary Israeli Arts and Culture* (2012) and editor of *The Arab Israeli Conflict in the College Classroom* (2019), as well as special issues of *Journal of Jewish Identities* (*JOJI*), *Nashim*, and *Shofar: An Interdisciplinary Journal of Jewish Studies*. Her articles on Israeli fiction, poetry, and film have been published in *Israel Studies*, *JOJI*, *Shofar*, and *Journal of Modern Jewish Studies*, among others. She is currently the Editor in Chief of *JOJI*.

DAN CHYUTIN is a Teaching Fellow at Tel Aviv University's Steve Tisch School of Film and TV and University of Haifa's MA Program in Film Culture. He has essays published or forthcoming in such peer-reviewed publications as *Cinema Journal, Shofar: An Interdisciplinary Journal of Jewish Studies. Journal of Film and Video, Jewish Film & New Media, Short Film Studies*, and *Journal of Jewish Identities* (*JOJI*).

Contributors

NETA ALEXANDER is Assistant Professor of Film and Media at Colgate University, New York. She has published articles in *Cinema Journal, Film Quarterly, Media Fields Journal*, and *Jewish Film & New Media*, among other peer-reviewed publications. Her first book, *Failure* (2020; cowritten with Arjun Appadurai), studies how Silicon Valley and Wall Street monetize failure and forgetfulness.

JOSH BEATY is a graduate of the University of Texas, Austin, and the University of Chicago and teaches courses on mass media at the University of Pittsburgh's Department of Communication. He is interested in the relationships among industrial practices, media spaces, and audience communities.

ANAT DAN is a PhD candidate at the University of Pennsylvania's Comparative Literature and Literary Theory Program, where her research is focused on Film and Media Studies, Continental Philosophy, and Environmental Humanities. Dan holds an MFA degree and an MA degree from the Steve Tisch School of Film and Television at Tel Aviv University.

NAVA DUSHI is Associate Professor of Film and Media Studies at Lynn University's College of Communication and Design. Her essays were published in the anthologies *Films with Legs: Crossing Borders with Foreign Language Films, Israeli Cinema: Identities in Motion*, and *Femininity and Psychoanalysis: Cinema, Culture, Theory*. She is a recipient of the American Israel Cooperative Enterprise Schusterman Israel Scholar Award and of a research grant awarded by the Florida Israel Institute.

SHMULIK DUVDEVANI teaches at the Steve Tisch School of Film and Television, Tel Aviv University; the Kibbutzim College of Education, Technology and Arts; and the Sam Spiegel Film School, Jerusalem. His book *First Person Camera*, which discusses Israeli personal documentaries (for which he coined the term *I-movies*), was published in 2010. He is currently working on a research project about Israeli modernist documentaries of 1960s and 1970s, with the assistance of a generous grant from the Israel Science Foundation (2012).

TOBIAS EBBRECHT-HARTMANN is Lecturer at the Department of Communication and Journalism and at the DAAD Center for German Studies at the Hebrew University of Jerusalem. He authored the books *Geschichtsbilder im Medialen Gedächtnis: Filmische Narrationen des Holocaust* (2011) and *Übergänge: Passagen durch eine deutsch-israelische Filmgeschichte* (2014), as well as articles for several journals, including *Memory Studies, New German Critique, Historical Journal of Film, Radio and Television*, and *Leo Baeck Institute Yearbook*. Currently, he is a consortium member of the EU-funded Horizon 2020 research and innovation project *Visual History of the Holocaust: Rethinking Curation in the Digital Age* (2019–2022).

JULIE GRIMMEISEN earned her PhD from the Department for Jewish History and Culture at Ludwig Maximilians University, Munich, and specializes in Israeli history and Gender Studies. Her recent publications include *Pioneers and Beauty Queens: Images of Women in Israel, 1948–1967* (2017, in German) and "'A Better Human Being': Diaspora Images of the New Israeli Woman" (*Journal of Israeli History*, 2019). Currently, she serves as Academic Director at the Consulate General of the State of Israel in Munich, Germany.

BOAZ HAGIN is Senior Lecturer and Chair of the undergraduate and graduate film studies programs at the Steve Tisch School of Film and Television, Tel Aviv University. His publications include the monographs *Death in Classical Hollywood Cinema* (2010) and (with Thomas Elsaesser) *Memory, Trauma, and Fantasy in American Cinema* (2012); the edited anthologies (with Raz Yosef) *Just Images: Ethics and the Cinematic* (2011) and *Deeper than Oblivion: Trauma and Memory in Israeli Cinema* (2013); and various articles for *Screen, GLQ, Cinema Journal, Camera Obscura, New Review of Film and Television Studies*, and other peer-reviewed journals.

ZACHARY INGLE received his PhD in Film and Media Studies from the University of Kansas and is Visiting Assistant Professor of Film at Hollins University in Roanoke, Virginia. Ingle has had articles published in *Post Script, Literature/Film Quarterly*, and *Journal of Sport History*, and his work on international cinema appears in several volumes in Intellect's Directory of World Cinema and World Film Locations series. He has also edited four books: *Robert Rodriguez: Interviews* (2012); *Gender and Genre in Sports Documentaries* and *Identity and Myth in Sports Documentaries* (both edited with David Sutera, 2013); and *Fan Phenomena: The Big Lebowski* (2014).

OHAD LANDESMAN is Lecturer in Film Studies at the Steve Tisch School of Film and Television, Tel Aviv University. His research focus is on documentary film and cinema in the digital age. He has published in several anthologies on documentary culture (most recently in *Vocal Projections: Sound and Documentary*, 2018) and in the peer-reviewed journals *Visual Anthropology Review, Studies in Documentary Film, Projections: The Journal for Movies and Mind*, and *Animation: An Interdisciplinary Journal*. Landesman is currently working on a monograph about documentary visits to Israel in the 1960s and 1970s, and on the coedited anthology *Truth or Dare: Selected Essays on Documentary Cinema*, which is to be published in Israel this year.

MARY N. LAYOUN is Emerita Professor of Comparative Literature at the University of Wisconsin, Madison. Her research interests include literature, culture, and politics; literature and history; visual culture; the modern novel; narrative; rhetoric; nationalisms; feminisms; East/West relations; and third-world literature. In addition to numerous articles on these and other topics, her books include *Travels of a Genre: Ideology and the Modern Novel* (1990) and *Wedded to the Land? Gender, Boundaries, & Nationalism in Crisis* (2001). She is currently working on a monograph on solidarity and the image.

YAEL MUNK is Senior Lecturer in Film and Cultural Studies at the Department of Literature, Language and the Arts, the Open University of Israel. She authored *Exiled in their Borders: Israeli Cinema between the Two Intifadas* (2013) and (with Nurith Gertz) *Looking Back: A Revised History of Israeli Cinema 1948–1990* (2015) and coedited *Stories from the Box*, a forthcoming volume on Israeli television drama. She has also published extensively in Hebrew, French, German, and English peer-reviewed journals on topics as far-ranging as Israeli and Palestinian cinemas, Holocaust studies, postcolonial theory, women's documentary, and gender studies in general.

YARON PELEG is Kennedy-Leigh Reader in Modern Hebrew Studies at the University of Cambridge. Peleg's scholarship includes the single-authored volumes *Derech Gever* (Shufra, 2003), *Orientalism and the Hebrew Imagination* (2005), *Israeli Culture Between the Two Intifadas* (2008), and *Directed by God: Jewishness in Contemporary Israeli Film and Television* (2016). He is also editor (with Miri Talmon) of the anthology *Israeli Cinema: Identities in Motion* (2011).

ARIEL M. SHEETRIT is Lecturer in Modern Arabic Literature and Arab Film at the Open University of Israel. She has published many scholarly articles on Arabic autobiography, fiction, and women's writing and on Palestinian film for such publications as *Journal of Arabic and Islamic Studies, Journal of Levantine Studies, Journal of Arabic Literature, Journal of Middle East Women's Studies*, and *Middle Eastern Studies*. Her most recent book is *A Poetics of Arabic Autobiography: Between Dissociation and Belonging* (2020). She is currently writing a book (with Yael Dekel) titled *In the Wake of War: Readings in Palestinian and Israeli Literature*.

YARON SHEMER is Associate Professor of Israel Cultural Studies in the Department of Asian and Middle Eastern Studies, University of North Carolina at Chapel Hill. In 2013, Shemer published *Identity, Place, and Subversion in Contemporary Mizrahi Cinema in Israel,* and his current research projects are "Neighboring Identities: The Jew in Arab Cinema" and a comparative study of Israeli and Palestinian political cartoons. Outside of his academic endeavors, Shemer has also produced and directed documentary films in Israel, Poland, and the United States, including *Pilgrimage of Remembrance: The Jews of Poland* (1988) and *The Road to Peace: Israelis and Palestinians* (1994).

PABLO UTIN was born in Buenos Aires and immigrated to Israel in 1996. He is author of the books *The New Israeli Cinema: Conversations with Filmmakers* (2008), *Lessons in Cinema* (2016), and *A Requiem for Peace: The Israeli-Palestinian Conflict in Israeli Cinema* (2017), coauthor of *Orson Welles* (2010), and coeditor of *The Transparent Look: Filmmakers on the Cinema of Eitan Green* (2008). Utin has taught classes on New South Korean Cinema, New Latin American Cinemas, Israeli Cinema, Alfred Hitchcock, and Short Film at Tel Aviv University's Steve Tisch School of Film and Television (from which he received his PhD degree), the Faculty of Arts at Beit Berl College, and Shenkar College of Engineering and Design.

RAZ YOSEF is Associate Professor and Head of the Steve Tisch School of Film and Television at Tel Aviv University. He is author of *Beyond Flesh: Queer Masculinities and Nationalism in Israeli Cinema* (2004) and *The Politics of Loss and Trauma in Contemporary Israeli Cinema* (2011) and coeditor of *Just Images: Ethics and the Cinematic* (2011) and *Deeper Than Oblivion: Trauma and Memory in Israeli Cinema* (2013). His work on gender and sexuality, race and ethnicity, ethics and trauma in Israeli visual culture has appeared in *GLQ, Third Text, Framework, Shofar, Journal of Modern Jewish Studies, Camera Obscura, Cinema Journal, Signs,* and *Israel Studies Review.*

INDEX

Page numbers in *italics* indicate figures.

9 780253 056399